harry gold

Oakland University

THE SOCIOLOGY
OF URBAN LIFE

PRENTICE-HALL, INC., ENGLEWOOD CLIFFS, NJ   07632

Library of Congress Cataloging in Publication Data

GOLD, HARRY
   The sociology of urban life.

   Includes bibliographies and index.
   1. Sociology, Urban. I. Title.
HT111.G 57   307.7′6   81-8539
ISBN 0-13-821371-2   AACR2

Editorial/production supervision by
Marina Harrison and Anne Armeny
Interior design by Marina Harrison
Cover design by Sue Behnke
Manufacturing buyer: John Hall

Printed in the United States of America

10 9 8 7 6 5 4 3 2 1

Prentice-Hall International, Inc., *London*
Prentice-Hall of Australia Pty. Limited, *Sydney*
Prentice-Hall of Canada, Ltd., *Toronto*
Prentice-Hall of India Private Limited, *New Delhi*
Prentice-Hall of Japan, Inc., *Tokyo*
Prentice-Hall of Southeast Asia Pte. Ltd., *Singapore*
Whitehall Books Limited, *Wellington, New Zealand*

contents

              Structure and Policies
              by Donald M. Levin   193

    Governing the Metropolis   194
    Urban Political Organization   200
    Modernizing Urban Government   209
    Selected Bibliography   211

Chapter 10   Urban Political Institutions: Informal Power
              Structure and Local Decision Makers
              by Donald M. Levin   214

    Urban Political Influences   214
    Community Leadership—Local Decision Makers   219
    Special Interest Groups   226
    The Influence of the General Public   231
    Selected Bibliography   234

Chapter 11   Urban Economic Institutions   236

    The Corporate Bureaucracy   237
    Innovations in Production, Distribution, and Consumption   239
    The Local Economy of Cities   243
    Employment Trends   244
    Occupational Specialization and the Division of Labor   244
    Occupational Groups in the Labor Force   246
    How Changes in the Labor Market Take Place   253
    Basic Assumptions of a Free Labor Market   254
    Barriers to Career Changes in the Labor Market   254
    Organic Solidarity and Ecological Interdependence in the Labor
    Market   256
    Selected Bibliography   259

Chapter 12   Welfare and Education as Emergent
              Urban Institutions
              by Jacqueline Scherer   260

    The Evolution of American Welfare   261
    Education: Historical Antecedents   273
    Urban Social Services: Policy Issues   279
    Selected Bibliography   280

preface

The SOCIOLOGY OF URBAN LIFE is designed as a comprehensive introduction to the field of urban sociology. Completing such a project is most challenging because of the vast diversity of accumulated theories, concepts, and empirical data which are currently available regarding all aspects of modern urban communities and urban life. The author of such a work is sometimes tempted to present an eclectic assortment of topics, in the hope that nothing significant will be left out. On the other hand, there is an equally compelling temptation to provide a more limited and focused perspective, with the risk that the greater selectivity of materials will provide a far less comprehensive overview of the field than usually called for by "survey" type courses common to urban sociology.

This present volume attempts to avoid the extremes suggested above. Of necessity, urban sociology remains a highly speculative and interpetive field, requiring the synthesis of a vast assortment of theories, concepts, and research findings. But such synthesis must provide a workeable balance between focus and breadth, and between extreme eclecticism and rigid systemization. This balance hopefully has been achieved here by the introduction of five major perspectives as the book's guiding frame of reference. They include: 1) the social change perspective; 2) the social organization perspective; 3) the ecological perspective; 4) the social problems perspective; and 5) the social policy perspective. These perspectives are implied or assumed throughout the book rather than spelled out in every instance, but they are defined and explained in more detail in the introductory chapter.

In addition to a guiding frame of reference, a variety of other student needs were taken into account in preparing the manuscript. These include an appropriate reading level, clarity of presentation, logical organization, sufficient explanation and illustration, and the need to maintain a high level of interest and stimulation. It is the author's premise that a well written, interesting, and clearly presented synthesis of current knowledge of urban processes and forms be available for many more people than just those seriously committed to becoming urban scholars or professional urban practitioners, and it was partially with this goal in mind that the present volume has been prepared.

I wish to acknowledge with deep depts of gratitude the many persons who wittingly or unwittingly contributed to the making of this book. First are the many former teachers who helped shaped my interest in and knowledge of the many dimensions of urban society—most notably, Amos Hawley, Albert J. Reiss, Albert J. Mayer, H. Warren Dunham, Harold Wilensky, Bazil Zimmer, Donald Marsh, and Mel Ravitz. Colleagues who read portions of the manuscript and made many valuable suggestions include Robert Gutman, William Faunce, Melvin Webber, Nahum Medalia, Richard Stamps, Donald Warren, Jesse Pitts, Donald Levin, and Jacqueline Scherer. W. C. Dutton, Jr., Edmond Burke Peterson, Charles Blessing, Norbert Gorwick, John T. Howard, Robert Hoover, Robert Carpenter, Bernard Frieden, and Robert Marans are among former colleagues, employers, or teachers in the field of urban planning who helped sensitize me to some of the applied and policy aspects of urban planning as a problem solving profession.

Special thanks and appreciation go to Donald Levin and Jacqueline Scherer for their more direct contributions to the book. Levin wrote Chapter Seven on the urban family and Chapters Nine and Ten on formal and informal political institutions. Scherer wrote Chapter Eight on urban religion and Chapter Twelve on urban welfare and education. Scherer also shares equal authorship with me in preparing Chapter Sixteen on the urban future and social policy. Needless to say, I alone accept full responsibility for the contents and any shortcomings of these chapters, as well as for the remaining parts of the book which I have exclusively authored.

I am grateful to Ed Stanford and Bill Webber of Prentice-Hall for their help and encouragement, and to the late Marion Wilson, Beth Watchpocket, and Denise Pattison for typing the manuscript. Finally, I wish to thank my son, David, who prepared some of the photographs, and my wife, Patricia, who assisted in ways too numerous to detail.

Harry Gold

PART I / INTRODUCTION

chapter 1

urban
sociology
as a field
of study

During the past century, America has changed from a predominantly rural society to one in which a great majority of its population now lives in urban areas. This transformation has had such far-reaching effects on the American way of life that its significance has not yet been totally comprehended by most Americans. Recent popular concern with the nature and quality of urban life seems to have been aroused by the turmoil of the 1960s and 1970s, when a series of urban crises claimed national attention, and many Americans began pressing for answers to questions about the nature and causes of urban problems and about the future of cities. As a result, urban sociology has recently become a field with considerable popular appeal to college and university students. What the neophyte student of urban sociology soon learns, however, is that the so-called current urban crisis is the product of a vast and complex evolutionary, or perhaps revolutionary, social process that has been continuously unfolding for many centuries. The student may also soon learn that urban sociology is a field of research with a rich and varied tradition going back at least a half-century, long before it assumed its current popularity. The boundaries and concerns of urban sociology have been in a continuous state of flux and growth during its development, and many sociologists are not certain that it makes sense to treat urban sociology as a distinct subspecialty set apart from general sociology. Because of the diversity and complexity of the subject

3

matter, the content of existing urban sociology texts differs widely, and the boundaries of the field are not readily apparent when one looks at the existing body of urban sociology literature.

The growing interest of legislators, government officials, journalists, community leaders, private foundations, research centers, and the general public, has resulted in a tremendous increase in the volume of urban research and writing. Millions of dollars have been poured into studies of virtually all aspects of urban life: population trends, changing patterns of residential and social mobility, poverty, housing, transportation and communications problems, race and ethnic relations, civil disorder, crime, city-suburban relationships, changing land-use patterns, municipal taxation and service delivery problems, pollution and other environmental problems, change in life styles and values—the list of urban-related topics is virtually endless.

The field of urban sociology has in fact grown so broad in its scope and in its overlapping concerns with topics associated with other disciplines and other subspecialties of sociology that some scholars have begun to doubt whether urban sociology really does have a clear focus of its own, independent of sociology as a whole (Gutman and Popenoe, 1970; Thomlinson, 1969). Very often, urban sociology courses and textbooks consist of a wide assortment of topics that do not seem to be connected to one another in any theoretically meaningful sort of way. Much of the writing, for example, relegates the urban community to a background context within which particular kinds of problems and behavior are considered, but the urban community itself is not the prime object of investigation. On the other hand, some textbooks and courses have become unduly restrictive in their efforts to provide a more rigorous or systematic frame of reference for urban sociology. They may focus exclusively on social stratification, social psychology, demography, or census tract analysis, at the expense of other equally important approaches or themes.

Of necessity, urban sociology still remains an interpretive, speculative field requiring much synthesis of empirical and theoretical materials from an extremely wide variety of sources. This book is no exception. It is an attempt to present the frames of reference that the author has evolved in his own courses in urban sociology and in his urban-related work experiences over the past several decades. The hope is that the book will do justice to what the author perceives as the mainstream of this difficult but exciting, challenging, and important field.

The field of urban sociology is so complex and diversified that it cannot be approached or completely understood from any single perspective or frame of reference. What is needed is a multidimensional approach that can provide the student with various perspectives to demonstrate the relationships between the various kinds of urban data and theory and clarify their meaning, without at the same time oversimplifying the complexities of the phenomena involved. To accomplish this goal, five major perspectives have been selected to provide the orientation for the remaining parts of the book. These are: 1) the *social change* perspective; 2) the *social organization* perspective; 3) the *ecological* perspective; 4) the *social problems* perspective; and 5) the *social policy* perspective.

Urban communities, like most social phenomena, are ever-changing entities. They may grow or decline, they may rearrange themselves internally, or their essential character may be altered over time. One cannot discuss present-day urban communities and urban life without asking such questions as: "How did these communities get to be the way they are?" "What are the existing forces likely to produce change?" Or "What are these communities going to be like in the foreseeable future?" Urban life as we know it is a relatively recent historical development, and there is no reason to believe that the urban community of tomorrow will be identical to the urban community of today. Because social change is ubiquitous to all social life, any effort to scientifically describe and explain current social realities is extremely difficult; and by the time existing social patterns that have been observed through social research can be analyzed and communicated by publication of the results (a process that may take at least several years) the original social patterns may have been significantly altered.

But to say that social change is ubiquitous is almost to say nothing, if the changes are not widespread or far-reaching in their consequences. The rhetoric of social change is currently in fashion, but if the concept of social change is widely and equally applied to all manner of conditions or is flagrantly abused, it may cease to have meaning or significance.

For our purposes, the most significant social change process is *urbanization*. Urbanization refers to the processes by which 1) the very first cities in history begin to emerge and develop in previously rural areas; 2) rural populations begin to move to cities; 3) urban communities continue to grow large and to absorb an ever-increasing portion of a society's or region's population; 4) the behavioral patterns of migrants to cities are transformed to conform to those that are characteristic of groups in the cities; 5) as cities grow larger, their structure and form become more complex and elaborately differentiated; and finally 6) urbanization transforms the nature of the entire society in which it occurs. Thus wherever urbanization takes place, it ultimately produces a radical transformation in the structure of the containing society.

The process of urbanization has been uneven throughout recorded history, moving slowly or not at all in some periods, accelerating rapidly in other periods, and declining in still others. In some periods of history urbanization has occurred so rapidly that it has assumed truly *revolutionary* proportions. Lest this be considered an exaggeration, it is important to identify the manner in which the concept of revolutionary change is being introduced here. Social revolutions involve nothing less than changes that drastically alter the structure of the entire society in which they take place. Thus the urban revolution, the industrial revolution, the democratic revolution, and so on, are all examples of radical transformations of the basic social patterns of the societies in which they occur.

Urbanization can be further described as revolutionary according to the following characteristics suggested by C. P. Wolf (1976) in his analysis of the structure of social revolutions:

Boston, like every other city, has changed through the years, as shown here in 1700, 1800, the turn of the century, and today. (Library of Congress and Massachusetts Dept. of Commerce and Development, Division of Tourism)

A. Irreversibility. A revolution is defined as "a relatively sudden set of changes that yield a state of affairs from which to return to the situation just before the revolution is virtually impossible." This applies aptly to urbanization, for while exceptions to the general rule occurred in earlier stages of urbanization, no society in the modern world has returned to a pre-urban state after having become highly urbanized. This is especially true wherever urbanization and industrialization have occurred simultaneously.

B. Suddenness. The most rapid changes in the process of urbanization have taken place in the nineteenth and twentieth centuries, and the appropriate time dimensions within which the revolutionary characteristics of urbanization can be observed must most often be counted in centuries and, at the very least, in decades. This may not seem to be very sudden to observers with a short sense of time, but against the total history of the human species, which has evolved over millions of years (less than one per-cent of the human race's total existence has occurred within the context of urban civilization), the adjective "revolutionary" is indeed appropriate.

C. Acceleration. If suddenness of change does not necessarily appear as revolutionary to some, drastic changes in the *rate* of change can be so considered. Again, as much of the work in this volume will emphasize, the rate or urbanization accelerated dramatically in the nineteenth century and in the first three-quarters of the twentieth century. In fact, the acceleration has been so rapid that urban experts are still attempting to measure and assess its characteristics and consequences, as does this volume also.

D. Discontinuity. Revolutionary changes are not usually smooth and continuous, but rather they create deep breaches in the continuity of the change process. New social arrangements and patterns occur that are often dramatically and completely alien to those that have previously dominated. Thus social revolutions may create upheavals and dislocations that disrupt people's habitual patterns of routinized behavior and require them to learn completely new ways of thinking and doing. Of course, much social strain and stress may be created in the process, which constitute the basis for some of the additional perspectives to follow.

THE SOCIAL ORGANIZATION PERSPECTIVE

This perspective deals with the basic forms of urban life that have evolved as a direct result of urbanization. Sociology as a discipline has probably made its largest contribution to this dimension of the urbanization process. The social organization of the modern urban community can be said to include a huge and complex network of individuals, groups, bureaucratic structures, and social institutions, which is further differentiated into a complex division of labor. The units of analysis can be ranked from the smallest and most simple to the largest and most elaborate, as follows:

The Individuals

The urban individual can best be described in terms of patterns of personality organization and individual life styles that are believed to have evolved in response to the conditions of urban life. Much of the early writing on the urban individual was based on the idea that the city produces distinct personality and behavioral characteristics that set urbanites apart from their rural counterparts. But recent writing on urban personality and life style has been more dynamic and has described mechanisms for coping with or adjusting to the urban complex, or the techniques of urban survival (Lofland, 1973). The concern with the individual also brings into focus many sociocultural dimensions, such as the positive or negative attitudes, values, beliefs, perceptions, and symbolic attachments that have come to be associated with urban life.

Primary Groups

These are small and intimate face-to-face groups, such as the family, couples, or intimate friendship groups. Of course, such groups are preurban in their origins and structure. Many scholars have speculated that as urban communities became larger and more elaborate, primary groups would be swallowed up or destroyed, and that all that would remain would be the segmented, impersonal, or dehumanized relationships thought to be characteristic of large bureaucratic structures (Popenoe, 1970). Yet primary groups have remained a viable part of urban social organization. While they appear to be necessary carry-overs from rural societies, their form and functions have changed in response to modern urban conditions. Such changes remain a focal point of much contemporary urban sociological research.

Neighborhoods, Social Networks, and Everyday Patterns of Interaction

Urban neighborhoods fall in the middle range of urban social organization, in terms of size and complexity. They are larger and more complex than primary groups, but are more informal and less complex than larger-scale bureaucratic organizations. Sociologists do not entirely agree on the significance of local neighborhoods for providing social bonds, arenas of social participation, meaning, or order to urban life at the local level, and there is a great deal of research and speculation on this topic. But recognition is growing that neighborhoods are an inherent part of the social fabric of modern urban communities and that a grasp of the social processes at work at this level of urban social organization is critical to a more complete understanding of urban social structure.

The same can be said of social networks, which are much more amorphous patterns of interaction than neighborhoods, as they are not necessarily tied to specific geographic locations, and they remain at a somewhat more primitive stage of classification and explanation in the sociological literature. Yet, social networks are coming to be recognized as more important than heretofore realized. The growing body of literature on the nature and functions of social networks in the urban community should be considered in any description or analysis of urban social organization.

Also at the intermediate level of social organization are the most transitory and diffuse patterns of urban social organization, which may be referred to under the general heading of collective behavior, for want of a better term. This includes the kind of interaction that routinely occurs in public and semipublic places, such as streets, sidewalks, parks, plazas, public buildings, theaters, meeting halls, and other gathering places. This public behavior sometimes takes the form of crowds, mobs, assemblies, audiences, spectators, or person-to-person encounters between strangers. Such topics have usually been considered within the framework of social psychology and are taken up in a separate chapter.

Voluntary Associations

Much has been said about the very high rates of participation in voluntary associations in contemporary urban America. Much has also been theorized about their structural characteristics and functions. For now, it is enough to say that voluntary associations are also at the middle or intermediate range of social organization, they are somewhat more formal and internally differentiated than neighborhoods or networks, and that they serve both instrumental and expressive functions that are not adequately met by any other level of social organization. They fill a gap in urban social organization by creating new blends of both primary group and bureaucratic forms of social organization.

Bureaucracy

Most large-scale and complex governmental and industrial organizations in the modern world can be characterized as bureaucratic in structure. Typically, bureaucratic organizations consist of an elaborate network of specialized roles or positions organized into a hierarchical division of labor. Each position has a definite sphere of competence, with specified task obligations, and a specified degree of authority or power. The table of organization of bureaucracies defines the scope and limits of their functions, and such organizations are usually bound by a written body of rules that governs the behavior of its members. The main significance of bureaucracy in the modern urban setting is that goods and services essential to the urbanite's well-being are increasingly available only in a bureaucratic context. In the popular mind, this trend is undesirable, since bureaucracies are often viewed as difficult to understand, difficult to utilize effectively, and highly impersonal and unresponsive to individual needs. The bureaucratic mentality is the object of much popular contempt and ridicule, and little has more political appeal than promises to eliminate bureaucratic red tape and costs. Yet, bureaucracy remains a very real element in the daily lives of most urbanites, and it is doubtful that large modern urban communities could continue to exist without some form of bureaucratic organization. Therefore the study of the forms and effects of bureaucracy remains essential to those who wish to understand the social organization of urban communities.

Social institutions

These are the largest and most abstract modes of social organization within the urban community. In the most general sense, social institutions consist of widely accepted patterns of behavior and expectations that evolve or are created as long-term solutions to the recognized needs of a community or society. Such basic institutions as the family or religion are preurban in their origins. Although their forms and functions may have changed drastically as a result of rapid urbanization, they continue to serve at least some of the recognized needs of modern urban communities. But many social critics question the degree to which institutions such as these have the capacity to respond effectively to the changing demands and opportunities of urban living, and their very survival is sometimes viewed as doubtful. Likewise, political and economic institutions are continually faced with the challenge of responding effectively to the ever-changing conditions of urban life. In addition, a host of more recent social institutions, such as mass communications, compulsory education, public welfare, commercialized leisure, and urban planning, have rapidly and dramatically emerged since the beginning of the industrial revolution. Institutional change may in fact be the key to the kind of revolutionary social changes that were earlier described as a product of rapid urbanization.

Alvin Boskoff (1970) has identified the main characteristics of social institutions: 1) they serve a specialized function or need; 2) they provide a

Economic institutions, such as the Chicago Mercantile Exchange, are constantly in need of meeting the demands of urban life. (Chicago Convention and Tourism Bureau)

set of guiding values that translate needs into specific objectives or goals; 3) they consist of a cluster of social roles and skills, which translate ultimate goals into specific duties and responsibilities for individuals; 4) they produce the development of a coordinated network of social roles through the formation of social groups of one sort or another (primary groups, voluntary associations, or bureaucracy); 5) they involve the participation of the entire community in this network of values, roles, and groups; and 6) the values and roles of dominant social institutions are internalized by a substantial portion of the population.

So defined, social institutions clearly are the most inclusive and extensive level of social organization that we have identified so far, and much of the description and analysis of contemporary urban life will be at this level throughout the book. According to Boskoff, major urban social institutions recently have been acquiring a greatly extended radius of influence and control in terms of geography and population. Since they tend to be the practical source of both stability and social change in modern urban communities, they are central to our understanding of current urban problems and of the many efforts to solve them. As social institutions proliferate, as they have in the modern urban-industrial age, newer problems of institutional conflict and power appear as some institutions become dominant at the expense of others. For the individual and for many groups, the conflicts of divided and contradictory institutional obligations, loyalties, and identities are new kinds of problems. On the whole, social institutions appear to represent groping trial and error adjustments to the complexities of urban living. The survival and well-being of modern urban civilization are to a large extent dependent on how successful urban social institutions respond to the challenges confronting them.

THE ECOLOGICAL PERSPECTIVE

At the most general level, ecology is concerned with the processes and forms of people's adjustment to their environment. The urban community is one major form that adjustment takes. More specifically, the study of territorially based systems, of which the urban community is the prime example, is also sometimes known as urban ecology. The urban community thus can be viewed as an *ecosystem*. As developed by Otis Dudley Duncan (1961), the concept of the ecosystem identifies four major classes of variables and specifies their relationships to one another and to the ecosystem as a whole. Duncan's four classes of variables are: 1) population; 2) environment; 3) technology; and 4) social organization. This concept of the ecosystem is useful for illustrating not only how each of these four classes of variables interacts with and contains implication for the others, but also helps us to understand the interrelatedness of urban life in a far more general way.

In the previous section the main dimensions of urban social organization have been described. The discussion to follow illustrates the main dimensions of the other three variables that comprise the ecosystem.

Population

One of the most significant characteristics of any urban community is the size of its population. For example, a community of 10,000 people differs tremendously in almost all respects from a community of 1,000,000 or more people. The size of a community's population may tell a good deal about its containing environment, its technology, and its social organization. In turn, the environment, technology, and social organization of a community may each or conjointly set ultimate limits on the size of its population.

The density, distribution, and rates of growth or decline of an urban population are additional population characteristics that affect and are affected by the other components of the ecosystem, as are also socioeconomic and age or sex characteristics. Rapid changes in any of the above characteristics of a community's population are surefire indications that significant changes are also taking place in its technology, social organization, or both.

Environment

The natural environment, including such elements as natural resources, climate, topography, soil conditions, and waterways, has always had an important bearing on the location in which cities originate and grow. In turn, these same geographic features may set ultimate limits on the size and density of the population in any given urban region. But in the process of accommodating to the local environment, an urban population may apply its technological, cultural, and social organization to modify the environment or its effects. Thus, hills may be leveled, canals dug, rivers diverted, swamps filled, foliage planted, fields irrigated, and buildings heated and air conditioned. The very existence of a population in a given geographic area and the resultant artificial spatial distribution of land uses that are derived from that population's daily activities become as much a part of the urban dweller's environment as the natural features mentioned above.

The more advanced are technology and social organization, the less limiting are the constraints imposed by the local physical environment. Thus people are able to use modern technology to build new urban communities in previously uninhabited and geographically inhospitable regions (such as in remote areas of Arctic Siberia or the tropical Amazon River basin) and to make these areas more directly accessible to established urban centers by newer forms of transportation, such as the airplane or automobile.

For a number of years, urban ecologists had neglected the natural environment as a topic of concern, and urban sociologists have been criticized for failing to deal adequately with the interrelationships between the physical environment and social factors. However, concerns about the depletion of natural resources and the pollution of air, land, and water by urban populations have recently become more widespread. As a result, new questions again are being raised about the potential constraint to future urban growth because of the increasingly evident effects of depletion and pollution on the natural environment.

Technology

The earliest cities could emerge only after technological improvements in agriculture made it possible to produce large enough surpluses in food supplies to support nonfarm populations. Since the beginning of urban life, success waves of technological development have enabled significant changes in the size, physical structure, and social organization of urban communities. It is no accident that the revolutionary growth in the size of cities and of the urban population since the beginning of the nineteenth century in Europe and North America paralleled the technological advances in manufacturing, transportation, communications, and economics brought about by the industrial revolution.

The metropolitan trend during this century toward the decentralization of city populations into sprawling suburbs and the redistribution of many industrial and commercial activities over an ever-expanding land area surrounding central cities has been greatly facilitated by modern scientific and technological advances, especially in the areas of transportation and communications. The extensive use of the automobile has eliminated the necessity of locating the place of work and residence in close proximity. Thus, those who were first able to afford the use of the private automobile were among the first urbanites to resettle on a large scale in suburban residential enclaves. Shopping centers, factories, and other business establishments were able to decentralize as they lessened their dependence on waterways, railroads, and an adjacent labor supply. The telephone, the motor truck, and the automobile made them readily accessible to their suppliers, their customers, and their employees at almost any location within the metropolitan complex. Of course, this expansion was also facilitated by the ready availability of low-cost energy and fuel supplies. As these become depleted, it is entirely possible that further urban growth and decentralization could be sharply curtailed.

This general pattern of decentralization is also probably both the source and product of changing values, such as industry's desire for more space, more attractive living conditions for its managers and employees, and an increasing emphasis on visible symbols of status, such as may be afforded by such amenities as green open space and landscaping, pleasingly visible architecture, and adequate parking facilities. A growing focus on the availability of increased leisure time and the most effective means for utilizing it is also one of the significant cultural manifestations of the technological advances of the twentieth century.

THE SOCIAL PROBLEM PERSPECTIVE

In one way or another, almost all contemporary social problems have been associated with the process of urbanization. Thus, a diverse set of problems such as those relating to crime, mental illness, broken family life, poor housing, poverty, unemployment, class conflict, racial and ethnic conflict,

The Nicollet Mall in Minneapolis is one of many malls in the U.S. that has contributed to the expansion of business and has made shopping easier. (Minneapolis Convention and Tourism Commission)

drug addiction, pollution, and a host of others are often grouped together under the ominous title of "the urban crisis." This tendency has been so pronounced in recent times that the temptation often arises to treat such problems as synonymous with the city itself. But to do so is misleading, because the city is much more than a simple compilation of its recognized social problems. To describe cities in terms of their problems is akin to trying to describe human beings in terms of their diseases! Neither is it accurate to suggest that urbanization is the main cause of most contemporary social problems. The relationship between a very broad and general social process such as urbanization and the much more concrete examples of social problems such as just listed is very difficult to observe directly, and the chain of events by which these two levels of social behavior can be said to be even remotely connected is complex and indirect. Nevertheless, the city and the metropolis are the settings in which many social problems have developed or intensified, and to understand these problems in their urban context is important.

A variety of current "urban" social problems will be discussed throughout this book, and several chapters will be devoted exclusively to some of the most widely recognized urban problems. This book does not intend, however, to deal with every possible aspect of the problems selected for inclusion, but mainly with those that are pertinent to their urban origins or setting. After all, this book is not designed as a text for a social problems course, and will not duplicate the many excellent social problems textbooks that are currently available. In a book such as this, with its focus on urbanization and its impact, it is important to explain what it is about crime, poverty, unemployment, racial and ethnic conflict, broken family life, or mental illness that make these problems "urban" in character. All of these problems have a long history and were prevalent in preurban societies. But they take on different forms and meanings in an urban society, and the urban sociologist has the added burden of identifying the theoretical or causal links between urbanization and the many "pathologies" commonly associated with modern urban life. This book will attempt to identify these linkages wherever possible and appropriate.

In introducing a social problems perspective, a note of caution is in order. It is much too easy to approach social problems in overly simplistic terms. To avoid this, the following characteristics of social problems must be taken into account.

First, not everybody shares the same views as to what the problems are, who suffers the most as a result of the problems, or the degree to which they represent crisis proportions. Banfield (1974), for example, suggests that what many urban experts refer to as an urban crisis is really not all that serious but merely represents the observers' state of mind. Whether widely recognized social problems represent mainly the perceptual problems of the observer or objective reality raises philosophical issues which are beyond the scope of this book. However, individuals occupying different positions in the social structure will tend to see problems differently and will be affected by them in different kinds of ways. Thus the affluent suburban dweller may see the problems of poor housing or poverty much differently than an unemployed inhabitant of an inner city slum. For all of the urban social problems discussed in this book, people's opinions and perceptions of their extent and consequences differ greatly.

Second, social scientists have not been conspicuously successful in identifying the main causes of major social problems, and a wide range of competing theories prevails at any given time among social scientists to explain the existence of any given problem. For example, crime may be variously explained as the result of rapid urbanization, broken families, spiritual breakdown, inadequate socialization, the competitive free enterprise system, blocked opportunity structure, poverty, poor housing, unemployment, peer group relations in the youth culture, the impact of the mass media, class conflict, poor law enforcement, individual biological or psychological traits, or any number of other hypothetical causes. However, social scientists almost universally agree that for any given problem, no *one* best explanation may exist. The causes are multidimensional and will vary for different groups or individuals under different sets of circumstances.

Finally, opinions vary tremendously on what, if anything, should be done to solve recognized social problems. Just as there may be no one best explanation for the existence of certain problems, there also may be no one best solution. Efforts to solve problems for some groups may in fact create new problems for others. Indeed, consensus on what to do about solving social problems is rarely, if ever, possible in highly complex and diversified urban industrial communities with their many competing interest and pressure groups. Nevertheless, the quest for solutions to urban problems continues to occupy the time, skill, and energies of many concerned individuals and groups at many levels of urban America.

THE SOCIAL POLICY PERSPECTIVE

The notion that problems ought to and can be solved or minimized is closely related to acknowledgement that problems exist. Indeed, the relationship between the recognition of a problem and the desire or ability to solve it is an aspect of many common sociological definitions of a social problem. For example, Horton and Leslie (1974) define a social problem as "a condition affecting a significant number of people in ways considered undesirable, about which it is felt *something can be done through collective social action.*"

For the urban problems identified and reviewed in this book, an impressively wide variety of groups and organizations—at the local, state, and national levels, as well as in both the public and private sectors of our society—have been attempting to propose or initiate policies and programs designed to change or ameliorate those urban problems that have caused the most public concern. These planned interventions represent a bewildering diversity of approaches of varying promise, about which both the student and teacher of urban sociology must have some knowledge to assess their significance. Planned interventions are rapidly becoming a part of the social fabric of urban communities, and thus they become an integral

As a result of war or political considerations, refugees have flowed to cities, adding to urban problems, as seen here in Hong Kong. (United Nations)

part of the data and ideas upon which the understanding of modern urban life is based.

Many approaches and policies for urban problem solving are too recent in origin or too untried to have yet demonstrated their effectiveness, and many of them generate considerable controversy among those who are directly affected, among the public at large, among public officials, as well as among those who are involved as professionals in urban service occupations. These controversies are often related to some very basic value conflicts about the way in which American democracy is expected or ought to work. For example, do we blame the environment or the "system" and forgive the person for the existence of major urban problems, or do we put the onus on the individual? Do we treat problems through institutional change or individually by client or case? Do we use a few universal schemes or do we opt for pluralistic efforts by separate social agencies? Are national measures the proper vehicle or are local community efforts more valid? Do we favor militancy, conflict, and confrontation, or more conciliatory and cooperative tactics? Do we need the input of additional professional experts, or should public opinion, no matter how poorly informed, be the basis for public policy decisions? Should the disadvantaged segments of urban society be given direct assistance, or is it better to stimulate the more "productive" segments of the society, with the hope that a "trickle down" process will ultimately benefit the needy? In American society, with its traditional strong emphasis on private enterprise, the question of who should attempt to bring about desired social change is always present. Is it the proper function of government to initiate, support, or operate programs designed to alleviate urban problem conditions? Or should these tasks be left to private groups or to the free play of the market place? Because of these controversies and value conflicts, most of which remain unresolved, the establishment of an effective urban policy for the United States has been an exceedingly complex and difficult, if not impossible, goal.

Moreover, despite efforts to guide social change through planned intervention, most social change, as we have described it in the other perspectives for this book, continues to proceed in unplanned or unanticipated ways. For example, many changes in attitudes, life styles, patterns of family living, religious, political, or economic institutions, or changes in the ecosystem still appear to be largely beyond the guidance or control of consciously planned intervention by institutional and social planners at this stage of history, no matter how great the efforts in these directions.

Nevertheless, urban and social planning are coming to the forefront as potentially important sources of future social change and have already had some impact in existing urban communities. Such efforts at planned social change are alluded to in many parts of this book. In particular, an entire chapter is devoted to some of the accomplishments, potentialities, and limitations of urban planning in the United States, as it has been practiced so far, and another chapter more speculatively focuses on some of the implications of social policy for the foreseeable urban future.

We have described the five major perspectives around which the contents of this book are loosely organized. Each of the perspectives has been introduced here as a useful frame of reference or theme for making sense out of the vast array of concepts and data presented throughout the book.

None of the five perspectives is mutually exclusive; all are overlapping and interdependent. For example, the social change perspective is highly relevant to the social organization, the ecological, and the social policy perspectives, as they have been described here. For some of the topics in the book, two or more of the perspectives may be more appropriate and given greater emphasis than in other chapters.

Also, the five perspectives are implied rather than explicitly spelled out in every instance. With a little thought, most readers should have no trouble recognizing them. Figure 1-1 identifies the perspectives emphasized in each subsequent chapter of the book and is presented in the following section.

THE QUALITY OF URBAN LIFE

Overriding and relating to all five of the perspectives is a more general concern with the quality of urban life in contemporary American urban society. The quality of life, of course, is a relatively impressionistic and subjective concept, meaning different things to different people.

In the last few decades, social scientists have attempted to measure

FIGURE 1-1 Applications of the five perspectives

CHAPTER	SOCIAL CHANGE	ECOLOGY	SOCIAL ORGANIZATION	SOCIAL PROBLEMS	SOCIAL POLICY
1 (Introduction)					
2	X*	X	X		
3	X	X	X	X	
4	X	X	X		X
5		X	X	X	
6			X	X	X
7	X		X	X	
8	X		X	X	
9			X	X	X
10			X	X	X
11	X		X	X	X
12	X		X	X	X
13	X	X	X	X	X
14	X	X	X	X	X
15	X	X	X	X	X
16	X	X	X	X	X

*X indicates the perspectives emphasized in each chapter.

objectively the quality of life through a variety of quantifiable social indicators, and some of these quantitative measures will be cited in various parts of the book. Our own use of this concept as a general frame of reference, however, is more subjective and speculative, and has to do with our effort to develop a more humanistic interpretation of what it is about urban living that creates positive satisfaction and a sense of well-being for some, dissatisfaction for others, and a desire to escape completely from the urban environment for still others. Hundreds of social observers and "urbanologists" have speculated for many years about the quality of urban life, and we claim no originality in this regard. But what we have attempted to do is to tie such speculation to the major perspectives upon which this book is built, and further to tie them to some of the accumulated wisdom and knowledge developed by urban sociologists over the past half-century or so.

Sociology, of course, is not the only discipline to have contributed to our understanding of the quality of urban life, and it is necessary to borrow data and ideas from other academic disciplines or fields of urban professional practice. History, anthropology, geography, economics, political science and public administration, psychiatry, law, journalism, architecture, social work, and urban planning have all made significant contributions to understanding and coming to grips with modern urban life. Insights and knowledge from these fields will be utilized in this volume whenever appropriate or feasible.

But it should be understood that this is primarily a work based on the accumulated contributions of experts who have called themselves or have been identified primarily as urban sociologists. Therefore, the following parts of this introductory chapter will consist of a brief review of the historical development of urban sociology as a field of study. Such a review should further clarify and illustrate the five major perspectives of this book and should further help the student appreciate the intellectual development of this diverse, complex, and challenging field.

THE DEVELOPMENT OF URBAN SOCIOLOGY AS A FIELD OF STUDY

Although there are individual exceptions, the classic writers who began and stimulated the serious analysis of urban life from sociological perspectives fall primarily into two major schools. The first developed in Germany and was centered in Heidelberg and Berlin. Its members were a remarkable group of scholars who produced a series of essays and books during the first quarter of this century, many of which remain influential to this day. The second school is commonly referred to as the "Chicago School" because its leading members were on the faculty of the University of Chicago. The ideas of the Chicago School, which were produced primarily in the period between the first and second world wars, also still pervade much of the writing of contemporary urban sociologists.

The German School

One of the earliest sociological efforts to understand the modern urban community was Max Weber's *The City*, published in Germany in 1905. In this work, Weber viewed the city as a total systematic unit of human life, distinguished by a complex order of social actions, social relations, and social institutions. To constitute an urban community, a human settlement has to consist of at least the following features: a fortification; a market; a complex legal system, including a court and a body of autonomous law; and an elected political administration. Weber's concept of the city is best understood in the context of the term "cosmopolitan." A cosmopolitan human settlement is one in which diverse individuals and life styles can coexist in the same community. To Weber, this definition is synonymous with the nature of the city itself: the city is that social form which permits the greatest degree of individuality and uniqueness in each occurrence or event produced within its boundaries. The city, then, represents much more than a single style of life. It is a constellation of social structures that can produce a multitude of life styles and encourage social individuality and innovation, and thus is the instrument of continuous social change.

Weber's work on the city is most valuable for the way in which it focused attention on urbanization as a fundamental process of social change and as a unique historical pattern. In this sense, the city represents a distinct and limited pattern of human life that could only appear under special conditions and at a certain time in history. To Weber, the ideal conditions conducive to the emergence of urban life were first produced in preindustrial Europe, which was characterized by the development and influence of rationality. In opposition to traditional action—which emphasizes what is handed down from the past—the cities of Western civilization emphasize rational action, which involves the calculated use of resources for the achievement of specified goals in the most economic way possible. Within this framework, Weber's work was comparative in that it recognized a great variety of forms of city life to be found in preindustrial Western societies as well as in non-Western societies. Nevertheless, the Western city, as Weber saw it, was itself going through a transformation that raised serious questions as to its capacity to survive in its present form. The urban community had lost, or was losing, its legal and political autonomy to the larger and more powerful nation-state, the urban citizenry was no longer united by a common purpose, and the internal structure of the city was approaching a state of decay. For Weber, the end of the modern Western city, as he knew it, appeared to be in sight.

The work of another German theorist, Oswald Spengler (1928), differed from Weber's in that Spengler believed that different stages of city development were indicative of the development of civilization as a whole in Western culture, and that the stages of growth in both were cyclical in nature. He believed that city cultures throughout history have had a clear pattern of growth and decay, and that the cities of his own time were a cancer. He saw them sapping off the sources of vitality and energy that were more characteristic of earlier periods of urban development when cities and their surrounding countrysides were of more equal strength and influence. In his major work, he prophesied that the large metropolitan centers of his day would meet the fate of ancient Rome, that modern cities would be destroyed by wars or other disasters, and civilized urban society would revert to a more barbaric form of preurban agricultural life. Then the whole cycle of urban growth would reinstitute itself, civilized life would return, again become overripe at the point where the city overpowers the country, and would once again collapse.

A major contribution of both Spengler and Weber was to postulate that a particular cluster of traits or characteristics is associated with each stage of urban growth, and that the cluster of hypothetical characteristics they identify represents the pure or "ideal" type for that stage of development. Thus, their work was an early effort to classify types of communities along dimensions such as age, size, function, or complexity of structure.

An even earlier effort to develop a typology of urban development was that of another German theorist, Ferdinand Tönnies (Nottridge, 1972). Tönnies's typology was spelled out in a book published in 1887 entitled *Gemeinschaft und Gesellschaft*. The title has no precise equivalent in English, but can be roughly translated into the terms "community" and "society." For Tönnies, these two concepts are opposites, and all human social relationships can be seen as divided between these two different types. *Gemeinschaft* relationships are found in the relationship between parents and children, within family and kinship groups, and between physically and socially close friends and neighbors who live and work together with close understanding and cooperation. The impression created by Tönnies is that *Gemeinschaft* relationships represent "natural will," are deep, warm, satisfying, and are most characteristic of peasant and agricultural communities. In contrast, *Gesellschaft* relationships are more impersonal, are bonded by contract rather than natural will, and tend to separate individuals and groups from one another by creating isolation, tension, and conflict. These relationships, it is implied, are characteristic of modern city life, and as the process of urbanization expands, *Gesellschaft* relationships will grow more dominant and will eventually displace *Gemeinschaft* relationships.

The German social theorist whose work probably had the most direct influence on the thinking of early urban sociologists in the United States was Georg Simmel, who was a friend and younger colleague of Max Weber. Simmel's work on the effects of urbanization was similar to that of Weber and the others reviewed above in that he utilized an "ideal type" method of analysis to describe the form that cities take. But Simmel differed from the others by emphasizing the psychological rather than the structural aspects of urban life. In his classic article, "The Metropolis and Mental Life," Simmel (1950) speculated that the size, density, and complexity of urban life would produce distinct personality traits and distinct mechanisms of human interaction, as city dwellers attempt to defend themselves from the excess of psychic or nervous stimulation Simmel thought to be characteristic of life in cities. Because of the exposure to constant shifts in internal and external situations in their daily round of life, city dwellers find it difficult to maintain an integrated personality, and the quality of interpersonal relationships in urban settings fails to insure consistency of behavior. Urban dwellers seek to protect themselves from the resulting state of over-stimulation by seeking anonymity, by adopting an attitude of sophistication, or by masking their feelings with a blasé or "cool" posture in response to psychic overload. The result is that calculated expediency and the rationale of efficiency takes the place of feelings as the basis for personal relationships in the city.

Simmel was unsure whether these changes in the characteristic modes of human interaction resulting from urbanization would lead to dispirited alienation or would liberate the urbanite for a more civilized and uplifting kind of human freedom. The great subtlety of Simmel's thinking at this early point in the development of ideas about urban life was that he did not foreclose the possibility of either or both of the above outcomes, and that he was willing to leave open for further exploration the potential for both good and evil that the giant and impersonal metropolis of his and later times might ultimately serve. Such exploration still goes on in modern urban sociology, since the issues raised by Simmel are still not satisfactorily resolved (Warren, 1973). Many of the materials included in this volume continue to confront the issues that Simmel originally posed.

The Chicago School

In the United States, the field of urban sociology was first widely recognized as a special subarea of sociology during the 1920s, and it was in 1925 that the annual meetings of the American Sociological Society were devoted almost exclusively to papers in the field of urban sociology (Burgess and Bogue, 1964). Actually, the development of urban sociology in this country has been most strongly influenced by the work of a group of scholars affiliated with the University of Chicago during a period beginning about 1915 to the present. Some of the greatest intellectual achievements of this group were accomplished in the 1920s and 1930s, establishing some of the main topical concerns of urban sociology, many of which are still highly relevant today. The most significant figures associated with the Chicago School were Robert Park, Ernest Burgess, Louis Wirth, and Robert Redfield. While these men were strongly influenced by the German School, their work shifted the development of urban sociology in different directions. Human ecology also evolved at the University of Chicago, becoming a subfield of sociology in its own right and sometimes viewed by its proponents as an alternative approach to the entire field of sociology. First, however, we shall consider the main contributions of the Chicago School.

The origins of the Chicago School can be traced back to an article by Robert Park entitled "The City: Suggestions for the Investigation of Human Behavior in the Urban Environment," published in 1916 (Burgess and Bogue, 1964). Formerly a journalist, Park had turned to sociology as a result of his fascination with many aspects of the social, economic, and political life of the city of Chicago. During his lifetime, that city had gone

The Chicago School was able to identify many of the urban problems during the 1920s and 1930s, many of which still apply today. (Chicago Convention and Tourism Bureau)

through a period of remarkable social changes, such as a very rapid population increase due to immigrants of many different ethnic and social backgrounds coming to the city in wave after wave. This growth was accompanied by noticeable social problems, such as the creation of overcrowded slum housing conditions, increased crime, municipal corruption, unemployment and poverty, and ethnic exploitation and segregation. Originally, Park approached these problems in the muckraking and reformist tradition of Lincoln Steffens and the whole school of journalism that Steffens represented. Much of the earliest urban research of Park and his followers was little more than the discovery and reporting to the public that the feelings and sentiments of those living in the newly forming ethnic slums were in reality very different from those imputed to them by the larger public, which had by that time already formed strong prejudices and patterns of discrimination toward the newcomers (Burgess and Bogue, 1964). Quite often, Park and other social scientists at the University of Chicago defended the immigrant groups publicly and spoke out for tolerance, understanding, and sympathy. When Park discovered that such efforts did not always lead to constructive change, his reformer or social work orientation gave way to an ambition to understand more fully and to interpret the social and economic forces at work in the city and their effect on the social and personal organization of those who lived there.

By the early 1920s, this shift toward more scientific analysis of city life led to the creation of a program of sociological field research, using the city as a laboratory for scientific study. The University of Chicago social scientists, with the assistance of their students, first undertook the task of discovering the physical pattern of the city. They made maps showing the spatial distribution of all kinds of social problems such as juvenile delinquency, mental illness, and prostitution. These were followed by maps showing the distribution of local facilities such as dance halls, movie theaters, rooming houses, and brothels. Soon their students began making maps of any social data that could be plotted. Two sociological classics that emerged from these early student field studies were *The Hobo,* by Nels Anderson, and *The Gold Coast and the Slum,* by Harvey Zorbaugh (Burgess and Bogue, 1964).

The research of this period was based on the assumption that the city had a characteristic social organization and a way of life that differentiated it from rural communities. Further, the city was composed of "natural areas," each having its own distinctive physical features, social institutions, or subcultures based on differences of income, occupation, ethnic background, religion, race, or other social characteristics. Park never tired of pointing out to his students how this process of differentiation conditioned almost every aspect of urban social life, and that the spatial segregation and differentiation of land uses and of groups of people were physical manifestations of social, psychological, and economic forces at work in the city as a whole.

Louis Wirth, whose book *The Ghetto* has become a classic, was another important figure in the Chicago School. He had absorbed many of the ideas of Park and Simmel, and while his work was not as original, he perhaps went further in systematizing, detailing, and extending urban theory. His article "Urbanism as a Way of Life" was an influential contribution in that it helped to further define the boundaries of urban sociology as a field of study. This article is still often reprinted as an introduction in more contemporary anthologies of urban sociology (Gutman and Popenoe, 1970; Fava, 1968). Wirth (1938) viewed the shift from a rural to a predominantly urban society as producing a profound change in virtually every phase of human life. While the city is the product of evolutionary rather than instantaneous growth and does not wipe out completely the previously dominant modes of folk society, which continue to have an imprint on urban social life, he believed that the city nevertheless does produce a distinctive mode of life. He perceived city life as the opposite of life in preurban folk communities. Wirth defined the city as "a relatively large, dense, and permanent settlement of socially heterogeneous individuals." It was the task of urban sociologists to discover the forms of social action and social organization that typically emerged in settlements of this kind. Wirth hypothesized that, as the size, density, and heterogeneity of city populations increased, the character of social relationships and social organization would also change. For example, the occupational division of labor would become more elaborate and complex, and the bonds between residents would grow weaker and more impersonal, superficial, and transitory. Urban dwellers would become more rational, sophisticated, and anonymous, their lives would be lived at a faster pace, and their contacts with other people would be physically closer but more superficial. Interest groups would multiply, producing a conflict of loyalties for urban dwellers, who, at the same time, would become more geographically and socially mobile.

Wirth suffered from the underlying pessimism about city life that afflicted many of the other German and Chicago sociologists, in the sense that he saw personal disorganization, mental breakdown, delinquency, crime, corruption, and social disorder as products of the "rootlessness" of growing urbanization. It has been difficult to test the validity of Wirth's observations about urban life, and many of them have been challenged by more contemporary social scientists. Yet Wirth's work still serves as a useful point of departure for much current urban research and as a useful focus on issues for the serious student of urban life.

Robert Redfield (1947) was an anthropologist at Chicago who had done much field work among villages and other rural communities in Mexico. His work broadened that of his colleagues by showing how their views of the modern city were based on their assumptions about life in nonurban, or "folk" societies. By combining analysis of the internal characteristics of cities, in the Chicago tradition, with the analysis of broader forces of social change and development that the German School emphasized, Redfield was able to show how the difference between urban and folk societies was related to the evolution of urban forms. Because of this synthesis, Sennett (1969) considers Redfield's contributions to be the most interesting to come out of the Chicago School. Redfield's main variables in showing change from folk society to urban society were the increase in cultural disorganization, the increase in secularization, and the increase in individualization. In effect, Redfield created a scale having at one end an "ideal type" with all the essential characteristics of a folk society and at the other end urban society. This concept has come to be referred to as the "folk-urban continuum" and has been widely quoted in the sociological literature as a point of departure for the study of urbanization (Hatt and Reiss, 1957). Redfield used this concept as the basis for an elaborate, sophisticated description of what happens to people as they become more urbanized. To Redfield, the move from folk to urban society was a process with a definite beginning and a definite end, with various stages in between, through which cities might pass while evolving. The form that the city might take at the end of the scale, according to Redfield, was also subject to change as a result of its relationships to other elements of the containing society.

Of course, many of the theories and conclusions of the earlier generations of contributors to the development of urban sociology as a field have been expanded upon, updated, revised, or discarded by subsequent generations of urban scholars, and many of their concerns will be reintroduced and reexamined in more detail in the chapters to follow, in the light of more recent thinking and research. But the early work of the contributors reviewed here was most influential in shaping the direction and topical concerns of much of contemporary urban sociology.

Within the framework of the five major perspectives previously discussed, *Part I* traces the evolution of cities from their origins in the pre-Christian era to the beginning of the twentieth century. Chapter Two provides a brief sociohistorical outline of urbanization up to the beginning of the industrial revolution in Europe. Only by reviewing preindustrial urban development in these earlier periods can one fully appreciate the significance of modern urban-industrial communities and understand how they got to be the way they are. Chapter Three begins with a discussion of the forces leading to the industrial revolution in Europe and the impact of industrialization on urban growth and development. It then proceeds to review the industrialization and urbanization processes in nineteenth-century America. While occasional international comparisons will be made, the remaining parts of the book from this point on will focus on urbanization in twentieth-century American society.

Part II describes and analyzes the basic forms of urban existence that have emerged in this century. Chapter Four identifies the revolutionary forms of metropolitan development and decentralization that have made the burgeoning suburbs as important as cities in the contemporary urban scene. This chapter also reviews many of the major theories of metropolitan structure and process, and it deals with some of the attempts to classify the component parts of the metropolis, such as cities, suburbs, natural areas, and slums. Chapter Five discusses middle-range levels of urban social organization; i.e., the structure and functions of local neighborhoods, social networks, and voluntary associations. Chapter Six examines the social-psychological aspects of the impact of urbanization on individual personality organization; some symbolic aspects of urban life; and a discussion of urban collective behavior (or everyday aspects of face-to-face interaction in urban settings).

Part III focuses on the recent history, current trends, and problems associated with the impact of urbanization and industrialization on some of the major social institutions of contemporary urban America. Chapters Seven and Eight analyze two social institutions that are pre-urban in their origins—the family and organized religion—which have changed drastically in the urban context and whose continued survival and well-being are being severely challenged. Chapters Nine and Ten deal with the political institutions of modern urban communities, with the former chapter focusing on formal government structures and policies and the latter on informal power structures and informal decision-making processes at the urban community level. More and more, urban political institutions are seen as crucial to efforts to solve urban problems and to help shape the future direction of urban development. Chapter Eleven analyzes modern urban economic institutions and describes in detail the characteristics and composition of the modern urban labor force, which has been changing rapidly in response to technological and other characteristics of rapid urbanization.

Formal educational and welfare systems are among the most recently institutionalized features of modern American urban communities, and they are assessed in Chapter Twelve. These two institutions are often at the heart of major controversies surrounding what, if anything, can and should be done to ease the stresses associated with urban living and what can be done to better prepare individuals with the appropriate skills, knowledge, and attitudes for successfully coping with urban living. These two institutions are increasingly responsible for attempts to improve the quality of life in urban communities, and their successes and failures are most important to understand in this context.

Part IV considers some of the most persistent and pressing social problems of American urban communities, assesses the planning approach to urban change and development, and closes with some speculation on the future of urban America. Chapter Thirteen explores the causes, extent, and consequences of various forms of crime, violence, and aberrant behavior in urban communities and considers the nature of the criminal justice system as a form of urban social control. Various proposals and policies designed to reduce urban crime and violence are discussed and evaluated, as is the *fear* of crime as a problem that has consequences probably as far reaching as the real incidence of crime itself. Chapter Fourteen deals with the problems of ethnic and racial minorities in urban America. Past trends, current realities, and controversies regarding public policy as a solution to problems of racial and ethnic conflict, segregation, or discrimination is discussed, with the greatest attention given to black Americans in large northern cities.

Chapter Fifteen provides a broad overview of the historical development and current realities of urban planning in America as an approach to improving the quality of communities by controlling or minimizing their most undesirable features. Urban planning is identified as a social movement, a legitimate function of urban governments, and as a technical profession. Some of the accomplishments, potentialities, and limitations of urban planning in such controversial areas as urban renewal and housing, the development of new towns, transportation planning, and metropolitan or regional planning is discussed, as well as some of the career patterns and opportunities for students hoping to enter the urban planning field.

Chapter Sixteen speculates on the future of urban America and considers some controversial policy alternatives that are expected to have considerable impact on the future of urban life. Upon these alternatives the survival of urban communities as we now know them may very well depend.

Chapter Seventeen, an epilogue, closes the book with a brief comparative overview of world urbanization in the industrialized and wealthier nations as well as in the underdeveloped parts of the world. The problems caused by rapid rates of urbanization in the Western world pale in comparison to those in Asia, Africa, and Latin America.

SELECTED BIBLIOGRAPHY

BANFIELD, EDWARD C. *The Unheavenly City Revisited.* Boston: Little Brown, 1974.

BERRY, BRIAN J. L. *The Human Consequences of Urbanization.* New York: St. Martin's Press, 1973.

BOSKOFF, ALVIN. *The Sociology of Urban Regions.* 2nd ed. New York: Appleton-Century-Crofts, 1970.

BURGESS, ERNEST W., and BOGUE, DONALD J., eds. *Contributions to Urban Sociology.* Chicago: University of Chicago Press, 1964.

DUNCAN, O. D. "From Social System to Ecosystem," *Sociological Inquiry* 31 (Spring 1961). pp. 140–149.

FAVA, SYLVIA F., ed. *Urbanism in World Perspective.* New York: Thomas Y. Crowell, 1968.

GUTMAN, ROBERT, and POPENOE, DAVID, eds. *Neighborhood, City, and Metropolis.* New York: Random House, 1970.

HATT, PAUL K., and REISS, ALBERT J., JR., eds. *Cities and Society.* New York: Free Press, 1957.

HAWLEY, AMOS H. *Urban Society.* New York: Ronald Press, 1971.

HORTON, P. B. and LESLIE, G. R. *The Sociology of Social Problems.* Englewood Cliffs, N.J.: Prentice-Hall, 1974.

LOFLAND, LYN H. *A World of Strangers.* New York: Basic Books, 1973.

MEADOWS, PAUL, and MIZRUCHI, EPHRAIM H., eds. *Urbanism, Urbanization, and Change: Comparative Perspectives.* Reading, Mass.: Addison-Wesley, 1969.

NOTTRIDGE, HAROLD E. *The Sociology of Urban Living.* London and Boston: Routledge & Kegan Paul, 1972.

POPENOE, DAVID. *The Urban-Industrial Frontier.* New Brunswick, N.J.: Rutgers University Press, 1970.

REDFIELD, ROBERT. "The Folk Society," *American Journal of Sociology* 52 (January 1947). pp. 293–308.

SENNETT, RICHARD, ed. *Classic Essays on the Culture of Cities.* New York: Appleton-Century-Crofts, 1969.

SIMMEL, GEORG. "The Metropolis and Mental Life." *The Sociology of Georg Simmel.* Trans. Kurt Wolff. New York: Free Press, 1950.

SMITH, MICHAEL P. *The City and Social Theory.* New York: St. Martin's Press, 1979.

SPENGLER, OSWALD. *The Decline of the West.* Vol. II. Trans. C. F. Atkinson. New York: Knopf, 1928.

THOMLINSON, RALPH. *Urban Structure.* New York: Random House, 1969.

WARREN, ROLAND L. *Perspectives on the American Community.* 2nd ed. Skokie, Ill.: Rand McNally, 1973.

WEBER, MAX. *The City.* Ed. and trans. D. Martindale and G. Neuwirth. New York: Free Press, 1958.

WIRTH, LOUIS. "Urbanism as a Way of Life," *American Journal of Sociology* 44 (July 1938). pp. 3–24.

WOLF, C. P. "The Structure of Societal Revolutions." In G. K. Zollschan and W. Hirsch, eds., *Social Change: Explorations, Diagnoses and Conjectures.* New York: John Wiley, 1976.

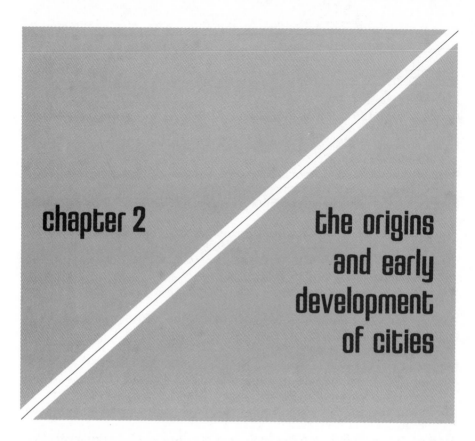

chapter 2

the origins
and early
development
of cities

This chapter will review some of the developments of the preurban era that made the emergence of cities possible. It will provide a brief sociohistorical outline of urbanization from the earliest cities of antiquity to the beginning of the industrial revolution in Europe, when the rates of urban growth began to take off at unprecedented speed. Only by reviewing preindustrial urban development can one fully appreciate the significance of modern urban-industrial communities and how they got to be the way they are.

It is difficult, of course, to know with any high degree of precision or certainty the exact nature of the earliest cities and urban life. What we do know comes largely from the work of archeologists and historians, who are constantly enlarging our knowledge with each new discovery of early urban sites and with each new find of ancient artifacts or documents. Modern techniques of excavating and interpreting such finds are improving so rapidly that it is almost impossible for the nonspecialist to stay abreast of such advances.

Rather than presenting a strictly chronological description of discrete historical events, our purpose here is to portray as broadly as possible what the conditions of urban life must have been like, in terms of population, environment, technology, social organization, and sociocultural characteristics. Also, we shall attempt to identify those forces working at various points in time that made each succeeding stage of urban development in preindustrial cities possible.

When the human species first appeared on earth is not exactly certain. The best estimates place the date anywhere between half a million and one million years ago. Current archeological findings may soon extend the estimated date even further back in time (Wenke, 1980). Nevertheless, estimates are more certain that the urban community as a form of human settlement did not develop until about 5,500 or 6,500 years ago, with the first cities of any consequence appearing sometime between 3500 and 4500 B.C. (Whitehouse, 1977). What is most significant about the above estimates is that they remind us that urban life has existed during only a tiny fraction of the history of humankind, encompassing perhaps less than one percent of human beings' total existence as a species. It took a very slowly developing but remarkable transformation of humans' way of life to produce the conditions that made the first cities possible, and one cannot overestimate how revolutionary were the changes necessary to support as many as several thousand people in permanent year-round settlements. Since this change occurred, the process of urbanization has been associated with continuous modifications in the conditions of human living ever since.

PREURBAN NOMADS AND THE FIRST PREURBAN PERMANENT SETTLEMENTS

Prior to the emergence of the first permanent year-round settlements, people lived in nomadic hunting and food-gathering bands, wandering from place to place in search of sustenance, without any permanent place of habitation. While climatic and environmental limitations on food supplies were an important barrier to permanent settlement in early human history, equally significant was the lack of adequate technological development and social organization. Not until people discovered the techniques of plant cultivation and the further technological development of agriculture, as represented by the domestication of animals, the development of the animal-drawn plow, the development of all kinds of tools (axes, fishing nets), the development of specialized skills, such as weaving and pottery making, and improvements in the techniques of fertilization and irrigation, did the first permanent towns and villages develop (Trigger, 1973).

Of course, these human inventions did not appear overnight and were thousands of years in the making. They seem to have first developed about 12,000 years ago in an elongated, semitropical zone reaching from central Asia through southeastern Asia and into northern Africa, where, with the discovery of plant cultivation, formerly nomadic hunting and food-gathering tribes drifted into permanent settlement in fertile river valleys and became increasingly dependent on cereal foods (Trigger, 1973).

In particular, the so-called Fertile Crescent region—which includes what is now Lebanon, Jordon, Syria, Israel, and parts of Iraq and Iran—is where the first year-round settlements were likely located. The village farming community of Jarmo, located in the Fertile Crescent, is the earliest

Reconstructions of life for the Cro-Magnons (about 30,000 years ago) and during Neolithic times (3rd century B.C.) reveal the development of early civilizations. (The American Museum of Natural History)

known example (Braidwood and Willey, 1962). It is believed that approximately 150 people lived at Jarmo at a population density of approximately twenty-seven people per square mile. Such density seems extremely low compared to the densities of modern American cities. But in contrast to earlier hunting and gathering societies in which at least one square mile was required to support a single individual, such concentration of population was a major achievement. There is evidence that the inhabitants of Jarmo had learned to domesticate goats, dogs, and possibly sheep. They grew barley and wheat, but they were still not able to supply all of their food needs in these ways. Thus, they still continued to engage in hunting and gathering for their livelihood.

Jarmo was inhabited from about 7000 B.C. to about 6500 B.C. While it appears that its technology advanced during this period, as evidenced by stone tools, weaving, and pottery at the excavation site, it is not known for certain why Jarmo and many similar agricultural settlements which had emerged and spread throughout surrounding regions over the next several thousand years failed to grow or survive. One of the most common explanations is that these earliest permanent settlements were easy prey to the marauding bands of nomads still occupying the regions in which they developed. In fact, a chronic state of warfare between the settled areas and the encircling nomadic groups probably existed for thousands of years (Hawley, 1971).

Paradoxically, the recurring needs for defense produced some of the most important innovations associated with the development of somewhat large and complex human settlements more accurately described as cities or towns. For example, defense requirements necessitated a development of organization beyond what was required for just the day-to-day food requirements. A military establishment with a clear-cut division of labor and a centralized command structure was created. A storable food surplus was required to maintain food supplies during periods of siege. This, in turn, required a system of taxation, initially applied against the agricultural product of the inhabitants, along with the organizational ability to enforce and administer the collection and distribution of the surpluses. Related developments in weapon making, record keeping, and administration thus became necessary. The construction of fortified places in which settlers could gather for mutual protection was one of the important physical manifestations of the need for defense, and often such fortresses are among the most visible excavated remains of settlements of this period. But even with these precautions, many of the early fortress settlements were overcome by force and perished (Hawley, 1971).

Those who successfully served as military chieftains in settlements that were able to survive probably emerged as rulers with broad power over the entire community. Such power often was passed from father to son over succeeding generations. A class structure appeared based on a dominating ruling family and a supporting cadre of functionaries superimposed on a large peasant class (Sjoberg, 1976). This social pattern is suggested by archeological remains of palaces, royal tombs and granaries, military garrisons, and the like, which are common to many of the earliest known permanent settlements.

The exact time and place at which the first cities of any consequence appeared are of some dispute, depending on what one defines as the characteristics of cities. A useful point of departure has been provided by Gordon Childe (1950), who characterizes the first classical urban revolution as producing cities consisting of some combination of the following features:

1. Permanent settlement in dense population aggregations.
2. A labor force of specialized nonagricultural occupations.
3. A system of taxation and capital accumulation.
4. Monumental public buildings (temples, palaces).
5. A ruling class.
6. A written language, with established techniques of writing.
7. The acquisition of predictive sciences—arithmetic, geometry, and astronomy.
8. A pattern of artistic expression.
9. A system of negotiated exchange (trade).
10. The replacement of kinship by residence as the basis for membership in the community.

Of course, not all of the early towns or cities had each of the above features to the same degree, or in the same combination. What is important is that Childe's list represents a most significant transformation from what had previously existed into what has commonly been referred to as the beginnings of human civilization.

MESOPOTAMIAN CITIES

The communities having what Childe has described as the characteristics of cities first appeared in Mesopotamia around 4000 to 3500 B.C. (McAdams, 1973). Forms of city life became well developed during the next thousand years or so, after which they began to decline. Some of the early cities were Ur, Eridu, Erech, Ubaid, Nippur, Lagash, Babylon, and Nineveh. Jericho, at the left bank of the Jordan River, also probably emerged during this same period (Hawley, 1971; McAdams, 1973).

Ur is believed to have been the largest of the known Mesopotamian cities (Childe, 1946). The excavated walls of Ur enclosed about 220 acres of land and the city is estimated to have had a population of about 24,000 people. Other Mesopotamian towns contained populations of up to about 20,000 people. By today's standards, these cities would be considered nothing more than small towns or villages. But Ur, with all its temples, canals, and harbors, was ten times the size of the earlier Neolithic agricultural villages, and must have been awesome in its time. McAdams (1973) estimates that even the largest cities of this period contained no more than 3 or 4 percent of all the people of the regions in which they were located. Agriculture as then practiced still required forty or fifty agricultural workers to supply sufficient food surpluses to support a single nonagricultural city dweller. Thus, the size of cities was (and still is) limited by how much food surplus could be produced, stored, and distributed by the available agricultural technology.

The description of Ur by its chief excavator, Sir Leonard Woolley (1952), tells us much about the physical and social structure of the typical Mesopotamian city. At the center of the town was a fortress which housed the ruling class and which included within its walls a palace, a temple, monastaries, convents, and granaries. The surrounding wall may have been as much for protection against the local people as against organized assaults from outsiders. Hawley (1971) suggests that the town's ruling classes were conquerors who had enslaved the local residents and built their wealth on the strength of exorbitant taxation of the peasantry. The artisans, the scribes, the domestic servants, and other retainers of the ruling class lived immediately beyond the inner fortress walls but were enclosed by the outer walls of the city. Within the outer wall there were sufficient gardens and pasture lands to enable the town to withstand a siege by its enemies. The streets were narrow and meandered like animal trails. Housing, which rose to two or three floors, was dense and congested. Each house was built around an inner court, with blank walls facing the street for defense purposes.

Ur was located at the confluence of the Tigris and Euphrates Rivers, and like other Mesopotamian cities, engaged in some intercity and interregional trade. The market place was not located within the city walls but was outside, adjacent to the river harbor. At first, trade was reluctantly accepted as a necessary evil, and traders and merchants were accorded marginal and inferior social status. The amount of internal trade was negligible, since most residents of the town furnished their own material requirements from their farmland and manors and had no special reason to buy or sell among themselves. Nevertheless, as agricultural surpluses began to be commonplace, trade became the most acceptable way of disposing of these surpluses. Eventually, successful trading activity came to be a desired end in itself, and trade already had become fairly extensive throughout the cities of the Mesopotamian region as early as 3000–2500 B.C. (McAdams, 1973).

Given the above description, Weber's (1962) definition of the classical city as a "fusion of fortress and marketplace" seems reasonable. Other scholars go further than Weber by also underscoring the importance of complex, universal religions as a functional characteristic of the earliest cities. Boskoff (1970), for example, describes the first urban wave (4500 B.C. to A.D. 500) as built on the triumvirate of *defense, worship,* and *commerce.* Normally, the priesthood shared power with the military officials, and, in some circumstances, the emergence of a priest-king was the product of a political-religious fusion among ruling families. Early urban communities were characterized by a bewildering variety of local cults, rituals, and gods; in general, each city was an isolated religious island.

While life in most Mesopotamian towns was ordinarily lived at a bare subsistence level, it must not be forgotten that warfare and conquest were often the means of enriching the town coffers. Thus, when a victorious king returned from forays rich with the spoils of war, he liberally distributed wealth to encourage the cultivation of learning and the creation of great works of art, such as sculpture, architecture, painting, and drama (Oppenheim, 1964). These periods of affluence, learning, and artistic creativity were probably sporadic and infrequent in the history of any one town. Nevertheless, the occasional plunder of war also enabled the Mesopotamian towns to make remarkable cultural advances of the kind listed by Childe. Writing and record keeping, systems of numbers, mathematical and astronomical calculations, systems for keeping time, law and administrative procedures, and many other elements of urban civilization all had their origins in Mesopotamian cities (Childe, 1950).

By the time that Mesopotamian cities had declined, for reasons that are not entirely certain, urban civilization had begun developing in other parts of the world. For example, urban societies had developed in the Indus River Valley of what is now West Pakistan and in the Yellow River Valley of China by about 2500 B.C. (see Pusalker, 1951; Eberhard, 1955–1956). In the Western Hemisphere, two urban civilizations, the Mayan of Central Mexico and the Incan in the Central Andes, had developed by about 1000 B.C. These appear to have developed independently from those emanating from the Middle East (McAdams, 1966). While all of the above urban civilizations were different from one another in many important respects, they all exhibited in some degree most of the essential characteristics of urban life enumerated by Childe.

EGYPTIAN CITIES

The cities of ancient Egypt probably represent the most direct diffusion of Mesopotamian culture and civilization. The first Egyptian cities appeared about 3300 B.C. and were remarkable for perpetuating a civilization with relatively few major changes for several thousand years (Clark and Piggott, 1965). Ancient Egyptian cities such as Memphis and Thebes were ruled by pharaohs who served in the dual role of god-king. The pharaoh was the head of a bureaucratic civil service structure that was quite elaborate and centralized for its time. He had at his service literate clerks or scribes who were trained in hieroglyphic writing and who used papyrus (paper) and ink, which were invented by the Egyptians. The bureaucracy had the power and skill to conduct an annual census of the population, collect taxes, and maintain a system of courts to enforce the laws of the ruling class. The Egyptians developed skills in medical sciences, such as anatomy, surgery, and pharmacy, and they invented a calendar similar to the one we use today. Notable examples of sculpture, painting, and architecture were also produced by full-time artisans and craftsmen who were in service to the pharaohs.

In some instances, the power of the pharaohs was so great that they were able to create completely new cities to reflect their own tastes and values. For example, the Pharaoh Ikhnaton (or Amenhotep the IV) of the eighteenth dynasty of the New Kingdom of ancient Egypt became dissatisfied with the existing religious, political, and cultural conditions that existed in the capital of Thebes when he assumed power around 1400 B.C. (White, 1949). Within a few short years, he built an entirely new city, which he called Akhetaton, and which he made the new capital of the Egyptian Empire. Under Ikhnaton's personal guidance the city flourished, creating new forms of religion, philosophy, art, and architecture that were thought to be many centuries ahead of their time. Many observers, for example, believe that the monotheistic religious philosophy that later became the basis for the Judaic-Christian religions can be traced directly to the original religious thought of Ikhnaton (Freud, 1957; White, 1949; Breasted, 1912).

While Ikhnaton's reign lasted less than twenty-five years and the city of Akhetaton was abandoned shortly after his death, late nineteenth-century excavations have provided a fascinating picture of what the city must have been like in its prime (see Steindorff and Seele, 1942). Resting on the west bank of the Nile on the plain of Amarna, the city was approximately two miles long and one-half mile wide. On the hills surrounding the city, burial places were laid out for high officials and favorites of the pharaoh, while more substantial rock-hewn tombs for the royal family were located in a more secure and remote desert valley some distance further.

In the city itself, at least five temples were built and dedicated to Aton, the sun god, the symbol of the pharaoh's new religion. The principal temple of Aton was physically connected to the royal palace and consisted of a series of open courts and halls, connected by pylons, in which altars were set up to receive sacrificial religious offerings.

The main palace had a large balcony across its facade upon which the pharaoh and his family would show themselves to the populace assembled in the large court in front of the palace. The private rooms of the palace were furnished with the "utmost spendor" and included paintings and mosaics of gaily colored stones, and the columns, walls, and pavements were decorated with the "most splendid color effects imaginable."

In the southern section of the city, the pharaoh had laid out for himself and his family a large pleasure garden with artificial pools, flower beds, groves of trees, a summer pavilion, a small temple, and numerous guardhouses. The interior rooms were also adorned with gaily colored columns and pavements painted with pictures of flowers, flying birds, and animals characteristic of the region.

An important part of the city was occupied by the villas of the high officials and administrators of Ikhnaton's regime. These were elaborate establishments, consisting of administrative buildings, stables, and storehouses, along with gardens and luxurious dwellings. All of them were designed according to the same plan. The walls of the houses were decorated with reliefs depicting the royal family, usually at worship in the presence of a sun disk representing Aton. The royal sculptor, Thutmose, who was active at the court of Ikhnaton and whose still greatly admired works adorned the temples and palaces of the city, also had a house in this section of the city.

But as was usually the case in Egyptian cities of this period, the slaves and workers who were engaged in the miserable work of hewing rock tombs, maintaining cemetaries, and other menial activities resided in tiny congested houses in a more crowded district of the city, separated and isolated from the residences, temples, and palaces of the ruling class by its own enclosure walls.

GREEK AND ROMAN CITIES

The cities of classic Greek and Roman civilizations are often considered the high points of ancient civilization, and modern societies are still in awe of their splendid cultural and technological achievements. Yet it must be remembered that most of the great Greek and Roman cities were nothing more than small towns by contemporary urban standards. For example, ancient Athens at its peak occupied less than one square mile, or fewer than 612 acres of land. This is less than half the size of the college campus at which this chapter is being written! Athens may have achieved a population as large as 150,000 people, but some scholars consider this estimate inflated and more indicative of the population of the entire city-state than of the city proper. Hawley (1971) is skeptical that cities such as Athens could have supported much more than 30,000 or 35,000 people in nonagricultural occupations, given the state of agricultural technology and land fertility at that time and place. Hawley also estimates that the normal reach of those cities' activities probably did not exceed a radial distance of three to ten miles.

By the fifth century B.C. Athens had become the metropolitan center of a well-organized city-state and a widespread trade network. Athens had turned to the sea for trade, for it was blessed with fine harbors. The city was filled with a growing number of craftsmen, merchants, sailors, and emmissaries from other lands. Athenians could legitimately boast of the cosmopolitan character of the city and its hospitality to traders and other friendly foreigners in its midst. Residents of the city were able to enjoy the products of other countries as well as their own. The expanding volume of trade made the introduction of coinage necessary for an efficient market place, and the Greeks were among the first peoples to develop the use of money as a widely accepted system of exchange (Hopkins, 1978).

Hawley (1971) suggests that the use of money in place of the older system of payment in kind or the exchange of a service for a service had the effect of sharpening the difference between social classes. The lack of money by those not fortunate enough to adapt to the new monetary system had the effect of divesting them of their lands, their personal property, and perhaps even their freedom (Hawley, 1971). Except for the elite, most

When Athens reached its peak in the 5th century B.C., its population was at most 150,000 and it occupied only one square mile, while today it numbers well over 2 million with an area of about 100 square miles. (Greek National Tourist Office)

Athens residents lived in conditions of overcrowding and squalor. Municipal services were poor and limited. Although the Greeks invented the concept of democracy, the rights of citizenship for most residents were limited to the right to worship at civic shrines. Citizenship was also limited to a small portion of the total population of the city-state. Since Athens was essentially a religious community, the lack of citizenship imposed strict limits on an individual's participation in public life. Yet, the concept of citizenship in a city-state was a great achievement in social organization, for it enabled various families, clans, and tribes to band together in larger aggregates than previously possible for mutual aid and protection. To a certain extent these functions benefited noncitizen residents as well. Without such innovations, Athens probably could not have become more than an agricultural village (Hopkins, 1978).

The physical structure of Athens was similar to other Greek city-states. The major city walls were built around a fortified hill called an acropolis, for defense purposes. The acropolis was also the site of major temples. All other major buildings, including those that served as a market place or meeting place, were located within the city walls. The housing for the wealthiest and most privileged citizens was within the walls, but all other housing was densely clustered immediately beyond the walls. Most of the streets of Athens outside the temple area were nothing more than unpaved winding lanes. But Piraeus, Athen's port city, did have a more efficient grid street pattern in which the streets intersected at right angles and at regular intervals.

The largest city of the ancient period was, of course, Rome. Estimates of its peak population have run as high as 1,200,000 people. Again, this probably errs on the high side, according to more reliable sources, and may include people who did not actually reside within the confines of the city. For the city proper, the maximum population size more likely was between 250,000 and 350,000 people (Russell, 1958). Such figures are difficult to confirm. But assuming that they are reasonably accurate, it is fascinating to consider that the cradle of the great Roman civilization at its peak was probably no larger than what is currently the forty-first largest American City, Omaha, Nebraska, or the fifty-sixth largest, Austin, Texas!

The city gained greater importance than ever before with the rise of the Roman Empire. No previous civilization was so extensively urbanized or was as successfully able to exploit the countryside in favor of city interests. The riches of the empire were drawn into the city through military conquest, tax collections, and exploitation of its colonies, farms, quarries, and mines (Braudel, 1976).

Rome was a crowded, congested city. Almost one-third of the space enclosed within the Aurelian Wall was devoted to streets, warehouses, the Campus Martius, and other public uses (Russell, 1958). The clutter visible in the remains of the Roman Forum is clear evidence of further congestion. The roads were crowded with hucksters and business stalls and with residents on their daily trips to market places. There was an extensive economic division of labor within and between crafts, such as tailoring, potting, or shoe making, and such specialists clustered on streets devoted to and named after each respective trade. The city was consumption oriented and commerce was the dominant daily activity. Most of the artisans and businessmen were organized into guilds through which they sought to monopolize their trades. Commerce was shored up by a supporting cadre of moneylenders, teamsters, warehousemen, bookkeepers, and others (Hopkins, 1978).

Rome had excellent examples of municipal planning, but they did not extend beyond the center of the city. While impressive public squares and public baths were provided, they were only for use by more affluent citizens and were not accessible to the great bulk of the population who were massed in squalid tenements reached only by a maze of narrow, crooked lanes. The magnificent main roads that connected the center of the city with its periphery were intended mainly as military thoroughfares or for ceremonial processions. As the city grew, the outer walls were torn down and rebuilt to include buildings that had developed on its outer rim. The city received its water supply from an extensive system of impressively engineered aquaducts, some of which still stand, and had an elaborately developed sewer system, at least in the more privileged residential areas.

Although Rome depended on imports from its hinterland, it also exported its innovations in engineering, law, and government. Its strong influence was felt in such provincial Roman cities as Paris, Vienna, Cologne, and London, which were laid out in a rectangular grid pattern similar to the standard Roman military encampments, which they originally were. All these cities displayed their common Roman origins in their forums, coliseums, public baths, and other municipal buildings (Hopkins, 1978).

The provincial towns of the Roman Empire began to decline during the fourth century A.D., and the fifth century marked the effective fall of the Roman Empire. Urban life, which had flourished in Europe and other parts of the empire, virtually disappeared as towns or cities were obliterated or reduced to agricultural villages (Gibbon, 1965). Even the city of Rome lost most of its population, with only about 20,000 people remaining to live among its ruins. For approximately 600 years thereafter, there was little or no evidence of any flourishing city life in most of Western Europe. This period, which was dominated by the decline of classical cities and the emergence of a feudal system, has been euphemistically referred to by some as the "Dark Ages" (Boskoff, 1970). Actually, the feudal system that dominated Europe from about the fifth to the tenth century A.D. had the following characteristics.

The settlement pattern comprised a multiplicity of small villages of no more than several hundred people each, among which were interspersed castles, monastaries, burgs, and ecclesiastical towns. Europe under feudalism was a patchwork of small domains, each of which was isolated from all others, and each of which was jealously guarded from external intrusions by local feudal lords. The lords offered local peasants protection from outside raiders, demanding in return their serfdom. Removed from outside influences, a rigid hereditary class structure emerged in which every person had an assigned place (Pirenne, 1939; Sjoberg, 1976). At the top was the family of a military overlord who controlled the land in each locality. The lands were subdivided among warrior vassals who subdivided their land allotments still further among lesser warrior vassals. At the bottom of the class structure were the serfs, whose condition of servitude was virtually slavery. During military conflict, each stratum was obliged to support the next higher stratum. The Church was an overriding institution, and church representatives and monastic orders frequently collaborated or competed with secular rulers for control of the social order. Scholars refer to feudal society as static, parochial, and ultraconservative in structure (Hawley, 1971; Sjoberg, 1976).

The prevailing economy was subsistence agriculture. The townspeople as well as the agriculturalists lived from the land. Virtually no market for foodstuffs existed, and food surpluses were rarely transported more than a few miles. Famines were recurrent, and people lived or died by what was produced in their own localities. Even the feudal lord often found it necessary to travel among his estates for sustenance, staying at each until the local food was consumed. Communications were poor and the movement of surpluses from adjacent areas was almost impossible.

Journeys over the existing highways were extremely hazardous, and few travelers ventured far without a group of armed guards for protection from roving bands of robbers. Even a journey of a hundred miles might fall under many different and probably hostile sovereignties, each with different rules, regulations, laws, weights, measures, and money. At every boundary, tolls had to be paid and fees extorted from the traveling merchant. All this served to maintain the insularity and isolation of each locality (Heilbroner, 1962).

Still, a few itinerant traders braved the dangers of travel to bring silks, linens, dyes, perfumes, and other luxury goods from the Near and Far East to those who could afford to buy them. Seasonal or annual fairs held outside the walls of the local towns were usually where traveling merchants displayed their wares or acquired additional merchandise to sell in a neighboring district. In turn, the fairs were exciting and festive occasions which afforded relief from the simple, self-sufficient routines of the townspeople, as well as an opportunity to barter the products of their own labor (Pirenne, 1939).

The feudal system in Europe prior to the tenth century clearly was characterized by declining urban growth. Cities were losing population, commerce was severely restricted, and the towns became "festering sores rather than cases of responsible community life" (Boskoff, 1970, p. 20). Towns had lost most of their urban functions and were shadows of their former selves, often surviving as little more than fortresses or ecclesiastic centers, rather than true cities. Yet they were an important historical prelude to the urban revival that followed.

THE RISE OF THE MEDIEVAL TOWN IN EUROPE

The revival of urban growth following the feudal order required a major stimulus, one that could produce dramatic new waves of urban growth and activity. The impetus most likely came from the rather sudden resurgence of trade stimulated by the medieval religious Crusades. Trade was never entirely absent from the European scene during the "Dark Ages," and it seems to have grown slowly along with slow increases in population, improvements in the food supplies, and the development of rural handicrafts. But the relatively slow growth of trade was dramatically accelerated in the eleventh century. As the crusaders assaulted the Moslem world, they ended the isolation of Europe from the Byzantine East. During the Crusades, they carried with them a demand for European goods for which they paid with the bounties of war. When they returned from the Byzantine Empire, the crusaders, enriched with the newly acquired wealth from plundered Byzantine towns, brought back into feudal Europe highly expanded tastes for the consumer goods and luxuries of the East. They also introduced Europe to new ideas about the uses of money, technology, and alternative styles of living (Hawley, 1971; Braudel, 1978).

Feudal Europe was receptive to the goods and coins carried by the crusader turned merchant, but it was not well prepared for the new notions of freedom, lack of commitment to the established order, sophistication, and wealth of the traders, who became fair game for anyone who could prey on them. Trade was still a hazardous, low-status occupation and was often received with contempt, suspicion, discrimination, and sometimes outright violence by feudal society. Nevertheless, trade expanded rapidly and flourished from the tenth century onward (Rörig, 1967).

With the rapid expansion of trade, along with accompanying improvements in agriculture, the population of towns increased and city life expanded rapidly. Many new towns appeared almost spontaneously, and older towns on suitable transportation and trade routes experienced rapid revival. Heilbroner (1962) estimates that nearly one thousand new towns were added to the settlement pattern of medieval Europe during the twelfth century and immediately thereafter.

The merchant settlements that had previously developed outside of town walls were often annexed to the towns during this period. They were later surrounded by their own walls, which were attached to those surrounding the towns. Adding to the growth of existing towns, these annexed merchant settlements, called faubourgs, were an early example of what we now call suburbs (Palen, 1975). The merchants gained new status as they came to be appreciated for the added economic value they brought to their towns. The feudal lords who benefited from new sources of monetary income began to take the merchants under their sponsorship and protection, and soon some of the wealthiest merchant "princes" became closely allied with the ruling classes (Herlihy, 1978).

For the most part, however, the merchants were becoming a respected and powerful middle class who sought to insure favorable economic position by demanding and receiving political safeguards from the ruling feudal authorities. The demands of the merchants included personal freedom to come and go as they pleased, to live where they wished, and to have wife and children emancipated from bondage to the whims of the nobles and ecclesiastic lords (Hughes, 1978).

The merchants, of course, were most interested in the right to unrestricted free trade, but in the course of gaining this privilege, a number of other economic, political, and legal innovations were initiated, leading to the emergence of a new set of municipal institutions that further freed the merchants and other townspeople from the rigid controls of the feudal order. The right to own and sell private property and land was established, as was the right to establish urban courts for settling commercial disputes. The latter helped to eliminate the tediously overlapping claims of numerous jurisdictions and the irrelevant complexities of many archaic laws. As civic order became a problem, the merchant classes developed and legalized local policy systems as well as uniform and rational penal codes. They freed themselves from the multiplicity of fees and tolls previously imposed by the lords and ecclesiastic authorities and won the right to levy their own excise and income taxes to pay for community services. Most important, they won the right to self governance, as represented by municipal charters and by an elected city council as the key administrative body of the towns (Braudel, 1976).

The merchants, along with money changers, innkeepers, weavers, metalsmiths, and other artisans constituted a new social class known as the *bourgeoisie*. This new class was the forerunner of the so-called middle classes of contemporary urban-industrial societies, and they were the antithesis of the feudal ruling classes. Under the guidance of the bourgeoisie, a political climate was created which was well described by a German expression that translates as "City Air Makes Man Free" (Palen, 1975).

What we now call the university was an interesting innovation first institutionalized in city settings during the twelfth and thirteenth centuries. The first universities or colleges were informal organizations of individuals proficient in the scholarly areas of law, theology, and medicine. The status of the early universities was quite marginal. They were housed in ramshackle buildings, and their assets consisted of a few precious manuscripts and "a motley assemblage of variously ill-prepared students... learning was personal, barely dignified" (Boskoff, 1970). Despite numerous difficulties, the Church, the merchants, and the ruling classes gradually came to accept and sometimes even subsidize the universities, since they were expected to satisfy the increasing demand for skills in law, medicine, and a growing variety of professional service occupations that were becoming increasingly necessary for people living in an urban environment.

THE PHYSICAL STRUCTURE OF MEDIEVAL CITIES

During the medieval period, only a small handful of cities, such as Paris, Florence, Venice, and Milan approached a population size of 100,000 (Braudel, 1976). Most were much smaller, hardly more than villages by contemporary standards. As was the case in earlier settlements, the wall remained an indispensable element of town structure. The thick walls, with their watchtowers and external moats, defined the available living space and provided a rough outline of the physical patterns of the cities. When the population increased, the walls were torn down and new city walls were built further out. Sometimes the resulting open space was used to construct ring roads or boulevards, such as the notable ring-line boulevards of Vienna or Paris (Palen, 1975). Except for the main thoroughfares, which led directly from the center to the town walls, the streets were narrow and winding and were densely lined with buildings that overarched or overhung the narrow streets. Streets and districts came to be differentiated by trades and crafts. The members of each occupation tended to cluster their residences and shops for mutual support and promotion of common interests. A trade or craft was a family concern, and the home was not separated from the place of work.

The two main focal points of the community were the cathedral, which represented the religious side of community life, and the palace, which represented community political life. The cathedral often stood beside a main gate in the town wall next to a large open space or plaza, the setting for religious festivals and gatherings. The political center was marked by the palace of the reigning royal family. Residences of other members of the ruling class were gathered closely around the palace. The poorer and more underprivileged members of the community were rele-

Carcassone, as shown above after its reconstruction in the 19th century by Viollet-le-Duc, is an example of a medieval walled town. (French Government Tourist Office)

gated to the outer edges of the town and sometimes beyond its walls. It is interesting to compare this pattern to that of contemporary American cities, in which just the opposite takes place: the poor live near the center, while the middle and upper classes, with some exceptions, tend to live at the periphery. Actually, most of the cities of the world today still tend to follow the medieval pattern of spatial distribution of the various socioeconomic strata, with cities in the United States remaining the notable exception. This is an important distinction that will be taken up in more detail in later chapters.

THE DECLINE OF THE MEDIEVAL CITY

Congestion and the lack of sanitary facilities made the medieval city a malodorous place. Sewage was dumped into the streets, and the remains of slaughtered animals were allowed to rot where they were dropped. Streets were unpaved, and water purification was an unknown skill. Consequently, garbage accumulated in large heaps and puddles, serving as food and a breeding ground for rats and other vermin. Mortality rates were extremely high, as various plagues attacked the urban population. For example, the Black Death alone decimated at least one-fourth of the entire population of

Europe in its first three years, between 1348 and 1350, and nearly one-third of the population of Europe succumbed to the disease during the fourteenth century (Hawley, 1971). The number of people in cities was so depleted that many of the cities were not able to continue functioning as viable social units. Havoc was intensified by people fleeing from areas where the plague was in full course and by people in other localities bitterly trying to shunt aside the flood of refugees. Trade was disrupted, organized community life was imperiled, and, in general, urban growth was drastically cut back during the fourteenth century.

It took more than a century for Europe to replace the population lost to the plagues, and the rural-based feudal system by that time had begun to disintegrate under the onslaught, never to regain its former prominence. By the fifteenth century, city life began to revive and urban populations began to grow again. By this time, new economic, political, and social forces were set in motion that were to lead to the industrial revolution, and to a growth in urban life so remarkable that in time it was to become the predominant mode of human existence in many parts of the world.

Before we proceed to the discussion of the urban-industrial revolution in the following chapter, one more important point should be made about the urbanization process. Not all of the social and technological changes associated with rapid urbanization have been accepted to the same degree or at the same rate of speed by all people exposed to these changes. Thus, at any given time, one can find individuals or groups of people who resist such changes and who do not represent the dominant modes of adjustment to the most advanced stages of urbanization in the regions in which they reside. For example, nomadic ways of life continued to persist in the Middle East long after cities became the center of Middle Eastern civilizations. Groups like the Bedouin still continue to pursue their nomadic tradition of rearing sheep and camels in the deserts of the Middle East—the region in which some of the earliest permanent year-round settlements and subsequent cities had first appeared (Kay, 1978).

Likewise, even in the most modern of urban communities, not all residents have adopted modern urban life styles, and every urban community contains people whose lives are still attuned to an earlier mode of adjustment. This "cultural lag"—or gap between technological and cultural advances and the resultant adjustments of customs, beliefs, and social practices—creates social strains in rapidly changing urban environments. Such strains are at the heart of many of the social problems associated with urban life that are explored in more detail throughout this book.

SELECTED BIBLIOGRAPHY

BOSKOFF, ALVIN. *The Sociology of Urban Regions.* 2nd ed. New York: Appleton-Century-Crofts, 1970.

BRAIDWOOD, ROBERT, and WILLEY, GORDON, eds. *Courses toward Urban Life.* Chicago: Aldine, 1962.

BRAUDEL, FERNAND. "Pre-Modern Towns." In Peter Clark, ed., *The Early Modern Town.* London: Longman, 1978.

BREASTED, J. H. *The Development of Religion and Thought in Ancient Egypt.* New York, 1912.

CHILDE, GORDON. *What Happened in History.* London: Penguin, 1946.

———. "The Urban Revolution," *Town Planning Review* 21 (1950).

CLARK, GRAHAME, and PIGGOT, STUART. *Prehistoric Societies.* New York: Knopf, 1965.

EBERHARD, WOLFRAM. "Data on the Structure of the Chinese City in the Pre-Industrial Period," *Economic Development and Cultural Change* 4 (1955–1956).

FREUD, SIGMUND. *Moses and Monotheism.* New York: Vintage, 1957.

GIBBON, EDWARD. *The Decline and Fall of the Roman Empire.* New York: Dell, 1965.

HAWLEY, AMOS. *Urban Society.* New York: Ronald Press, 1971.

HEILBRONER, ROBERT. *The Making of Economic Society.* Englewood Cliffs, N.J.: Prentice-Hall, 1962.

HERLIHY, DAVID. "The Distribution of Wealth in a Renaissance Community: Florence: 1427." In Philip Abrams and E. A. Wrigley, eds., *Towns in Societies: Essays in Economic History and Historical Sociology.* London: Cambridge University Press, 1978.

HOPKINS, KEITH. "Economic Growth and Towns in Ancient Antiquity." In Abrams and Wrigley (1978).

HUGHES, DIANE O. "Urban Growth and Family Structure in Medievel Genoa." In Abrams and Wrigley (1978).

KAY, SHIRLEY. *The Bedouin.* New York: Crane and Russak, 1978.

MCADAMS, ROBERT. *The Evolution of Urban Society: Early Mesopotamia and Prehispanic Mexico.* Chicago: Aldine, 1966.

———. "Patterns of Urbanization in Early Southern Mesopotamia." In Ruth Tringham, ed., *Urban Settlements: The Process of Urbanization in Archeological Settlements.* Andover: Mass.: Warner Modular Publications, 1973.

OPPENHEIM, LEO A. *Ancient Mesopotamia: Portrait of a Dead Civilization.* Chicago: University of Chicago Press, 1964.

PALEN, JOHN J. *The Urban World.* New York: McGraw-Hill, 1975.

PIRENNE, HENRY. *Medieval Cities.* Princeton, N.J.: Princeton University Press, 1939.

PUSALKER, A. D. "The Indus Valley Civilization." In R. C. Mahumdar, ed., *The Vedic Age.* Bombay: Bharatiya Vidya Bhaven, 1951.

RÖRIG, FRITZ. *The Medieval Town.* Berkeley: University of California Press, 1967.

RUSSELL, J. C. *Late Ancient and Medieval Population.* Philadelphia: American Philosophical Society, 1958.

SJOBERG, GIDEON. "The Nature of the Pre-Industrial City." In Clark (1976).

STEINDORFF, GEORGE and SEELE, K. C. *When Egypt Ruled the East.* Chicago: University of Chicago Press, 1942.

TRIGGER, BRUCE. "Determinants of Growth in Pre-Industrial Societies." In Tringham (1973).

WEBER, MAX. *The City.* New York: Collier, 1962.

WENKE, ROBERT J. *Patterns in Prehistory.* New York: Oxford University Press, 1980.

WHITE, LESLIE A. *The Science of Culture.* Chapter IX. New York: Grove Press, 1949.

WHITEHOUSE, RUTH. *The First Cities.* New York: Dutton, 1977.

WOOLLEY, LEONARD. *Ur of the Chaldees.* London: Penguin, 1952.

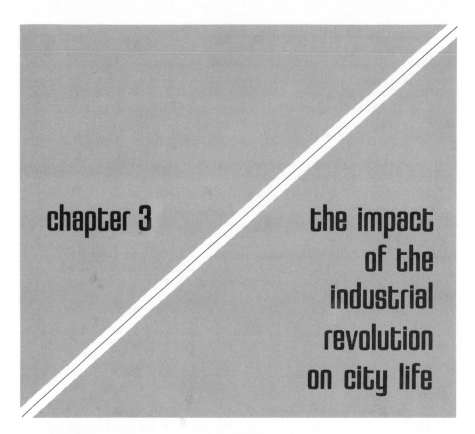

chapter 3

the impact
of the
industrial
revolution
on city life

The nineteenth century has been widely characterized as the age of the industrial revolution. The nineteenth century has also been aptly described as the period in which the proliferation and growth of cities reached explosive proportions. These two trends have been so intertwined that the concept of the *urban-industrial revolution* is often used to describe the unprecedented transformation in human society that took place during this period. So many of the patterns and problems of modern urban life are the consequences of the nineteenth-century industrial revolution that we must begin with an analysis of this development as a basis for understanding the major themes of the remaining portions of this book.

Actually, the industrial revolution was the product of a diversity of social, economic, and technological changes that began in Europe about the fifteenth century. These changes combined in such a way during the nineteenth century in Europe and North America as to make rapid industrialization inevitable.

THE MARKET ECONOMY

Perhaps the most important prerequisite to industrialization was the emergence of a market economy. A market economy is one in which the process of exchanging goods and services is based on an impersonal and standardized monetary system. In modern industrial societies, this feature of the market economy is so institutionalized that it is taken for granted. In a preindustrial society in which a market economy had not yet emerged, trade was conducted by bartering, a ritual involving much haggling over the value of the respective goods to be exchanged. Of course, such a system was time consuming and inefficient, and it limited the volume of commodities that could be exchanged in any given time period. Also, the residents of such a society would have been shocked to learn that many services which were to them too sacred or personal to have monetary value, such as buying food or drink in a restaurant, getting a bed in a hotel or motel, paying nurses to take care of us when we are sick, or paying a counselor for marital or sexual advice, are impersonally bought and sold on the open market in contemporary industrial societies.

From the perspective of urban sociology, the commercialization of land and labor are among the most significant characteristics of a market economy. The idea that land was no longer a sacred trust, to be maintained and transmitted by families from one generation to another, but was a commodity to be sold to the highest bidder, or to be used for the most efficient or monetarily profitable purpose, would have been considered repugnant and strongly resisted by most feudal landlords (Heilbroner, 1962). Yet the impersonal and routinized sale of real estate, and the resultant frequent change in land use, are important characteristics of modern urban-industrial communities.

Likewise, the emergence of a market economy requires that, to participate in the market for goods and services, one must have cash at his or her disposal. In the preindustrial medieval economy, at least 60 or 70 percent of the actual working population labored as serfs without anything resembling full payment in money (Heilbroner, 1962). With the emergence of a market economy, however, no longer was labor part of an explicit social relationship in which one person (serf or apprentice) worked for another (lord or guildmaster) in return for lodgings and other nonmonetary subsistence. Labor now became a commodity, to be exchanged for the best monetary reward, in the form of the wages it could bring. The substitution of an impersonal wage system for the reciprocal obligations and responsibilities between serf or apprentice and lord or guildmaster also undermined some of the stability and security workers experienced under the feudal system and placed them at the mercy of whims and fluctuations in the labor market. Thus, the greater risk of unemployment was introduced as one of the more problematic characteristics of the market economy. This problem will be discussed in more detail later in this chapter.

THE RISE OF CAPITALISM

One of the ideas basic to capitalism is private ownership of the means of production, and their operation for profit by private entrepreneurs competing in a free and open market. In the modern western world, it would be difficult to overestimate the impact of the profit motive as an inducement to industrialize or the importance of capital investment as an underlying prerequisite to industrialization.

Sociological perspectives on capitalism have tended to emphasize the *culture* of capitalism, the values that sustain and reflect the economic organization of capitalism as it developed in Europe and North America. For example, Wilensky and Lebeaux (1958) have attributed the values of American capitalism to the rational, acquisitive, self-interested individuals who subscribe to the following beliefs:

1. Those who work hard and have ability will be rewarded with success (this not only includes income and economic wealth, but also power and occupational prestige—along with the life styles these permit).
2. Success is the reward of virtue: virtue will bring success. Failure (if it is not a temporary way station to success) is a sin and reveals a lack of virtue.
3. When the lazy, incompetent, and unvirtuous attain success, it is merely a matter of luck: it could happen to anybody, but it does not happen too often.
4. The test of reward should be the ability to contribute to the productive and other purposes of free enterprise. There should be unequal reward for unequal talents and unequal contributions.

Weber (1930) has pointed out how certain values that emerged as features of the Protestant Reformation in Europe were conducive to the expansion of capitalism and economic rationality. High value is placed on an active rather than a contemplative life, unremitting labor is considered both a moral virtue and a moral obligation, and the individual who engages in highly productive labor is asserted to have found favor in the eyes of God. Thus, success, profit, and wealth are virtues. They are vices only if they lead to idleness and dissipation.

While Weber did not attempt to prove a causal relationship between Protestantism and the rise of capitalism, the Protestant outlook undoubtedly was a powerful motivation for productive work and did historically coincide with the expansion of technology and production associated with the industrial revolution. However, the increase in secularism and growing faith in science that arose during the same period should not be minimized.

NATIONALISM, COLONIALISM, AND IMPERIALISM

Between the fifteenth and nineteenth centuries in Europe, one tumultuous change of particular importance for the progress of industrialization was the movement toward political unification and the rise of the nation-states. This led to greater centralization of government controls of city and country alike as elaborate administrative bureaucracies arose, partly in response to the need or desire to promote and regulate economic growth and expanded trading areas (Hawley, 1971). One consequence of this trend was increased growth in the political capitals of the emerging nation-states.

Thus, cities such as Paris, London, Warsaw, Moscow, Lisbon, Vienna, and Copenhagen had attained populations of 100,000 or more by the middle of the seventeenth century. In turn, the resultant urban growth itself became the basis for expanded trade.

The expansion of trade in the European nation-states encouraged Europeans to search farther and farther for new markets and riches. They established colonies for this purpose in Africa, Southern Asia, South America, and North America from the fifteenth century onward. This was made possible in part by some of the technological advances in transportation and navigation, as well as by their superior military technology. Once the large colonial empires were established, it was no accident that the centers of these empires became the focal points for greater industrialization and urbanization, such as the growth of London, Manchester, and Birmingham as population and industrial centers for the British Empire.

THE MACHINE AND THE FACTORY SYSTEM
OF PRODUCTION

All of the above forces combined during the latter part of the eighteenth century to make the introduction of the factory system of production both desirable and feasible. The substitution of steam-powered machinery for animate sources of energy, previously supplied by humans in the form of tools or as extensions of their own limbs, was the earliest and most significant direct manifestation of the industrial revolution. The factory system of production, utilizing steam-driven machinery, first emerged in England in the 1780s in the textile industry as machines were gradually substituted for hand tools in the related processes of spinning and weaving cotton and woolen fabrics.

Until the factory appeared, the household was the scene of nearly all industrial labor. In England, the dominant means of production just prior to the industrial revolution was the "cottage" or "putting out" system, in which an employer owns the raw materials and gives them out to various craft workers who produce finished products through processes carried out in their homes (Smelser, 1959). The worker then returns the goods to the employer, and, if they are not yet finished, the employer passes them on to other workers, who also engage in various craft processes at home. The employer is a capitalist in the sense of owning the materials during the processes of production and advancing wages to the workers.

As this system expanded, the employer eventually owned the tools or other equipment used during production. In many instances, the employer owned the cottages used by the workers, which were rented to them completely equipped for both production and family living. This cottage system brought a number of workers under a moderate degree of supervision and direction by their employers, but on the whole the system did little to standardize the nature of industrial work. The rates and efficiency of production differed vastly from employer to employer and from cottage to cottage since each worker still had a large degree of control over the pace and style of his or her work, as was the case in earlier stages of craft production (Usher, 1920).

What the factory system did was to bring large numbers of workers together under the same roof in buildings devoted solely to their work and under the direct surveillance and control of the employers. Increasingly, the pace of work became regulated by the requirements of the power-driven machinery, restricting much of the freedom that the worker enjoyed under the putting out-system. Workers at first resisted the organization of work in the factories, and a central problem for the new industrialists was to attract labor to their factories, especially when the factory system of production became very profitable and the demand for industrial manpower had greatly expanded. Since much of the factory work required far less skill than the crafts it replaced, the problem was essentially how to get rural, peasant peoples off the farms and into city-based industries (Wilensky and Lebeaux, 1958).

In the earliest days of the industrial revolution, coercion often played the main role in labor recruitment, with people being virtually pushed into factory work as much as they were voluntarily attracted by the great opportunity before them. In England, the *enclosure* movement, which culminated in the eighteenth and early nineteenth centuries, is an example of such coercion. The commercialization of land and property made the landed aristocracy, increasingly squeezed for cash, begin to see their estates as sources of monetary revenue. Aided by acts of Parliament (which was partial to commercial and industrial interests during that period), they began consolidating small strips of peasant-occupied grazing land into larger units to produce cash-producing crops for a growing city market. As the common grazing fields, which the peasants had previously shared with the owners for their mutual subsistence, were enclosed, the peasant tenants found it increasingly difficult to support themselves and were gradually pushed off the land (Heilbroner, 1962).

The enclosure process provided a powerful force for the destruction of the medieval village and its communal ties. By dispossessing the peasant, it created a new kind of landless labor force, without traditional forms of nonmonetary subsistence. Under the English Poor Laws of the early nineteenth century, the many destitute people wandering about the country were thrust into the workhouse if they did not take jobs voluntarily, and anyone who left a job without his employer's written permission was subjected to the same treatment. Thus, the peasants were compelled to find work for wages wherever it might be available: most likely in the growing industrial cities of London, Manchester, Birmingham, Sheffield, and Liverpool.

URBAN POPULATION GROWTH IN EUROPE

At the beginning of the nineteenth century, England was the most urbanized society in Europe. Using a minimum population size of 20,000 to designate urban places, the population of Europe was less than 5 percent urban in 1800. At that date, England and Wales had a population that was 17 percent urban. Urban growth accelerated dramatically in England during each decade of the nineteenth century and had doubled by the middle of the century. By the last decade of the century, more than one-half of the English population lived in cities of 20,000 or more people. As Table 3-1 illustrates, urbanization also increased throughout much of the European continent during the nineteenth century, but at a slower rate than in England.

.The growth in the number of larger cities, with a population of 100,000 or more, is also a useful index of urbanization. In Europe only twenty-three cities had a population of 100,000 or larger in 1800, but by the end of the century 143 cities were in this category. While the total population of Europe slightly more than doubled during the nineteenth century, the population of the larger European cities of 100,000 or more increased tenfold during the same period (Hawley, 1971).

The early European industrial cities, although producing much in the way of new wealth, were characterized by overcrowding and unbelievably poor sanitary conditions. Diseases and epidemics were common and mortality rates were high. Social critics have portrayed these cities as devoid of beauty, without parks or pure water supplies, public lighting or drainage, since such amenities were considered frivolous by the early industrialists. Discussing the slums, poverty, cruelty, and misery, the Hammonds (1925) have described the early English factory towns in these terms:

> The towns had their profitable smoke, their profitable disorder, their profitable ignorance, their profitable despair . . . . The new factories and the new furnaces were like the Pyramids, telling of man's enslavement, rather than of his power; casting their long shadow over the society that took such pride in them.

A series of reforms began to take place in England around the middle of the nineteenth century that ameliorated some of the worst of the conditions described above, and urban-industrial cities continued to grow and thrive throughout England and the rest of Europe. But by this time the main thrust of urban growth had begun to shift to North America, and we will devote the remaining parts of this chapter to this development.

PREINDUSTRIAL URBAN GROWTH IN AMERICA

Except for the Aztec, Mayan, and Incan civilizations of Mesoamerica, which were centered in densely populated communities, no indigenous cities existed in North America when the first European colonists began to arrive. The new towns created by the early settlers led rather than followed the settlement of the rest of the country. The earliest centers to extend beyond village proportions were ports and trade centers, such as New York, Philadelphia, Boston, Baltimore, and Charleston. Early town growth was slow, and as late as 1790 (the year the first United States census was

TABLE 3-1 Proportions of total populations in cities of 20,000 or more inhabitants (selected countries and dates)*

YEAR*	ENGLAND-WALES	HOLLAND	GERMANY	BELGIUM	ITALY	AUSTRIA	HUNGARY	SWEDEN	FRANCE
1800–01	16.9%	—	—	—	4.4%	3.6%	2.3%	3.0%	3.9%
1810–11	18.1	—	—	1.3%	—	—	—	—	—
1820–21	20.8	20.1%	—	—	—	—	—	—	—
1830–31	25.0	—	—	—	—	—	—	—	4.5
1840–41	28.9	—	—	—	—	4.2	—	—	—
1850–51	35.0	21.7	—	5.2	6.0	—	4.6	3.4	6.0
1860–61	38.2	—	12.5%	—	—	—	—	—	—
1870–71	42.0	—	—	—	—	—	—	—	6.7
1880–81	48.0	—	18.1	—	—	9.6	—	—	—
1890–91	53.6	31.3	21.9	13.2	13.3	12.0	11.2	10.8	9.1

*Dates are approximate.

SOURCE: A. F. Weber, *The Growth of Cities in the Nineteenth Century*, Columbia University Press, 1899, pp. 47–119.

Philadelphia was one of the five cities with more than 10,000 people in the late 18th century. (Painting by Clyde O. De Laud, Philadelphia Board of Public Education)

taken) the five cities listed above were the only ones in the United States with populations of more than 10,000 people. In all, only twenty-four towns or cities in the United States had more than 2,500 people, and at that date no city in the United States had yet achieved a population as large as 50,000. Only 5 percent of the total population of 3,929,000 lived in towns or cities (Table 3-2).

During the first several decades of the nineteenth century, the number of new towns and the urban population slowly but steadily increased as commerce continued to accelerate and as a steady stream of European immigrants settled in the existing cities or set up new communities in the expanding Western and Southern territories. Table 3-2 illustrates the population growth of principal American cities between 1790 and 1830. By then, New York had become the largest, with just less than a quarter of a million inhabitants. New York and Philadelphia were the only two with a population of more than 100,000 people, and just under 9 percent of the total population lived in cities or towns.

The urbanizing process in America began to move faster in the period from 1830 to the beginning of the Civil War. As the national population increased and migration to the West accelerated, the need for new and larger cities grew still more rapidly. Part of the urban increase resulted from a new flux of immigrants who settled in the established cities of the Northeast as well as in the new Western cities. The pattern of urban growth

TABLE 3-2 Populations of principal U.S. cities, 1790 to 1830*

CITIES	1790	1800	1810	1820	1830
New York	33,131	60,515	96,373	123,706	202,589
Suburbs			4,402	7,175	39,689
Totals			100,775	130,881	242,278
Philadelphia	28,522	41,220	53,722	63,802	80,462
Suburbs	15,574	20,339	33,581	45,007	80,809
Totals	44,096	61,559	87,303	108,809	161,271
Boston	18,320	24,937	33,787	43,298	61,392
Suburbs			4,959	10,726	18,104
Totals			38,746	54,024	85,568
Baltimore	13,503	26,514	46,555	62,738	80,620
New Orleans		9,000	17,242	27,176	46,082
Cincinnati		750	2,540	9,642	24,831
Charleston	16,359	18,924	24,711	24,780	30,289
Albany	3,498	5,349	9,356	12,630	24,209
Washington		3,210	8,208	13,247	18,826
Providence	6,380	7,614	10,071	11,767	16,833
Pittsburgh	376	1,565	4,768	7,248	15,369
Richmond	3,761	5,737	9,735	12,067	16,060
Salem	7,917	9,457	12,613	12,731	13,895
Portland	2,239	3,704	7,169	8,581	12,598
Troy		4,926	3,895	5,264	11,556
New Haven	4,487	4,049	5,772	7,147	10,180
Louisville	200	359	1,357	4,012	10,341
Newark			5,008	6,507	10,953
Total of Urban Residents	202,000	322,000	525,000	693,000	1,127,000
Number of Towns over 2500	24	33	46	61	90
Percent Urban	5.1	6.1	7.3	7.2	8.8
Total U.S. Population	3,929,000	5,308,000	7,240,000	9,638,000	12,866,000

*U.S. Census Office, *Seventh Census: 1850* (Washington, D.C.: U.S. Government Printing Office, 1951), p. liii; U.S. Bureau of the Census, *Thirteenth Census: 1910* (Washington, D.C.: U.S. Government Printing Office, 1911), *Population,* I, p. 80; U.S. Bureau of the Census, *Seventeenth Census: 1950* (Washington, D.C.: U.S. Government Printing Office, 1951), I, U.S. Summary, Table 15.

in America during this period differed from that in Great Britain in that it was still being spurred by commercial rather than industrial development (McKelvey, 1973). In turn, the enormous growth of trade and the expansion of trading areas were facilitated by major innovations in land and water transportation. The steamship came into general use, first on river and coastal routes, then in transoceanic service. The adoption of steam-driven trains as a principal means of land travel advanced rapidly as the railways began to provide a continent-wide transportation network linking the hinterlands to the existing urban centers. Overland trips that had been measured in days and weeks now could be accomplished in a matter of hours. The invention of the telegraph also speeded the flow of trade by making possible more closely timed buying and selling transactions over larger and larger territories.

By 1860 the principal outlines of the urban settlement pattern east of the Mississippi had been completed, and most of the present larger cities in that region now having a population of 100,000 or more were already established. West of the Mississippi, St. Louis and San Francisco had already become urban centers. Still, New York (including the borough of

Brooklyn) was the first and only American city to have produced a population of more than a million by that date, and the greatest spurt in city growth was yet to come. Table 3-3 illustrates the growth of American cities from 1830 to 1860. Although urban growth as a portion of the total United States population had more than doubled during this period, less than 20 percent of the population resided in cities in 1860, and it was still too soon to refer to the United States as an urban society.

THE INDUSTRIAL REVOLUTION IN AMERICA

The full force of the industrial revolution finally reached America in the 1860s. Since it followed the industrial revolution in England by more than a half-century, it was no longer a new phenomenon, and American cities already possessed the essential ingredients for rapid industrialization. Economic historians are divided as to whether the Civil War promoted or hindered industrialization (McKelvey, 1973), but northern industrialists did begin producing steel, coal, and woolen goods at faster rates to gain from the inflated profits stimulated by the demands of war. The return of hundreds of thousands of men from military service also helped generate new demands for facilities and services. The nation's net income from

TABLE 3-3 Populations of principal U.S. cities, 1830 to 1860*

CITIES	1830	1840	1850	1860
New York	202,589	312,700	515,500	813,600
Philadelphia	161,271	220,400	340,000	565,529
Brooklyn	15,396	36,230	96,838	266,660
Baltimore	80,620	102,300	169,600	212,418
Boston	61,392	93,380	136,880	177,840
New Orleans	46,082	102,190	116,375	168,675
Cincinnati	24,831	46,338	115,435	161,044
St. Louis	5,852	14,470	77,860	160,773
Chicago		4,470	29,963	109,260
Buffalo	8,653	18,213	42,260	81,130
Newark	10,953	17,290	38,890	71,940
Louisville	10,340	21,210	43,194	68,033
Albany	24,209	33,721	50,763	62,367
Washington	18,826	23,364	40,001	61,122
San Francisco			34,776	56,802
Providence	16,833	23,171	41,573	50,666
Pittsburgh	15,369	21,115	46,601	49,221
Rochester	9,207	20,191	36,403	48,204
Detroit	2,222	9,012	21,019	45,619
Milwaukee		1,712	20,061	45,246
Cleveland	1,076	6,071	17,034	43,417
Total of Urban Residents	1,127,000	1,845,000	3,543,700	6,216,500
Number of Towns over 2500	90	131	236	392
Percent Urban	8.8	10.8	15.3	19.8
Total U.S. Population	12,866,000	17,069,000	23,191,800	31,433,300

*Derived from U.S. Censuses in 1850, 1860, and 1910 (Washington, D.C.: U.S. Government Printing Office).

Factories thrived throughout the Northeast during the late 19th century, as did the one above in Fall River, Massachusetts. (Library of Congress)

manufacturing increased 77 percent during the 1860s, placing it ahead of all industrial nations for the first time (McKelvey, 1973). Expanded rates of productivity in cities that were rapidly becoming manufacturing centers, such as Scranton, Jersey City, Cleveland, Indianapolis, Newark, Milwaukee, Rochester, Cincinnati, Buffalo, and Pittsburgh, contributed to urban growth as immigrants flocked to these cities and others in search of the new economic opportunities promised by the potential of industrial work.

Growth was by no means confined to the manufacturing cities, since other cities also began to take on more specialized functions, complementary to those of manufacturing. Thus, many cities became centers of trade, administration, education, or recreation and leisure, and they too shared in the tremendous population expansion of the latter part of the nineteenth century (Hawley, 1971).

The United States population mushroomed from 31 million in 1860 to 92 million in 1910, with most of the increase going to the cities. Until the 1880s, much of the growth was provided by Irish, German, or Scandinavian immigrants, most of whom were skilled and literate. They were able to take advantage of the Homestead Act and become farmers. Beginning in the 1880s, migration shifted from northern and western Europe to southern and eastern Europe, becoming mostly Italian, Greek, Croat, Czech, Slovak, Slovene, Polish, Hungarian, Rumanian, and Russian by nationality (Wilensky and Lebeaux, 1958). Many of the newer immigrants were unskilled peasants who came to the industrial cities and had to adjust simultaneously to urban and industrial ways of life. More will be said about this problem later.

As in England, the burgeoning manufacturing cities were often dirty, noisy, overcrowded, and congested with pollution-producing factories. They were certainly not attractive by today's standards, to say the least.

Pittsburgh has often been pointed out as a prototype of the American industrial cities of the latter nineteenth century. A description written in 1884 vividly depicts the city:

> Pittsburgh is a smoky, dismal city at her best. At her worst, nothing darker, dingier or more dispiriting can be imagined.... The smoke from her dwellings, stores, factories, foundries and steamboats, uniting, settles in a cloud over the narrow valley in which she is built, until the very sun looks coppery through the sooty haze.... It has thirty-five miles of factories in daily operation, twisted up into a compact tangle, all belching smoke, all glowing with fire, all swarming with workmen, all echoing with the clank of machinery.... In a distance of thirty-five and one-half miles of streets, there are four hundred and seventy-eight manufactories of iron, steel, cotton, brass, oil, glass, copper and wood, occupying less than four hundred feet each.... These factories are so contiguous in their positions upon the various streets of the city, that if placed in a continuous row, they would reach thirty-five miles... (Glazier, 1884, pp. 332–334).

The demand for housing often greatly exceeded the supply, and the concentration of large numbers of people in relatively small land areas made itself felt in intolerable living conditions and repeated epidemics of major proportions in some cities. Buildings with no sanitary facilities beyond the privy and the gutter were being crowded together in such a way as to leave many dwellings virtually without light and air. In New York, for example, a law prohibiting the building of residential rooms without windows was not passed until 1879 (Gold, 1965). None of the large cities made adequate public provision for disposal of sewage until late in the nineteenth century, and even in 1900 Philadelphia and St. Louis had twice as much street mileage as sewer mileage. In the same year Baltimore, New Orleans, and other cities were still relying on open gutters for drainage. Frequently, cities were prompted to construct sewer systems only by social catastrophe. Memphis, for example, did not take this step until after the city had been practically depopulated by a yellow fever epidemic in 1879 (Gold, 1965).

In many other ways a large gap existed between the needs of a growing urban population and the capacity or willingness of the local urban municipalities to supply solutions to those needs. At the beginning of the industrial revolution, municipal fire and police departments had not yet become fully institutionalized as legitimate ongoing functions of local government, and these services were still sometimes being offered by volunteers, or to private subscribers by profit-oriented private companies. With few notable exceptions, many industrial cities were devoid of public parks or playgrounds until very late in the nineteenth century.

POVERTY, UNEMPLOYMENT, AND INDUSTRIAL UNREST

In the early days of the industrial revolution, the workers' job security was often precarious. This was partly because most manufacturing industries were concentrated in large numbers of rather small family owned and managed units engaged in fierce competition with one another, making the owner's lot precarious as well. In addition, the fortunes of business were subjected to wide fluctuations between various booms and depressions that were probably more severe than those in modern regulated economies. Thus, despite relatively high wages, industrial workers were often faced with long periods of unemployment and with much work and residential dislocation, since they moved frequently from firm to firm, industry to industry, and city to city. Since the provision of financial aid through public welfare or unemployment insurance was an idea whose time had not yet come, the unemployed were left to the whims and limitations of church supported and other private charities or were left to their own meager resources for subsistence.

There is some evidence that many of the immigrants who came to the cities in search of wage labor were never successful in this endeavor and became vagabonds, vagrants, hoboes, or beggars (Glaab, 1963). Others survived through marginal economic activities, such as rag picking and bone gathering. A New York State report of 1857, based on a survey of slum areas in Manhattan and Brooklyn, describes one such group:

> "Rag-pickers' Paradise" is inhabited entirely by Germans, who dwell in small rooms in almost fabulous gregariousness.... We were told of a colony of three hundred of these people, who occupied a single basement, living on offal and scraps, ... their means of livelihood, degraded as it is, is exceedingly precarious, especially in severe winters, when snow storms, covering the ground, hide the rags, shreds of paper, etc., on the sale of which they subsist. In such seasons the children are sent out to sweep crossings or beg, and many of the most adroit practitioners on public charity are found among these urchins, who are generally marked by a precocity and cunning, which render them, too often, adepts in vice at the tenderest ages.... The colonies sally out at daybreak with their baskets and pokers, disperse to their respective precincts, and pursue their work with more or less success throughout the day. On their return, the baskets, bags and carts are emptied into a common heap. Then, from the bones and scraps of meat, certain portions are selected wherewith to prepare soups. The rags are separated from bones and sorted, washed and dried ... after which rags and bones are sold—the former to adjacent shopkeepers who live by the traffic, at about two cents per pound, and the latter for thirty cents per bushel.

> When it is recollected that the process of washing filthy rags, collected from the gutters, sinks, hospital yards, and every vile locality imaginable, is conducted in the single apartment used for cooking, eating, sleeping, and general living purposes, by the tenants (sometimes a dozen in one room)... and where to these horrible practices are superadded the personal filth, stagnant water, fixed air, and confined, dark and damp holes, all characteristic of the tenant-house system,... it is no wonder that these unfortunate people are yearly decimated; it is not strange that the cholera and other epidemics have, as we are told, made frightful havoc among them in past years (Glaab, 1963, pp. 277-278.)

The kind of poverty described above, plus other newly emerging insecurities of industrial life—the new dependence on the employer, the obsolescence and dilution of skills, the difficult adaptation to factory discipline, the new insecurity of old age—added to a long period of labor unrest and protest in the latter part of the nineteenth century. The decade of the 1880s, for example, produced a near-revolutionary upheaval. Following the accelerated tempo of industrialization and several periods of depression, wage cuts, and unemployment, labor protest began to sweep the land. This involved the skilled and unskilled, women and men, the native born and the foreign born in a rush to organize into labor unions. General strikes, sympathy strikes, consumer boycotts, and working class political movements became the order of the day. Reactive employer associations were quickly formed and countered in kind with lockouts, blacklists, armed guards, and detectives (Wilensky and Lebeaux, 1958). This was also the time of the famous bomb explosion on Haymarket Square, which touched off a period of hysteria and police terror in Chicago, which was, incidentally, one of the fastest growing cities in America during the same decade.

During this period many rural and small-town Americans began to see the cities as a serious menace to their concept of civilization. This was in part based on a native-born, Anglo-Saxon, Protestant, puritan reaction to the somewhat more permissive life styles and values of the immigrants from predominantly Catholic European countries. Thus, the saloon and the resulting intemperance were frequently cited, along with the growing inequities in the class structure, as an unfortunate and dangerous by-product of urbanization and industrialization. Josiah Strong (1885, p. 128–138) an influential reformist Congregationalist minister of the day, stated what he saw as the "dangers" of the city:

> Socialism not only centers in the city, but is almost confined to it; and the materials of its growth are multiplied with the growth of the city. Here is heaped the social dynamite; here roughs, gamblers, thieves, robbers, lawless and desperate men of all sorts, congregate; men who are ready on any pretext to raise riots for the purpose of destruction and plunder; here gather foreigners and wage-workers; here skepticism and irreligion abound; here inequality is the greatest and most obvious, and the contrast between opulence and penury the most striking; here is suffering the sorest. . . .

Strong and other critics seriously questioned whether the existing social, economic, and political institutions could survive the revolutionary forces they saw operating in American cities at that time (Glaab, 1963). The ferment of labor and radical movements of this period provided impetus for reform and social welfare. Many of these reforms were ultimately achieved early in the next century, with the enactment of factory codes requiring proper ventilation and sanitary appliances, workmen's compensation laws, bars on contract labor, child labor laws, the shortening of the work day, and many other reforms that culminated in the New Deal days of the 1930s. But these reforms must be seen in the context of late nineteenth-century urban-industrial unrest, agitation, and protest, epitomized by the social stresses and strains of the 1880s.

In spite of the many social strains, a large number of technological innovations developed in the nineteenth century that enabled cities to grow still larger and more populated. Until the horse-drawn railway made its appearance early in the century, city transportation was largely pedestrian. This limited the spread of settlement, as factories, commercial establishments, and the homes of workers all had to be within walking distance of one another. Whenever cities expanded beyond this scope, it was as a series of adjacent cells rather than as a unified whole (Hawley, 1971). The horse-drawn railways permitted a wider spread of settlement, along with a greater differentiation and specialization of such land use activities as manufacturing, commerce, and residency. Hawley views the emergence of a central business district serving an entire large city as related to this improvement in the means of transportation. The advent of the electrified street railway later in the century made possible an even greater concentration of people at a given place in a smaller amount of time, widening the spread of settlement more than ever.

The growing importance and concentration of the central business district was facilitated by the adoption of iron and steel frame construction

Alexander Graham Bell demonstrated his invention of the telephone in 1877. in Salem, Massachusetts. (Library of Congress)

in architecture, which allowed the construction of high rise buildings, some rising to eight and ten stories in cities such as Chicago, New York, and St. Louis in the 1860s and 1870s (McKelvey, 1973). The successful development of a safe and reasonably fast passenger elevator encouraged the effort to build even taller buildings, and by the close of the century the skyscraper had become a dramatic and indelible feature of the skylines of both New York and Chicago, a pattern that has since been emulated in countless American and world cities.

The telephone, invented in the 1870s, won such immediate favor that numerous cities soon had telephone lines in operation. The great benefits it provided by speeding communications were partially matched by the application of electricity to street lighting and finally for indoor use with the development of the incandescent electric light bulb. As well as providing still greater opportunities for industrial development, the telephone and the electric light found immediate use in the expanding department stores that were appearing in the downtown sections of the largest cities, and these developments of course helped to transform the shopping habits of many urbanites (McKelvey, 1973). Still another invention of this period that helped to create an urgent demand for skyscrapers and a greater concentration of office workers in the downtown areas was the typewriter, which, along with the telephone, greatly expanded the volume of communications in commerce and industry. Thus, innovations such as these enabled the city centers to expand vertically as well as horizontally.

SOCIAL INNOVATION

So far, we have described nineteenth-century industrialization primarily in terms of major economic, technological, and physical changes in the form and content of city life. But social changes were equally significant. For example, many of the older body of rules, procedures, and understandings that guided the commonplace behavior of preindustrial village residents as they pursued their everyday needs were no longer adequate to the exigencies of urban life. Older institutional arrangements had to be overhauled and new institutions had to be created to accommodate the new forces at work.

Many of the resultant social innovations that took place in American cities arose because the growing cities were becoming populated mainly by European-born and native-born rural migrants who were encountering the complexities of city life for the first time. They had no knowledge of how to live in the new context or of the demands that would be placed on them. The skills necessary for successful accommodation were not easy to acquire, and this process often took a generation or more. Nevertheless, the trial and error efforts of the immigrants in forging a new urban life did help produce a number of innovations, many of which have survived to thrive in contemporary urban society.

Some of the most significant social innovations came from structural changes in the family. The specific causes, forms, and consequences of these changes are too complex to be considered in detail here and will be examined more extensively in a later chapter. But one important change was a direct result of migration and the conditions under which it took place. The literature on immigration is filled with examples of extended families and even of almost entire villages leaving the old country or rural areas and arriving intact to begin a new life in the city (Handlin, 1951). For the most part, however, the larger family units dissolved at the points of departure. The main pattern was one of younger members migrating as married couples or unattached individuals, leaving their older relatives behind. Migration tends to be selective of young people; thus, the population of the rapidly growing industrial cities came to be made up preponderantly of persons in the fifteen to thirty-five age bracket (Hawley, 1971). For the first time, many of these young people were left to their own wits and resources, free from the surveillance, controls, or guidance of the older members of their families and villages. Even the children living with immigrant parents discovered that many of the family customs and traditions were not adequate guides for coping with the demands or opportunities of urban-industrial life. For example, the tradition of passing occupational roles from father to son withered as it was discovered that the father's agricultural background and limited knowledge of the more specialized industrial, commercial, and professional occupations were not helpful. The increased separation of work and residence helped to increase the gap between the generations, as did other extrafamilial institutions like compulsory education. Traditional forms of "love control" such as the dowry system, arranged marriages, and chaperonage likewise withered under the onslaught of city life.

One interesting innovation to come out of this set of circumstances was the youth-oriented immigrant settlement house. Initially staffed by middle- and upper-class volunteers, these organizations were the forerunner of the various public and privately sponsored social agencies and their full-time professionally trained staffs that are now a well-institutionalized feature of urban society. Hull House in Chicago was an early and prime example. Jane Addams, a founder of Hull House, was a notable reformer well ahead of her time and active in various movements to improve the quality of life in the immigrant slums. She was an acute observer of young people as they moved about the streets of the city pursuing their newfound urban interests. Of particular concern to her was what she saw as the lack of adequate community-sponsored recreational facilities for young working ·people, who were being exploited in this area by the dispensers of commercialized leisure. In a book published shortly after the turn of the century, this is how she described the problems of the city's youth:

> In the medieval city the knights held their tourneys, the guilds their pageants, the people their dances, and the church made festival for its most cherished saints with gay street processions. . . . Only in the modern city have men concluded that it is no longer necessary for the municipality to provide for the insatiable desire for play . . . . A further difficulty lies in the fact that industri-

alism has gathered together multitudes of eager young creatures from all quarters of the earth as a labor supply for the countless factories and workshops, upon which the industrial city is based. Never before in civilization have such numbers of young girls been suddenly released from the protection of home and permitted to walk unattended upon city streets and to work under alien roofs . . . . Never before have such numbers of young boys earned money independently of the family life, and felt themselves free to spend it as they chose in the midst of vice deliberately disguised as pleasure . . . .

In every city arise . . . "gin palaces" . . . in which alcohol is dispensed, not only to allay thirst, but ostensibly to stimulate gaiety, it is sold really in order to empty pockets. Huge dance halls are opened to which hundreds of young people are attracted, many of whom stand wistfully outside a roped circle, for it requires five cents to procure within it for five minutes the sense of allurement and intoxication which is sold in lieu of innocent pleasure . . . . We see thousands of girls walking up and down the streets on a pleasant evening with no chance to catch a sight of pleasure even through a lighted window, save as these lurid places provide it. Apparently the modern city sees in these girls only two possibilities, both of them commercial: first a chance to utilize by day their new and labor power in its factories and shops, and then another chance in the evening to extract from them their petty wages by pandering to their love of pleasure . . . .

One of the most pathetic sights in the public dance halls of Chicago is the number of young men, obviously honest young fellows from the country, who stand about mainly hoping to make the acquaintance of some "nice girl." They look eagerly up and down the rows of girls, many of whom are drawn to the hall by the same keen desire for pleasure and social intercourse which the lonely young men themselves feel.

Perhaps never before have the pleasures of the young and mature become so definitely separated as in the modern city (Addams, 1910, p. 3–21).

As sympathetic and enlightened as Jane Addams was for the times, the above passages reflect turn of the century upper-middle-class values in equating commercialized recreation with vice and sin. But from the modern sociological perspective of functionalism, implicit in these descriptions of the saloons and dance halls is that an important need or want was being fulfilled, and that these establishments were the forerunners of a significant urban institution. Out of the same set of circumstances, one can see the rise of professional athletics (the first professional baseball clubs, all of them in urban-industrial cities, were first franchised before the turn of the century, and professional prizefighting had already become a popular urban sport), vaudeville and the musical stage, the motion picture, jazz and popular music, radio and the phonograph. All of these were forms of popular entertainment created to satisfy the tastes and needs of the same youthful urban mass described by Jane Addams. While some of these forms of popular entertainment may have originated to satisfy creative or artistic urges as well, the most successful of them proved to be highly profitable to their providers and were the basis for a multimillion-dollar popular entertainment industry.

"The Cliff Dwellers," painted in 1913 by George Wesley Bellows, depicts city life at that time. (Los Angeles County Museum of Art, Los Angeles County Funds)

To a degree, one can also see organized crime syndicates in American cities arising from the same set of circumstances, as some members of various immigrant groups one after another became involved in the marginal and sometimes illegal business of satisfying wants that were otherwise taboo or suppressed by the conventional puritan morality of the day, such as gambling, alcohol, drugs, prostitution, and pornography (Bell, 1953). It is no accident that the leading prizefighters, ball players, singers, movie actors, comedians, and organized crime figures often came from the same family, neighborhood, or immigrant group and intermingled socially as they rapidly climbed the ladder of success that these new and expanding urban industries provided. In some cases, the same individuals have moved freely across the boundaries of professional sports, show business, and organized crime in the process of pursuing a popular and readily available vision of "making it big" in American society.

By the first decade of the twentieth century, all of the main features of

TABLE 3-4 Population of cities that reached 100,000 by 1910*

CITIES	1860	1870	1880	1890	1900	1910
Albany, N.Y.	62,367	69,422	90,758	94,923	94,151	100,253
Atlanta, Ga.	9,554	21,789	37,409	65,533	89,872	154,839
Baltimore, Md.	212,418	267,354	332,313	434,439	508,957	558,485
Birmingham, Ala.			3,086	26,178	38,415	132,685
Boston, Mass.	177,840	250,526	362,839	448,477	560,892	670,585
Bridgeport, Conn.[1]	13,299[1]	18,969	27,643	48,866	70,996	102,054
Buffalo, N.Y.	81,129	117,714	155,134	255,664	352,387	423,715
Cambridge, Mass.	26,060	39,634	52,669	70,028	91,886	104,839
Chicago, Ill.	109,260	298,977	503,185	1,099,850	1,698,575	2,185,283
Cincinnati, Ohio	161,044	216,239	255,139	296,908	325,902	363,591
Cleveland, Ohio	43,417	92,829	160,146	261,353	381,768	560,663
Columbus, Ohio	18,554	31,274	51,647	88,150	125,560	181,511
Dayton, Ohio	20,081	30,473	38,678	61,220	85,333	116,577
Denver, Colo.		4,759	35,629	106,713	133,859	213,381
Detroit, Mich.	45,619	79,577	116,340	205,876	285,704	465,766
Fall River, Mass.	14,026	26,766	48,961	74,398	104,863	119,295
Grand Rapids, Mich.	8,085	16,507	32,016	60,278	87,565	112,571
Indianapolis, Ind.	18,611	48,244	75,056	105,436	169,164	233,650
Jersey City, N.J.	29,226	82,546	120,722	163,003	206,433	267,779
Kansas City, Mo.	4,418	32,260	55,785	132,716	163,752	248,381
Los Angeles, Cal.	4,385	5,728	11,183	50,395	102,479	319,198
Louisville, Ky.	68,033	100,753	123,758	161,129	204,731	223,928
Lowell, Mass.	36,827	40,928	59,475	77,696	94,969	106,294
Memphis, Tenn.	22,623	40,226	33,592	64,495	102,320	131,105
Milwaukee, Wis.	45,246	71,440	115,587	204,468	285,315	373,857
Minneapolis, Minn.	2,564	13,066	46,887	164,738	202,718	301,408
Nashville, Tenn.	16,988	25,865	43,350	76,168	80,865	110,364
New Haven, Conn.	39,267[1]	50,840[1]	62,882[1]	81,298	108,027	113,605
New Orleans, La.	168,675	191,418	216,090	242,039	287,104	339,075
New York, N.Y.[2]	1,174,779	1,478,103	1,911,698	2,507,414	3,437,202	4,766,883
Manhattan Borough	813,669	942,292	1,164,673	1,441,216	1,850,093	2,331,542
Bronx Borough	23,593	37,393	51,980	88,908	200,507	430,980
Brooklyn Borough	279,122	419,921	599,495	838,547	1,166,582	1,634,351
Queens Borough	32,903	45,468	56,559	87,050	152,999	284,041
Richmond Borough	25,492	33,029	38,991	51,693	67,021	85,969
Newark, N.J.	71,941	105,059	136,508	181,830	246,070	347,469
Oakland, Cal.	1,543	10,500	34,555	48,682	66,960	150,174
Omaha, Nebr.	1,883	16,083	30,518	140,452	102,555	124,096
Paterson, N.J.	19,586	33,579	51,031	78,347	105,171	125,600
Philadelphia, Pa.	565,529	674,022	847,170	1,046,964	1,293,697	1,549,008
Pittsburgh, Pa.[3]	77,923	139,256	235,071	343,904	451,512	533,905
Portland, Oreg.	2,874	8,293	17,577	46,385	90,426	207,214
Providence, R.I.	50,666	68,904	104,857	132,146	175,597	224,326
Richmond, Va.	37,910	51,038	63,600	81,388	85,050	127,628
Rochester, N.Y.	48,204	62,386	89,366	133,896	162,608	218,149
St. Louis, Mo.	160,773	310,864	350,518	451,770	575,238	687,029
St. Paul, Minn.	10,401	20,030	41,473	133,156	163,065	214,744
San Francisco, Cal.	56,802	149,473	233,959	298,997	342,782	416,912
Scranton, Pa.	9,223	35,092	45,850	75,215	102,026	129,867
Seattle, Wash.		1,107	3,533	42,837	80,671	237,194
Spokane, Wash.				19,922	36,848	104,402
Syracuse, N.Y.	28,119	43,051	51,792	88,143	108,374	137,249
Toledo, Ohio	13,768	31,584	50,137	81,434	131,822	168,497
Washington, D.C.[4]	61,122	109,199	177,624	230,392	278,718	331,069
Worcester, Mass.	24,960	41,105	58,291	84,655	118,421	145,986

[1] Population of town; town and city not returned separately.

[2] Population of New York and its boroughs as now constituted.

[3] Includes population of Allegheny as follows: 1900, 129,896; 1890, 105,287; 1880, 78,682; 1870, 53,180; 1860, 28,702; 1850, 21,262; 1840, 10,089; and 1830, 2,801.

[4] Population as returned from 1880 to 1910 is for the District of Columbia, with which the city is now coextensive.

*U.S. Bureau of the Census, *Thirteenth Census: 1910* (Washington, D.C.: U.S. Government Printing Office, 1913), I, p. 80.

an urban-industrial civilization were in place and intact. In 1910, fifty American cities had a population of 100,000 or more people. New York City had a population of nearly five million people, and Chicago, demonstrating phenomenal growth, increased its population twentyfold in half a century: from 109,260 in 1860 to 2,185,283 in 1910. Table 3-4 illustrates population growth in the fifty largest American cities from 1860 to 1910. Approximately 46 percent of the nation's ninety-two million people lived in cities in 1910, compared to less than 20 percent in 1860.

The nation had not yet fully accepted or assimilated the significance of the changes that had been taking place, but reform movements were underway to minimize some of the more undesirable features that the urban-industrial revolution had wrought, mainly in the areas of housing, sanitation, public health, recreation, zoning and planning, education, social service, and municipal government. These will be considered in greater detail in later chapters.

By this time, the first social-scientific studies of urban life had begun to appear. Adna Weber's (1899) *The Growth of Cities in the Nineteenth Century* and the field studies reported in the Hull House Papers, which go back to 1895 (Burgess and Bogue, 1964), were among the most significant of the early efforts at objective empirical analysis of urban life and forms. Similar work had been going on in New York City and in other cities that had undertaken social surveys or investigations of slums. The first formal studies of the city by professional sociologists began in the decade of World War I, as previously discussed in Chapter One. These efforts were in welcome and refreshing contrast to the more biased and impressionistic forms of observation that had prevailed earlier. As Ernest Burgess, one of the key figures in the development of urban sociology, has suggested: "Although he was not there first, the sociologist made a big difference in urban research. It was sociology that emphasized science and the importance of understanding social problems in terms of the processes and forces that produce them" (Burgess and Bogue, 1964, p. 4).

SELECTED BIBLIOGRAPHY

ADDAMS, JANE. *The Spirit of Youth and the City Streets.* New York, 1910. (Cf. Glaab, 1963.)

BELL, DANIEL. "Crime as an American Way of Life," 13 *Antioch Review* (Summer 1953). pp. 131–154.

BURGESS, ERNEST W., and BOGUE, DONALD J., eds. *Contributions to Urban Sociology.* Chicago: University of Chicago Press, 1964.

GLAAB, CHARLES N. *The American City: A Documentary History.* Homewood, Ill.: Dorsey Press, 1963.

GLAZIER, WILLARD. *Peculiarities of American Cities.* Philadelphia, 1884. (Cf. Glaab, 1963.)

GOLD, HARRY. "The Professionalization of Urban Planning." Ph.D. dissertation, University of Michigan, 1965.

HAMMOND, JOHN L., and HAMMOND, BARBARA. *The Rise of Modern Industry*. 2nd ed. London: Methuen & Co., 1925.

HANDLIN, OSCAR. *The Uprooted*. Boston: Little, Brown, 1951.

HAWLEY, AMOS H. *Urban Society*. New York: Ronald Press, 1971.

HEILBRONER, ROBERT L. *The Making of Economic Society*. Englewood Cliffs, N.J.: Prentice-Hall, 1962.

MCKELVEY, BLAKE. *The Urbanization of America: 1860–1915*. New Brunswick, N.J.: Rutgers University Press, 1963.

————. *American Urbanization: A Comparative History*. Glenview, Ill.: Scott, Foresman, 1973.

SMELSER, NEIL. *Social Change in the Industrial Revolution: An Application of Theory to the British Cotton Industry*. Chicago: University of Chicago Press, 1959.

STRONG, JOSIAH. *Our Country: Its Possible Future and Its Present Crisis*. New York, 1885. (Cf. Glaab, 1963.)

THERNSTROM, STEPHAN, and SENNETT, RICHARD, eds. *Nineteenth Century Cities: Essays in the New Urban History*. New Haven, Conn.: Yale University Press, 1969.

USHER, ABBOTT PAYSON. *The Industrial History of England*. Boston: Houghton Mifflin, 1920.

WEBER, A. F. *The Growth of Cities in the Nineteenth Century*. New York: Macmillan, 1899.

WEBER, MAX. *The Protestant Ethic and the Spirit of Capitalism*. Trans. T. Parsons. London: George Allen & Unwin, 1930.

WILENSKY, HAROLD L., and LEBEAUX, CHARLES N. *Industrial Society and Social Welfare*. New York: Russell Sage, 1958.

PART II

BASIC FORMS OF URBAN LIFE IN THE MODERN METROPOLIS

chapter 4

the metropolitan revolution: anatomy of the metropolis

Until the twentieth century, the city was the dominant form of urban development. Throughout recorded history, the distinction between city and country was a clear one, since cities were seen as self-contained entities with easily recognizable boundaries. Although such compact and densely settled cities and towns still exist, the appearance and growth of the metropolis and its eventual dominance of the national landscape is the principal theme of American urban development during the first three-quarters of the twentieth century. Like nineteenth-century urbanization, the process of twentieth-century metropolitanization has been so rapid that there has been a cultural lag in public awareness of and response to what is happening. This partially explains the urban crises of the 1960s and 1970s. Americans had become part of a predominantly metropolitan society even before they had become fully aware that they were members of a society that was no longer rural but largely urban.

FACTORS LEADING TO METROPOLITAN GROWTH

The industrial revolution, which brought large numbers of rural and foreign migrants to American cities in the latter part of the nineteenth century, had persisted well into the early part of the twentieth century. By

1920 more than one-half of the United States population lived in urban areas. Until that time, most of the growth had been concentrated in the largest cities, which had been growing in numbers and density, and this trend had produced serious problems of overcrowding in residential, industrial, commercial, and public facilities. The health and sanitation problems created by the concentration of large numbers of people in relatively small land areas often made living conditions impossible. In effect, the big cities were bursting their seams.

Also creating problems was the uncontrolled competition for scarce urban space, which often led to the incompatible uses of adjacent parcels of land, represented by the intrusion of unsightly, noisy, and congestion-producing commercial and industrial activities into residential areas and an ever more intensive utilization of the land, without regard for such consequences as increased pressures on already overburdened transportation, sewage, water, and utility systems, recreation facilities, and so on. Residential areas tended to deteriorate and become dilapidated in the expectation by many landowners that eventually such properties would succumb to the inevitable pressures of more intensive and economically more productive industrial and commercial uses. In fact, much slum clearance supposedly undertaken for the benefit of the affected slum dwellers actually hastened the conversion of residential areas into nonresidential uses (Gans, 1962; see also Chapter Fifteen).

What happened in this process was that residential land values became so high that many middle-income families were either forced to live in substandard housing at excessive cost or were forced to leave the central cities in order to find suitable housing within a reasonable price range. Of course, the housing problem became even more difficult for the many low-income and minority groups caught in the squeeze between high-cost substandard housing in the central cities and the social barriers that excluded them from the suburban housing market (see Chapter Fourteen). For these groups the overcrowded slums were the only available alternative (see the discussion of slums later in this chapter).

In contrast to the plight of the city dweller, the migration of those who have moved to outlying suburban areas is a much larger and more significant trend toward decentralization of the growing urban population. This has produced a *metropolitan* pattern of urban settlement. Recent metropolitan development not only represents a decentralization of the residential population, but also includes a redistribution of many industrial, commercial, and cultural activities over an ever-expanding land area surrounding the central cities.

This trend has been greatly facilitated by scientific and technological advances of this century, especially in the areas of transportation and communications. The extensive use of the automobile has eliminated the necessity of locating the place of work and residence in close proximity. Thus, those who were first able to afford private automobiles were among the first urbanites in large numbers to resettle in suburban residential enclaves, well separated from the more hectic, noisy, or other unpleasant aspects of the central business district or factory (earlier suburbs of more limited population were built along rail commuter lines). Shopping centers, factories, and other business establishments were able to decentralize as they lessened their dependence on waterways, railroads, and an adjacent labor supply. The telephone, the motor truck, and the automobile made them readily accessible to their suppliers, their customers, and their employees at almost any location within the metropolitan complex. More recently, helicopters increasingly have been used to provide this same service. Much of the industrial and commercial decentralization thus made possible was probably a response to the larger quantities of cheaper land in outlying suburban fringes. However, this general pattern of dispersion and decentralization is also probably a result of changing values, such as industry's desire for more space, more attractive living conditions for its executives and employees, and an increasing emphasis on visible symbols of status, such as may be afforded by the availability of green open space, pleasingly visible architecture and landscaping, and adequate parking facilities (Boskoff, 1970).

THE EXTENT OF METROPOLITANIZATION

Identifying the boundaries or assessing the extent of metropolitan growth and development is difficult because the term is rather imprecise and because there are no standard agreed-upon definitions of what is metropoli-

Early commuters were faced with virtually the same problems as today's commuters. (Michigan Dept. of State, State Archives)

tan. Some descriptions, for example, portray the sprawl of metropolitan growth in these commonly recognizable but impressionistic visual terms:

> Seen from above, the modern city edges imperceptibly out of its setting. There are not clear boundaries. Just now the white trace of the superhighway passes through cultivated fields; now it is lost in an asphalt maze of streets and buildings. As one drives in from the airport or looks out from the train window, clumps of suburban housing, industrial complexes, and occasional green spaces pass by; it is hard to tell where city begins and country ends (Handlin and Burchard, 1963, p. 1).

In recent decades, the most commonly accepted definitions and estimates have become those developed by the U.S. Bureau of the Census. According to current Census Bureau standards, the Standard Metropolitan Statistical Area (SMSA) is the appropriate metropolitan unit. SMSAs are defined as counties containing one or more city of at least fifty thousand population, plus adjacent counties meeting specified criteria of urban character that are economically and socially integrated with the county containing the central city (see Bollens and Schmandt, 1975, pp. 2-6, for a more detailed discussion of this definition and its limitations). So defined, many metropolitan areas ignore the political boundaries of cities and some even sprawl across the boundaries of several states.

The Census Bureau first used the concept of SMSA for the 1950 Census. Thereafter, the criteria for SMSA status has been slightly revised each decade it has been used. This makes intercensus comparisons of metropolitan growth rather difficult. For example, applying 1970 SMSA definitions to earlier decades would yield slightly larger estimates of the metropolitan population and the total number of SMSAs than would applying 1950 definitions (Hawley, 1971, pp. 249-252). Nevertheless, it is still possible to provide a reasonable illustration of the extent of metropolitan growth during the present century by using data derived from several census reports.

As Table 4-1 illustrates, only sixty-one urban centers in the United States qualified as metropolitan at the beginning of this century, according to 1950 definitions. These centers contained slightly less than one-third of the total United States population. In each succeeding decade, the number of such areas rose, quadrupling by 1970. The metropolitan population as a portion of the total United States population also increased rapidly in each decade between 1900 and 1970. Thus, by 1970, there were 243 SMSAs, in which slightly more than two-thirds of the United States population resided. By 1977 there were 276 urban centers meeting current SMSA criteria. It is expected that the 1980 census will indicate still more growth in the number of metropolitan areas and in the total size of the metropolitan population of the United States.

Metropolitan growth generally has consisted of the movement of people and activities from the center of urban concentrations outward toward the periphery over an ever-expanding radius of land. However, this is not to imply that such dispersion is randomly devouring raw land, because metropolitan development in the United States is highly concen-

TABLE 4-1 Metropolitan growth in the United States: 1900-1977

YEAR	NUMBER OF SMSAs	POPULATION OF ALL SMSAs (IN THOUSANDS)	SMSA POPULATION AS A PERCENT OF U.S. POPULATION
1900	61	23,558	31.0
1910	97	42,012	45.6
1920	112	52,505	49.5
1930	143	66,712	54.1
1940	150	72,576	58.5
1950	191	88,964	58.8
1960	212	112,385	61.3
1970	243	139,000	68.6
1977	276	—	—

SOURCES: *U.S. Census of the Population,* 1960: Standard Metropolitan Statistical Areas, PC 3, 1DI; *U.S. Census of the Population,* 1970: Number of Inhabitants, United States Summary, PC 1-A1; and *HUD Newsletter* 4 (May 28, 1973). Estimates for 1900 based on 1950 U.S. Census criteria for SMSA status; 1910-1960 estimates are based on 1960 U.S. Census criteria for SMSA status; and 1970 and 1977 estimates are based on 1970 U.S. Census criteria for SMSA status.

trated within specific regions of the country, with vast portions of the total land area still relatively undeveloped or unpopulated. Census Bureau figures indicate that approximately three-quarters of the population is concentrated on less than 2 percent of the nation's total land area, with most of this concentrated in the SMSAs (United States Department of Commerce News, U.S. Government Printing Office, April 21, 1972, p. 1). About one-half of the U.S. population is concentrated in only eight of the fifty states—California, Illinois, Michigan, New Jersey, New York, Ohio, Pennsylvania, and Texas.

One important consequence of metropolitanization is that it tends to blur traditional rural-urban differences, particularly in the rural areas immediately adjacent to the metropolitan centers. As metropolitanization gathers momentum, it reaches out to link and absorb formerly rural areas on the periphery of the metropolis. In the 1960-1970 decade, population growth rates of rural communities and villages within a fifty-mile radius of metropolitan areas was twice that of similar places at greater distances from metropolitan areas and well above that for the nation as a whole (National Research Council, 1975, p. 40). No longer are the rural areas of America primarily agricultural. Rural residents are increasingly being employed in a range of nonfarm occupations. In 1970, although 27 percent of the nation's population was still classified as rural, five out of every six rural people were nonfarm. In no state in the entire country was the majority of the rural population still in the farm category (National Research Council, 1975, p. 39). A two-way flow of migration between urban and rural places is now commonplace, as is daily commuting between metropolitan areas and their surrounding rural areas. The latter is particularly feasible for those with immediate access to the interstate highways that now connect many metropolitan areas with their rural fringes and that considerably shorten the time for such commuting trips.

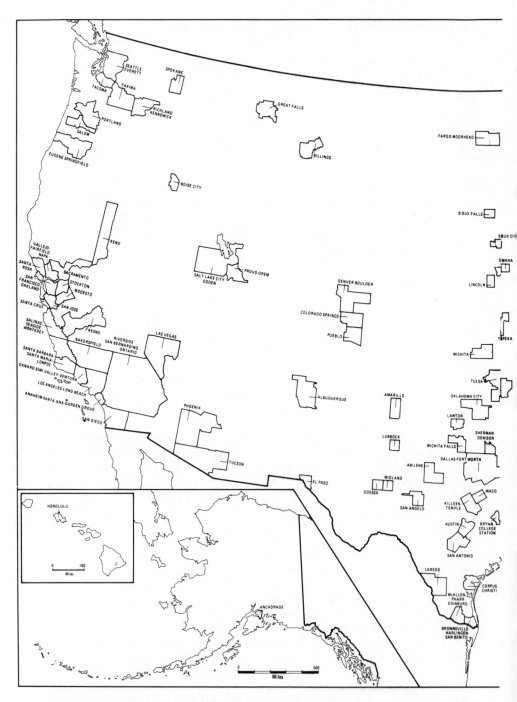

FIGURE 4-1 Based on map prepared by Bureau of the Census, U.S. Department of Commerce. Areas defined by Office of Management and Budget, August 1973. Population data compiled from 1970 Census of Population.

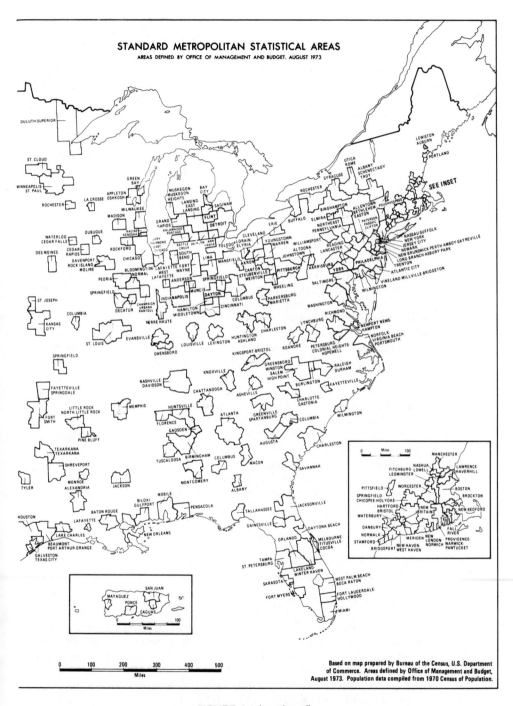

STANDARD METROPOLITAN STATISTICAL AREAS
AREAS DEFINED BY OFFICE OF MANAGEMENT AND BUDGET, AUGUST 1973

Based on map prepared by Bureau of the Census, U.S. Department of Commerce. Areas defined by Office of Management and Budget, August 1973. Population data compiled from 1970 Census of Population.

FIGURE 4-1 (*continued*)

Changes in the time-distance factor serve as a useful index to the ways in which modern time-saving means of transportation have furthered the expansion of the radius of and frequency of interaction between metropolitan areas and their hinterlands. The distance that can be traveled in sixty minutes provides a reasonable basis for illustration. Before the arrival of the automobile, the sixty-minute radius of cities seldom exceeded six miles. The automobile extended the one-hour travel distance to approximately twenty-five miles. With the advent of freeways and other highway system improvements, the sixty-minute commuting distance to major places of recreation and employment has risen to approximately thirty-five miles in most metropolitan areas. In those parts of the United States where metropolitan areas are relatively close together, almost all of the rural population is now within this sixty-minute time-distance. Approximately 95 percent of the country's population, both rural and urban, now lives within the daily commuting field of the central city of a metropolitan area (National Research Council, 1975, p. 10).

The farm population of the United States has diminished to less than 5 percent of the total. Farming has also become more of a business enterprise and has declined markedly as a distinctly rural way of life. Widespread ownership of automobiles, telephones, radios, and television sets by farm people, along with greater access to other mass media sources, have given rural residents access to the same information, attitudes, and opinions available to urbanites. In almost every sphere of their lives, the residents of rural areas, with few exceptions, are now served by urban-type institutions. Therefore, whether a person resides in a rural or a metropolitan area is less and less a useful basis for identifying distinctive patterns of behavior. More and more it becomes reasonable to speak of the United States as an urban society in which a shared urban culture is the predominant pattern. Of course, regional variations in life styles and other behavioral patterns continue to exist, but they are probably less significant than those related to such characteristics as socioeconomic status, age, occupation, education, or ethnic background. Such variations all occur within the framework of an encompassing urban civilization of which they are an integral part.

THE ANATOMY OF THE METROPOLIS

The growth of the metropolitan community involves the spatial redistribution of population and land use activities, as the central cities expand outward from their centers. This growth process also helps to produce a complex sociogeographic division of labor among the component parts of the metropolitan community. Each part or subarea of the community becomes clearly differentiated from the other parts, in terms of its physical characteristics or the characteristics of its population. In turn, a complex network of interdependencies is created as each part or subarea develops its own specialized functions essential to the functioning of the entire community.

Architectural features are among the characteristics of "a natural area" within a city. (Fred Klus/Gouvernement du Québec, Ministère du Loisir, de la Chasse, et de la Peche)

These concepts are among the basic assumptions of the ecological approach to urban analysis, which entails understanding how these component parts are organized and coordinated into a recognizable and integrated ecological entity in response to the more general patterns of metropolitan growth and dispersion. Much of the classic urban ecological research and theory has been devoted to the task of mapping and analyzing the spatial, functional, and symbiotic relationships among the component parts of the modern metropolis. To date, no completely acceptable standardized nomenclature has evolved for delineating and classifying local areas within the metropolitan community, and this has proved to be a difficult task for the professional urbanologist as well as the nonspecialist. Thus, concepts such as "city," "suburb," "local community," "neighborhood," "slum," "inner city," "urban fringe," "grey area," "satellite," or "ghetto" are so imprecise that they often mean different things to different people. Nevertheless, some attempts at classification do stand out, and a review of some of them is in order here.

Burgess's Concentric Zone Theory

First advanced in the early 1920s, Burgess's concentric zone theory is widely regarded as one of the classic statements of urban growth and differentiation. Burgess (1925) saw growth and differentiation of metropolitan areas in the United States as occurring in gradually extended concentric zones, each characterized by a typical pattern of land use. These zones were produced as the result of expansion outward from the central business district of the central city. The *central business district* is the first or inner zone, comprising skyscrapers, department stores, hotels, and other forms of retailing, light manufacturing, or commercialized leisure. The second zone, which surrounds the central business district (CBD), is called the *zone of transition* because it is subject to change caused by encroaching business and industrial land uses expanding beyond the CBD. This zone is described by Burgess as a mixture of residential and nonresidential uses. The residents tend to be a heterogeneous assortment of low-income groups, immigrants, and unconventional types or social outcasts such as prostitutes, addicts, or criminals, interspersed with some high-income groups living in luxurious "Gold Coast" style apartments. Zone three is the *zone of workingmen's homes,* occupied mainly by second-generation immigrant blue-collar workers, who are higher in socioeconomic status than most of the zone of transition dwellers, but who are still not fully assimilated into the middle class. The fourth zone is the *zone of middle class dwellers,* comprising mainly professional people, small businesspersons, managerial types, and other white-collar workers. The fifth zone, the *commuter's zone,* is the area consisting of suburbs or satellite cities on the outer periphery of the central city. In large metropolitan areas, this zone may form a ring from thirty to sixty miles beyond the central business district. Burgess's title for this zone implies an efficient transportation network allowing city workers to arrive daily from and escape nightly to bedroom communities beyond the political boundaries of the central city.

Burgess did not insist that his theory was empirically accurate as a physical description of any given city, and he recognized that physical barriers, such as hills, rivers, lakes, or transportation lines, could produce variations from his model. Rather, the concentric zone theory is an idealized concept designed to identify in dynamic terms general processes of city growth and differentiation over time, with minor variations, in most modern industrial cities in the United States.

Hoyt's Sector Theory

Homer Hoyt (1939) developed the sector theory as an outgrowth of a study of 142 American cities conducted during the depression years. Hoyt hypothesized that instead of forming concentric zones around the center of the city, the city tends to grow in sectors along the major transportation arteries outward from the center, creating a pattern akin to an octopus with tentacles extending in various directions, or in the shape of a multipointed star. Hoyt assumed that most residential, commercial, and industrial development of urban areas was distributed in a definite pattern within these sectors. He viewed the location and movement of various socioeconomic levels of the residential population as the key factor in patterning urban growth. As the cities grow in population, the upper-income groups move outward along a particular street or transportation line, so that upper-income residential areas tend to be located on the outer edges of the sector. In turn, lower-income groups tend to inherit or invade the aging and frequently deteriorating portions of the sector that have been or are being thus abandoned. The theory is similar to the concentric zone theory in that the socioeconomic status of the population varies from low to high as one moves from the center of the city to the periphery, the main difference being that this occurs in sectors shaped like the cut of a pie radiating outward from the center rather than within concentric zones encircling the center of the city. A more detailed summary of Hoyt's sector theory includes the following elements: 1) industrial areas do not develop in a circle around the CBD but also follow transportation lines, such as railroads, waterways, or highways; 2) upper-class residential areas first emerge near retail or administrative centers, and tend to follow established commuter routes toward desirable residential sites on scenic high grounds or along scenic lakes, rivers, forests, or parkways. They also tend to grow in the direction of open and undeveloped countryside rather than toward areas restricted by preexisting developed areas or natural barriers.

Harris's and Ullman's Multiple-Nuclei Theory

Harris and Ullman (1945) argue that cities developed around a series of centers serving a variety of different functions and located at several points within their boundaries, rather than producing a single center at the heart of the city. Thus, cities may develop retail centers, wholesale centers, residential centers, and the like, each representing the concentration of a specific activity at a particular location that may be best suited for that activity. They argue that multiple centers develop as a result of the following four factors: 1) certain activities require specialized facilities, such as water, sewerage, parking, or accessibility, and they tend to concentrate in the vicinity of these facilities, wherever they may be; 2) similar activities benefit from locations close to one another, and they group together for mutual advantages, as in the cases of high fashion retail shops, law offices, or the headquarters of financial institutions; 3) certain unlike activities may be incompatible or disadvantageous to one another—for example, locating a glue factory in the middle of a prime residential area would be considered highly offensive to the citizens of such an area and probably would be forbidden by local zoning codes; 4) for many activities, such as storage facilities or warehousing, land in the CBD or other choice locations may be too expensive or may not be sufficiently advantageous to warrant the costs of competing with other potential users for the use of such locations (Harris and Ullman, 1945).

The multiple nuclei theory does not specify a particular pattern for the distribution of centers within the urban area, but implies instead that each city develops its own special pattern as a result of its unique historical circumstances. Thus, there is no typical way in which multiple centers arrange themselves in relationship to one another.

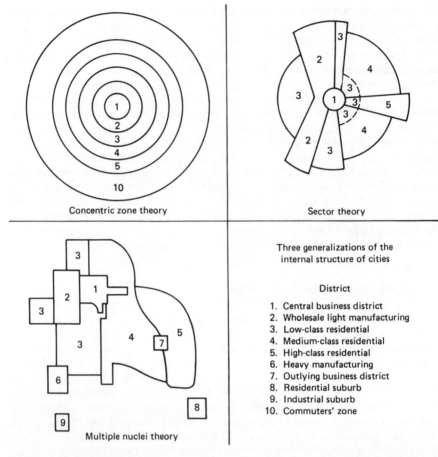

Concentric zone theory

Sector theory

Three generalizations of the
internal structure of cities

District

1. Central business district
2. Wholesale light manufacturing
3. Low-class residential
4. Medium-class residential
5. High-class residential
6. Heavy manufacturing
7. Outlying business district
8. Residential suburb
9. Industrial suburb
10. Commuters' zone

Multiple nuclei theory

FIGURE 4-2   Classic theories of metropolitan growth and structure (C. D. Harris and Edward L. Ullman, *Annals,* 242, November 1945, 7-17).

A Critique of the Classic Theories of Growth

All three of the theories just discussed have been widely accepted by social scientists, but not without considerable criticism. Most of the criticism centers on the assumption that these theories were intended as literal generalized descriptions of the spatial patterning of cities. The multiple-nuclei theory, which does not specify concrete patterns, escapes this particular criticism. But empirical examination of particular cities that do not seem to fit any of these theoretical schemes, especially the concentric zone theory and to a lesser extent the sector theory, is often cited to cast doubt on their accuracy or validity. For example, Firey (1947, pp. 41–68) found both the concentric zone and sector theories inadequate for the city of Boston. Davie (1937, pp. 133–161) conducted a detailed study of New Haven, Connecticut, and examined land use maps for twenty other cities.

He found considerable heterogeneity within zones and many irregularities of pattern. He concluded that the idea of a symmetrical distribution of land uses in concentric rings was overly simple. Caplow's (1952, pp. 544–549) findings in Paris and a study of Budapest by Beynon (1943, pp. 256–275) are examples of studies of European cities that have found exceptions to the concentric zone pattern of development.

Hawley (1971, p. 101) concludes that criticisms like these have been provoked by a too literal interpretation of the zonal hypothesis, and much of the objection might have been obviated had it been conceived of in more general terms as an ideal typology of growth rather than as a concrete descriptive model. Moreover, empirical studies have supported the concentric zone theory. Blumenfeld's (1949, pp. 209–212) examination of Philadelphia strongly confirmed the dominance of the concentric zone pattern in that city, although he found only three main zones rather than five. Schnore and Jones (1969) have found that a rough approximation of Burgess's model does apply to older and larger American industrial cities, primarily in the Midwest and Northeast.

In the latest word on this subject, Berry and Kasarda (1977, p. 90) suggest that if the concentric, sector, and multiple-nuclei schemes, as illustrated in Figure 2, are conjointly overlaid on the land use and population maps of any city they reveal weblike patterns of neighborhoods whose social, physical, and economic patterns exhibit both concentric and axial dimensions. Thus, they conclude, the three classic principles of internal structure of cities are "independent, additive descriptions of the social and

Paris is an example of the exception to the concentric zone pattern of development. (Air France Photo)

economic character of neighborhoods in relation to each other and to the whole" (ibid.).

Perhaps the most valid criticism of the classic ecological theories is that they are unidimensional in the characteristics assumed to be distributed within the metropolitan complex. More recent ecological theory and research are based on the assumption of a multiplicity of characteristics, each of which may be spatially distributed somewhat differently than the others. Some of these more advanced ecological attempts to describe the characteristics and functions of subareas within the metropolis are described below. But whatever the criticisms of the concentric zone theory, the sector theory, or the multiple-nuclei theory, they are still widely cited in the current sociological literature on urbanization, and they constitute a useful introduction and point of departure for more refined and detailed urban analysis.

Social Area Analysis

Social area analysis is a technique for describing and assessing the spatial distribution of many key variables that allegedly delineate significant subareas or social areas of the urban community. The objective is to classify and compare small sections of the metropolitan community on the basis of their main social attributes. The basic units for analysis are census tracts. These are areas of approximately 4,000 persons, drawn up by the U.S. Census Bureau for the purpose of providing census data for relatively small and compact segments of the urban population. Most of the larger metropolitan areas are composed of at least several hundred census tracts. The concept and techniques of social area analysis were originated by Shevky and Bell (1955), using census data from the Los Angeles and San Francisco SMSAs. Shevky and Bell identified what they concluded were the three main dimensions of urban society and used available census data to construct the following indexes:

1. *Social Rank.* This represents the socioeconomic status of an area, as measured by its occupational and educational levels.
2. *Urbanization.* Shevky and Bell define urbanization in terms of the family structure of an area. This measure is derived from the fertility rates of women, the proportion of gainfully employed women, and the percentage of the area housing in single family dwelling units.
3. *Segregation.* This index is based on the ecological or spatial separation of racial and ethnic groups.

These indexes make it possible to provide a social profile for each census tract of the metropolitan area and to compare their relative standing for each of the three major social dimensions just described. For example, one tract might be high in social rank and segregation but low in urbanization, another tract might be high in segregation and urbanization but low in social rank, and so on.

The proponents of social area analysis (Bell, 1959) argue that the approach is useful to social scientists because it provides a simple and systematic method for delineating urban neighborhoods and communities having different social characteristics. In addition to facilitating comparative studies of the social areas of different cities at one point in time, changes within a given area over time can also be systematically examined by this approach. The approach can be used to examine the relationship between social rank, urbanization, or segregation, and an almost unlimited variety of measurable phenomena, such as crime rates, rates of mental illness, voting or religious behavior, life styles, and property values.

But social area analysis, like the theories preceding it, is not without its detractors. Some critics (Duncan, 1955; Hawley and Duncan, 1957; Van Arsdol et al., 1958) view the approach as lacking both an adequate theoretical rationale and sufficient empirical utility. For example, no clear theoretical relationship is specified between the basic concepts of social rank, urbanization, and segregation, and the particular census tract variables used in constructing the index. Likewise, it is argued, there is no particular advantage in using these social area indexes instead of individual census measures, which may give considerably better results. In fact, these critiques imply that the indexes are nothing more than arbitrary groupings of variables without a clear-cut rationale for their selection. Nevertheless, social area analysis was a useful step in systematically measuring the multidimensionality of the modern urban community, and it helped to pave the way for more sophisticated and elaborate methods of urban research.

Factorial Ecology

Rees (1970) has suggested that the use of many more variables detailing the socioeconomic characteristics of census tract populations constitutes a logical expansion of social area analysis. Through the more sophisticated methods of factor analysis, the fundamental patterns of variations in the data can be isolated, whether or not they conform to the main dimensions of social area analysis. "Factorial ecology" is the term now used to characterize studies applying factor analysis to ecological study. In this sense, factorial ecology is a more sophisticated elaboration and outgrowth of the social area analysis approach.

One of the major results of factorial ecology has been the comparison of preindustrial urban ecological systems with those found in modern industrial communities, such as comparisons between Chicago and Calcutta (Berry, 1971; Rees, 1972) designed to show what common spatial structural characteristics occur in cities in different parts of the world. But there have been other major studies of single cities based on factorial ecology (Smith, 1973, pp. 40–44). Rees's (1970) study of Chicago is one of the best illustrations of factor analysis of an American city. Rees compiled data based on fifty-seven socioeconomic and demographic variables for 222 subareas of the Chicago SMSA and performed a factor analysis. The first factor represented socioeconomic status, as measured by occupation, education, and income. The second factor dealt with stages in the life cycle and was based on family size, age, and housing type. The third factor comprised race and

TABLE 4-2   Criteria of social well-being and variables used in Tampa study

CRITERIA AND VARIABLES		
I ECONOMIC STATUS		
i) *Income*		
1 Income per capita ($) of persons 14 and over 1970	+	(1)
2 Families with income less than $3000 (%) 1970	−	(1)
3 Families with income over $10,000 (%) 1970	+	(1)
4 Persons in families below poverty level (%) 1970	−	(1)
ii) *Employment*		
5 Unemployed persons (% total workforce) 1970	−	(1)
6 Persons aged 16–24 working less than 40 weeks (%) 1969	−	(1)
7 White-collar workers (%) 1970	+	(1)
8 Blue-collar workers (%) 1970	−	(1)
iii) *Welfare*		
9 Families on AFDC program (%) Oct. 1971	−	(2)
10 Persons aged 65 and over on Old Age Assistance (%) Oct. 1971	−	(2)
II ENVIRONMENT		
i) *Housing*		
11 Average value of owner-occupied units ($) 1970	+	(1)
12 Owner-occupied units valued less than $10,000 (%) 1970	−	(1)
13 Average monthly rental of rented units ($) 1970	+	(1)
14 Rented units with monthly rentals less than $60 (%) 1970	−	(1)
15 Units with complete plumbing facilities (%) 1970	+	(1)
16 Deteriorating and dilapidated houses (%) 1971	−	(3)
ii) *Streets and Sewers*		
17 Streets needing reconstruction (% of total length) 1971	−	(4)
18 Streets needing scarification and resurfacing (% of total length) 1971	−	(4)
19 Sanitary sewer deficiencies (% of total area) 1971	−	(5)
20 Storm sewer deficiencies (% of total area) 1971	−	(4)
iii) *Air Pollution*		
21 Maximum monthly dustfall (tons/sq. mile) 1969	−	(6)
22 Average suspended particulates (μgm/m ^{3}/day) 1969	−	(6)
23 Maximum monthly sulfation (mg SO $_4$/100 cm ^{2}/day) 1969	−	(6)
iv) *Open Space*		
24 Area lacking park and recreation facilities (%) 1971	−	(7)
III HEALTH		
i) *General Mortality*		
25 Infant deaths (per 1000 live births) 1970	−	(8)
26 Death rate (per 10,000 persons 65 or over) 1970	−	(8)
ii) *Chronic Diseases*		
27 Cancer deaths (per 100,000 population) 1970	−	(8)
28 Stroke deaths (per 100,000 population) 1970	−	(8)

(continued)

resources, as indicated by census tract measures of blacks as a percentage of total population, and the proportion of the total census tract population in low-status employment, with low incomes, and living in substandard housing. These three factors taken alone accounted for 45.1 percent of the variance in the original fifty-seven variables. What is significant here is that Rees's study of Chicago as well as other factorial studies of American cities (Berry and Kasarda, 1977, p. 123) have succeeded in isolating and reinforcing the importance of the social area indices originally proposed by Shevky—socioeconomic status, family status, and ethnic status. Berry and Kasarda (ibid.) also conclude that there is some fit of each of these three dimensions with the essential features of the classic spatial models previously discussed.

TABLE 4-2 (*continued*)

	CRITERIA AND VARIABLES		
29	Heart disease deaths (per 100,000 population) 1970	−	(8)
30	New active tuberculosis cases (per 10,000 population) 1970	−	(8)

IV EDUCATION
   i) *Duration*

31	Persons aged 18–24 with 4 or more years high school or college (%) 1970	+	(1)
32	Persons over 25 with 8 years or less school (%) 1970	−	(1)
33	Persons over 25 with 4 years high school (%) 1970	+	(1)
34	Persons over 25 with 4 years college (%) 1970	+	(1)

V SOCIAL DISORGANIZATION
   i) *Personal Pathologies*

35	Narcotic violations arrests (per 10,000 residents) 1971	−	(9)
36	Venereal disease cases (per 10,000 population) 1970	−	(8)

   ii) *Family Breakdown*

37	Families with children, having husband and wife present (%) 1970	+	(1)
38	Persons separated or divorced (% ever married) 1970	−	(1)

   iii) *Overcrowding*

39	Dwellings with more than 1.0 persons per room (%) 1970	−	(1)

   iv) *Public Order and Safety*

40	Criminal violation arrests (per 1000 residents) 1971	−	(9)
41	Juvenile delinquency arrests (per 10,000 residents) 1971	−	(9)
42	Accidental deaths (per 100,000 population) 1970	−	(8)

   v) *Delinquency*

43	Juvenile delinquency arrests by residency (per 10,000 population) 1971	−	(9)

VI PARTICIPATION AND EQUALITY
   i) *Democratic Participation*

44	Registered voters (% population 18 and over) 1971	+	(10)
45	Eligible voters voting in mayoral election (%) 1971	+	(10)

   ii) *Equality*

46	Racial distribution index 1970	−	(1)
47	Income distribution index 1970	−	(1)

SOURCES OF DATA: (1) *1970 Census of Population and Housing.* (2) Division of Family Services, State of Florida. (3) Hillsborough County Planning Commission. (4) Department of Public Works, City of Tampa. (5) Sanitary Sewers Department, City of Tampa. (6) Hillsborough County Pollution Control Commission. (7) Metropolitan Development Agency, City of Tampa. (8) Hillsborough County Health Department. (9) Police Department, City of Tampa. (10) Supervisor of Elections, City of Tampa.

The Social Indicators Movement

Both factorial ecology and social area analysis have been criticized for relying almost exclusively on the content of census reports for their data. Smith (1973, p. 43) has identified one major omission in all of these studies; an adequate representation of social pathologies or social problems of urban centers, which are not directly available in census reports. Thus, some of the important conditions of human existence that may also be spatially differentiated are not included in these approaches. Smith argues for the need to tackle the problem of area variations in "social well-being" within urban centers, in the context of whether socially undesirable conditions are getting better or worse over time. This can be done by combining some of the techniques developed in the factorial ecology approach with sets of data that more accurately and fully reflect social well-being or the quality of life than do the contents of census reports; for example, measures of physical and mental health, crime and violence, delinquency, child abuse, drug addiction, alcoholism, dependency, suicide, life expectancy, and the like.

The gradual recognition of this situation has led in recent years to what has been referred to as the "social indicators movement" (Smith, 1973, p. 52). Alternatively described as "social accounting," "social reporting," or "monitoring social change," social indicators measure conditions as they vary in space and time. Social indicators may apply to nations, states, or regions, but their inter- and intracity applications are what concern us here.

One key illustration of the application of intracity social indicators research is a study of Tampa, Florida (Smith and Gray, 1972). In this study, forty-seven variables were assembled to measure the spatial distribution of six major criteria of social well-being within the city: 1) economic status; 2) environment; 3) health; 4) education; 5) social disorganization; and 6) participation and equality. The forty-seven variables are listed in Table 4-2. In contrast to earlier efforts at social area analysis, most of the variables were provided from local sources rather than from U.S. census reports. The data illustrated in Table 2 embody many important conditions having a bearing on the quality of individual life and provide a useful measure of the general concept of social well-being.

Figure 4-3 illustrates the general spatial patterning of social well-being in Tampa, as indicated by combining the results for all of the variables listed in Table 4-2. The darkly shaded areas are those poorest in the general indicators of well-being. They appear to be concentrated around the central business district and within the innermost parts of the northeastern sector of the city, while the "better" areas tend to occupy the opposite sector. Relatively poor conditions are also found in isolated census tracts in the extreme northern and southern parts of the city.

Not coincidentally, the areas indicating the worst conditions had at the time of this study already been designated as the target of various public projects aimed at permanently raising the socioeconomic and physical living standards of the most deprived population groups of the city.

Smith (1973) argues that one basic advantage to mapping social indicators in this way is that one can achieve a more humanistic view of the internal differentiation of cities. This may lead to the examination of the basic mechanisms of urban systems that give rise to the extreme disparities in the quality of life in the different areas of American metropolitan centers.

One of the shortcomings of this approach, as is also the case with the other attempts to identify the component parts of the urban community previously discussed, is that such study can become an end in itself, without enough concern for the kind of direct social action aimed at improving the unsatisfactory conditions that the social indicators movement has the potential for precisely identifying (Plessas and Fein, 1971, pp. 43–44). The eventual usefulness of the social indicators movement depends on the

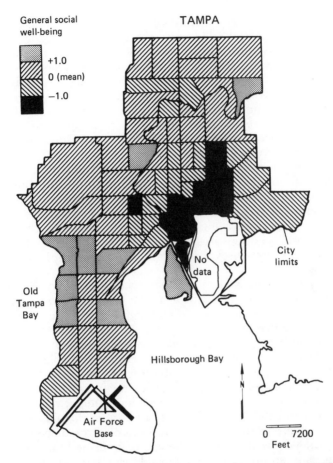

General social
well-being

+1.0

0 (mean)

−1.0

TAMPA

City
limits

No
data

Old
Tampa
Bay

Hillsborough Bay

N

Air Force
Base

0   7200
Feet

FIGURE 4-3   Standard scores on a general indicator of social well-being, based on data on all 47 variables listed in Table 4-2. (David M. Smith, *The Geography of Social Well-Being in the United States: An Introduction to Territorial Social Indicators,* New York: McGraw-Hill, 1973, p. 126.)

ability and willingness of urban planners, policy makers, and the general public to incorporate measures of social well-being into programs of direct social action designed to improve the quality of life in urban communities.

IDENTIFYING LOCAL AREAS IN THE METROPOLIS:
THE SLUM AS A SPECIAL CASE

In contrast to scientific efforts to classify subareas of the metropolis, lay descriptions and definitions tend to be imprecise and impressionistic. For example, the primarily suburban students in a large urban sociology course taught by the author were recently asked to define the essential characteristics of an urban slum and to identify those parts of the nearby city of Detroit that best represented their concept of it. The responses were vague on both counts. Many of the perceptions had to do with the physical condition of the housing, while others focused on the social characteristics of the residents. At one extreme, some students labeled the entire city a slum, while at the other, some were unwilling to consider any part of the city a slum. Within these extremes, the responses were varied. The variations in perception were as great among those who claimed to know the city well as among those who were only remotely familiar with the city. The responses were only slightly less varied when these same students were asked to identify and describe the "inner city." Yet these students strongly agreed that the slums represented a serious social problem about which something should be done. The most common response was that massive slum clearance was the only realistic solution. When asked to define the criteria by which areas would be designated as slums for the purpose of slum clearance, the students' responses were again imprecise, impressionistic, and widely varied.

On the surface, social area analysis, factorial ecology, or social indicator analysis would seem to provide a more rational and precise method for identifying areas for the purposes of planned social and economic changes such as slum clearance or urban renewal. To a certain extent, some large American cities already have applied techniques similar to these to systematically classify local subareas for conservation, rehabilitation, or massive demolition. To devise a reasonable set of objective measures upon which to build an empirical description of an urban residential slum is relatively simple, although tedious. Such an index might very well be based on the number of dwelling units within an area in dilapidated condition, the degree of overcrowding within housing units, the degree of absentee ownership of local dwelling units, the age of housing in a neighborhood, rental value, and so on. It is even possible to construct an index of the characteristics of slum dwellers, based on income, employment, or a wide variety of other available indicators of social well-being.

But such measures lack one important ingredient, which has to do with the attitudes and values of the residents. If the residents of a given area do not consider it to be a slum or even an undesirable place to live, to impose such a label might not always be fair or wise. The West End of Boston is a case in point. This area was designated a slum by city officials several decades ago and scheduled for massive rebuilding. This required the massive relocation of its then current residents. What was overlooked was that this was a cohesive and stable ethnic community to which its residents were strongly tied by sentiment and tradition (Gans, 1962). Subsequent studies of those who were involuntarily relocated to other parts of the community indicated that there was much psychological suffering and a profound sense of loss as a result of this displacement from what was to them a good community that satisfactorily met most of their real and perceived needs (Fried, 1963).

What has often happened is that when such areas have been targeted for slum clearance, city officials have been bombarded with resistance from the residents of such areas who do not consider their own neighborhood to be a slum or to need such drastic treatment as massive demolition. Obviously, in these cases, there is a large discrepancy in the perception of what constitutes a slum exists between the city officials on the one hand and the residents on the other. In disputes like these, the question of whose perception and judgment should prevail often becomes an emotionally charged political issue that is difficult to resolve to the satisfaction of the competing interest groups involved.

Thus, efforts to identify areas as slums should include measures of the attitudes and sentiments of their dwellers, in addition to more formal measures of physical condition or socioeconomic status. It seems reasonable to apply this label only to those areas considered *undesirable places to live by their own inhabitants,* as well as by outsiders.

A TYPOLOGY OF SLUMS

Actually, those areas of the city generally regarded as slums by outsiders contain diverse social groups and perform a variety of functions for the metropolitan community as a whole. Some of the more easily recognized slum subcultures and the functions they perform can be identified as follows:

Urban Villages

These include immigrant groups who settle in distinct areas of the city and who carry on the peasant life of their native communities. These areas are characterized by traditional family structures, local institutions such as ethnic churches, newspapers, social service agencies, restaurants, and commercial establishments. Ethnic groups in these areas may form a strong identification with the local neighborhood and its institutions, which in turn may serve as a source of stability, cohesiveness, and social control for that group. They supply a stable labor supply for the metropolitan labor market, and may become identified with particular occupations, depending on their skills, previous experience, and the opportunities currently available. Urban villages may provide a source of cultural diversity for the larger community with their ethnic restaurants and food shops, arts and crafts, and social customs. One of the most important functions of urban villages in American cities is that because they have been the port of entry for millions of impoverished and dispossessed migrants from rural areas or other lands they enhance socialization and assimilation for these people as they become accustomed to their new urban environment.

Skid Row

The inhabitants of these areas tend to be "skidders" or failures from other walks of life, such as chronic alcoholics, drug addicts, or vagrants. They usually are older, unattached, isolated males—the so-called "homeless man" of an earlier period of sociological literature (Burgess and Bogue, 1964). Rooming houses, flop houses, and transient hotels are the principal kinds of housing for these inhabitants, and the local institutions include social service agencies such as the Salvation Army, pawnshops, saloons, employment agencies, and the police. These areas function to segregate their inhabitants from other parts of the community where they usually are not tolerated. But contrary to the lay image of the residents of these areas as bums, they are often an important source of day labor for the central business district as janitors and maintenance workers, restaurant workers, street cleaners, and the like. One can see large lines of skid row inhabitants in front of local employment agencies looking for day work, and many local businesses depend on them for certain types of work. In a more negative sense, the skid row areas may also serve as a kind of burial ground where their homeless and aging population awaits death.

Young Adults

Slum areas of large American cities are inundated with many kinds of young people: students at metropolitan universities, colleges, and specialized trade schools, divorcees, childless newlyweds, unmarried couples, or young singles who have left their parents' homes to begin life on their own or to locate near their work. Such areas may serve as stepping-stones to social mobility for young people beginning careers in urban occupations. While their residence may be temporary, many local institutions cater to their needs, including movie theaters, discothèques, coffee shops, dating bureaus, parks, bars, and other meeting or gathering places.

Nonconformists

Bohemian, beatnik, hippy, gay, are labels that have been intermittently used to describe avant-garde or innovative behavior. Predominantly young adults, such groups have often congregated in inner city areas such as Greenwich Village, Haight-Ashbury, or the Left Bank of Paris. These areas provide escape from the controls or constraints of the conventional middle classes and an opportunity to experiment with new forms of expression in music, poetry, drama, literature, painting, filmmaking, fashion, politics, or sexual behavior. Very often the cultural innovations created in these settings pave the way for ultimate general acceptance by the larger society, and their creators have sometimes become mass media celebrities. Thus, such areas are a source of cultural diversity for the larger society and may afford many individuals a release from the constraints and frustrations of more conventional life styles.

The "Underworld"

Pornography, prostitution, gambling, drug distribution, and other "vices" tend to be concentrated in slum areas, where they are offered by a variety of underworld professionals, hustlers, or exploiters. Usually unattached individuals, they may or may not reside in the areas in which they operate. In some cities, special districts are set aside for these activities to prevent them from spreading to other areas where they are unwanted. Such areas may serve as a tourist attraction and a boost to the local economy, often attracting conventions and visitors from outside the metropolitan area. They also may provide an occasional outlet or escape from the frustrations and constraints experienced by the residents of local middle-class areas (who at the same time may work hard to keep such activities out of their own neighborhoods!).

The Ghetto

These areas provide homes for those who are not permitted to live anywhere else in the local community. Traditionally, this concept applied to the segregated Jewish communities of central and northern Europe of the preindustrial period, but in the United States the term has been increasingly applied to segregated Black, Oriental, Spanish American, or other ethnic communities, whether or not such segregation is entirely involuntary.

Other Groups

Finally, slum areas may be desirable to other groups who have none of the characteristics just described simply because of their convenience to the central business district or other centrally located activities. Or they may serve as a convenient meeting place for strangers who wish to carry on all sorts of activities with a maximum of privacy and a minimum of surveillance.

The main point in this discussion of urban slums is that to make simple generalizations about the characteristics of local areas of a metropolitan community is not easy. They tend to be more heterogeneous than commonly supposed. Most current popular stereotypes or images of areas such as the slums are often inaccurate, oversimplified, and unwarranted.

CITIES AND SUBURBS: A COMPARATIVE VIEW

Of all the efforts to classify the component parts of the modern metropolitan area, none are as significant or widespread as the efforts to compare the central cities of metropolitan areas with their suburban "rings" or "belts." Some of the reasons for this particular concern are obvious. While the traditional past concerns of urban sociologists had focused on the city, most of the large cities in the United States had matured by the period immediately following World War II and had begun to experience rapidly declining growth rates. Between 1950 and 1970, many of these cities had in fact begun to lose population. The 1980 Census has revealed an additional loss in the central city population as a portion of the total United States population, as well as a net loss in the total number of Americans living in the central cities of SMSAs.

In contrast, almost all urban growth in the United States in the past several decades has been in the suburbs. During the 1960s the suburbs surpassed the cities as the predominant form of urban development, as the total population of the suburbs became larger than that of the cities they surround for the first time in recorded history. Schwartz (1976, p. vii) estimates that there are now over thirteen million more people in the suburban rings than in the cities they surround, and that this gap promises to widen. Thus, suburbanization represents the newest form of urbanization, but more importantly, it is widely considered to be a distinct form of urbanization representing a sharp departure from the earlier development of the cities from which they have expanded. If, in fact, cities and suburbs are distinctly different forms of human settlement, then twentieth-century suburbanization is as revolutionary a change as was the urban-industrial revolution of the nineteenth century, with as great a potential for transforming the entire character of American society. It is in this context that city-suburban comparisons are highly significant.

Sociological comparisons of cities and suburbs generally have been made at several levels. The first has to do with ecological comparisons, which focus on differences or similarities in physical land use patterns, or which attempt to identify the economic function each area serves for the larger containing metropolitan community. The second focuses on differences or similarities in the demographic characteristics of the populations of cities and suburbs, such as socioeconomic status, household formation, and race and ethnicity. The third area of comparison has to do with differences or similarities in attitudes, life styles, or social behavior. For now, we will focus predominantly on the first two levels of comparison.

Much of the earlier literature on suburbs (see Kramer, 1972; Schwartz, 1976) described them impressionistically as "bedroom communities" or "dormitories" for managerial- or professional-level male white-collar workers who commuted daily to and from their place of employment in the central city. In this literature, the suburbs were hotbeds of fertility in the sense that child rearing was among their most important functions, the suburban housewife remaining at home to fulfill this function while her spouse was away at work. Physically, the suburbs served primarily a residential function for middle-class or higher-level families who could afford the perceived advantages of single family homes on large well-landscaped lots segregated from the noise, overcrowding, congestion, pollution, and other perceived disadvantages of living in the city. Thus, they were distinguished from the central cities by the socioeconomic status and the familial or child-rearing status of their residents.

Some of the literature has focused on zoning restrictions and other efforts by suburban residents to protect the uniqueness of their communities from encroachment by urban types of land use development, such as factories, commercial areas, multiunit apartment house developments, or lower status or racially different populations. Another common theme was the homogeneity of the population in conforming to common values

and behavior. "The suburb," said Riesman (1957, p. 134), "is like a frater-
nity house at a small college ... in which like-mindedness reverts upon
itself as the potentially various selves in each of us do not get evoked or
recognized." Whyte (1956) described the suburbs as the proving ground
for a new social ethic—a mindset emphasizing teamwork in place of
individuality—which had been nurtured among the young executives of
the large corporations who inhabited the mass-produced postwar suburbs
such as Park Forest, Illinois, or Drexelbrook, Pennsylvania. He detected in
these suburbs a unique and unparalleled similarity in the lives of their inhabitants.

Yet much of the current reevaluation of the suburbs calls into serious
question these images of the suburbs as homogeneous and distinct from the
cities upon which they depend. Critics in recent years have labeled the
above notions of suburbia "the suburban myth." Out of a series of post-
1960 studies (see Kramer, 1972; Schwartz, 1976) came the realization by
many social scientists that suburbia is a dynamic setting, its social, institutional, and demographic structure becoming more diverse, complex, and
urban than previously realized. Kramer (1972), for example, argues that to
employ the term "suburb" to suggest a single type of place, or to imply that
there is an overarching pattern of suburban social organization is to greatly

Suburbs, such as those surrounding Portland, Oregon, have become the predominant form of
urban development in the past decades. (Portland Chamber of Commerce Photo)

overgeneralize. Thus, as a descriptive sociological term, "suburb" has little meaning.

Schnore (1972) has found that many significant differences exist between the socioeconomic status of central city and suburban populations but that no one type of city-suburban differential applies to all metropolitan areas. He has identified several major types of patterns according to income differentials. The most common type is that in which the highest and lowest income groups are overrepresented in the central city and the middle income group is overrepresented in the suburbs. The next most frequent type is that in which high-income groups are suburbanized while low-income groups are concentrated in the central city. But another type has high-income groups concentrated in the central city while low-income groups reside in the suburbs. Using years of education completed as a criterion, Schnore identified at least six types of differences between cities and suburbs, again supporting the notion that there is no one single pattern of differences between cities and suburbs. Schnore suggests that the size and the age of the metropolitan community are major factors producing different types of city-suburban differentials. Studies of working-class suburbs (Berger, 1971), low-income black suburbs (Kramer, 1972), and new mass-produced suburban communities such as Levittown, New Jersey (Gans, 1967), also challenge the traditional suburban myth with their findings that do not conform to the stereotype of a homogeneous and undifferentiated middle class suburban population.

To date, there has been no really adequate effort to systematically classify the many diverse types of suburban development. The most basic attempt is that of Schnore (1963, pp. 77–86), who distinguishes two main types of suburbs–employing and residential. Employing suburbs are highly industrialized, providing a large portion of their working population with jobs in the local community. Residential suburbs are those containing relatively few industrial or commercial activities and which therefore have a resident working population that must commute to workplaces outside the local suburb. Comparing these two types of suburbs in the New York SMSA by using census data, Schnore found that employing suburbs had a higher percentage of foreign-born, nonwhite, and aged residents than residential suburbs, and were more likely to be losing population or growing at a slower rate of increase. Conversely, residential suburbs were higher in socioeconomic status, with a larger percent of their populations in white-collar occupations, with more formal education, and with higher incomes than residents of employing suburbs. Also, the inhabitants of residential suburbs were more likely to occupy their own single-family housing units of a newer vintage than those of the employing suburbs. Schnore also identified a third, intermediate type of suburb, containing elements of both the employing and residential.

Pollster Louis Harris (*Time*, March 15, 1971, pp. 14–20) has used a typology limited to residential suburbs, which is based on whether or not the suburb is expanding or has reached its peak in growth as well as in socioeconomic status. The types are: 1) affluent bedroom; 2) affluent settled; 3) low income growing; and 4) low income stagnant. Thorns (1972) has developed a typology for suburbs in the United States and England based on social class; whether or not the suburb was planned in its development; and the distinction between residential and industrial suburbs suggested by Schnore. This typology lists 1) middle-class planned residential; 2) working-class planned residential; 3) middle-class unplanned residential; 4) working-class unplanned residential; 5) middle-class planned industrial; 6) working-class planned industrial; 7) middle-class unplanned industrial; and 8) working-class unplanned industrial. Boskoff (1970, pp. 113–119) has developed a six-part typology: 1) the traditional upper-class suburb; 2) the identity-conscious suburb; 3) the mass-produced suburb; 4) the suburban slum; 5) the stable variegated suburb; and 6) the industrial suburb.

These typologies are incomplete and their usefulness obscure, but they all acknowledge the growing disparity and complexity of modern suburban development. An important question raised here is that in view of an increase in the heterogeneity of suburban life and forms, are some of the traditional distinctions between cities and suburbs beginning to disappear? To put it another way, are the suburbs beginning to be more and more like the cities?

There is no doubt that the suburbs have been "invaded" in recent decades by a large influx of city-like facilities and amenities: shopping centers, which often exceed central city department stores in the volume of business they do and in the variety of merchandise they carry; a wide variety of ethnic shops, restaurants, and social services; cultural facilities such as civic centers, concert halls, movie theaters, art galleries, and museums; bars and nightclubs; athletic clubs and stadiums; hospitals and clinics; high rise office buildings and hotels; and multiunit housing developments, such as apartment houses, row houses, and condominiums. Also on the increase in the suburbs is the portion of the population living in household units other than families with young children. These include single adults, childless couples, the divorced, and the aged. For many suburbanites, frequent trips to the central city for employment or urban goods or services are no longer necessary, for they are now to be found conveniently near home.

Urban problems have also invaded the suburbs: traffic congestion and air pollution; rising crime and delinquency rates; deteriorating housing in some of the aging neighborhoods; poverty and unemployment. According to an HUD Newsletter (January 10, 1972, p. 4), the number of poor suburban residents increased more than did the central city poor during the 1960–1970 decade. It is fair to conclude that suburbia no longer affords, if it ever did, complete escape from the conditions of city life that many Americans have long sought.

But important differences between cities and suburbs probably do continue to exist. Schwartz (1976, pp. 333–339) argues that in spite of the many criticisms and contrary evidence, the so-called suburban myth does contain a persistent degree of accuracy. Most suburbs continue to remain segregated white enclaves, while urban blacks remain largely in segregated communities within the central cities. Almost all economic expansion in the last several decades has taken place in the suburbs, while the economies of many large central cities have begun to decline. While the variations in the economic status of both city and suburban populations are great, overall differences between the general economic well-being of city dwellers and suburbanites still remain. Finally, but not least important, many traditional stereotypes and misconceptions have created a climate of conflict between many large cities and their suburban rings. Mutual antagonisms, prejudices, fear, and mistrust often inhibit cooperative solutions to the problems that afflict cities and suburbs alike. Some of these problems will be addressed more fully in later chapters.

POSTMETROPOLITAN URBAN DEVELOPMENT: MEGALOPOLIS

This entire chapter has been devoted to the emergence of metropolitan patterns of urban development, the implications of which are not yet fully understood. But in this last half of the twentieth century, a new and larger *super*metropolitan form has emerged and is just beginning to be recognized. This newer form involves the overlapping and penetration of previously separate metropolitan areas. This overlapping creates a continuous band of urban and suburban development, stretching for hundreds of miles in some regions. These expanded, supermetropolitan areas are sometimes referred to as "conurbations," or are more commonly called "megalopolis." Originally a classic Greek concept, the term megalopolis was applied by Gottman (1961) to a region of the northeastern seaboard that extends about 600 miles from southern New Hampshire to northern Virginia and extends up to 100 miles inland from the Atlantic shore to the foothills of the Appalachian mountains. Sometimes called "BosWash," this megalopolis encompasses all of Massachusetts, Rhode Island, Connecticut, New Jersey, Delaware, and the District of Columbia, as well as large sections of Maryland, New York, and Pennsylvania. It includes approximately one-fifth of the entire United States population. Another megalopolis can be identified as emerging in the Great Lakes region, stretching from Milwaukee through the Chicago metropolitan area across northern Indiana, northern Ohio, and southern Michigan, encompassing Detroit, Flint, Toledo, Cleveland, Akron, and possibly Pittsburgh. Still a third megalopolis stretches along the West Coast from San Diego to San Francisco.

It is difficult for the average person to grasp the concept of megalopolis or personally to identify with this type of development in any significant way. To date, little systematic scientific analysis of megalopolis as a new form of urban settlement has been attempted. The need to understand more fully and to come to grips with megalopolis as a new dominant force in American society is suggested in these passages by Gottman (1961, pp. 5–16):

> The old distinctions between rural and urban do not apply here any more.
> . . . In the area, then, we must abandon the idea of the city as a tightly settled

and organized unit in which people, activities, and riches are crowded into a very small area clearly separated from its non urban surroundings. Every city in this region spreads out far and wide around its original nucleus; it grows amidst an irregularly colloidal mixture of rural and suburban landscapes; it melts on broad fronts with other mixtures, of somewhat similar though different texture, belonging to the suburban neighborhoods of other cities. . . . This region serves thus as a laboratory in which we may study the new evolution reshaping both the meaning of our traditional vocabulary and the whole material structure of our way of life . . . . So great are the consequences of the general evolution heralded by the present rise and complexity of Megalopolis that any analysis of this region's problems often gives one the feeling of looking at the dawn of a new stage in human civilization . . . . Indeed, the area may be considered the cradle of a new order in the organization of inhabited space. . . . Megalopolis stands indeed at the threshold of a new way of life, and upon solution of its problems will rest civilization's ability to survive.

SELECTED BIBLIOGRAPHY

BELL, WENDELL. "Social Areas: Typology of Urban Neighborhoods." In Marvin Sussman, ed., *Community Structure and Analysis,* pp. 61–92. New York: Thomas Y. Crowell, 1959.

BERGER, BENNETT M. *Working Class Suburb.* Berkeley: University of California Press, 1971.

BERRY, BRIAN J. "Comparative Factorial Ecology," Supplement to *Economic Geography* 2 (1971).

———, and KASARDA, JOHN D. *Contemporary Urban Ecology.* New York: Macmillan, 1977.

BEYNON, ERDMAN D. "Budapest: An Ecological Study," *Geographic Review* 33 (1943): 256–275.

BLUMENFELD, HANS. "On the Concentric-Circle Theory of Urban Growth," *Land Economics* 25 (1949): 209–212.

BOLLENS, JOHN C., and SCHMANDT, HENRY J. *The Metropolis: Its People, Politics, and Economic Life.* 3rd ed. New York: Harper & Row, Pub., 1975.

BOSKOFF, ALVIN. *The Sociology of Urban Regions.* 2nd ed. New York: Appleton-Century-Crofts, 1970.

BURGESS, ERNEST W. "The Growth of the City." In Robert E. Park, Ernest W. Burgess, and Roderick D. McKenzie, eds., *The City.* Chicago: University of Chicago Press, 1925.

———, and BOGUE, DONALD J., ed. *Contributions of Urban Sociology.* Chicago: University of Chicago Press, 1964.

CAPLOW, THEODORE. "Urban Structure in France," *American Sociological Review* 17 (1952): 544–549.

DAVIE, MAURICE. "The Patterns of Urban Growth." In G. P. Murdock, ed., *Studies in the Social Sciences.* New Haven, Conn.: Yale University Press, 1937.

DUNCAN, OTIS DUDLEY. "Review of Social Area Analysis," *American Journal of Sociology* 61 (1955): 84–85.

FIREY, WALTER. *Land Use in Central Boston.* Cambridge, Mass.: Harvard University Press, 1947.

FRIED, MARC. "Grieving for a Lost Home." In Leonard J. Duhl, ed., *The Urban Condition,* Chapter 12. New York: Basic Books, 1963.

GANS, HERBERT. *The Urban Villagers.* New York: Free Press, 1962.

———. *The Levittowners.* New York: Vintage Books, 1967.

GOTTMAN, JEAN. *Megalopolis: The Urbanized Northeastern Seaboard of the United States.* New York: Twentieth Century Fund, 1961.

HANDLIN, OSCAR, and BURCHARD, JOHN. *The Historian and the City.* Cambridge, Mass.: Harvard University Press, 1963.

HARRIS, CHAUNCY, and ULLMAN, EDWARD. "The Nature of Cities," *Annals of the American Academy of Political and Social Science* 242 (1945): 7–17.

HAWLEY, AMOS. *Urban Society: An Ecological Approach.* New York: Ronald Press, 1971.

———, and DUNCAN, OTIS DUDLEY. "Social Area Analysis: A Critical Appraisal," *Land Economics* 33 (1957): 337–345.

HOYT, HOMER. "The Structure and Growth of Residential Neighborhoods in American Cities." Washington, D.C.: U.S. Federal Housing Administration, U.S. Printing Office, 1939.

KRAMER, JOHN, ed. *North American Suburbs: Politics, Diversity, and Change.* Berkeley, Calif.: Glendessary Press, 1972.

NATIONAL RESEARCH COUNCIL. *Toward an Understanding of Metropolitan America.* San Francisco: Canfield Press, 1975.

PLESSAS, D. J., and FEIN, R. "An Evaluation of Social Indicators," *Journal of the American Institute of Planners* 38 (1971): 43–51.

REES, P. H. "Concepts of Social Place: Toward an Urban Social Geography." In Brian J. Berry and F. Horton, eds., *Geographic Perspectives on Urban Systems.* Englewood Cliffs, N.J.: Prentice-Hall, 1970.

———. "Problems of Classifying Subareas within Cities." In Brian J. Berry, ed., *City Classification Handbook.* New York: John Wiley, 1972.

RIESMAN, DAVID. "The Suburban Dislocation," *Annals of the American Academy of Political and Social Science* 314 (1957): 123–146.

SCHNORE, LEO F. "The Socioeconomic Status of Cities and Suburbs," *American Sociological Review* 28 (1963): 76–86.

———. *Class and Race in Cities and Suburbs.* New York: Markham, 1972.

———, and Jones, Joy K. "The Evolution of City-Suburban Types in the Course of a Decade," *Urban Affairs Quarterly* 4 (1969): 421–422.

SCHWARTZ, BARRY, ed. *The Changing Face of the Suburbs.* Chicago: University of Chicago Press, 1976.

SHEVKY, ESHREF, and BELL, WENDELL. *Social Area Analysis.* Palo Alto, Calif.: Stanford University Press, 1955.

SMITH, DAVID M. *The Geography of Social Well-Being in the United States: An Introduction to Territorial Social Indicators.* New York: McGraw-Hill, 1973.

———, and Gray, R. J. "Social Indicators for Tampa, Florida." Urban Studies Bureau, University of Florida, 1972. Mimeographed.

• THORNS, DAVID C. *Suburbia.* London: MacGibbon & Dee, 1972.

VAN ARSDOL, MAURICE; CAMILLERI, SANTO; and SCHMIDT, CALVIN. "The Generality of Urban Social Area Indexes," *American Sociological Review* 23 (1958): 277–284.

WHYTE, WILLIAM H., JR. *The Organization Man.* New York: Anchor Books, 1956.

chapter 5 / neighborhoods, networks, and associations

Early sociological observations concerning the social organization of urban communities tended to emphasize either social disorganization or the lack of adequate organization. A widely accepted "theory of social disorganization" fed on the apparent evidences of disorganization in urban slums and other urban subareas. On the one hand, there was the primary group, as represented by the family and closely knit peer groups. On the other, there were the increasingly bureaucratic large-scale institutions of modern urban society, such as the modern corporation or nation-state. What was missing, according to this perspective, was the adequate organization of communal life that lies between these two extremes—the local neighborhoods, social bonds, or formal associations that were thought to provide meaning, purpose, and order to life at the local level. Popenoe (1969, p. ix) has stated this general perspective succinctly:

> The modern citizen finds a limited sense of personal and communal identity and meaning around his immediate family, peers, and private interests (such as his occupation): similarly he is "plugged in" fairly well to his nation-state—indeed this is the only group in modern times, aside from his family, for which an individual is prepared to give his life (although this social fact seems presently to be on the decline). There is a profound lack of feelings of general identity and sense of community in *the middle range*, however, between the levels of family-occupation-corporation and nation-state. There are too few social ties and concerns bonding together the variety of social groups and

individuals at the local and regional levels. A man's private and family concerns are too narrow and limited, his national concerns too abstract and depersonalized, to generate a strong commitment to the general welfare in the arena of the urban-industrial community.

But the modern urban community, it has now been established, is a highly intricate social, ecological, and economic organization. Its social structure includes all of the simpler forms of social organization, such as the family (see Chapter Seven), and the more complex forms, such as those having bureaucratic characteristics. However, it also includes a varied web of social organization at the middle range of size and complexity. These middle-range elements, sometimes lumped together under the general rubric of "community" or "primary group," are an inherent part of the social fabric of modern urban communities, and recognition is growing that a grasp of the social processes at work at these levels of urban social organization is critical to the more complete understanding of urban social structure. As Wilensky (1958, p. 136) notes, "a lively primary group life survives in the urban area, and primary controls are effective over wide segments of the population. The alleged anonymity, depersonalization, and rootlessness of city life may be the exception rather than the rule."

Some of the middle-range forms of social organization, such as the neighborhood or friendship groups, are of course preindustrial in their origins, but they continue to survive in modified forms in the modern era. Others, such as voluntary associations, have evolved more recently in the context of urban-industrial development. Still others, such as social networks, have always existed but remain amorphous and at a primitive stage of classification and explanation in the sociological literature on urbanization. The shape and characteristics of all of them are still subjectively identified, and some urban sociologists of an ecological bent are prone to minimize their significance. Nevertheless, we intend to review some of these concepts and supporting research materials in this chapter, since they do have much bearing on the quality of life in urban areas.

THE URBAN NEIGHBORHOOD

The first problem encountered in any effort to synthesize present knowledge about the urban neighborhood is the existence of varied and inconsistent definitions of the term "neighborhood." Glass (1948, pp. 150–170) recognized this problem when she presented two alternative definitions. The first describes the neighborhood as "a distinct territorial group, distinct by virtue of the specific physical characteristics of the area and the specific social characteristics of its inhabitants." This historically popular conception, as advanced by Park and his followers, assumed that, as particular kinds of individuals clustered together in metropolitan areas, they produced unplanned "natural areas." In a more recent example of this approach, Abrahamson (1976, pp. 154–160) seems to reject the more amorphous social psychological definitions of the neighborhood in favor of designating physically well-defined census tracts as neighborhoods, in the manner of social area analysis (see Chapter Four).

Glass's second definition describes the neighborhood as "a territorial group, the members of which meet on common ground within their own area for primary group social activities and for organized and spontaneous social contacts." Carpenter (1933, p. 357) had earlier provided a more elaborate version of this second conception:

> The most distinctive characteristics of a neighborhood are its relations with a local area sufficiently compact to permit frequent and intimate association and the emergence of such association of sufficient homogeneity and unity to permit a primary or face-to-face social grouping endowed with a strong sense of self-consciousness and capable of influencing the behavior of its several constituents.

Other problems with the concept of neighborhood arise from efforts to precisely delimit neighborhood boundaries. Some observers (see Mann, 1965; Hawley, 1971, p. 196), particularly community planners, sometimes equate the boundaries of neighborhoods with those of local schools. For example, the radius around an elementary school within which elementary students reasonably can be expected to walk to and from school may be one such approximation. Ross (1962) suggested that the boundaries of commonly recognized and commonly labeled subcommunities, such as Beacon Hill or the Back Bay areas of Boston, are appropriate determinants of neighborhood units. Caplow and Forman (1950, pp. 357–366) employed as a working definition of neighborhoods in Minneapolis "a family dwelling unit and the ten family dwelling units most accessible to it." Suttles (1972) identified the typical city block as one useful frame of reference for neighborhood analysis, while the parochial ethnic group was identified as another.

Clearly, there is no commonly agreed upon definition of a neighborhood or the appropriate boundaries of neighborhood units. But Keller (1968, pp. 91–92) has suggested that four approaches may have been used most predominantly by social scientists in both theoretical and applied studies of the urban neighborhood. These four approaches are summarized as follows:

A. The Ecological Neighborhood Approach. From this perspective, a neighborhood is a physically delimited area having an ecological position in a larger area and particular physical characteristics arising from natural geographic conditions and from a particular configuration of land uses. "Natural areas," such as skid rows, waterfront areas, cultural centers, or red light districts are apt illustrations of this conception of neighborhood.

B. The Neighborhood Resources Approach. This approach focuses on the specific physical resources of an area, such as stores, housing, schools, clubs, and offices, which may suggest the special functional role that the neighborhood serves for its own residents. Of course, resources in a given

A street festival in "Little Italy," New York, contributes local culture to the neighborhood as well as the city. (Marc Anderson)

neighborhood may also be used by outsiders who do not reside in the local area, and such outside use of the neighborhood for recreational, business, or cultural purposes may contribute heavily to the general character of the neighborhood.

     C. The Symbolic Neighborhood.   This approach views a neighborhood as representing certain values both for the residents and for the larger community. Thus, a neighborhood may evoke value-laden images such as social solidarity, political cohesion, lawlessness, ethnic or religious compatibility, or prestige of its residents, as well as the aesthetic quality (cleanliness, quiet, or beauty) of its physical features. What is important here are the meanings that a neighborhood evokes in the minds of the resident or nonresident observers, whether or not such symbols are based on "objective reality."

     D. The Subcultural Neighborhood.   The history of the social, economic, and ecological factors operating in a given neighborhood tend to give that neighborhood its own special cultural atmosphere, which may persist over a long period of time. Once the cultural characteristics of an area become well established, they usually persist over decades, despite the turnover of individuals residing there. For example, a well-established ethnic neighborhood may retain its essential ethnic character generation after generation. Likewise, a middle-class suburb or a highly transient skid row area may each have a history that produces a collective quality of life persisting over decades and that is not necessarily modified by individual variations in the actions of its residents.

The problems of definition aside, the most crucial questions for those professionally interested in the analysis of neighborhoods have been along these lines: 1) What are the useful social functions of the neighborhood; for its inhabitants on the one hand, and for the larger containing community on the other? 2) What are the particular mechanisms or social processes through which the functions of the neighborhood are achieved or maintained? 3) What are some of the internal or external forces that maintain sound and viable neighborhoods, and what are some of the forces that threaten their disintegration? 4) What are some of the significant variations among different types of neighborhoods, with respect to their structural characteristics, social processes, or functions? 5) What is the future prospect for the urban neighborhood, in terms of growth, stability, or decline? 6) What, if anything, can or ought to be done in the way of deliberate social planning to improve urban neighborhoods as effective units of social participation or social action?

THE FUNCTIONS OF NEIGHBORHOODS

The urban neighborhood in the modern metropolitan complex can be seen as fulfilling many functions not necessarily served at other levels of urban social organization. Warren (1977) identifies at least six major functional roles for the neighborhood: 1) as an arena for interaction; 2) as a center for interpersonal influence; 3) as a source of mutual aid; 4) as a base for formal and informal organizations; 5) as a reference group; 6) and as a status arena.

The Neighborhood as an Arena for Interaction

This function has to do with the informal interchanges of physically proximate residents within the neighborhood as a whole. Warren makes a useful distinction between these neighborhoodwide patterns of interaction and those more narrowly limited to next-door neighbors or close friendship groups. They may include casual greetings or visits with those members of the neighborhood with whom one does not necessarily have a close or intimate relationship. These exchanges imply an attitude of cordiality or neighborliness. This provides the individual with a sense of belonging to the neighborhood and mitigates some of the depersonalizing influences commonly ascribed to the urban environment.

The Neighborhood as a Center for Interpersonal Influence

Face-to-face contacts with neighbors may provide a means of defining the norms of child rearing, education, or socioeconomic aspirations that the larger society generates. Forms of social influence, such as ostracism or

This New York City scene shows interaction and interpersonal influence within a neighborhood. (Marc Anderson)

rewards based on social acceptance and the attendant definitions of conforming or deviant behavior, can take place in more detail in the neighborhood than in the more diffuse institutions of the larger community. This is particularly true when neighborhood interaction is frequent and intense. In a "two-step flow of communication," local opinion leaders who are exposed to the mass media and other extraterritorial influences pass along these influences to those in the population who are relatively isolated from them. The transmitting or filtering role of local opinion leaders provides mechanisms for integrating the individual into the larger society and for preventing the breakdown of local norms; the neighborhood opinion leaders may provide at the local level the selective integration of values disseminated from the larger community.

The Neighborhood as a Source of Mutual Aid

Studies have documented the extent to which exchange of help between those living in close proximity in urban areas is a frequent and important activity. The rapid response of neighbors is essential when such aid is not available from other sources, such as relatives or formal organizations. Despite the proliferation of social service agencies (see Chapter Twelve), such bureaucratic organizations often lack the ability to respond promptly and flexibly to many emergencies (for example, approximately 75 percent of all disaster rescues are made by neighbors). A study of fatherless families found that mutual aid was extensive for employed mothers, and that minor exchanges—borrowing or lending groceries or small amounts of money, baby-sitting, or shopping—were frequent for both hus-bandless and married mothers. Only 16 percent did not report such ex-changes. The local neighborhood's role as a center for mutual aid may take the form of protection against outside intrusions as well as serve as a substi-tute for external support. Thus, refusing to give information to authorities or to aid institutions viewed as alien to local neighborhood values is impor-tant protection for the values of local residents. When there is a sudden disaster, for example, or when the cost of seeking resources outside the neighborhood is excessive, or when protection from external social institu-tions alien to the local area is involved (some observers see this as a negative or divisive function), mutual aid may play a significant role for many urban families.

The Neighborhood as a Base
for Formal and Informal Organizations

Many voluntary associations (discussed in more detail later in this chapter) are organized at the neighborhood level. They may compete with other social units in the neighborhood or they may link the neighborhood to the larger community by promoting the participation of local residents. Neighborhoods are often characterized by frequent population turnover, and local voluntary associations often speed the assimilation of newcomers into the neighborhood. Depending on the character of such organizations, they need not conflict with other neighborhood social units, such as the family, or prevent individuals from forming close ties with neighbors more informally. If a neighborhood can integrate individuals quickly through voluntary associations, rapid population turnover need not produce a lack of neighborhood cohesion. Under some circumstances, local associations provide a means for mobilizing people to engage in efforts at social change. By defining what otherwise might be a diffuse sense of dissatisfaction felt by local groups, neighborhood organizations may stimulate rather than retard participation in social movements.

The Neighborhood as a Reference Group

Although many studies suggest that informal and formal contacts are more extensive in most urban neighborhoods than commonly supposed, the fact that many neighbor contacts are ephemeral and low in intensity suggests that the influence exerted by neighbors is often subjective. Im-plied in the term "reference group" is that many individuals may be guided and changed in their behavior and values by what they understand to be the values of a perceived social entity. In this way, people's self-images may be shaped by what they think others think of them. The social climate of a neighborhood may lead individuals to seek out others who agree with them and thereby reinforce the attitudes they already hold. But merely believing that a majority of one's neighbors agree with one may have the same effect.

The Neighborhood as a Status Arena

Perhaps the least explored function of the neighborhood is its importance as a status-conferring entity. Status symbolism, in terms of both the housing or prestige of a given neighborhood, may be valued by outsiders, but insiders may use such symbols to protect themselves against invidious status comparisons by outsiders. The neighborhood may act as a mirror of personal achievement and well-being by screening out definitions of class or status that are irrelevant at the local level and by providing an area within which status claims derived from the larger society are "cashed in" in terms of housing quality, life style, or other highly visible symbols of social status. As status centers, neighborhoods enable local opinion leaders to act as agents of status bestowal or appraisal for the entire neighborhood, particularly when positive status is not forthcoming from the larger community.

Using these six functional categories in a sample of twenty-eight local black neighborhoods in the Detroit area, Warren (1975) found that these neighborhoods fulfilled various combinations of the functions for their residents. In addition, a comparison of white and black neighborhoods also supported the notion that the functions were fulfilled in white neighborhoods, but in different combinations than in the black neighborhoods.

TYPES OF NEIGHBORHOODS

Not all urban neighborhoods are equally effective in fulfilling the functions just described, nor do all of the residents of the most cohesive neighborhoods participate in the interactional activities characteristic of their particular neighborhood. For, as Fischer (1976, p. 121) suggests, the fate of social relations in general does not depend on the fate of neighborly relations. In answer to the rhetorical challenge, "Who needs neighborhoods?" he suggests that some persons certainly do, but many also seem to do well without them.

Some studies support the notion that patterns of participation in neighborhood activities vary widely from one kind of neighborhood to another. For example, Fava (1959) has found that suburban residents in the New York metropolitan area exhibited a higher degree of neighboring than did inner city residents. In the suburban areas, activities such as informal interaction between neighbors, entertaining, and collective efforts at problem solving took place more frequently than they did in the inner city neighborhoods. But another body of literature supports the theory that the neighborhood is more likely to be meaningful as an arena of participation for lower-income groups for whom limited education, ethnic dissimilarity, minority group status, or poverty limit the opportunities for participation in the larger community (Hawley, 1971, pp. 194–197). Those groups with greater resources or statuses are better able to spread their radius of interaction over a wider range of the metropolitan area and therefore need not submit to the limited choices in the immediate neighborhood or to dependence on their neighbors for social contacts.

To account for some of these kinds of differences in neighborhoods and patterns of neighborhood participation, some observers have attempted to develop typologies, which take into account different patterns of neighborhood social organization and different patterns of residents' orientation toward neighbors and neighborhoods. Borrowing concepts from the work of Warren (1977), Suttles (1972), Dentler (1968), Shostak (1969), Litwak and Fellin (1968), and others, we have identified several types of neighborhoods as representing a reasonable composite of the most salient types of local neighborhoods in the modern American metropolis:

The Integral Neighborhood

This type of neighborhood represents the ideal for those who see stable, well-organized local neighborhoods maintaining strong integrative links to the larger communities of which they are a part as essential to the well-being of urban communities. In this type of neighborhood, people are extremely cohesive, they know each other reasonably well, they frequently interact with one another, and they belong to many local organizations, such as block clubs, community councils, P.T.A.s, and other locally oriented voluntary associations. In all, these are extremely active neighborhoods with much face-to-face interaction and participation in the organized activities of the local area.

But the residents of such neighborhoods also actively support the norms and values of the larger community and participate actively in its affairs. Behavioral indicators, such as voting in elections and maintaining contact with the political institutions of the larger community, indicate some of the external links to the larger communities, as do memberships in informal groups or formal voluntary associations that are not in the local neighborhood. Thus, the integral neighborhood is not only a very cohesive center of local activity, but it is a cosmopolitan center as well.

The integral neighborhood is most effective in mobilizing both local and external resources when it attempts to solve local problems or responds to challenges caused by changes taking place in the larger community. This neighborhood type has been well illustrated in Whyte's (1956) study of Park Forest and in Seeley, Sim, and Loosley's (1956) study of Crestwood Heights. Both of these communities were middle- or upper-middle-income suburban communities, which are among the most likely candidates to become integral neighborhoods, but some big city neighborhoods with more heterogeneous socioeconomic characteristics also appear to have taken on the characteristics of integral neighborhoods.

The Anomic Neighborhood

With respect to the amount of social cohesion, the anomic neighborhood is at the opposite end of the scale from the integral neighborhood. It is the most completely disorganized and atomized type of residential area described in the earlier body of sociological literature. It lacks established patterns of participation in community affairs and a common identification with either the local area or the larger community. Such settings usually reflect mass apathy and lack of involvement in any form of collective action (Warren, 1977).

Estrangement from the values of the larger community manifests itself in nonvoting and indifference to the goals of the larger community. The anomic neighborhood would be least likely to influence, mobilize, or alter the values of its residents through any efforts at social control or planned social intervention. The very absence of social organization might suggest the emergence of values defined as deviant by the larger community. But the more reasonable hypothesis is that residents of the anomic neighborhood are not engaged in active resistance to the values of the larger society as a result of alienation, but are rather displaying passive behavior of a diffused nature. (Warren, 1977). But as suggested at the beginning of this chapter, this type of neighborhood occurs less frequently than commonly supposed in the traditional conventional wisdom. However, at least some anomic neighborhoods may be found in urban communities. But they are the exception rather than the modal type of urban neighborhood in the American metropolis.

An important variation of the anomic neighborhood is the transitory, or *stepping-stone*, neighborhood, in which the residents keep to themselves, avoid local entanglements, or fail to participate in or identify with the local community. But in this case, the motives for noninvolvement may be that, because of strong economic or status aspirations, the members of a given family must devote their energies to working, getting more education or training, and a variety of self-improvement efforts. Such commitments usually mean that both husband and wife and their working or school-age children simply have little time, energy, interest, or opportunity for participating in neighborhood activities. According to Warren (1977), this may help to explain the low rates of participation in some working-class, blue-collar suburbs, where the strong desire to work up and out of such areas may lead the residents to view strong neighborhood links and activities as a threat or barrier to their aspirations.

The Defended Neighborhood

Suttles (1972) has resurrected the concept of the defended neighborhood from the earlier work of Park and Burgess and their followers. The concept identifies neighborhoods in which the residents seal themselves off from outside intrusions through the efforts of well-organized gangs, restrictive convenants, sharply defined and enforced boundaries, or by a forbidding reputation. The most obvious earmark of the defended neighborhood is street corner gangs claiming their "turf" and warding off strangers or anyone else not a proper member of the neighborhood. It is here that one finds vigilante community groups, militant neighborhood conservation groups, a high incidence of uniformed doormen or security guards, and the frequent use of door buzzers and television monitors. According to Suttles (1972, p. 245), these defensive tactics indicate the "general apprehension of inner city dwellers, rich and poor alike, and the necessity for each of them to bound off discrete areas within which he can feel safe and secure."

The defended neighborhood is not necessarily delineated by the physical features of the area, but rather by "cognitive maps" that the residents form in their own minds for describing not only what their own and other areas of the city are like but also what they think they ought to be like. Suttles argues that these cognitive maps, which may be shared by the residents of a given neighborhood, serve a useful function because they are part of the social control apparatus of urban areas and are of special importance in regulating spatial movement to avoid conflicts between antagonistic groups. Cognitive maps of a neighborhood provide a set of social categories for differentiating between those people with whom one can or cannot safely associate and for defining the concrete groupings within which certain levels of social contact and social cohesion are based. The basis for such cognitive differentiation may be ethnicity, race, socioeconomic level, life style, or the like.

Historically, defended neighborhoods have tended to be concentrated in the central cities of the large metropolis and to consist primarily of lower-income groups. These are the areas where ethnic and racial cleavages are the most apparent (see Chapter Fourteen for a more extended discussion of these problems) and where population density and transiency are the highest. These residents have the greatest need for a set of cognitive guidelines by which they can safely navigate within their own residential areas. As Suttles states (1972, pp. 244–245), "It is here that the defended neighborhood should have its greatest appeal and serve best to mollify the imagined or real dangers which exist in the inner city."

Empirical illustrations of what can be described as defended neighborhoods are boundless. Zorbough's *The Gold Coast and the Slum,* Whyte's *Street Corner Society,* Gans's *Urban Villagers,* Thrasher's *The Gang,* and Shuttles's own more recent studies of the Near West Side of Chicago (1968) are all excellent descriptions of defended neighborhoods in the inner areas of big cities. But some studies of stable blue-collar working-class suburbs have also identified characteristics similar to those associated with Shuttles's concept of defended neighborhoods (see Shostak, 1969; Berger, 1960).

One structural characteristic of defended neighborhoods is that a certain amount of social cohesion ensues when residents must band together from time to time in joint actions to protect the neighborhood from what they consider to be undesirable intrusions or changes. These may consist of the actions of outside agents of the community, such as politicians, industrialists, realtors, or city planners, who threaten to change the physical character of a neighborhood. The residential "invasion" of a neighborhood by outside groups of differing ethnic, racial, socioeconomic, or behavioral characteristics also may be seen as threatening or resisted by neighborhood groups. For example, the movement of hippies, gays, prostitutes, cults, or therapeutic groups (such as Synanon) into stable low-income working-class neighborhoods is often met with fierce organized resistance by local neighborhood groups organized for this purpose.

Another more subtle characteristic of defended neighborhoods is that the residents may share secrets and myths stemming from the gossip and rumors of informal interaction. Such half-truths and bits and pieces of information may add up to a sort of subculture shared by the residents and may give them a common identity. Their views of their own neighborhood and of the outside world may not correspond to the views of the officials of the larger community or to that of outsiders in general, and their behavior and attitudes may appear to be deviant or nonconforming to outsiders. This characteristic reinforces the cohesion and differentiation of the defended neighborhood and its isolation from the larger community.

The Contrived Neighborhood

With the advent of city planning, urban renewal, public housing, and expanding markets for housing in the suburbs, a relatively new form of neighborhood is now appearing—mass-scale housing developments that are created and built in the same architectural mold virtually overnight. Public housing projects, apartment and condominium complexes, and suburban single-family housing subdivisions are among the best examples. The most striking feature of these "planned" neighborhoods is the relatively extreme homogeneity of both its physical characteristics and the socioeconomic status of its residents. Residential homogeneity is almost assured because the screening of new occupants is centralized in the hands of a single realtor, developer, or manager. The cultural uniformity of the residents tends to make these areas even more segregated than defended neighborhoods. Although racial or ethnic segregation in these newer developments may not be acceptable policy or permitted by law, one can now find entire developments restricted to child-rearing families, singles, childless couples, or retirees of the same general socioeconomic levels. The contrived or artificial neighborhood has easily distinguishable boundaries, which are reinforced by its unified architectural design and a single source of development. These neighborhoods also have a ready-made name and image usually created by the developers, which is adopted as the official name of the area by the residents. Such designations may be a source of pride, as in the case of prestigious subdivisions, or a source of deprecation, such as the case of some low-income public housing projects in areas commonly referred to as slums.

Suttles describes the contrived neighborhood as a variation of the defended neighborhood in the functions it serves for its residents. The main difference, however, is the extreme specialization and homogeneity in the social characteristics of the residents. Also, when the contrived neighborhood selects residents with cosmopolitan life styles (see Chapter Six for a description of cosmopolitan life styles), it may take on the social characteristics of the integral neighborhood. In other words, the residents may form strong bonds to both the local neighborhood and the larger containing community. Gans's (1967) study of Levittown is a good illustration of a relatively cosmopolitan contrived neighborhood. Many observers have described virtually all suburbs as specialized contrived neighborhoods, but this clearly is not the case and is but another example of the suburban myth described in Chapter Four. The extremely specialized contrived neighborhood is still not clearly identified in the sociological literature, and its significance is still not clearly understood. Much more research needs to be done on the nature and significance of specialized contrived communities.

The Neighborhood as Staging Area

Much of what goes on in many local neighborhoods is not necessarily initiated by local residents but is rather the product of the interplay of groups and interests with a much larger base in the surrounding city or, indeed, in the national society. Thus, certain kinds of neighborhoods often become the staging area for national dramas, in which local residents play only secondary roles. Neighborhoods likely to become staging areas for the activities of outside interest groups are likely to be seen by these outsiders as in the midst of crises such as poverty, crime, or social unrest which, if left unchecked, could have an undesirable effect on the entire containing community. Thus, such neighborhoods are likely to become the staging areas for action by municipal, federal, or private social agencies bent on altering the character of the local neighborhood through planned intervention.

The concept of the neighborhood as a staging area was introduced by Dentler (1968) in his analysis of Ocean Hill-Brownsville, a troubled neighborhood in the New York City borough of Brooklyn. Dentler has identified organized helping professions in the fields of health, education, labor unions, industrial corporations, political parties, municipal bureaucracies, and private foundations as all having a high stake in producing changes in this neighborhood through various strategies of planned intervention. The local neighborhood thus becomes a stage upon which these outside interest groups engage in a contest to act out their complex strategies in cooperation, competition, or conflict with one another. Dentler argues that the neighborhood as such a staging area is something less than a cohesive or viable community.

In addition to the "colonization of the underclass," Dentler suggests that another incentive for neighborhoods to become staging areas is economic. Subcommunities that have an aging or declining industrial or commercial base, or are declining in their capacity to provide a tax revenue base, may be targeted for industrial or commercial redevelopment by powerful industrial, commercial, or governmental interest groups outside the local neighborhood. In either of the above cases, the residents, no matter how great their efforts may be to control the destiny of their own community, may find those efforts blocked by larger forces over which they have no control. Or they may discover that their efforts are caught up in larger contests that may distort or destroy any real possibility of local control. Yet Dentler holds out the hope that the conflicts that frequently occur as neighborhoods become staging areas could also have the side effect of strengthening residents' interest and participation in the affairs of their neighborhood, as is apparently what eventually happened in Ocean Hill-Brownsville.

WHO NEEDS NEIGHBORHOODS?

The above review of different kinds of neighborhoods fails to establish that the local neighborhood is a well-organized social entity in all cases, or that it is a powerful influence in the lives of all urbanites. As easy-to-use transportation facilities, such as the automobile or mass transit, or communications facilities such as the telephone have become more available to urbanites, many have become increasingly liberated from the close ties and constraints of the local neighborhood. As Wellman (1977, pp. 221–223) observes:

> It is fruitless to concentrate on the neighborhood as the fundamental area of personal relations. Too many people are moving beyond its confines for too many personal relationships. Being concerned only with developing neighborhood interaction works against having the liberating effects of being able to select one's own intimates and acquaintances from a metropolis-wide pool of applicants. Neighborly relations must be seen in perspective as only one special aspect of urban personal ties. . . . [A] concentration on neighborhoods as the central basis of personal relationships has become anachronistic and is doomed to failure.

But it is also true that many examples of successful neighborhoods can be found on the urban scene and that they continue to serve useful and necessary functions for their residents and often for the larger community. To some social observers, the integral or the defended neighborhood still remains the epitome of the ideal community, and some have a strong ideological commitment to preserve and strengthen the neighborhood as a unit of social action. Warren (1977), for example, argues that well-organized neighborhoods can positively contribute to social change in the following three ways:

1. Neighborhoods can provide an appropriate program unit for governmental and private efforts at planned social intervention.
2. Given the high rate of built-in social change in a mass, industrial, bureaucratic society, neighborhood primary groups may be able to respond to conditions of urban life more flexibly and effectively than formal organizations.
3. Neighborhood organizations can play a major role in clarifying and defining the solutions to urban problems by clearly differentiating among problems with a local focus that are amenable to solution by local self-help and self-determination and those problems that clearly require wider bases of mobilization and collective action.

Warren advocates a strong community organization movement aimed at converting individual needs and interests into a collective source of influence and to mobilize people at the neighborhood level to bring about

The Tucson Community Center brings entertainment to the city and provides conventioneers a place to meet. (Tucson Convention and Tourist Bureau)

effective change. To further this aim, Warren has coauthored the *Neighborhood Organizers Handbook* (Warren and Warren, 1976), designed to train both professionals and volunteers in the techniques of community organization, which has become a significant subspecialty within the social work profession (see Chapter Twelve).

Many successful instances exist of neighborhoods that have been helped by innovations in community organization, but whether or not such efforts can successfully protect or improve local neighborhoods in the face of the larger community and societal forces threatening to alter them or minimize their significance remains to be convincingly demonstrated. In the next section, we will discuss patterns of social interaction in the urban community that may in fact be replacing the neighborhood as an object of concern among social scientists.

SOCIAL NETWORKS

It is increasingly clear that many urbanites maintain informal social contacts in a wide variety of settings that do not conform to the boundaries of primary groups and territorial-based neighborhoods on the one hand, or on large-scale formal organizations on the other. Thus, one may develop informal social relationships on the basis of friendship, common occupation or social class, old school ties, or common leisure-time pursuits or hobbies.

Wellman (1977) argues that many kinds of personal relationships in the city have become "despatialized." His research in Toronto's East York area, for example, found that a city-dweller's intimates (relatives, friends, and acquaintances) live all over the entire city. Few people to whom the city-dweller felt close actually lived in the same neighborhood. The large majority lived in other parts of metropolitan Toronto or outside of the metropolitan area.

Fischer (1977) suggests that each individual in the urban community is the center of a web of social bonds that radiates outward to the people one knows intimately, those one knows well, those one knows casually, and to the larger community beyond. These kinds of social bonds are increasingly coming to be called *social networks*. Fischer suggests that to understand the individual in the larger urban community, it is increasingly necessary to understand the fine mesh of social relations between the person and the society.

The concept of social networks is not restricted to the boundaries of the urban community. Even the most seemingly formal institutions, such as large bureaucratic organizations, are in many ways the framework within which social networks of personal ties are developed. In another example, the election of Jimmy Carter as President brought mass media attention to his home state of Georgia and to the social bonds among groupings of certain residents of the Deep South, commonly referred to as "good ole boy" networks. A small but growing number of sociologists and anthropologists have identified the concept of social networks in urban settings as a promising new area of theory and research for better understanding the total fabric of modern urban life. Scherer (1972, p. 115) describes social network analysis as "an exciting and stimulating possible means of understanding human relationships in situations where the usual social structures are not observed and contacts appear scattered and diffused."

The concept of social network arises in part from the work of Elizabeth Bott (1971), who initially defined a social network as a social configuration in which some, but not all of the component external units maintain relationships with one another. She further used the term "close knit" to describe a social network in which many of the people a person knows tend to reach consensus on norms, exert consistent informal pressure on one another to conform to the norms, to keep in touch with one another, and if need be, to help one another.

This form of social network is also found in Liebow's (1967) study of street corner groups in a low-income neighborhood, and in the work of Scherer (1972, pp. 111-113), who mapped the social networks of a group of fifty-two nonresidential students of a technological college in central London. Scherer's study found many variations and differences in the range of contacts and the number and depth of the relationships that were identified.

Scherer's finding, along with the question of how close knit the networks were, implies that social networks may vary widely in such characteristics as their size, duration of membership, or the content, frequency, and intensity of contact. Lauman (1973, pp. 114-115) has distinguished "loose knit" or "radial" networks from close-knit networks as those in which the persons involved have little need for uniform opinions and are likely to have relatively low affective involvement and commitment to their relations with one another, because their common interests and concerns are likely to be more specialized and more severely circumscribed than in close-knit networks. He implies that while loose-knit networks will share less intimate information than close-knit ones, they are more significant in contemporary urban society because they are more flexible and more adaptive to the demands of a continuously changing society whose members are likely to be geographically and socially mobile. Granovetter (1973) identifies networks based on relatively weak social ties, such as those based on marginal social contacts, such as sporadic or accidental contacts with former co-workers, old college friends, or people who get together several times a year at conferences or conventions. Journalist Vance Packard (1972) suggests that even sports or hobby enthusiasts can form these "weak" networks that may be meaningful to them over the years, even if the network members live hundreds of miles apart. While such weak social ties may be amorphous and transitory, it can be argued that they form an integral part of the fabric of modern urban life.

Warren (1977) adds to the still evolving typology of informal social networks by identifying "proximity anchored helping networks" as those that emerge in response to specific problems the people in a given area may face. This type of network may provide the mechanisms for solving local problems that are not supplied by any other type of urban social organization. He suggests that this type of network may become the basis for more permanent and institutionalized patterns of social organization, such as block clubs, community councils, or other types of voluntary associations. Thus, social networks can be viewed as linked to neighborhoods and other territorial based subunits of the urban community and as serving the same kinds of functions. But this is only one special application of the social network concept, and social networks can be identified at all levels of the social organization of urban communities, including nonterritorial forms of urban social organization.

APPLICATIONS OF SOCIAL NETWORK ANALYSIS

The analysis of urban social networks is sociologically significant for several reasons. First, social networks can be seen as extremely useful for the individual by providing a diversity of social contacts from which one can choose those that best accomplish one's desires and goals. Second, social networks may be seen as providing the thread that holds the urban community together as a social system. The analysis of social networks can offer descriptions of the urban system's structure and function. Third, social network analysis provides the means by which traditional assumptions about the nature of urban social life can be more adequately tested and perhaps challenged. For example, the traditional view that urban life is highly disorganized, atomistic, or lacking social bonds has been brought into much doubt and criticism by studies of social networks.

But one of the most significant findings of network research is the growing appreciation of the role social networks play in providing informal communications and informational systems that link individuals not only to one another but to other networks and to the larger containing community (Wigand, 1977). Eames and Goode (1977, p. 242) suggest that cities may ultimately be viewed as "a network of networks," whereby identifiable personal networks coalesce into more formal groups and institutions and ultimately the entire urban structure. Studies of mass communications have identified a two-step flow of information that works this way: a few opinion leaders obtain information or messages about products and adopt points of view about issues reported in the mass media; they influence others who have come to respect their judgment. This model of communications can be extended to include the possibility that through a wide web of separate but overlapping social networks, such information or messages ultimately becomes widely diffused throughout an entire community.

In such ways, such innovations as changing fashions of dress, self-help health measures (diets or the use of drugs), patterns of voting, patterns of leisure-time activities, or the patterns of migration by ethnic groups may become widely diffused among large segments of the urban population. These may be a direct result of the informal mechanisms for communicating information and ideas supplied by a widespread participation in social networks. For example, in one classic study of the diffusion of medical innovations in several cities, Coleman (1966) found that doctors who were friends and professional associates of other physicians were more likely to prescribe a new drug earlier than doctors who were somewhat isolated from their colleagues, but that through more loosely constructed communications channels, the use of the new drug eventually spread to increasingly wider circles of physicians.

Likewise, some anthropologists have used network analysis to examine the process of migration to urban societies and found that social networks were very important in mitigating the more traumatic aspects of rural to urban migration (Eames and Goode, 1977; Fischer, 1977). What happens is that many migrants travel to cities where they already have kin or friends who may have transmitted information in advance as to what to expect in the city. Upon arrival, the migrant is assisted by the associates in his network, who provide help in finding housing and jobs and may introduce him or her to more people. The migrant's social network then expands as he or she adds new members, such as fellow workers, neighbors, and those who are met casually in shopping places, public eating places, or places of recreation. In these ways, the migrants are assimilated into networks involving mutual aid, exchange of goods and services, and diffusions of ideas and information, as well as emotional support and sociability for its own sake. Social networks also serve similar functions for already urbanized individuals or nuclear families making city-to-city, city-to-suburb, suburb-to-suburb, or suburb-to-city moves.

It seems reasonable to conclude this very brief discussion of informal social networks in the urban community by suggesting that while they are among the most diffuse and impressionistically identified forms of urban social organization, they may be the initial stages of newer institutionalized patterns of nonterritorial urban life.

VOLUNTARY ASSOCIATIONS

Voluntary associations are those more or less formally organized groups whose membership is by choice. They are the most structured of the middle-range forms of social organization considered in this chapter. Any time two or more persons identify a common interest that cannot be satisfactorily pursued individually or through preexisting forms of social organization, including those previously discussed in this chapter, the potential arises for the creation of a voluntary association. Social clubs, special interest groups, hobby groups, occupational associations and unions, political committees, and the like are well-known examples. The modern urban community is sprinkled with thousands of such groups, which have become increasingly important components of urban social organization. The 17,000 nationally or regionally organized associations listed in the *Encyclopedia of Associations* (1972) are probably a small fraction of the total number.

Voluntary associations have been particularly characteristic of American urban life since its earliest manifestations. For example, de Tocqueville, a notably perceptive observer of the American scene, wrote as early as 1831:

> In no country in the world has the principle of association been more successfully used or applied to a greater multitude of objects than in America. Besides the permanent associations which are established by law...a vast number of others are formed and maintained by the agency of private individuals (de Tocqueville, 1946, p. 106).

Voluntary associations may vary greatly in size and jurisdiction, ranging from small neighborhood units consisting of a relatively small handful of members residing in close proximity, to large nationally organized units with thousands of members and with many local chapters or branches in all regions of the country. The Boy Scouts, League of Women Voters, American Red Cross, or AFL-CIO are examples of the latter. They may also vary in the complexity of their organizational structures, with some producing elaborate hierarchies or divisions of labor and elaborate formal rules or constitutions, while others appear to be rather haphazardly and informally organized. In general, voluntary associations can be viewed as an intermediate type of social organization, more formally organized than primary groups but less formal than highly bureaucratized organizations. They are experimental blends of both types of social organization, neither of which has been judged as entirely adequate by itself to provide the range and quality of organization deemed necessary for coping with the complexities

The American Heart Association contributes to the health of the community by conducting blood pressure screenings in shopping malls and other public places. (American Heart Association National Center, Dallas, Texas)

of urban living. Thus, they supplement but do not displace primary groups and highly formalized bureaucratic institutions.

Much speculation has arisen on the motives for participation in voluntary associations. For example, they may offer warmth and friendship, particularly when such needs are not satisfactorily supplied by primary groups. They may serve as a source of personal identification, as illustrated by the uniforms, emblems, or titles associated with fraternal orders, lodges, or social clubs. They may provide enhanced social status or upward mobility to status-conscious individuals who may consider the prestige of an association as an inducement to join, or they may provide social contacts with persons who are in a position to supply jobs, services, recognition and visibility, or other rewards. Members may join to protect a common vested interest or to apply pressure to outsiders to produce desired social change.

One important distinction among voluntary associations identifies *expressive* associations as providing their members regular opportunities for self-expression, creativity, or diversion in some special field of interest or hobby that can be commonly shared. *Instrumental* associations, on the other hand, are created to accomplish specific objectives within the larger community, through lobbying, demonstrations, public relations campaigns, and other techniques of persuasion that can roughly be labeled as political in character. Thus, voluntary associations at the local or national levels may spring up to promote or to block a specific piece of proposed legislation, to promote a specific moral cause, to protect or enhance the character of a local community or neighborhood, to protect taxpayers' or property owners' interests, or to further the interest of a specific social institution, such as education, religion, industry, or health care. For example, the traditional cliché "You can't fight city hall" is more often than not countered by the actions of well-organized voluntary associations designed to do just that! (See Chapter Ten.) To the extent that instrumental associations are often the basis for a successful social movement, they must be counted among the most significant sources of (or barriers to) planned social change in urban-industrial societies.

PARTICIPATION IN VOLUNTARY ASSOCIATIONS

Although voluntary associations are widely distributed throughout the United States, this does not guarantee that all urbanites will necessarily become joiners. Extensive research on rates of participation in voluntary associations provides increasing evidence that membership in voluntary associations has not been equally attractive to all of the urban subgroups. One of the most important variables determining who participates in voluntary associations appears to be social class. Available studies generally indicate that people with high income and occupational status tend to participate more extensively in associations than individuals of lower socioeconomic status. While the results of studies undertaken in different communities at different times show slightly different patterns, the general picture is one in which well over one-half of those with middle- or upper-class status participate in some degree in voluntary associations, while significantly less than one-half of those with lower- or working-class status participate. Among those who do participate, the number of associations with which they are affiliated also rises in direct relationship to socioeconomic status.

Boskoff (1970, pp. 188–189) explains the above differences in rates of participation in terms of who is most motivated by the goals of an urban culture. He suggests that voluntary associations are supported by middle-class people because they share a basic social stability, as reflected in "respectable" or responsible occupations, moderately long residence in the urban milieu, and optimism about long-run community prospects. This is accompanied by an emphasis on personal and community progress, as reflected in concern for education and upward mobility and a somewhat greater involvement in service organizations of one kind or another. In contrast, he speculates, lower-status people seem to have a more limited identification with urban values, and therefore have less appreciation of voluntary associations as a normal part of their existence. In turn, the frustration, pessimism, and uncertainty of achieving success of recent urban migrants of lower socioeconomic status is in part a result of noninvolvement and participation in voluntary associations, which may lead to a state of anomie. Boskoff concludes that by providing a continuing source of morale for the supposedly heartless, impersonal, and fragmented urban community, voluntary associations bolster the social and psychological stability of an otherwise precarious middle class.

What is not clear in the literature on neighborhoods, networks, and associations is the relative importance of each to the urbanite, and the degree to which each can serve as a reasonably satisfactory substitute for the others in providing a sense of belonging to the larger community (as implied earlier in this chapter, neighborhoods and voluntary associations may or may not coexist to serve mutually complementary or supportive functions). But it is far more certain that those individuals who have no ties to either neighborhoods, social networks, or voluntary associations are the most likely to conform to the traditional image of the personal isolation, loneliness, and depersonalization depicted in the earlier urban literature.

Not considered in this chapter have been the most transitory and diffuse patterns of urban social organization, which may be referred to under the general heading of "collective behavior," for want of a better term. This includes the kind of behavior that occurs in public and semipublic places, such as streets, sidewalks, parks, plazas, public buildings, theaters, meeting halls, and other gathering places. This public behavior sometimes takes the form of crowds, mobs, assemblies, audiences, spectators, or person-to-person encounters between strangers. Such topics usually have been considered within the framework of social psychology and thus have been examined in Chapter Six.

SELECTED BIBLIOGRAPHY

ABRAHAMSON, MARK. *Urban Sociology.* Englewood Cliffs, N.J.: Prentice-Hall, 1976.

BERGER, BENNETT. *Working Class Suburbs.* Berkeley: University of California Press, 1960.

BOSKOFF, ALVIN. *The Sociology of Urban Regions.* 2nd ed. New York: Appleton-Century-Crofts, 1970.

BOTT, ELIZABETH. *Family and Social Networks.* 2nd ed. New York: Free Press, 1971.

CAPLOW, T., and FOREMAN, R. "Neighborhood Interaction in a Homogeneous Community," *American Sociological Review* 15 (June 1950): 357–366.

CARPENTER, N. "Neighborhoods." *Encyclopaedia of the Social Sciences,* p. 357. New York: 1933.

COLEMAN, JAMES S., et al. *Medical Innovation.* Indianapolis: Bobbs-Merrill, 1966.

DENTLER, ROBERT A. "Brownsville: Community or Staging Area?" *Center Forum,* November 13, 1968: pp. 12–14.

DE TOCQUEVILLE, ALEX. *Democracy in America.* New York: Knopf, 1946, Vol. II.

EAMES, E., and GOODE, J. G. *Anthropology of the City.* Englewood Cliffs, N.J.: Prentice-Hall, 1977.

FAVA, SYLVIA F. "Contrasts in Neighboring." In W. M. Dobriner, ed., *The Suburban Community,* pp. 122–130. New York: Putnam's, 1959.

FISCHER, CLAUDE S. *The Urban Experience.* New York: Harcourt Brace Jovanovich, 1976.

_____, et al. *Networks and Places.* New York: Free Press, 1977.

GANS, HERBERT. *The Levittowners.* New York: Vintage Books, 1967.

GLASS, RUTH. *The Social Background of a Plan.* London, 1948.

GRANOVETTER, MARK S. "The Strength of Weak Ties," *American Journal of Sociology* 79 (May 1973): 1360–1379.

HAWLEY, AMOS H. *Urban Society.* New York: Ronald Press, 1971.

KELLER, SUZAN. *The Urban Neighborhood.* New York: Random House, 1968.

LAUMAN, E. O. *Bonds of Pluralism.* New York: John Wiley, 1973.

LIEBOW, ELLIOTT. *Tally's Corner.* Boston: Little, Brown, 1967.

LITWAK, E., and FELLIN, P. "The Neighborhood in Urban American Society," *Social Work* 13 (July 1968): 72–79.

MANN, PETER. *An Approach to Urban Sociology.* New York: Humanities Press, 1965.

PACKARD, VANCE. *A Nation of Strangers.* New York: McKay, 1972.

POPENOE, DAVID, ed. *The Urban-Industrial Frontier.* New Brunswick, N.J.: Rutgers University Press, 1969.

ROSS, H. L. "The Local Community: A Survey Approach," *American Sociological Review* 27 (February 1962): 75–84.

SCHERER, JACQUELINE. *Contemporary Community: Illusion or Reality?* London: Tavistock, 1972.

SEELEY, J. R.; SIM, A. R.; and LOOSLEY, E. W. *Crestwood Heights.* New York: Basic Books, 1956.

SHOSTAK, ARTHUR. *Blue Collar Life.* New York: Random House, 1969.

SUTTLES, GERALD D. *The Social Construction of Communities.* Chicago: University of Chicago Press, 1972.

_____. *The Social Order of the Slum.* Chicago: University of Chicago Press, 1968.

WARREN, DONALD I. *Black Neighborhoods.* Ann Arbor: University of Michigan Press, 1975.

_____. "Neighborhoods in Urban Areas." In Roland L. Warren, ed., *New Perspectives on the American Community.* 3rd ed. Skokie, Ill.: Rand McNally, 1977.

_____, and WARREN, ROCHELLE B. *The Neighborhood Organizer's Handbook.* Notre Dame, Ind.: University of Notre Dame Press, 1976.

WELLMAN, BARRY. "Who Needs Neighborhoods?" In Roland L. Warren, ed., *New Perspectives on the American Community.* 3rd ed. Skokie, Ill.: Rand McNally, 1977.

WHYTE, WILLIAM H., JR. *The Organization Man.* New York: Simon & Schuster, 1956.

WIGAND, ROLF T. "Communication Network Analysis in Urban Development." In W. E. Arnold and Jerry L. Buley, eds., *Urban Communication.* Cambridge, Mass.: Winthrop, 1977.

WILENSKY, H. L., and LEBEAUX, CHARLES N. *Industrial Society and Social Welfare.* New York: Russell Sage, 1958.

chapter 6

the social psychology of urban life

Social psychological dimensions of urbanization often have been treated as a residual or derivative component of urban social systems. As such, they have often been cursorily examined or neglected altogether in many textbook treatments of urban sociology. Compared to other urban sociology topics, little systematic effort has been made to detail the social psychology of urban life, even though much of the early theorizing about urbanization focused on questions of social psychological significance, and much contemporary field research has been conducted in this area. Yet our understanding of the fabric of life in an urban context is not complete without some consideration of how individuals experience or give meaning to their lives as urbanites, and how they interact with others within a context of commonly shared meanings and symbols on the one hand, or within a context of a diversified range of attitudes, values, and perceptions on the other. This chapter is devoted to a review of social psychological topics, such as the impact of urbanization on individual personality structure, urban life styles, everyday patterns of interaction in public places, and the symbols and imagery of urban life. Our position is that, far from being residual or derivative components, these dimensions of urban social systems contribute as heavily to an understanding of the quality of urban life as do the other components of urban ecosystems—population, environment, technology, and social organization.

One of the questions that has long intrigued social scientists and other observers of the urban scene is whether or not the impact of urbanization is powerful enough to produce distinct differences between the personality characteristics of urban and nonurban dwellers. To the extent that human personality is shaped by sociocultural influences of all sorts and is not exclusively a product of physiological or biological factors, it seems reasonable to conclude that the urban environment constitutes one such major sociocultural influence. Wirth (1938) and Simmel (1950) are the best-known examples of sociologists who used this kind of deductive reasoning to postulate ideas about the personality characteristics that were believed to derive from the conditions of urban living, as they saw them. For the most part, they saw the city as highly disorganizing and disruptive for the individual, creating a wide variety of psychological pathologies. They hypothesized that friction, irritation, nervous tension, and personal frustration would increase in response to the greater size, density, and heterogeneity of the urban population and the more rapid tempos of urban life. Wirth, for example, argued that "personal disorganization, mental breakdown, suicide, delinquency, crime, corruption, and disorder might be expected under these circumstances to be more prevalent in the urban than the rural community" (1938, p. 162). Such reasoning for a long time has been the conventional wisdom of urban sociology, although usually the early proponents had not backed their conclusions with empirical analysis. More recent empirical research, as reviewed in the following section, has cast doubt on the validity of the theory that urban dwellers are any more prone to mental illness than rural dwellers, and the findings point to other sociocultural variables as potentially more significant than rural or urban residence as causative factors.

Classifying and Measuring Mental Illness

Instruments for measuring rates of mental illness in a population have been equally varied, and different indicators produce different results. One of the most frequently used measures of the incidence of mental illness has been hospitalization or confinement to a facility for the mentally ill. Using this approach, Goldhamer and Marshall (1962) computed the rate of admission to hospitals for psychosis in the state of Massachusetts between 1840 and 1940. They reasoned that since that particular time period was a century of greatly increasing urbanization, mental health rates should also have risen accordingly. Their findings at first glance seemed to support this conclusion, as rates of admission for psychosis more than doubled over this period, from 41 per 100,000 in 1840 to about 85 per 100,000 in 1941. However, controlling for age, Goldhamer and Marshall found that for those between twenty and fifty years of age there was no

City life can produce friction and irritation in day to day living. (Harry Gold)

significant change in admission rates during the entire century studied, and that only persons over fifty experienced higher admission rates. This difference probably is accounted for by the fact that it was easier for rural and farm people to care for the older mentally ill members of their families at home than it is for city people living in less spacious or in isolated accommodations. Thus, the findings of this study did not support the theory that mental illness has increased with greater urbanization.

In another classic study using rates of hospitalization as an index, Faris and Dunham (1939) plotted the residential distribution of all patients admitted to public and private mental hospitals from the city of Chicago and computed rates of hospital admission for various diagnostic categories of mental illness. While no urban-rural comparisons were made, the study did demonstrate the significant fact that hospitalized mental illness was not randomly distributed through the city. Highest rates were found near the center of the city, in areas of high population mobility and low socioeconomic status. Conversely, the lowest rates were from the stable residential areas of higher socioeconomic status.

But there are major shortcomings of hospitalization as an indicator of mental illness, which apply to the kind of studies cited above. Hospitalization rates are inadequate unless all mentally ill members of the population have roughly an equal chance of being hospitalized or confined. To the extent that rates of hospitalization can be influenced by such factors as closeness or accessibility to a mental hospital, the availability of bed space in such facilities, differences in tolerance for symptoms of mental illness among subgroups of the population, or by the existence of alternatives to hospitalization, hospitalization rates will be poor indicators of the true rate of mental illness in a population. Gibbs (1962) compared rates of mental hospitalization to some noninstitutional indicators of the amount of psychopathology in the population, using data from the forty-eight continental states. Using such measures as deaths from mental disorder, deaths from suicide, deaths from duodenal ulcer, deaths from alcoholism, and the number of homicide victims under four years of age as indicators of psychopathology in the population, he found that rates of mental hospitalization were *not* closely related to noninstitutional indicators.

Other studies of community mental health have been based on sample surveys, in which the respondents are asked to assess their own personality adjustment. In some cases the results are then coded and rated by professionals skilled enough to classify the findings in psychiatric or psychological terms. One of the most thorough surveys of personal adjustment using this approach was reported by Gurin, Veroff, and Feld (1960). Researchers from the University of Michigan Survey Research Center interviewed a large national sample of adults who were representative of the total population in terms of sex, income, education, occupation, and place of residence. Nearly 25 percent of those interviewed had at one time in their lives felt sufficiently troubled to need help, mainly in the areas of marriage, parenthood, work, and personal psychological problems. Feelings of general dissatisfaction were widespread among the respondents and showed no consistent relationship to place of residence. Differences by place of residence were fewer than those based on education, income, and sex. In effect, the survey found no greater symptoms of poor mental health among the residents of metropolitan areas than among those residing in the less urbanized areas of the United States.

The Leightons (1957) surveyed a rural county and found that over half of the population had at some time or other exhibited psychoneurotic symptoms and that 77 percent reported having had psychosomatic disorders to a significant degree. A study of the Hutterites, a closely knit religious sect residing primarily in the nonindustrial, nonurban parts of the Midwest, indicated a sufficient rate of psychoses and other untreated types of mental illness to challenge further the conventional view that people living in stable, self-contained rural communities are less likely to experience symptoms of mental illness than those living in larger urban communities (Eaton and Weil, 1955). Likewise, Lewis's (1951) study of a small Mexican agricultural village found considerable evidence of violence, cruelty, suffering, and strife both within the village and in its relations with other villages. Far from being harmonious and free of stress, the residents of such rural communities may be subject to as great a degree of anxiety and personal adjustment problems as those residing in urban areas. Studies of the incidence of schizophrenia among primitive people living in preliterate and tribal societies (see N. J. Demareth, 1955; Tsung-yi Lin, 1959) indicate that the various psychoses are widely prevalent in such societies, contrary to common belief.

Clearly, there is no simple yes-or-no answer to the very complex questions as to whether modern urban civilization has led to an increase in the amount of mental illness in the population. The research results to date do not support such a conclusion, but the possibility cannot yet be completely discounted. In general, the amount of mental illness in any society or population will depend upon the genetic composition of the population, the prevalence of certain types of trauma or pathogenic processes in early family life, the kinds of stresses to which adults are exposed late in life, cultural definitions of mental illness, and the exercise of potential controls, which may limit the development of symptoms. The relative weights and particular forms of factors and the degree to which the various urban and nonurban environments are contributing factors have not yet been conclusively established.

Variations in Mental Health within Metropolitan Areas

Although the data comparing mental illness in urban areas with that in rural areas are inconclusive, it is far more certain that within metropolitan areas mental disorders are not evenly distributed and vary widely from subarea to subarea or group to group. Also, the distribution of particular types of mental disorders, such as the psychoses, neuroses, and psychosomatic disorders, is widely varied.

Social class appears to be one of the most important factors related to variations in rates of mental illness. The Midtown Manhattan Study (Srole, 1975) was one of the more notable attempts to assess the relationship between mental health and social class. In this study, approximately 1,700 white adult residents of mid-Manhattan between the ages of twenty and fifty-nine were randomly selected for a several-hours-long interview in their homes. The interview asked questions about depression, immaturity, psychosomatic illness, and so on. Two psychiatrists, from whom information that might identify the socioeconomic class of the respondents was withheld to prevent possible class biases from influencing the results, independently rated the number and severity of the reported psychological symptoms and placed each person into one of four mental health categories: 1) well; 2) mild symptom formation; 3) moderate symptom formation; and 4) psychologically impaired. The well group had no significant symptoms, while the impaired group had symptoms of mental illness severe enough to handicap them greatly in coping with everyday life. The mild and moderate groups were between these two extremes: they indicated some degree of psychological difficulty, but they were able nevertheless to carry on their adult activities successfully. The results did not demonstrate a relationship between mental health and such variables as immigrant generation status, national origins, religious identity, or urban-rural origins. The age of the respondents and their marital status was only moderately correlated with the mental health ratings. But of all the variables considered, social class was by far the best predictor of mental health and mental illness. In the lowest socioeconomic stratum of the sample, only 4.6 percent of the respondents were rated as well or free of symptoms, in contrast to the 30 percent of the highest socioeconomic stratum who were symptom free. While only 12.5 percent of the highest socioeconomic stratum was rated as psychologically impaired, nearly half (47.3 percent) of the lowest stratum was classified as impaired. Thus, the members of the lowest status group were four times more likely to be severely impaired psychologically than the highest status group, and were six times less likely to significantly escape the symptoms of mental illness and enter the "well" category.

Another major study demonstrating a strong relationship between social class and mental illness was conducted in New Haven, Connecticut, by Hollingshead and Redlich (1958). The study was based on data for at least 98 percent of the residents who were receiving psychiatric care at the time of the survey. This included not only those who were hospitalized but also those who were receiving outpatient care from private practitioners and clinics. Dividing the community into five social classes, the study found that the prevalence of treated psychosis was more than three times greater in the lowest class than in the highest class. Also, once a lowest-class patient is diagnosed as psychotic and committed to a mental hospital, he or she tends to remain hospitalized nearly twice as long as patients in the highest social class. For neurosis, the relationship to social class was just the reverse, with higher rates positively associated with higher social status.

Life Style and Adjustment to Urban Life

The question of what it is about lower-class status in an urban environment that produces a negative impact on mental health, in contrast to higher-status groups that seem more successfully to escape the most debilitating impact, cries for a reasonable explanation. While no simple answer is possible, the most fruitful approach lies with the concept of *life style*. Life styles abound among various urban groupings, some of which bear at least some relationship to social class. If any particular urban style of life can be seen as a means of accommodating to the conditions of urban life, or as an adjustment to ease the stresses and strains of urban living, then it can also be argued that some ways of life provide a better fit than others to the demands of urban living. From this perspective, the problem lies not so much with the particular conditions of the urban environment as it does with the way in which groups of people adjust or accommodate to this environment.

Gans (1968) has presented a discussion of five urban ways of life, based mainly on social class and on stages of the family and life cycle, which

These people are coping with a hot summer day in a city pool. (Marc Anderson)

suggests how analysis of life styles may provide clues to the quality of adjustment to urban life. The first life style is that of the *cosmopolites*. Cosmopolites include those who consciously choose to reside in an urban environment to participate in the cultural activities the city has to offer, which are highly important to them. They occupy varying socioeconomic levels, but tend to be intellectuals and professionals or artistically inclined. The *unmarried and childless* constitute a second life-style grouping. Such groups tend to cluster in apartment house areas that also provide an active night life, such as singles bars and other places of entertainment. These groups participate actively in the varied activities of the city. Their residence in the city may be transitory, however, as many of them move to single-family housing in the suburbs when and if they enter the child-rearing stages of their life cycle. The third major life style is that of *ethnic villagers* (see Chapter Four for a discussion of this life style in another context). Ethnic villagers are immigrant or migrant groups who attempt to carry on in urban enclaves the peasant life of their native regions. They create their own close-knit social structures, which help cushion or isolate them from what they consider to be the harmful effects of the city, including other competing ethnic or racial groups whom they may attempt to prevent from encroaching on their "own" neighborhoods. The fourth group, the *deprived*, are those who are in the city largely because of the handicaps of extreme poverty, emotional problems, or racial discrimination, which leave them with no alternatives but to remain in deteriorating housing or blighted neighborhoods in the worst areas of the central cities. The final group, the *trapped* and the downwardly mobile, consists of those who cannot afford to move when a neighborhood changes for the worse and those who can no longer compete economically for good housing, such as retirees on fixed pensions or widows who have lost the income of a breadwinner. Such groups may suffer a visible loss of status and well-being as their situations grow worse with the changing circumstances of their environment.

Of the five life styles suggested by Gans, only the last two represent the types of social and personality disorganization that traditionally have been associated with urban living. The deprived and the trapped or downwardly mobile are subjected to stresses and strains for which they may not have the psychic or material resources to cope successfully. Under such circumstances, it is no wonder that such groups represent a large segment of the lowest socioeconomic levels that usually have the highest mental illness rates in the cities.

The ethnic villagers are often protected from the disorganizing effects of urban life. But under rapidly changing circumstances, such as are caused by the encroachments of urban renewal or invading external groups that may rapidly change the character of their neighborhood, even the ethnic villagers may be dramatically subjected to new stresses or strains beyond their control. Thus, whether or not the ethnic villagers do, in fact, produce a style of life ideally suited to the conditions of urban living remains circumstantially problematic.

The urban singles have received a good deal of attention from the mass media in recent years. Singles bars with their nightly crowds of unattached young people looking for "one night stands" or short-term affairs without long-term commitments, and large singles-only apartment complexes that function in ways similar to a resort hotel are part of the popular image of a supposedly fun and carefree "swinging" life style. While sociological documentation is somewhat scanty for this group, there is no certain reason to suspect that such a life style is particularly conducive to satisfactory adjustment to city life or to superior personality integration in the urban context. On the other hand, neither is there clear evidence that young singles are more prone to serious personality disorders than other life style segments of the urban population. Palen (1975, pp. 125–126) describes the life styles of singles as more humdrum in reality than popular images suggest. For example, most of the young singles are faced with the everyday problems of making a living, finding a decent place to live, making friends, eventually finding a suitable mate, and so on. Hardly social or economic radicals, they are in Palen's view "trying to achieve essentially middle class material goals without being able to rely on many of the usual institutional supports for their activities."

A study by Starr and Carns (1973) of singles in their early and mid-twenties who were working in Chicago indicated that most singles do not live in singles apartment complexes and that such groups had no community roots in the housing areas or neighborhoods in which they resided. In addition, the singles bars that were often frequented did not necessarily serve as satisfactory substitutes for an active community involvement, and interest in frequenting such places would drop off rapidly after six months or so, or by the time the respondents began to reach their late twenties. As Palen (1975, p. 127) remarks, few singles can take for long the forced conviviality and the strained and artificial social patterns of the singles bars. Even among many singles, singles bars are sometimes referred to as "meat markets" that can produce only shallow and one-dimensional relationships. For most working singles, the work place is a more effective site for meeting people and forming relationships than places of residence or places of entertainment. At any rate, the question of the degree to which Gans's unmarried and childless category cushions its members from disorganizing aspects of urban life remains largely unanswered, except that the detachment of the singles from undesirable commitments or obligations probably does protect them from some of the kinds of problems experienced by the "deprived" or the "trapped."

The cosmopolitans have received the least attention in the sociological literature on urban life styles. This is unfortunate, for it is among this group that one must look in order satisfactorily to answer the question, Is a truly urban life style emerging? One can argue that problems of community or personality disorganization are most commonly associated with those urban groups with the least urbanized life styles. On the other hand, those groups that have made a satisfactory adjustment to urban life, are attuned to its opportunities and demands, and actively partake in the unique activities the city has to offer, tend to be ignored as objects of inquiry because they are not at the core of commonly perceived social problems. A more extended discussion of cosmopolitan life styles is therefore in order.

Cosmopolitan Life Style as an Urban "Ideal Type"

Just as Wirth and Simmel had earlier postulated a set of traits or characteristics that would provide a composite view of the urban personality as an "ideal type," so we intend here to postulate a set of characteristics or traits representing our view of an ideal type model of a cosmopolitan life style. In contrast to the views of Wirth, however, our model does not assume that personality pathology or disorder is the inevitable product of urban living. It asserts instead that under certain circumstances an urban life style can be perceived that provides a "best fit" with the conditions and demands of urban living, and that is positive in the sense that it maximizes the pleasures and satisfactions of urban living. At the same time, this model of a cosmopolitan life style protects the individual from undesirable distortions of his or her personality in the process. What we are trying to do is to identify those life-style characteristics or traits most likely to be associated with good mental health in the metropolitan setting. While such a model is still largely speculative, we shall cite some of the arguments that seem to reinforce it. The cosmopolitan life style we present is not representative of the majority of people currently residing in urban areas. In fact, most current urban dwellers probably are not fully attuned to or satisfied with the conditions of urban living that they now experience and would prefer to live in another kind of environment (see the concluding section on public opinion). Most urban dwellers have not yet accommodated themselves to urban living by the adaptation of life styles which in our view provide the best fit or accommodation to living in metropolitan communities. Instead, it is useful to think of the cosmopolitan life style as a potential about which we can find a number of examples from among limited segments of the urban population. The following elements comprise our model of the cosmopolitan life style.

Knowledgeability.   A wide knowledge of the urban community and its resources is an essential characteristic of this life style, if one is to benefit fully from urban life. One must know what cultural, economic, and service facilities are available and be able to use them. For example, if one wishes to pursue a career in an urban environment, one must be familiar with many of the occupations making up an urban labor force, be familiar with the qualifications or training necessary for any given occupation, know where to apply for such positions or for the opportunity to train for them, and know the most effective routes to arrive at a given work site at the most reasonable cost of time, money, and distance. If one wishes to enjoy cultural and social activities, one must know what is available, the time and place, and the criteria for admission. Finding a good doctor, dentist, counselor, attorney, auto mechanic, hairdresser, or other dispensers of desired professional services, and knowing where to find other people with similar interests or with whom one may wish to associate are further examples of the need to be knowledgeable of the urban environment in order successfully to live a cosmopolitan life style.

Such knowledge can be acquired in two ways. The first involves completing some period of formal education and becoming literate enough to use formal informational systems such as libraries, newspapers and magazines, directories, maps, and printed instructions. The inability to use telephone directories, read instructions on application forms, follow printed instructions, or to read signs or maps can be highly frustrating and discouraging to the functionally illiterate, and the need for a relatively high level of literacy to function effectively in an urban environment has long been widely recognized. The second source of such knowledge comes through experience with living in an urban environment. Thus, those who have been born and reared in an urban environment or are descendants of urban dwellers are more likely to have the appropriate kinds of knowledge than those who are recent migrants from nonurban environments. Through experience, urban dwellers may acquire a kind of "street wisdom" enabling them accurately to judge potential rewards or dangers and to avoid situations their experience tells them may be undesirable.

Skill.   The old adage "Practice makes perfect" applies here. One must develop skills in using urban resources, such as knowing how to find places or ask for directions, getting on or off of escalators, elevators, subway cars, and buses, filling out questionnaires and forms, communicating with others in situations where exchanges of information are necessary, and dealing with bureaucratic functionaries to receive desired services. Skill and knowledgeability are closely connected since the skills necessary for successful urban living can best be acquired through various combinations of experience and formal education. In many large cities, the public schools have begun to facilitate this process through such devices as field trips, apprenticeships, and other skill-oriented forms of training (see the chapter on health, education, and welfare). Lofland (1973, pp. 158–159), in a somewhat different vein, views the appropriate knowledge and skills as a prerequisite for having fun or adventure in the urban setting, characterizing such experiences as exhilarating or exciting for sophisticated urbanites. As she remarks, they "sometimes find it enjoyable to seek out a little danger, to court a little fear, to engender a little anxiety. They sometimes find it enjoyable, that is, to go adventuring."

Tolerance.   To the extent that urban communities contain diverse peoples with unlike social characteristics and behavior patterns, successful accommodation to urban living would seem to require a high degree of tolerance and flexibility. Becker and Horowitz (1972), in writing of the high degree of tolerance shown for "deviance" in the city of San Francisco, identify a "culture of civility" which they believe to be relatively uncommon in many other American cities. An implicit "live and let live" kind of social contract exists where "straights" do not become outraged by "freaks" and the latter have a greater degree of freedom for engaging in their preferred life styles, provided they do not go beyond certain implicit but agreed-upon boundaries. As the city becomes widely known for allowing certain kinds of deviants or eccentrics to live with a degree of acceptance and a minimum of harassment, it continues to attract more of these unconventional types, who, in a mutual display of tolerance for one another, tend to increase the overall tolerance levels of the city as a whole.

Karp, Stone, and Yoels (1977) suggest that Becker and Horowitz's model of civility in San Francisco is too static and does not take into account the possibility that tolerance sometimes disintegrates when ultra life style groups begin to test the limits of a community's tolerance by pushing their deviance to unacceptable extremes. Fischer (1971, pp. 847–856) qualifies the relationship between urbanization and the amount of tolerance for such groups as racial or ethnic minorities by suggesting that tolerance for diversity is probably more a byproduct of the social characteristics of the residents of a given community than it is of community size. Our purpose here, however, has not been to demonstrate the association between tolerance and urbanization, but rather to suggest that some degree of moral relativity and tolerance for diversity may protect individuals from the strains and frustrations of dealing with a wide range of people who might be unacceptable to them, but with whom they are unable to avoid contact, experienced by those who are more rigidly intolerant or prejudiced. The recent crusade by Anita Bryant in Miami, Florida, against the gay community would be one visible example of what we mean. Whether or not a high

Tolerance is necessary for all city dwellers. (Marc Anderson)

degree of tolerance is a widespread reality in the current urban scene, it is a reasonable characteristic of a cosmopolitan life style as we are defining it here.

A sense of humor about the many inconsistencies, paradoxes, and dilemmas of urban living certainly eases the adjustment process, and we include this characteristic as a component of a tolerant and flexible cosmopolitan attitude. It is no accident that professional comedians are among the top celebrities of the mass media world of entertainment and are often admired as individuals who are helpful in relieving the stresses of urban living through their comedy. Eulogies presented at the recent passing of such long-established stars as Jack Benny, Groucho Marx, or Peter Sellers attest to this fact.

Self-awareness. The urbanite is daily confronted with a bewildering variety of choices and is constantly bombarded with one form of persuasion or another, be it demands on time, energy, or income. Some observers have described the conflict of making choices from the bewildering assortment of urban alternatives as somewhat akin to the conflict of choosing what to eat in a well-stocked cafeteria. In this case, the range and variety of choices available to the individual probably does increase with the size of the community. To make intelligent choices, the individual must be aware of his or her own abilities, limitations, likes and dislikes, and needs. One must be aware of how one's own needs can best be satisfied and be able to make the appropriate choices from among the competing alternatives. One must be able to take on satisfying relationships and activities as well as to abandon those that are detrimental to one's own well-being. Also, the ability to "travel light," not excessively burdened by the obligations of property or tradition, in order to pursue one's own interests, might very well constitute a component of a cosmopolitan life style. Thus, a "take it or leave it" attitude toward people or things potentially can supply a degree of freedom and mobility for those who are most in tune with the wide range of opportunities afforded in an urban environment.

Meaningful Work Roles. Having an occupational role that is meaningful, prestigious, and visible in the urban context may be among the more important dimensions of a cosmopolitan life style, particularly in an urban-industrial society. A blacksmith, snake charmer, or horse trader may be accorded very little social standing by urbanites, but an attorney, television talk show host, disk jockey, journalist, actor, musician, social worker, physician, police officer, or public official may be recognized as being in an occupation that makes a useful or interesting contribution to the quality of urban life. Such areas as politics and government, science, education, the professions, business management, the arts, social and health services, and popular entertainment would meet our criteria for inclusion here as a component of a cosmopolitan life style. While many of the workers in these areas have above average incomes, the amount of money earned at an occupation is not the prime consideration here (although having an adequate income is necessary). The sense that one is engaged in work that is pertinent to the interests of the community, however, can provide a better sense of belonging to and participating in the urban community than an occupation having no apparent link to what is widely perceived to be important. (See the chapter on urban economic institutions for further analysis of urban work roles and the urban labor force.)

Positive, Appreciative Attitudes. Finally, liking the urban environment, its crowds, its physical development, its facilities, its amenities, and its resources, and having a positive attitude toward participating in the cultural activities of the urban community are essential ingredients of a cosmopolitan life style. This dimension comes closest to what Gans had in mind when he first suggested the idea that a cosmopolitan life style goes further than most in cushioning the individual from the harshest, most unpleasant, and most disorganizing aspects of urban living. One interesting example of this aspect is the delight with which many urbanites enjoy "people-watching" or "rubbing elbows" in crowded and busy urban settings. New York's Greenwich Village, Central Park, and Rockefeller Plaza are examples that immediately come to mind. In the suburbs, one can see the newer enclosed shopping malls serving this same function for many of their users.

While we are not asserting that a cosmopolitan life style, as we have described it above, is representative of the populations now residing in urban settings, nevertheless many of the components of such a life style are relatively commonplace. One can find many examples of the attitudes and behavior associated with a cosmopolitan life style being considered desirable goals. Cosmopolitan attitudes and behavior are implicit in the programs of many public school systems and institutions of higher learning, they are integrated into the child-rearing practice of many urbanites, and countless examples can be found among mass media heroes and celebrities. Widely known celebrities such as John Lindsay, Joyce Brothers, Gore Vidal, Johnny Carson, Woodward and Bernstein, Walter Cronkite, Joe Namath, Hugh Hefner, David Susskind, Woody Allen, Sammy Davis, Jr., and the Kennedy family are among those that have occurred to the author's students as they attempted to associate the concept of a cosmopolitan with models commonly visible in the mass media. Also identified were fictional television series heroes, such as Baretta, Kojak, Police Woman, and Marcus Welby.

We also are not asserting any claims of moral superiority for a cosmopolitan life style in comparison to other alternatives; such moral judgments are best left to the reader. We do believe, however, that a concern for the mental health and well-being of persons residing in an urban setting should lead to further investigation of the relationship between life style and personality adjustment in the context of specific social and physical urban environments.

EVERYDAY BEHAVIOR IN PUBLIC PLACES

Some of the most transitory and diffuse patterns of urban social organization may be referred to under the general heading of "collective behavior," for want of a better term. This includes the kind of behavior that occurs in public and semipublic places, such as streets, sidewalks, parks, plazas, public buildings, theaters, meeting halls, and other gathering places. This public behavior sometimes takes the form of crowds, mobs, assemblies, audiences, or spectators. What is important here is that such patterns of collective behavior generally involve person-to-person encounters between strangers. The sheer volume of such potential interaction between strangers in a large city is illustrated by Whyte (1974), who has determined that on one short city block on New York City's Lexington Avenue—between 57th and 58th streets—some 38,000 people pass by on an average weekday.

Ever since the earlier writing of Simmel (1950), who believed the everyday tempo of city life significantly affects the social psychology of urbanites, many observers have tended to couch the everyday interaction of strangers in public urban places in highly negative terms. For example, they have often been described as uncivilized, insensitive, indifferent, uncaring, or blasé, if not downright rude or overaggressive. One widely shared negative image has been restated by anthropologist Edward Hall (1969, p. 174):

> Virtually everything about American cities today . . . drives men apart, alienating them from each other. The recent and shocking instances in which people have been beaten and even murdered while their neighbors looked on without even picking up a phone indicates how far this trend toward alienation has progressed.

Open and flagrant examples of pilfering and looting that sometimes takes place during natural disasters such as floods or during technological breakdowns such as the electric power blackout in the New York metropolitan area in July 1977, feed further the image of everyday city life as potentially chaotic and disorganized.

The problem with these images, however valid they may be in some instances, is that they do not adequately explain how everyday city life is possible in any form. Millions upon millions of urbanites manage to go about their daily business of living in a routinized pattern with a minimum of disruption. This, in spite of the negative factors, suggests that there may be some degree of order to the process, no matter how fragile it may appear. In the last decade or so a number of scholars have begun to readdress themselves to the interaction patterns of everyday public behavior to discover whether order or regularity underlies such behavior, and whether such behavior has meaning that can be made sense of by the participants (or at least by objective social observers). Much of this work has emanated from the followers of Goffman (1963, p. 4), who has suggested that the informal rules of conduct in streets and other public places where people commonly gather should be the object of inquiry if one wishes to understand fully the most diffuse forms of social organization that constitute everyday urban behavior.

Lofland (1971) maintains that public ordered life between strangers is possible because urbanites successfully have created what she calls a workable social contract or a public "social bargain." This is based on the need recognized by urbanites that they must protect one another so that all can carry on the business of living. According to Karp, Stone, and Yoels (1977, p. 110), this social bargain demands that persons cooperate with one another enough to insure some intelligibility and order in their everyday lives, while seeking at the same time to keep their involvement with one another at a manageable minimum. Urbanites must take others into account at the same time that they seek to protect their personal privacy. They are required to strike a balance between involvement, indifference, and cooperation with one another as they seek to minimize involvement and maximize social order. At a more concrete level, the empirical question they put forth is "What are the types of normative conventions followed by city persons that maximize intelligibility and predictability in their relations with others while simultaneously maximizing their own sense of privacy in public?" (Karp, Stone, and Yoel, 1977, p. 113.)

Some recent research by Wolff (1973), based on close, careful observations in natural settings, nicely demonstrates how everyday urban life is ordered along the lines just suggested. He studied pedestrian behavior on 42nd Street in Manhattan, and was able to show through a series of video tape pictures that a number of consistent patterns of accommodation were made by the supposedly autonomous strangers in the streets, which demonstrated a high degree of cooperation among them. These patterns have been summarized as follows:

1. Step-and-slide pattern. As persons pass one another, there is a "slight angling of the body, a turning of the shoulder, and an almost impercepti-

ble slide step—a sort of step and slide." The interpretation here is that pedestrians cooperate with one another by twisting their bodies so as to minimize the amount of physical contact.

2. The head-over-the-shoulder pattern. Pedestrians maintains a head over the shoulder relationship with persons walking less than five feet in front of them to see what is occurring ahead, while at the same time avoiding stumbling onto the feet of the persons in front.

3. The spread effect. This involves persons walking in the same direction distributing themselves over the fullest width that the sidewalks will allow. Presumably, this maximizes the efficiency of movement.

4. Detouring. This occurs when a person forced to detour around another person returns to the original path once the detour has been accomplished.

5. Avoiding perceptual objects. People tend to treat perceptually distinct parts of the sidewalk surfaces, such as grating, as obstructions to be avoided whenever possible.

6. Monitoring. Persons tend continually to monitor the immediate environment in order to avoid collisions, as well as to evaluate the potential behavior of others. They scan the faces of persons coming from the opposite direction and turn or stop in response to out of the ordinary facial expressions that may signal some unusual situation to be monitored.

Karp (1973) has studied the behavior of people in Times Square pornographic bookstores and movie theaters, supposedly the epitome of an anonymous inner city area. He found that the people, who were engaged in somewhat unconventional behavior, were nevertheless concerned with being defined as "proper" by total strangers in their immediate vicinity, and would adjust their behavior accordingly. They would attempt to hide, obscure, or shield their interest in buying or using pornographic materials from those strangers who might be around them before entering a pornographic bookstore or theater. Once inside, the normative structure seemed to demand a careful avoidance of either eye or physical contact with other customers. Karp concluded that the persons in this semipublic urban setting were involved in a highly structured social situation in which the norms of privacy were highly standardized and readily understood by the participants.

Lofland (1971, p. 226) has suggested that people will use a variety of ways to protect their self-esteem when in the presence of strangers in public places. She states that "if a person is to exist as a social being . . . there must be some minimal guarantees that in interaction with others he will receive the affirmation and confirmation of himself as a 'right.'" She mentions the following as major techniques or devices used by persons in public places to protect their self-images under the scrutiny of strangers: 1) checking for readiness—persons will check their appearance, making sure that their hair is in place, zippers are zipped, etc., before entering a potential encounter situation; 2) taking a reading—this involves stopping to take stock of the social setting before entering it; 3) reaching a position—once having decided on the spot or the point they wish to occupy, persons tend to make a direct approach to that spot in as inconspicuous a way as possible in order to avoid remaining under the social spotlight longer than is absolutely necessary.

Karp, Stone, and Yoels (1977, pp. 112–113) interpret some of these regularities of encounters in public places by suggesting that society provides a baseline of knowledge in the form of rules or norms which provide a shared meaning to the participants, in spite of slight variations of meaning from person to person or situation to situation: "Without this common-sense sharing of knowledge, social order would be impossible. Such social knowledge is extremely far-reaching, encompassing literally thousands of social conventions." However, they also recognize that the meaning of any social act is situationally specific, and that knowledge must be continually reevaluated as one moves from one social setting to another.

Another body of literature focuses on the fact that different cities will produce markedly different patterns among strangers in such public spaces as streets, sidewalks, or parks. Cities differ in their attitudes to the suitability of using the streets for walking, "people-watching," or other similarly pleasurable participation in the public life of the community. Detroiters, for example, many of whom view their own central business district as unsafe for pedestrian activity, will often comment on the pleasant, safe, and pleasurable ambience of street life of nearby Toronto. Goffman (1963, p. 200) and others have compared the ambience of public streets in Paris with those in England and the United States. He refers to the greater "looseness" of the streets of Paris, where one can eat from a loaf of bread while walking to and from work or become heatedly involved in a passionate conversation. These variations in patterns are often accompanied by varying images of different cities as enjoyable places in which to live or visit. Speaking of Paris, Hall (1969, p. 175) observes:

> Paris is known as a city in which the outdoors has been made attractive to people and where it is not only possible but pleasurable to stretch one's legs, breathe, sniff the air, and take in the people and the city. . . . It is noteworthy that the little streets and alleys too narrow to accept most vehicles not only provide variety but are a constant reminder that Paris is for people.

Observers such as Jane Jacobs (1961) and William H. Whyte (1974) focus on those areas within cities that are widely known to provide a diversity of activities and that draw people to them for differing degrees of contact, excitement, or enjoyment with the many other people similarly attracted. Boston's North End, Greenwich Village and the midtown areas of New York City, San Francisco's Fisherman's Wharf, or the Yorkville area of Toronto are among such places. Jacobs suggests that the density and diversity of such areas as well as the effective use of space are the basis for an active, interesting street life, and she criticizes much of current city planning for not taking these aspects of urban design into account (see Chapter Thirteen). Whyte calls for the creation of parks and plazas having an abundance of moveable seating placed in the areas of highest activity or where those using them can conveniently view interesting activities or objects. Widened sidewalks for greater pedestrian access and comfort, pleasant landscaping, and the availability of food vendors are some of the amenities advocated by Whyte as ways of enhancing the quality of those areas of highest pedestrian activity. Whyte's observations of such areas in midtown Manhattan over a four-year period showed an increase in the number of persons using open spaces and parks, more street entertainers, and more people eating outdoors or having impromptu street conferences. As his article concludes, "schmoozing, smootching, noshing, ogling are getting better all the time. The Central City is alive and well" (1974, p. 30). The value of such observations is that they also may help to explain why many city areas are perceived negatively as depersonalized, lonely, or potentially dangerous; they can be explained by the absence of characteristics or amenities such as those just described. Thus, there may be some lessons here for the design or redesign of many urban spaces in large metropolitan communities that are now perceived to lack such positive qualities.

Karp, Stone, and Yoels, upon whose work this section has drawn heavily, provide an apt conclusion for our brief discussion of the social organization of everyday urban life:

> The city can be a humane, personal place. If we agree upon the value of creating even more humane cities, we must understand the normative demands of public interaction. We must understand the limitations and poten-

Street musicians entertain passers-by during a lunch hour in New York City.

tialities of public city life. To do that, we must not casually take at face value the readily accessible and commonly expressed images of city life promoted by the mass media and frequently sustained by our most distinguished literary and philosophical figures. If our conceptualizations of the urban environment become too rigid (or too narrow), we severely restrict the range of possible experiences that urban residents may undergo (1977, p. 127).

THE SYMBOLISM AND IMAGERY OF URBAN LIFE

To develop a completely objective, value-free view of urban communities and urban life is probably impossible, for people's attitudes to them are strongly subjective. The modern city is an object of hatred for many people, but it is also a love object to many others. Still others may have more ambivalent, love-hate sentiments toward the city. The modern city may be perceived or valued in extremely wide variety of ways, including the following:

> As a feast—a place of novelty and excitement, of fashion and style, of ideas and artifacts, a center of sumptuous consumption, of diversity and delight. As a den of iniquity—a place where vice and crime abound, and political corruption rides high.

> As a fountainhead of service—a place where health and wealth, the arts and sciences, the educational and welfare services reach their highest levels. As a center of loneliness—a place where man is depersonalized, anonymous, alone, rootless, afraid, uniquely separated from his fellow men (Wilensky and Lebeaux, 1958, p. 116).

Gist and Fava (1974, p. 573) suggest that it is important to describe what is known of the sentiments and symbols attached to cities, if only to avoid possible attitudinal biases that may color research on urban life. Moreover, such imagery can have real consequences on policy decisions concerning the urban community. For example, if the city is seen as so evil, decayed, or anachronistic that it is beyond salvation, then it may be neglected or abandoned as an object of further investment or planned social intervention. On the other hand, if it is seen as totally satisfactory in its present form, then the perception very well might be that no further social intervention, other than perhaps the free play of "natural" market forces is necessary. According to this perspective, the city can easily deal with its own contingencies without help from external agencies (see Banfield, 1974; Greer, 1962; Downs, 1976; Caputo, 1976). Perceptions between these two extremes, which are the most reasonable from our point of view, are more likely to be that urban communities are worth preserving, but that in many cases they need massive intervention and social guidance if they are to remain workable and livable.

Many popular images of the city and attitudes toward urban life have been commonly expressed in the mass media, public opinion surveys, popular music, literature, and films. Our purpose here is briefly to summarize some of the main dimensions of these popular sentiments. Of course, social scientists have produced their own images of urban life, but these have been the major focus of other parts of this book.

Popular Music

The folklorist Botkin (1954) has found that American cities possess a folklore that has grown up around landmarks, streets, neighborhoods, expressed in the form of folk, jazz, or popular music. Much of it also expresses a positive attachment for urban sights and sounds, or a longing for a city or place left behind by a geographically mobile wanderer. The music of the late jazz composer and conductor Duke Ellington, for example, includes many compositions expressing positive affection for his adopted hometown of Harlem, as illustrated by such titles as "Drop Me Off in Harlem," "Harlem Upbeat," "Echoes of Harlem," "Harlem Speaks," "Heart of Harlem," "A Tone Parallel to Harlem," or "Harlem Airshaft" (Ellington, 1973).

The other side of the coin is expressed in the city blues, such as the St. Louis, Kansas City, Beale Street, or Memphis blues, which cry out of being down and out, lonely, or abandoned by a loved one in the "cold, impersonal" city. Popular songs such as "I Left My Heart in San Francisco," "Give My Regards to Broadway," "I'll Take Manhattan," "Moon Over Miami," "I Love Paris," or "Chicago, My Kind of Town," all express a sentimental desire to return to an urban scene associated with pleasant memories of one sort or another. Charosh (1968) more specifically refers to these types of songs as "home songs." It has also been suggested that much of the country and western music that has recently become popular, particularly in the cities of the South, Southwest, and the industrial North, attracts an audience of "urban hillbillies" for whom the themes of much contemporary country western music probably remind them of the problems they faced in their recent urban migration (Wilgus, 1971).

One thing that is interesting about popular, folk, or jazz music with an urban theme is that it invariably focuses on the city or on specific subareas of the city. But so far none of it deals with the larger types of metropolitan complexes discussed in Chapter Four. Evidently the larger metropolitan unit is too large, too new, too abstract, or too amorphous to have yet taken its place as an object of sentimental identification. We have yet to hear popular expressions of attachment to these larger units in song titles such as "I Left My Heart in the San Francisco Metropolitan Statistical Area," or "Give My Regards to the Bos-Wash Megalopolis."

The City in Popular Literature

The novel and contemporary feature films are two important sources of urban symbolism. In them the city may simply be a setting in which the plot unfolds, or it may be an important part of the story line itself. Early in the nineteenth century a body of literature already existed that depicted the American city as a backdrop for heartless commercialism, poverty, crime and evil, loneliness, and personal defeat. The works of Melville, Hawthorne, and Poe, for example, portray the city as a source of nightmares and other frightening personal experiences. Around the turn of the century, the burgeoning industrial cities of the Northeast and Midwest were viewed with distaste by popular authors such as Upton Sinclair, Frank Norris, and Theodore Dreiser. Prominent social critics such as Jane Addams and Joshua Strong wrote of the city in nonfictional terms with equal distaste (see Chapter Three).

In the 1930s and 1940s John Marquand's novels involving upper-class Bostonians (*The Late George Apley*) or transplants from rigidly stratified small towns to the more open social class structure of big cities (*Point of No Return, H. M. Pulham, Esq.*) provided a satirical view of the class structure of New England towns, large and small, while Meyer Levin's "The Old Bunch" and James T. Farrell's *Studs Lonigan* vividly portrayed peer group relations among the adolescents and young adults of Chicago's well-defined hyphenated American ethnic subcommunities. F. Scott Fitzgerald portrayed the naïveté of Midwesterners transplanted into the more cynical and worldly urban East (*The Great Gatsby*), and much of John O'Hara's work (*Appointment in Samarra, Rage to Live, Butterfield Eight, Ten North Frederick*) often contrasted Manhattan with his semifictional hometown of Gibbsville, Pennsylvania, from which financially able natives would occasionally escape to carry on nefarious activities in the anonymous big city.

In the 1950s, Saul Bellow's semiautobiographical *The Adventures of Augie March* evoked a vivid sense of Chicago as the environmental setting in which a young man comes of age. Mordecai Richter's *The Adventures of Duddy Kravits* used the city of Montreal in much the same way in his similarly titled novel. The city as Armageddon has been another theme of some novels, with Nathaniel West's *The Day of the Locust* a case in point. In this work, Los Angeles is the setting in which a set of unrelated circumstances eventually comes together in such a way as to produce senseless mass violence and self-destruction among hordes of people crowded in the streets at the premier of a Hollywood movie. Doris Lessing's *Memoirs of a Survivor* projects the ultimate collapse and destruction of the fabric of urban life in response to a breakdown in the ecological order upon which the survival of the city depends. Similar themes are repeated in countless popular science fiction works.

The City in Films

Many of these novels also have been re-created as motion pictures. The motion picture medium has been most effective in borrowing materials from short stories, novels, and the theater for plot materials, but it has created original material of its own as well. While not always attuned to the artistic intent of the authors of these sources, the film medium does have the added advantages of sight and sound. Films provide a more realistic and intense sense of the cityscapes and scenes in which the plot action takes place. Such settings are often created in a film studio, but more and more films are produced on location in the appropriate city or cities. One common film cliché is to begin by zooming in on the skyline of the film's city setting to create a more authentic sense of place of the story's locale. The skyscrapers of New York, the hills, bridges, and bays of San Francisco, and the streets of Los Angeles have probably been used most often for this effect in American films. But what is important is the idea that popular movies, whatever the sources of their plots, are a rich and diversified source of urban imagery. For many filmgoers, films shot on location in such cities as Los Angeles, New York, Chicago, San Francisco, Boston, Miami, Honolulu, Seattle, or Denver are their only direct contact with such places and may be one of the most important influences on their impressions of these places. Television tends to use these same locales for their urban-based serials or specials and thus may have a similar positive or negative impact on the viewer.

Public Opinion

The most common method of measuring the attitudes of the general public has been through national sample surveys, commonly referred to as public opinion polls. In recent years, several such polls have begun to survey Americans' attitudes to living in cities. For example, some of these polls have asked people to indicate the size or type of community in which ideally they would prefer to live. Two polls conducted in the early 1970s seem to suggest that a large majority of people would prefer to live in the country or small towns and suburbs rather than in large cities. One Gallup survey (1973) found only 13 percent of the respondents preferring city living to suburbs, small towns, or farms, while the U.S. Commission on Population Growth (1973) found only 14 percent choosing large cities over smaller cities, towns, or the countryside. These results point to a rather strong antiurban bias, even though a substantial majority continues to reside in urban areas. While most people indicated they were generally satisfied with the quality of life in the communities in which they lived, in another Gallup poll (1974) the residents of metropolitan communities of a million or more population were slightly less satisfied than the residents of places under 2,500 population: 83 percent of the residents in the smaller areas expressed satisfaction, compared to 71 percent in the larger areas. That many big city residents would prefer to live in smaller communities but do not choose to do so would seem to suggest that attitude surveys are not a reliable predictor of actual behavior. A more reasonable explanation, however, is that many people are reluctant urban dwellers who feel they have no real choice because of occupational ties to the metropolitan labor force or other economic circumstances that prevent their moving to less urbanized areas.

Some surveys have pinpointed dissatisfaction with particular aspects of urban living rather than total disillusionment. For example, Fischer (1976, p. 173) reports the results of several studies suggesting that distrust of other people tends to increase with community size. The same survey also showed that anxiety about crime increases with city size. Only 14 percent of rural respondents felt that it was unsafe to walk outside at night, while 57 percent of the respondents who resided in the center cities of large metropolitan areas felt that it was unsafe (Fischer, 1976, p. 95). Likewise, big city residents are more than twice as likely as rural residents to think it important to lock their doors when they leave home (Marans and Rodgers, 1975).

While the balance of public opinion tends to swing toward negative views of urban living, such views are not universally shared and a significant minority of Americans are prourban. Some studies (Mazie and Rawlings, 1972) suggest that those who are highly educated, employed in professional and white-collar occupations, young or elderly, childless couples, or interested in the cultural activities of the city tend to have positive attitudes toward city living and are more likely already to be living in urban environments. These are the cosmopolites discussed in an earlier section of this chapter. To the extent that current demographic trends point to an increase in the portion of the total population expected to have such social characteristics, it seems reasonable to speculate that an increase in cosmopolitan life styles among the population will eventually lead to more positive attitudes toward urban living among a wider portion of Americans than is now the case. Certainly some real or perceived improvements in the conditions of urban living that are now deemed unsatisfactory—such as a decrease in the crime rate—would probably serve to enhance this prospect. (See Chapter thirteen.)

SELECTED BIBLIOGRAPHY

BANFIELD, EDWARD C. *The Unheavenly City Revisited.* Boston: Little, Brown, 1974.

BECKER, HOWARD, and HOROWITZ, IRVING L. *Culture and Civility in San Francisco.* New Brunswick, N.J.: Transaction Books, 1972.

BOTKIN, B. A., ed. *Sidewalks of America.* New York: Bobbs-Merrill, 1954.

CAPUTO, DAVID A. *Urban America: The Policy Alternatives.* San Francisco: W. H. Freeman and Company Publishers, 1976.

CHAROSH, PAUL. "The Home Song." In Sylvia F. Fava, ed., *Urbanism in World Perspective.* New York: Thomas Y. Crowell, 1968.

DEMARETH, N. J. "Schizophrenia among Primitives." In Arnold Rose, ed., *Mental Health and Mental Disorder.* New York: W. W. Norton & Co., Inc., 1955.

DOUGLAS, JACK. *Understanding Every Day Life.* Chicago: Aldine, 1970.

DOWNS, ANTHONY. *Urban Problems and Prospects.* 2nd ed. Skokie, Ill.: Rand McNally, 1976.

EATON, J., and WEIL, R. *Culture and Mental Disorders.* New York: Free Press, 1955.

ELLINGTON, EDWARD K. *Music Is My Mistress.* Garden City, N.Y.: Doubleday, 1973.

FARIS, ROBERT, and DUNHAM, H. WARREN. *Mental Disorders in Urban Areas.* Chicago: University of Chicago Press, 1939.

FISCHER, CLAUDE S. *The Urban Experience.* New York: Harcourt Brace Jovanovich, 1976.

———. "A Research Note on Urbanism and Tolerance," *American Journal of Sociology* 76 (March 1971): 847–856.

GANS, HERBERT J. "Urbanism and Suburbanism as Ways of Life." In Sylvia F. Fava, ed., *Urbanism in World Perspective.* New York: Thomas Y. Crowell, 1968.

GIBBS, JACK P. "Rates of Mental Hospitalization," *American Sociological Review* 27 (1962).

GIST, NOEL P. and FAVA, SYLVIA. *Urban Society.* New York: Thomas Y. Crowell, 1979.

GOFFMAN, ERVING. *Behavior in Public Places.* New York: Free Press, 1963.

GOLDHAMER, HERBERT, and MARSHALL, ANDREW W. *Psychosis and Civilization.* New York: Free Press, 1962.

GREER, SCOTT. *The Emerging City.* New York: Free Press, 1962.

GURIN, G.; VERROFF, J.; and FELD, S. *Americans View their Mental Health.* Ann Arbor: University of Michigan Survey Research Center, 1960.

HALL, EDWARD T. *The Hidden Dimension.* Garden City, N.Y.: Doubleday, 1969.

HOLLINGSHEAD, AUGUST B., and REDLICH, FREDERICK. *Social Class and Mental Illness.* New York: John Wiley, 1958.

JACOBS, JANE. *The Death and Life of Great American Cities.* New York: Random House, 1961.

KARP, DAVID A. "Hiding in Pornographic Bookstores: A Reconsideration of the Nature of Urban Anonymity," *Urban Life and Culture* 4 (January 1973): 427–451.

KARP, DAVID A.; STONE, GREGORY P.; and YOELS, WILLIAM C. *Being Urban: A Social Psychological View of City Life.* Lexington, Mass.: Heath, 1977.

LEIGHTON, A. H., et al., eds. *Explorations in Social Psychiatry.* New York: Basic Books, 1957.

LEWIS, OSCAR. *Life in a Mexican Village: Tepoztlan Restudied,* Urbana: University of Illinois Press, 1951.

LIN, TSUNG-YI. "Effects of Urbanization on Mental Health," *International Social Science Journal* 11 (1959): 24–33.

LOFLAND, LYN. "Self Management in Public Settings: Part I." *Urban Life and Culture* 1 (April 1971): 93–117.

_____. *A World of Strangers.* New York: Basic Books, 1973.

MARANS, R. W., AND RODGERS, W. "Toward an Understanding of Community Satisfaction." In Amos Hawley and V. Rock, eds., *Metropolitan America in Contemporary Perspective.* New York: Halstead, 1975.

MAZIE, S. M., and RAWLINGS, S., eds. *Population, Distribution, and Policy.* Washington, D.C.: U.S. Government Printing Office, 1972.

PALEN, J. JOHN. *The Urban World.* New York: McGraw-Hill, 1975.

SIMMEL, GEORG. "The Metropolis and Mental Life." In Kurt H. Wolff, *The Sociology of Georg Simmel.* New York: Free Press, 1950.

Smithsonian Collection of Classic Jazz (from record guidebook). Washington, D.C.: Smithsonian Institution, 1973.

SROLE, LEO, et al. *Mental Health in the Metropolis.* rev. ed. New York: Harper & Row, Publishers, 1975.

STARR, JOYCE R., and CARNS, DONALD E. "Singles and the City: Notes on Urban Adaptation." In John Walton and Donald E. Carns, eds., *Cities in Change.* Boston: Allyn & Bacon, 1973.

WHYTE, WILLIAM H. "The Best Street Life in the World," *New York Magazine* 15 (July 1974): 26–33.

WILENSKY, HAROLD L., and LEBEAUX, CHARLES N. *Industrial Society and Social Welfare.* New York: Russell Sage, 1958.

WILGUS, D. K. "Country Western Music and the Urban Hillbilly." In A. Parades and E. J. Steckert, eds., *The Urban Experience and Folk Tradition.* Austin: University of Texas Press, 1971.

WIRTH, LOUIS. "Urbanism as a Way of Life," *American Journal of Sociology* 44 (July 1938: 1–24).

WOLFF, MICHAEL. "Notes on the Behavior of Pedestrians." In Arnold Birenbaum and Edward Sagarin, eds., *People in Places: The Sociology of the Familiar.* New York: Praeger, 1973.

PART III

URBAN
SOCIAL
INSTITUTIONS

chapter 7

the family
in the
urban world

BY DONALD M. LEVIN

The family may be the oldest and longest surviving of all human institutions. In preurban societies, the family held the dominant position in community life, if in fact it was not synonomous with the community itself. As urban civilization began to emerge, the earliest cities were the first human communities that were organized on a basis other than kinship. But the family remained firmly entrenched in the social traditions and authority structure of preindustrial urban societies for many centuries. Indeed, it was often thought of as a "sacred" institution, beyond question or criticism.

Although it took many forms in different societies, the family in preindustrial cities generally has been characterized as based on extended kinship or blood ties that, through lineage, link several generations and various networks of relatives under the same system of family controls and bonds, often under the same roof. The extended family conferred status and prestige, supplied individual members with occupational roles and identities, and arranged marriages at an early age for the youngest family members (Sjoberg, 1960).

Ever since the modern urban-industrial revolution, however, the family has been going through many important organizational and functional changes. The family is no longer the dominant social institution in the social order of the modern urban-industrial community, and it has lost many of its traditional functions to competing institutions. The nuclear or conjugal family, consisting of husband, wife, and their immediate off-spring, has largely displaced the extended family as the principal family unit, and even the nuclear family has been subjected to new stresses and demands. In fact, the very survival of the family as a key social unit is in doubt, according to some observers, and there have been many gloomy predictions of the inevitable decline and disintegration of the family as we know it. For example, recent projections by the Harvard-MIT Joint Center for Urban Studies anticipate that the so-called conventional nuclear family of mother, father, and young children living together will constitute just over 25 percent of all American households by the year 1990, and that by that time, there will be a substantial increase in single parent and other nontraditional households, including single men and women living alone or as unmarried couples (Christian Science Monitor, May 27, 1980).

In this chapter, we will examine the American family in its contempo-rary urban setting and speculate how the family, for better or worse, has adapted to some of the technological, economic, environmental, and social forces associated with the urban-industrial revolution of the past century or so. Some of the newer alternative or nontraditional family patterns that have emerged in recent decades in the metropolitan community will also briefly be discussed.

CONTRASTING TYPES OF FAMILY ORGANIZATION

In their studies of various types of societies, anthropologists have identified an immense variety of family forms and patterns of organization. We will discuss only two of the more important of these variations to provide a basis for understanding the urban family as it appears today. The smallest type of family organization is the *nuclear* family, consisting of a husband and a wife and one or more of their offspring. This is the basic form predominat-ing in American society and, as such, is also referred to as a *conjugal* family type. Here the stress is on marital ties, with the individual's primary duties directed to the immediate family. In contrast, the *extended* or *consanguine* family stresses kinship or blood ties (those of parents, children, brothers, and sisters), and several generations live together, observing traditional roles. In the consanguine family, individualism is discouraged—the family as an entity is far more important than any single person. According to Stewart and Glynn, this type of family is "well adapted to an agricultural society where tradition is strong and change is slow and where all members must work together to survive. . . . It gives a sense of belonging and secu-rity although the individual must subordinate his desires to the good of the family group" (Stewart and Glynn, 1971, p. 181). In an agricultural society, the consanguine family works together as an economic unit. Social mobility for the individual does not exist, as a person's status in the community is clearly fixed by the family into which he or she is born.

With industrialization, a different type of family format is needed—a format in which mobility and individualism are required and encouraged. Hence, the nuclear family, lean and small in size, more mobile and adaptable to change, is particularly suited to an urban environment where economic subsistence depends on the larger society outside of the family. The nuclear family is physically free to go where jobs are available and the head of the family is not tied to the status ascribed by the extended family. At the present time the majority of the people in the world do not belong to nuclear families, but several writers have noted that the worldwide trend in this direction is unmistakable. From his analysis of family patterns in diverse societies in the twentieth century, Goode concluded that "the alteration appears to be in the direction of some type of conjugal family pattern—that is, toward fewer kinship ties with distant relatives and a greater emphasis on the nuclear family unit of couple and children" (Goode, 1963, p. 1). In summarizing the general changes that accompany this movement, Leslie includes the following: 1) free choice of spouse; 2) more equal status for women; 3) equal rights of divorce; 4) neolocal residence (couple living independent of their extended kin group); 5) bilateral kin (tracing descent through both the male and female lines); and 6) the equality of individuals against class or caste barriers (Leslie, 1973, p. 67).

The factors prompting this movement can be explained not only in

Members of today's nuclear family have more responsibilities due to modern day stresses. (P. Greenwood/United Nations)

terms of urbanization and industrialization, but also must be seen in terms of ideological beliefs—egalitarianism, democracy, progress, and survival. The underdeveloped regions of the world have little choice. As populations expand, a subsistence agricultural economy must give way to a more efficient arrangement where industrialization is sought as the means of increasing productivity and wealth. With the rapid diffusion of knowledge, the peoples of these regions are no longer satisfied with the status quo. Social change is actively sought, using as models the industrialized societies of the West. To accommodate this change the traditional consanguine family has lost its relevance and a new pattern is sought.

CHANGING FUNCTIONS OF THE FAMILY

As the extended family gave way to the more adaptable nuclear family other changes also followed in the transition from an agricultural-rural to an industrial-urban society. Many of these changes, such as the increasing divorce rate, the new alternatives for sexual expression both within and outside of marriage, the diffusion of traditional sex roles, or the growing emphasis on hedonistic endeavors are often cited as evidence of the family's disorganization and decay. These patterns could also be viewed equally well as responses to changes that have occurred in other areas of the social structure. The social system is a complex, integrated network of roles and norms that operate in a symbiotic relationship with one another. To understand any single institution, such as the family, we must see how that institution interacts with the other parts of the social network.

Without getting into an elaborate analysis of how this change has actually evolved over the past two hundred years or so, let us summarize some of the basic alterations that have occurred in those societies, such as the United States, that have become highly urbanized. The urban family, unlike its traditional predecessor, is more limited in the basic societal tasks it is willing or able to assume. While many of the older family functions still exist, their scope and relative importance have changed. For example, procreation and childbearing are still largely organized within the family nexus but the emphasis today is on fewer children, planned parenthood, and siblings closer together in age. In addition, radical changes in sex roles, the legitimacy of the wife and mother career concept, and the growth of day care centers have either affected or been affected by these other changes.

Writers in the family field pay a good deal of attention to the changing function of the American family. Perhaps the most obvious of these changes has occurred in the area of economics. The contemporary family, for the most part, is no longer a self-sufficient economic and production unit even though it has increased in importance as a consuming unit. One set of authors, in describing this change, suggests that the old way probably contributed to greater stability: "The family no longer earns its living together—a strongly integrative function—but is more inclined to compete in the spending of the income, a somewhat divisive function" (Stewart and Glynn, 1971, p. 186). In addition to moving the work place and occupational roles outside of the home, the urban family has also shifted other functions to more specialized secondary agencies. No longer primarily responsible for educational and religious matters, the family has become more broadly a cultural entity. Recreation, protection, and care of the aged, while still remaining to some degree family functions, have also been replaced by other social groups.

At one time a popular theme in the literature was to use the loss of function analysis in support of the argument that the family is disintegrating as a viable social institution. William F. Ogburn (1955), one of the early writers on this topic, perceived that industrialization and urbanization had changed the family from a relatively self-sufficient institution to one whose main function was the distribution of affection and the formation of personality. Pitrim Sorokin (1937, p. iv), in an even more pessimistic appraisal of the future, predicted that the family was moving toward a point where it would become "a mere incidental cohabitation of male and female," while the home becomes "a mere overnight parking place mainly for sex relationships." Using historical analysis, Carle C. Zimmerman (1947) saw the family as moving along and changing according to the nature of the larger society which it served. This change involved the transition from "the trustee family" (individualism subordinated to the welfare of the family group) to "the domestic family" (an intermediate type in which familism and individualism are in balance) to "the atomistic family" (familism is replaced by individualism). When the last stage occurs, individualism gives way to societal decay and the process begins again with the reemergence of the trustee family. In effect, Zimmerman is arguing for a return to the moral values and norms of the traditional family if society would escape the inevitable decay that comes with rampant individualism.

Most scholars have questioned the conclusions of these writers. Instead of arguing that family change was symptomatic of moral decay and eventual disintegration, the prevailing attitude seems to be that the family is adapting and modifying itself to the changing society of which it is part. Looking at the total social structure, not just the family, these scholars point out that many human relationships are structured to meet human needs; the family is but a part of the total system.

THE CHANGING AMERICAN FAMILY

Leslie (1973, pp. 210–214) identifies three major forces that have been influential in molding the character of the American family: the frontier; large-scale immigration and urbanization; and industrialization. The frontier was important because it provided an outlet for a socially mobile society whose people were seeking new opportunities. The presence of this outlet for opportunity encouraged young people to leave their family households; consequently, the frontier is credited with breaking up family units and increasing the isolation of the nuclear family. Furthermore, the resultant family breakups tended to lessen patriarchal control as the young pioneers were freed from extended family patterns of authority. Women were given more equal status on the frontier, at least in a de facto way, because the isolation and rigors of life required the diffusion of work roles on the basis of need rather than on tradition.

As the country prospered, large-scale immigration provided the masses who were to inhabit the expanding cites of the nineteenth century. These new immigrants brought their own family traditions and norms with them and somewhat resisted assimilation into the mainstream of American life. With increased economic opportunity and the lessening of ethnocentric barriers, intermarriage, first along nationality lines and then along religious lines, began to increase. Today, the American pattern of family life is somewhat of a mosaic, still maintaining distinct ethnic and cultural variations and, when cross-cultural intermarriage has occurred, presenting an amalgamation of different cultural strains and unique historical experiences. Immigration has thus contributed to the heterogeneity of American life in general and family life in particular, making it difficult to broadly generalize about the American family without recognizing the existence of these cultural variations.

Among the many consequences that urbanization and industrialization have produced, Leslie (1973, pp. 213–214) identifies the following:

> ... the prospect of factory employment freed young adults and unmarried men and women from direct dependence upon their families. As their wages made them financially independent, the authority of the head of the household weakened further. Urbanization also brought the development of such specialized commercial establishments as hotels and rooming houses, restaurants, bakeries, grocery stores and laundries, making it possible for many persons to live apart from families altogether. This situation had special significance for women who no longer had to marry in order to have a place to live and who no longer had to stay married simply because there was no alternative. The divorce rate began to rise.
>
> Finally, children ceased to be economic assets and became liabilities instead. Although there was a period of the use and abuse of child labor, legal regulations gradually removed children from the job market. At the same time, formal educational requirements were increasing, lengthening the period of dependence upon parental support. Living space in the cities was crowded and expensive; child-care was demanding. The birth rate began to fall.

As we discuss the consequences of urbanization we should mention that we are talking not only about a process but also about a phenomenon that has had impact on those not directly involved with the process itself. Depending on the criteria used, it is safe to say that the United States population is at least 75 percent urban and, accordingly, when we speak about the American family we are speaking about an urban model that represents the dominant experience of the majority of Americans. However, even for those people not associated as urban inhabitants in a demographic sense, the process of urbanization has had an impact on their total life experiences, including family organization and interaction. Gist and Fava (1974, p. 483) describe the reciprocal nature of this process:

> The concept of urbanization has a dual meaning. In one aspect, it is demographic, referring to the increasing proportion of population in a country or region who reside in cities. In another aspect, it has reference to the process whereby people are influenced by the values, behavior, institutions, and material things that are identified as urban in origin and use. It is well to keep this dual meaning in mind; yet the two meanings are invariably related. As a country or region becomes more urbanized in the demographic or ecological sense, the people, rural and urban alike, are increasingly influenced by the process.

In the next section we will look at some examples of how this process has affected American families.

FAMILY ORGANIZATION AND INTERACTION

Societal Values and Family Interaction

The advent of an industrial-urban society in America has brought with it the lessening influence of religion institutions and values on behavior and the resultant drift toward secularism. In this new society, rationalized and scientific norms have tended to replace traditional responses and modes of interaction. Role behavior, which was fixed and predictable, now becomes segmented and flexible. Individuals are given much greater freedom to direct their own behavior according to values that tend to focus on materialistic and worldly concerns. The sacred society provided a basis of cohesion in which consensus was the ultimate product of the socialization system. Consensus is not easily achieved in the urban society, where the cultural heterogeneity of the group more often favors a form of symbiosis as the basis for providing whatever group cohesion does exist.

Accompanying these basic changes we also see a gradual reliance on secondary group associations as opposed to primary associations. These secondary relationships, which often involve fragmented roles, become the basis of much social interaction. Group memberships multiply as people are free to seek new associations, thereby finding support for behavior that would be unacceptable within the restraining environment of the primary group. In addition, the various social institutions become less integrated with one another with the result that social behavior seen within the family or government, for example, tends to operate with greater autonomy and independence from the external restraints at work in traditional society. Unlike the older society, the new society is highly accepting of change—in fact, actively seeks change, is innovative, dynamic, and oriented to the future.

Needless to say, these changes have had a tremendous impact on the family as an institution and how the members of this institution interact with each other. Individualism, for example, has become an important value for the American family. This value, which is a direct reflection of the values of the total society, is closely integrated with the economic system that promises mobility and success for those who are free to seek opportunity where it exists.

Closely related to individualism is the belief that marriage and family life should produce happiness for the family members. This complex of values generally includes material comfort, fun, hedonism, self-indulgence, and security. Unlike earlier beliefs, which viewed marriage as a religious commitment or as an economic obligation, marriage and family life that are centered upon the production of happiness tend to be less stable and permanent, since the very definition of happiness is an elusive and highly changeable concept. Implied in this definition of marriage is the assumption that marriages that do not produce happiness are perhaps not worth saving. An outgrowth of this assumption, at least in America, is the provision of easier procedures for obtaining divorce so that the individuals who have not found happiness may be free to continue the pursuit.

In a classic article, John Sirjamaki (1948) describes additional values and normative beliefs that have influenced family functioning. These include the belief that marriage should be based upon love and free choice, that life has most to offer the young, and that childhood should be protected and prolonged. Other writers talk about companionship or togetherness as family values, describing the belief that marriage partners should not only see themselves as economic collaborators or child-rearers but also as friends, confidantes, and individuals who find fulfillment and growth by sharing experiences together. Many of these values and beliefs actually are contradictory and, instead of producing family solidarity and stability, have contributed to much confusion, dissatisfaction, and conflict as individuals have attempted to adjust their personal needs to a rapidly changing social system.

Courtship and Mate Selection

Mate selection in the traditional family was rarely a matter of choice. Marriages were either arranged in terms of socioeconomic realities or came about through a rather restricted courtship process in which the field of eligible marital partners was limited by the isolated nature of rural life and by strict moral codes and normative expectations. The traditional family, supported by the extended kin groups, could be counted on to enforce first acceptance of the chosen mates, and then, to a certain degree, harmony within the home. Industrialism and urbanization brought a change to all of this. As the city develops and prospers, young people, motivated by the larger cultural values of progress, mobility, and success, leave their homes and families to take advantage of the opportunities available to them in urban communities. No longer restricted by traditional values and norms, new patterns of mate selection emerge and new social and economic influences prevail that contribute to the ultimate decision as to who marries whom.

With a few isolated exceptions, dating has replaced all other institutions for mate selection in urban society. This phenomenon, which began in earnest in the United States after the first World War, became the process by which the individual is exposed to a field of eligible marital partners from which a choice is ultimately made—a choice allowing the individual ideally to meet his or her emotional, psychological, status, and sexual needs. Discussing the factors that contributed to this twentieth-century social process, Kephart (1966, p. 290) writes:

> Migration from farm to city, large-scale employment of girls and women, coeducation, the rise of commercialized amusements and recreation, increases in leisure time, the phenomenal spread of the automobile, the popularization of vacation spots—all of these factors tended to facilitate the association and intermingling of young people. And within a few generations the courtship process had changed from a brief period of rather formal association with a very few individuals of the opposite sex, to a prolonged period of informal association with scores of partners, under conditions in which the only restrictions were those which were self-imposed. As these conditions came to prevail, and as the "love bug"—aided by Hollywood—began to bite with increasing frequency and severity, the modern American game of dating was born.

One must not believe, however, that urbanization has democratized the mate selection process by creating an open, egalitarian system of dating. The choice of a mate in the urban setting, while much less restrictive than was the case in the traditional society, is still not a random process where any single individual has equal access to any other single individual as a prospective spouse. Sociologists have long recognized the importance of propinquity as a dominating factor in mate selection. Since propinquity with regard to residence or work location is closely related to socioeconomic status and has implications for associations, it follows that young people are brought into contact mainly with those from similar class, racial, and religious backgrounds. While this type of restrictive interaction was more operative several years ago when ethnic neighborhoods and the institutions that served these neighborhoods tended to be more cohesive than today, the argument that propinquity creates the social conditions that direct people to marry endogamously is still valid.

The American school, particularly the public coeducational high school, has become one of the prime agencies for meeting potential spouses. For those who have not found a marriage partner during their high school or college years, the opportunities for heterosexual contacts have to be more deliberately sought out, since the occupational setting frequently fails to provide an abundant source of such contacts. Even in a job situation where an almost equal number of each sex is employed, few unmarried individuals may be available. New modes of meeting people develop which more or less replace the more traditional avenues available during the adolescent and young adult years. This is especially true for the middle-class, well-educated young people whose affluence provides them with the mobility to take advantage of these new outlets. Starr and Carns

High schools provide opportunities for establishing strong friendships and meeting potential spouses. (Freda Leinwand/ Monkmeyer)

(1973, p. 155) comment that "never before has the city seemed so organized in its readiness to accommodate the young. Most cities appear to have an abundance of singles bars; some have co-ed singles apartment houses. Ads for singles weekends and excursions pad out the travel sections of big city newspapers.... All this would seem to suggest an unprecedented institutionalization of this new life style in cities." At any rate, the number of single young people under thirty is expected to reach the highest level of this century by 1990 (Christian Science Monitor, May 27, 1980).

The Marriage Relationship

To generalize about the marriage relationship that exists within the contemporary American urban family is a most difficult undertaking since many subcultural variations must be taken into account. If one compares the role expectations that ultimately affect the nature of the marital relationship on any axis of variation, such as ethnic or class affiliation, it is apparent that they are defined differently, and their complementary structure varies according to the particular mode of family organization characteristic of that class or ethnic group. Marriage in contemporary urban society has emerged as a social system separate from that of the family and, as one writer describes it, "reflects a key aspect of the American value system, namely, the freedom and the rights of the person over ascribed institutional ties that would compromise his freedom of choice" (Martinson, 1970, p. 301).

The differentiation process that has led to the recognition that marriage and the family represent different social systems is a product of the changes brought about through industrialization and urbanization. Since the family no longer rests on ties to property, to location, to land, or to extended family, the stability of the family, its success or failure, depends on the compatibility of husband and wife. The mass urban society has transferred many of its basic functions from the family to other institutions where these functions are met within large-scale secondary group associations. The result for the individual is a greater sense of alienation, anonymity, fragmented and impersonal role relationships, and a lack of intimacy between people. As the individual's various social relationships in this type of milieu become more transitory, the relationship between husband and wife takes on added significance. According to Schneider (1969, p. 483):

> It is the ability of the husband and wife to adjust to each other, to compromise their difficulties, which is crucial in our family system. Since so much hinges on the conjugal relationship, mates must be chosen in terms of personal preference; e.g., in terms of romantic attraction, sexual compatibility, and personality affinity. Even if there were no reasons of an ideological nature, it is doubtful whether a system of arranged marriages could work in our society.

The demands and expectations thus placed on middle-class marriages in America have created conditions that tend to make the marriage relationship more tenuous and volatile than was true during an earlier period. Now that marriage is more a matter of emotional rather than economic necessity, marriages not marked by a high degree of intimacy and emotional commitment are frequently regarded as failures.

In addition to the emotional needs placed on the marital relationship, another characteristic of contemporary marriage, frequently discussed in the literature, pertains to the diffusion of roles expected by the participants in the relationship. The highly individualistic, technologically advanced culture of modern urban America has created a climate where husbands are no longer the undisputed masters and neither men nor women are always sure of what is expected of them or what they expect of their spouses in the marriage. Though women largely have gained equality with men, at least in middle-class families, the nature of the equality remains vague and undefined. To some the equality follows the traditional division of labor model where the man is the economic provider and the wife assumes the child-caring and housekeeping role. To others it means that the division of labor should be accommodated according to the temperaments and needs of the spouses. Husbands and wives do not always agree what the roles should be, with the result that a good deal of confusion, conflict, and dissatisfaction may result. Given the pluralistic nature of urban society and the freedom of the individual to be exposed to varied subcultural influences, people are continually coming into contact with new interpretations of what marriage should be and what obligations, if any, the participants have toward each other. Nurtured in a climate of individualism, egalitarianism, and personal fulfillment and given viability in a social system that has opened educational opportunity for all and where economic restrictions against the working woman have been greatly reduced, these new interpretations have altered the nature of the marriage relationship and have made it less stable and predictable than in traditional society.

Child rearing in America has gone through several stages as the country matured from an isolated rural society to a highly industrialized, urban nation. Prior to the Civil War, children were treated rather formally and were expected to defer in all matters to the commands of their parents. As important contributors to the economic productivity of the family they were also expected to be industrious, with little time given to frivolity or formal education. With the development of the factory system and the rapid growth of cities in the second half of the nineteenth century, the locus of work for more and more families shifted away from the home. Children were in great demand as laborers and it was not considered unreasonable to require them to work a twelve- to fourteen-hour day. By 1900, which was the peak year in the employment of children, about one in four boys between ten and fifteen was working, and about one in ten of the girls (Schneider, 1969, p. 499). According to Kenkel (1966), children during this era were socialized to develop such traits as self-control, self-denial, self-sufficiency, a strong desire to get ahead, and a willingness to take risks. They were thus being prepared to live in a competitive society where survival depended on one's ability to work within the system.

Today the picture has radically changed. Child labor laws, mandatory school attendance, technological advances, increased wealth, and the emergence of scientific child-rearing theories are only some of the factors that have altered the status of children and have affected attitudes as to how they should be socialized for adult roles. The task of being a parent in urban America is a complex and often ambiguous undertaking for many, frequently causing confusion and discouragement. Unlike traditional society, where roles and expectations between parents and their children tended to be specific and unquestioned, today's urban parents, particularly in middle-class families, are faced with some of the questions that LeMasters (1974, p. 53) raises in his role analysis of parenthood: When should children be punished? What is meant by "harsh" child-rearing methods? Should fathers try to assume more authority with their children or less? Is it true that modern parents are largely responsible for the increase in juvenile delinquency in the United States? Is it true that mothers who work outside of the home are virtually sentencing their children to delinquency or mental illness or both? Is the American mother as bad as the best sellers say she is? Do parents ever have the right to be different whether society or the child's peer group likes it or not?

Much of this ambiguity can be attributed to the "child experts" who gained prominence in the United States after World War I. The behavioral sciences (psychiatry, sociology, anthropology, and psychology) gained increased attention and respectability as the practitioners from these fields became "worshipped as the high priests of child rearing" (Pohlman, 1969, p. 102). Americans came to depend more and more on the advice of scientific experts as to how to raise children. The problem is that this advice has changed rather dramatically over relatively short periods of time, leaving many in a state of bewilderment over which patterns of behavior would be most desirable. In a review of child-rearing research, Brofenbrenner (1958) reveals that during the first half of the twentieth century middle-class parents tended to be more strict with their children than working or lower-class parents, but by the fifties they had crossed over and become more permissive. Schulz (1972, p. 262) believes that the trend toward permissiveness by middle-class parents now appears to be abating in favor of sterner discipline, but no hard research is available to prove this one way or the other. Skolnick (1973, p. 303) concludes that "ironically, attention to the experts among middle-class people seems to raise anxiety rather than reduce it. Research on middle-class mothers ... suggests that the more awareness a mother has of the child-rearing literature, the more uncertain she feels that she is doing the right thing."

In addition to the ambiguity of the parental role, LeMasters (1974, pp. 174–177) discusses additional examples of the impact urbanization has had on American parents. The pluralistic nature of the city has meant that parents and their children have had to function in close proximity with others of diverse racial, religious, and ethnic backgrounds. The child thus becomes exposed to all sorts of "competing models" and may question why his or her own parents think and behave as they do and, in so doing, may undermine the authority held by the parents. The increased leisure of urban youth also creates problems in that large amounts of "spare time" have to be accommodated and may conflict with the work schedules both of fathers and employed mothers. The urban school calendar with its long summer vacations is a carry-over from a rural society and has never really been adapted to the realities of urban life.

Increased leisure time and close physical proximity in the city have also helped to contribute to the development of a more powerful youth peer group than existed in a rural society where most of the time of young people was absorbed by work on the farm. The associations formed within these groups often becomes translated into new norms of behavior and loyalties that challenge the power and influence of parents and produce conflicts that have come to be described by the term "the generation gap." In assessing the power of the youth peer group, David Riesman (1950, p. 82) writes: "There has been an enormous ideological shift favoring submission to the groups.... The peer group becomes the measure of all things; the individual has few defenses the group cannot batter down."

Other examples of urban impact cited by LeMasters (1974, pp. 174–177) are: 1) the impersonality and anonymity of the city—a condition that limits the parents' ability to be knowledgeable about the child's interactions; 2) the pervasive nature of urban mass media frequently portraying values that may not be in harmony with the values the parents would like their children to adopt; and 3) the urban ghetto which, in the case of the less affluent minority-group parents, imposes the overwhelming problems of having to raise children in a society where schools and other public services are not maintained at desirable levels and where housing is almost universally substandard.

In all fairness, however, the urban community offers many advantages for child rearing compared to rural areas. For the affluent and those adaptable to the urban way of life, the city provides a variety of educational opportunities geared to a diverse clientele, including the handicapped and others with special learning problems. It also has available a better system of social welfare services, better medical and public health facilities, and offers a climate more tolerant of racial and religious minorities, with a greater chance for vertical social mobility. In discussing some of these positive aspects of urban life, LeMasters (1974, p. 177) notes:

> It is an interesting fact that the minority group that has achieved the highest socioeconomic position in the United States—the Jews—is almost entirely metropolitan in residence. And contrary to what millions of Americans think, the majority of these Jewish families entered the socioeconomic system at the bottom. It was the utilization of urban services, such as the urban university, that enabled them to attain a comfortable position in our society.

Family and Occupational Roles

As previously discussed, work roles and family roles in traditional nonurban societies are not sharply delineated from each other. In urban societies, the situation is just the opposite—the actual performance of the work role may be quite distinct from the family role and, indeed, these two roles may, at times, be in conflict with each other. In most American families the occupational role of the father becomes the dominant element in his life and has important consequences for the other members of the family as well as for himself. Not only is the male socialized in early life to anticipate that his adult life will be organized around work, but women also are indoctrinated to place strong emphasis on the importance of the male work role. For example, Benson (1968, p. 271) reports a study conducted with women in which two-thirds of them considered the bread-winner role to be the man's most important function, with husbanding and child rearing coming in a poor second and third.

The income provided by the husband through his occupation is obviously of crucial importance to the family in determining its stability and standard of living. When income is low or sporadic, the husband's authority and influence in the family is seriously challenged and the wife has less vested interest to keep the marriage intact. In her study on the correlates of dissatisfaction in marriage, Rennie (1970, p. 61) found that income was more closely related to marital dissatisfaction than was either education or occupation, "probably because it has an independent and very concrete impact on the couple's daily life. Other aspects of social status count for relatively little if the family's income is not adequate to its needs."

Among the lower socioeconomic groups in urban society, we see vivid proof of the effect that inadequate income has upon family life. The urban poor who compose these groups consist mainly of displaced rural migrants or the children of such migrants who originally came to the city because they or the relatives who preceded them hoped they could find work and the opportunity for a better life. Even if they cannot find work they remain, living on welfare and the help of kinfolk. While some choose to return to rural areas, most stay on because the alternatives in rural America offer them even less. Their plight is described by one writer who says: "Whether in the rural area or in the city, they have few usable skills; they are willing to work but our society no longer needs their labor. They are surplus people in the countryside; they are surplus people in the city, and they live on surplus food" (Fullerton, 1972, p. 192).

Oscar Lewis (1965) has described these people as living in the "culture of poverty" where, under the conditions of the modern urban world, they have developed a set of patterns and attitudes that are functionally useful for survival. Unlike the masses of the poor throughout the world who live in stable societies with tribal or peasant cultures that are integrated and self-supporting, the urban poor represent an anomaly surrounded by affluence. According to Lewis (1965, p. xliv), "The culture of poverty is both an adaptation and a reaction of the poor to their marginal position in a class-stratified, highly individuated, capitalistic society. It represents an effort to cope with feelings of hopelessness and despair which develop from the realization of the improbability of achieving success in terms of the values and goals of the larger society."

These are people who do not feel that they have control over their own destiny and therefore are not oriented to the deferred gratification pattern characteristic of middle-class groups. Horton and Leslie (1974, p. 366) describe the impact that this culture has for family relationships:

> A strong sense of marital and filial duty is unlikely to arise among men who see little realistic prospect that they will ever be able to support a family decently, no matter how monumental their efforts. Where men are at best undependable providers, a woman may weaken her control over her household if she marries the man she is living with, and thus lose her ability to throw him out if he mistreats her. Consequently, there are many casual and temporary unions, with the woman as the central figure in the family and the "husbands" only marginally involved. Divorce, nonsupport, desertion, sexual promiscuity, and illegitimacy are common, are not strongly disapproved, and are functionally useful in meeting needs of the people involved.

While this evaluation may be somewhat simplistic and too highly generalized, it is meant to convey the idea that the life style of the poor in family and other associations is frequently a rational and functionally necessary product of their economic status. This condition is true of other social classes as well. Aldous (1969, p. 712) has found in her research that the companionship family is most frequently found in the lower middle class, where men are frequently employed in dull, repetitive, and unrewarding jobs. These men, "far from seeking to carry over job-related behaviors to the family often look to their homes as havens from job monotonies and as sources of the satisfactions lacking in the occupational sphere."

What is implied in the above research and many other studies that have attempted to explore the relationship that exists between occupations and family living is that occupation is a strong determinant of class and status position and these positions, in turn, become subcultures carrying with them habits, values, perceptions, attitudes, and behavior. That a family belongs to a particular class or status group may influence many structural and functional features of that family, such as the number of children, the role of the father, the position of the mother, the role of the aged, or the vulnerability of the family to crisis. A man's occupation is thus more than just income. It has an impact on the prestige enjoyed by the family members in the community and is an important determiner of the family's life style—where they will live, with whom they will associate, educational experiences provided for the children, what they will do for recreation, and many other items of a similar nature. Furthermore, occupation determines the amount of time which the job-holder will spend in the home and can create tensions and strains that may be transferred to family life in many subtle and not so subtle ways. It is not possible within the scope of this chapter to review the many studies that have been done illustrating the relationships between occupation and family life but, suffice it to say, these studies show that occupational impact is experienced at every level of the social stratum.

Married Women Who Work

No discussion about family occupational roles would be complete without considering the growing participation of married women, with or without dependent children, in the labor force. More than one-half of all married women with dependent children now have paid jobs outside the home, and the portion is expected to continue growing. In 1960, the percentage of husband-wife households with only one partner gainfully employed outside the home was 43 percent of the total of such households. According to a Harvard-MIT Center for Urban Studies projection, only 14 percent of all husband-wife households will have less than two breadwinners by the year 1990 (Christian Science Monitor, May 27, 1980). Married women not only are participating in the labor force in greater numbers, but the trend is also toward a greater number working at full-time rather than part-time jobs than ever before. In 1980, about 25 percent of family income was contributed by working wives (the figure is this low mainly because of women's participation in lower-paying or part-time jobs). But even though women have traditionally earned only about 60 percent of what men earn, working wives' contributions to family income are expected to rise to about 40 percent of family income by 1990 (Christian Science Monitor, May 27, 1980). Part of this gain potentially will come about through expected greater equality of earnings, but it will also be due to the greater proportion of married women working full-time.

This continuing trend can be accounted for in several ways. The rapid expansion of the economy after World War II combined with the low birth rates in the fifteen-year period prior to that period produced a severe labor shortage, opening a great number of positions to women. In addition, improved technological, marketing, and medical advances have changed the nature of household tasks, freeing women for work outside of the home. Control over fertility has also been an important enabling and

Most married women with dependent children are now part of today's labor force. (Irene Springer)

motivating factor. As these social changes were taking place, society also saw the development of new sex role definitions as women were achieving higher levels of education and competence in fields that were once foreign to them. With the changing social climate and the stimulus provided by the women's movement came a new sense of awareness and greater demand for economic equality by both men and women. Women were now given greater freedom than ever before to seek creative and achievement goals independent of their traditional homemaking role. This freedom came not only because of men's greater acceptance for these new roles but because women themselves were experiencing fewer inner conflicts and emotional restraints about seeking employment outside of the home. Of course, the desire for improvements in family standards of living in a period of rising prices should not be overlooked as another important incentive for married women seeking full-time paid work.

Much research has been done and a good deal more is currently underway to measure the effect that working wives and mothers have had on family life. In an attempt to summarize some of these studies, Nye and Berardo (1973, pp. 291–293) have come up with the following generalizations: 1) there are no large differences between children of employed and unemployed mothers; 2) employed mothers tend to exercise more power in family decisions; 3) there tends to be more conflict between spouses in families in which the wife is a provider; 4) the health of employed women tends to be better than that of those not employed; 5) mothers who are providers are more likely to experience guilt feelings concerning their roles as mothers; 6) younger women tend to like the provider role better than older women; 7) holding age constant, the fewer household duties the woman must perform personally, the more likely she is to occupy a provider role; and 8) the more marketable her skills the more likely the wife will be employed.

Given the current social climate and increased economic demand together with the perennial desire for "the good life," it seems safe to predict that an increasing proportion of married women will be seeking employment. Urban communities have already adapted to this trend and will continue to do so by providing more day-care centers, after-school recreation and supervision services, and other facilities and services designed to assist the married woman to accommodate the dual roles of mother and provider. There are those who predict dire consequences for the institutions of marriage and the family if this trend continues, but as of now the harmful consequences anticipated have not been substantiated.

Alternative Family Patterns

As urban society expands and intensifies, the pattern of family life that is characteristic of this environment will be forced to adapt itself accordingly. What now exists and will probably continue to proliferate is not one single family pattern but many, each reflecting the heterogeneity and pluralism that are the dominant characteristics of urban life. Family living has now become an arena of experimentation and innovation, unfettered by many of the traditions of the past. Among some of the more commonly identified alternative family patterns are the following:

A. Living Together.   This trend has accompanied decreasing marriage rates and increasing divorce rates. Households consisting of unmarried couples are now commonplace enough to be taken for granted. In 1976, approximately 1,320,000 unmarried couples were reported to be living in two-person households. This is twice as many such unmarried couples living together as just six years earlier (U.S. Census, February 8, 1977).

B. Open Marriage.   This pattern involves far more individual flexibility than the traditional marriage and allows marriage partners greater freedom for pursuing individual interests, friendships, and even extramarital sexual relationships outside of the marriage itself. Strong advocates of this pattern argue that flexible marriages are more realistic than traditional closed marriages in that they do not demand that the partners fill all of each other's emotional, psychological, intellectual, and physical needs. However, others question whether open marriages are less stressful or problem free than traditional marriages. Palen (1979), for example, mentions jealousy and feelings of hurt and bitterness as obvious difficulties of such marriages.

C. Group Marriage. This is an arrangement in which two or more men are married to two or more women. While such group marriages may have received much attention in popular gossip and in the mass media, such unions are probably quite unstable and extremely rare (Melville, 1980). Little research has been done on the subject, but one such study was able to identify only 101 group marriages in the United States, one-third of which were no longer in existence by the time the researchers were able to complete their interviews of the participants (Constantine and Constantine, 1973).

D. Swinging. This is a variation of group marriage and involves married couples engaging in group sex with a larger, almost random number of partners who party together in orgylike fashion. The actual amount of swinging is not known, but it is probably much less common than popular stereotypes or middle-class fantasies would suggest (Palen, 1979).

Palen (1979) correctly concludes that while all of the alternative marriage patterns have received popular attention way out of proportion to their actual incidence, family structures on the whole are more open and flexible today than they have been in the past. He further concludes that family relationships are in some ways "less tied to social or economic pressure than they used to be, and a greater variety of life-styles is tolerated, allowing for greater individual freedom and development."

THE URBAN FAMILY—FUTURE PROSPECTS

Alterations in social structure will always be difficult to predict, but nevertheless certain trends seem well established and, unless reversed by unforeseen circumstances, will probably continue to shape the structure and relationships of the urban family.

Nye and Berardo (1973, pp. 633–641) describe some of these trends and offer the following predictions based on what they see: 1) as the economic expansion of the United States continues family affluence will continue to rise with accompanying positive effects on family relationships; 2) the number of employed wives entering the labor force will continue to increase; 3) child-care services will be more readily available, especially for low-income families; 4) the marriage rate and the number of new families formed will increase; 5) the trend toward increasing divorce and remarriage rates will continue—more and more marriages in the future will be second marriages for one or both spouses; 6) age at marriage will increase—due, in part, to the greater equality being given to women, whose range of alternatives in the occupational world will expand; 7) the family of the future will be more equalitarian—there will be a greater accentuation of the companionate family with its diffusion of power; 8) the sex norms will more closely approximate a single standard for both men and women; and 9) more leisure time will be available for all family members.

Other writers offer predictions that do not necessarily agree with these. Forecasting is obviously a hazardous undertaking and will produce a variety of prognostications, depending on the orientations and insights of the individuals involved. What we can be certain about is that whatever emerging family forms and relationships develop, they will not be the last. We can also be sure that the family of the future will not be without problems. Some will respond readily to the social change that is an inherent part of urban life while others will resist such change, preferring to hold on to traditional values and behavior patterns that have become functional to them. Describing the effects of social change in the urban setting, Horton and Leslie (1974, p. 237) conclude: "Even when the changes are not actively opposed, people are disoriented by them. They are torn between loyalty to the values of old and acceptance of new, supposedly better ways. The conflict rages between groups and within individual personalities."

SELECTED BIBLIOGRAPHY

ALDOUS, JOAN. "Occupational Characteristics and Male's Role Performance in the Family," *Journal of Marriage and the Family* (November 1969).

BELL, R. R. *Marriage and Family Interaction.* Homewood, Ill.: Dorsey Press, 1975.

BENSON, LEONARD. *Fatherhood: A Sociological Perspective.* New York: Random House, 1968.

BERELSON, BERNARD. "The Value of Children: A Taxonomical Essay." In J. Gipson Wells, ed., *Current Issues in Marriage and the Family,* pp. 168–175. New York: Macmillan, 1975.

BROFENBRENNER, U. "Socialization and Social Class Through Time and Space." In Eleanor E. Maccoby et al., eds., *Readings in Social Psychology,* pp. 400–425. 3rd ed. New York: Holt, Rinehart & Winston, 1958.

CONSTANTINE, L., and CONSTANTINE, J. *Group Marriage.* New York: Macmillan, 1973.

ESHLEMAN, J. ROSS. *The Family.* Boston: Allyn & Bacon, 1974.

FULLERTON, GAIL P. *Survival in Marriage.* New York: Holt, Rinehart & Winston, 1972.

GIST, NOEL P., and FAVA, SYLVIA F. *Urban Society.* New York: Thomas Y. Crowell, 1974.

GOODE, WILLIAM J. *World Revolution and Family Patterns.* New York: Free Press, 1963.

HOFFMAN, LOIS W., and NYE, F. IVAN. *Working Mothers.* San Francisco: Jossey-Bass, 1975.

HORTON, PAUL B., and LESLIE, GERALD R. *The Sociology of Social Problems.* 5th ed. Englewood Cliffs, N.J.: Prentice-Hall, 1974.

KENKEL, WILLIAM F. *The Family in Perspective.* New York: Appleton-Century-Crofts, 1966.

KEPHART, WILLIAM M. *The Family, Society, and the Individual.* 2nd ed. Boston: Houghton Mifflin, 1966.

LEMASTERS, E. E. *Parents in Modern America.* rev. ed. Homewood, Ill.: Dorsey Press, 1974.

LESLIE, GERALD R. *The Family in Social Context.* New York: Oxford University Press, 1973.

LEWIS OSCAR. *La Vida: A Puerto Rican Family in the Culture of Poverty—San Juan and New York.* New York: Random House, 1965.

MARTINSON, FLOYD M. *Family in Society.* New York: Dodd, Mead, 1970.

MELVILLE, KEITH. *Marriage and Family Today.* 2nd ed. New York: Random House, 1980.

NYE, F. IVAN, and BERARDO, FELIX M. *The Family.* New York: Macmillan, 1973.

OGBURN, WILLIAM F. *Technology and the Changing Family.* New York: Viking, 1955.

PALEN, J. JOHN. *Social Problems.* New York: McGraw-Hill, 1979.

POHLMAN, E. H. *Psychology of Birth Planning.* Cambridge, Mass.: Schenkman, 1969.

REISS, IRA L. *Family Systems in America.* 2nd ed. Hinsdale, Ill.: Dryden Press, 1976.

RENNIE, KAREN S. "Correlates of Dissatisfaction in Marriage," *Journal of Marriage and the Family* 32 (February 1970).

RIESMAN, DAVID. *The Lonely Crowd.* New Haven, Conn.: Yale University Press, 1950.

SCHNEIDER, EUGENE V. *Industrial Sociology.* 2nd ed. New York: McGraw-Hill, 1969.

SCHULZ, DAVID A. *The Changing Family.* Englewood Cliffs, N.J.: Prentice-Hall, 1972.

SIRJAMAKI, JOHN. "Culture Configurations in the American Family," *American Journal of Sociology* 53 (May 1948): 464–470.

SJOBERG, GIDEON. *The Preindustrial City.* New York: Free Press, 1960.

SKOLNICK, ARLENE. *The Intimate Environment.* Boston: Little, Brown, 1973.

SOROKIN, PITRIM A. *Social and Cultural Dynamics.* New York: American Book, 1937.

STARR, JOYCE R., and CARNS, DONALD E. "Singles in the City." In Helena Lopata, ed., *Marriages and Families,* pp. 154–161. New York: D. Van Nostrand, 1973.

STEWART, ELBERT W., and GLYNN, JAMES A. *Introduction to Sociology.* New York: McGraw-Hill, 1971.

UDRY, J. RICHARD. *The Social Context of Marriage.* Philadelphia: Lippincott, 1966.

U.S. BUREAU OF THE CENSUS. *Current Population Reports: Marital Status and Living Arrangements, 1976.* Washington, D.C., February 8, 1977.

U.S. BUREAU OF THE CENSUS. *Statistical Abstracts of the United States.* 91st ed. Washington, D.C., 1972.

ZIMMERMAN, CARLE C. *Family and Civilization.* New York: Harper & Row, Publishers, 1947.

chapter 8

religion
in the
urban
community

BY JACQUELINE SCHERER

Many theologians have called for a reexamination of traditional religious practices and beliefs as they exist today in urban societies. Some argue that churches have not changed as quickly or as deeply as is necessary to confront key modern issues. Religious institutions often appear to be bypassed by other social institutions, and important individual and societal concerns do not appear in church agendas. The process by which religious institutions are separated from other social arrangements and lose influence throughout many areas of life is known as *secularization*. Historically, secularization and urbanization have been linked together, and the goal of this chapter is to show how each process has influenced the other.

CLASSICAL THEORIES

Two main themes in sociological theory link the process of secularization with the massive transformations that occur when societies change from rural to urban. The first is that of Emile Durkheim (1915), who believed that social change often causes social disorganization and loss of influence, weakening traditional institutions and making them less effective in resolving new problems. Another view is that of Max Weber (1958), who coined the term "demystification" to characterize the effect of scientific explanation on traditional religious ideas. Magic and religious dogma are no longer the foundation for understanding but are replaced by intellectual modes of inquiry employing rational objective analysis. Areas of social activity that had been previously dominated by religious authority are controlled by other institutions that appeal to scientific and rational expertise as the basis of knowledge.

The term "secularization" is confusing because it has been used in several different ways. First, secularization refers to the separation of religious institutions from other social arrangements, as in the break between church and state, the distinction made between religious and economic activities, and the loss of religious influence in educational institutions. A second meaning of the term suggests fewer public religious practices, such as attending church services or formal prayer. Third, secularization as developed by Weber refers to the decline in beliefs about the supernatural and a downgrading of mystical and spiritual explanations essential to most religious belief systems.

To measure secularization in any one of these meanings is difficult. Historical comparisons of religious activities are inaccurate because our records of the past are incomplete. Also, church membership had a different connotation when the church was a political and economic institution in the lives of ordinary people. Recent surveys estimate a decline in adult attendance at weekly services in the United States from 49 percent in 1958 to 43 percent in 1968 (Gallup Poll, 1968). Present estimates indicate that approximately 40 percent of all Americans attend religious services regularly. This figure varies greatly, however, among different denominations and urban situations. Information about religious affiliation is not collected in the U.S. census, so that attendance figures are gathered by individual churches, making it difficult to check for accuracy and reliability. Other urbanized countries have national figures that document the decline in attendance. Weekly attendance has changed in England from 25 percent in 1900 to 15 percent in 1965 (Argyle, 1975, p. 11). Other evidence supporting the decline of religious influence in modern societies is the loss of status of the clergy, the rise in the number of people who claim no religious affiliation, the overwhelming use of scientific knowledge as the basis of decision making and explanation, and the continued develpoment of specialized organizations that restrict the scope of religious institutions.

Secularization is further complicated because any definition of the process depends upon the definition of religion adopted. If religious participation is defined as attendance at a formal worship service, secularization refers only to attendance. But other measurable dimensions of religion identified by social scientists are: a system of belief or dogma; ritual and ceremonial activities; and membership in some kind of association or fellowship. Efforts to evaluate these dimensions have proven very difficult.

Whatever definition one adopts for religion—and there are many—religious questions clearly deal with problems of ultimate values and meaning. Religion is expected to provide both assistance and explanations of profound human concerns, as well as to establish a fundamental understanding of life and death. Throughout history, the answers given to such important questions have been as varied as the organizational arrangements developed by religious groups. Although most churches adopt some reference to a supernatural being or spiritual power, modern ideologies such as humanism or communism may serve as spiritual substitutes, providing meaning and direction in the lives of individuals and groups without appealing to God or the supernatural. One definition of religion that includes all of these ideas is that of Geertz (1968, p. 643):

> A religion is a system of symbols which acts to establish powerful, pervasive, and long-lasting moods and motivations in men by formulating conceptions of a general order of existence and clothing these conceptions with such an aura of factuality that the moods and motivations seem uniquely realistic.

Religious organizations are the usual social means for expressing and interpreting religion. Like other institutions, religious institutions are independent of contemporary members and survive individual personnel changes: they deal with the collective features of religious organizations and belief systems that are complex in the extreme, varying from formal structures of ecclesiastical authority to informal groups. Urban religious institutions are more differentiated than their rural counterparts because urban environments are generally more complex. The belief that the country is more religious than the city cannot always be supported, however. Sociologist Peter Berger (1969) argues that the departure of the supernatural is more likely to occur in modern, urban societies, but a continued interest in religious institutions can be observed in all urban societies.

We must conclude that the strength of religious institutions is a complicated matter, reflecting more than geography or even the economic development of societies. To understand the survival of churches in urban areas is to recognize that religious institutions have responded to a variety of demands, both personal and social, in different ways. This process has entailed transformation, adaptation, and innovation in both religious organization and beliefs.

URBAN ADAPTATIONS TO RELIGIOUS INSTITUTIONS

A major factor that has stimulated religious adaptations in urban contexts has been the diversity of populations living together. Different religious opinions encouraged the growth of more tolerant attitudes toward those who believed differently from one another. In addition, more sophisticated ideas about science and trade that were accepted in cities influenced religious thinking among many church members and stimulated new theological scholarship. As already noted, the rationalism characteristic of social relationships in urban areas was a key factor in the development of

Religious pluralism characterizes the modern urban community throughout the world. (Mexican National Tourist Council, United Nations, Greater Vancouver Convention 8 Visitors Bureau)

bureaucratic and rational authority structures. Churches developed organizational arrangements similar to those found in other areas of social life operated by specialists with management expertise.

Another feature of the urban milieu was the competition among different religious messages. Church members could choose among creeds, worship styles, and fellowship groups. In some instances, churches competed for new members by using the same kinds of marketplace techniques that producers employ to sell ordinary products. Members were able to compare and contrast their religious institution with others, making religious membership a choice rather than a birthright or a permanent identification.

URBAN FEARS

Religious leaders often found the urban scene threatening and hostile to traditional church views. One response to this perceived threat was to emphasize old-fashioned values and strict adherence to dogmatic interpretations of human beings and God. This emphasis was reflected in the growth of fundamental churches and evangelical religious movements urging people to return to the teachings of the Bible. It was as if fundamental and dogmatic religious ideas could shield urban dwellers from dangerous features of cosmopolitan life. An example of the kinds of tensions reflected in many of these struggles was the famous Scopes trial in 1921. The scientific theory of evolution taught in a local high school was debated in light of the biblical explanation of creation. The evolution controversy provided a rallying point around which many diverse fears could be articulated. Interestingly, in the 1970s evolution erupted again in debates over school textbooks, once more providing a focus for those who believed that science, social change, and urbanization would threaten established and traditional views.

The fundamentalist theme is particularly strong in American Protestantism, and a strong antiurban bias has been powerful in many Protestant groups. Often it was related to the desire to preserve small religious community life and the "purity" of rural values.

The fear of the city as a dangerous and destructive place can also be seen in the concerns of religious leaders. Even when many of these church members moved into urban areas themselves, they brought their fears and dislike of the city along, and sought to replace small towns with neighborhood groups or church communities. Another effect of the religious bias against the city was to exaggerate the fears of immigrant groups who were predominantly urban, largely Catholics and Jews.

Signs of an antiurban attitude are still evident. For example, church services are scheduled at ten or eleven o'clock on Sunday mornings to fit the rural pattern; farmers can complete their chores and get dressed for the ride to church. This may not be the most practical time for a service in modern societies, but the tradition continues. "The death of God" movement publicly denounced the symbolism of rural existence as one inappropriate for the contemporary urban dweller.

Another response to the urban influence has been the persistence of an organizational form known as the sect that retains the small-town quality of rural churches. Sects have been particularly attractive to rural migrants who find themselves locked into large urban societies for which they are not prepared psychologically or financially. Located at the bottom of the social scale, often poor, uneducated, and with very little hope, some turn to small religious groups organized in a personal style. The religious message of these groups promises eternal rewards to compensate for earthly suffering. Members of sects often meet in stores or in private homes; they can be seen preaching on street corners and passing out religious literature from house to house.

Another important effect of rural attitudes among church leaders was to encourage clergy and lay members to help those suffering in the godless cities through charity work. The social gospel preached in the late nineteenth century urged concern with the plight of those unfortunates who were led to sin in the evil metropolis. An example of this concern was the Young Men's Christian Association. Like the Young Women's Christian Association that followed later from England, these groups tried to assist urban youth in many ways. The Salvation Army brought its missionary zeal to the suffering "down and outs" in the poorest parts of the city. Christian movements were influential in the early settlement houses, and were centers for early reformers, particularly in Chicago. In 1925 Paul Douglass studied 1,044 city churches and concluded that the city church is "an evolved rural church" (Cully and Harper, 1969, p. 83). From this religious base, support for Prohibition grew in urban areas.

In the turbulent sixties religious institutions continued to help relieve suffering among the elderly, the blacks, and the poor caught in more recent migrations to American cities. Paradoxically, the antiurban bias has both stimulated and slowed social action efforts, particularly among wealthy suburbanities or religious leaders who believe in the inherent depravity of cities and wish to remain uncontaminated.

FUNCTIONAL ANALYSES OF URBAN RELIGIOUS INSTITUTIONS

Another way to understand how religious institutions have responded to changes brought about through urbanization is to examine the changing social functions of these institutions. In hunting and agricultural systems, religion is usually the center of group life. To Durkheim, religious rituals were the affirmation of the group's existence, and religious beliefs the foundation of all social order. Religion provided a cultural cement composed of common values, understandings, and ideologies which brought people together. Durkheim adopted the term "collective conscience" to refer to group morality. He called attention to an important sociological insight that religion has social purposes as well as spiritual messages; or, in his terms, religion is a social fact with social consequences.

When viewed in the context of villages and tribes, Durkheim's ideas were supported by the many ways in which religion did provide a unifying center for all social activity. Even today, in small towns and villages the church remains physically in the center of community life and dominates group socialization activities. In urban areas, however, Durkheim's theory becomes severely strained. Two or three churches of different denominations may exist side by side and compete for members. Often one group is actively opposed to the beliefs of another group. Clearly, religion can divide and separate groups as well as unite them. Durkheim's theory requires modification as an explanation for religious functioning in urbanized societies, a task that has occupied urban scholars for over seventy-five years.

One modification has been to examine urban religious institutions as the source of unity for a particular group rather than between different groups. For example, churches have served as cultural centers for different ethnic groups in American history. Churches were homes for people of one nationality in a mixed society, providing a place where religious beliefs and cultural traditions could be shared. A Polish-Catholic parish, a Russian-Jewish synagogue, or a German Lutheran church are examples of the ties between religious participation and ethnic cultures. According to sociologist Will Herberg (1955, p. 85), an ethnic group is "a form of self-identification and self-location" that is linked to religious affiliation. Andrew Greeley (1972, p. 115) goes even further by noting that, instead of "Americans belonging to churches because they believe in religion, there may be a strong tendency for them to believe in religion because they belong to churches." When the group is without a geographic center, such as a village, and when an established national church cannot provide cultural unity, religious institutions preserve ethnic association.

The sense of belonging is an important part of religious affiliation within a heterogeneous population. Religious groups can provide primary relationships in a complex impersonal world, meeting a human need for fellowship and coming together with others who share similar views on significant issues. Belonging is recognized as one of the most important factors in church membership. Churches are thereby part of the web of affiliations that help to solidify the individual's social bearings. Because church membership is voluntary, individuals can withdraw or change religious affiliations as well as identities in ways that were not possible when a single religious perspective dominated the environment. Catholics who no longer attend Mass regularly may no longer think of themselves as Catholic or Italian. If the individual decides his or her personal and group needs are satisfied within the church, support is given freely; but support can be withdrawn just as freely if such needs are not met. Freedom of choice has important consequences on the clergy, on church financing, and on the ability of the organization to change or modify activities.

Today, some urbanities find the most attractive features of belonging to a church are psychological. The church provides comfort in times of trouble, security in times of fear, and companionship in times of loneliness. This comfort theory of religion suggests that the primary function of religion in urban society may be the enrichment of individual lives rather than social groups. The term "privitism" describes an orientation toward religious participation based upon the belief that religion is a private concern. One of the ways in which urban religious institutions differ from their rural counterparts is an emphasis on religion as a personal, voluntary, and private matter rather than as an issue of public policy. The personal dimension appears to be reinforced where laws on the separation of church and state discourage public identification with one denomination, and where alternative religious messages are easily available.

Although most urban citizens recognize the private benefits obtained from religious institutions, sociologists also believe that these institutions are important in maintaining social control. Religious justifications for regulating many areas of social behavior, particularly in matters of morality in key life areas, such as sex, marriage, birth, and death, are the subject matter of rituals symbolizing the religious meaning of life. Among small groups, agreed-upon religious values and the ability to know well most of the people with whom one interacts make it possible for informal social pressures to control social behavior. To use such methods in urban areas is difficult, although some evidence suggests that active participation in any religious organization helps the individual to be more disciplined. Because any one denomination in the city cannot exert the power that led to social conformity in nonurban situations (Argyle, 1975), religious influence on social order diminishes.

Elizabeth Nottingham (1971) has tried to view the changing functions of religious institutions in conjunction with the stage of development of societies. Thus, in a society characterized as small, isolated, and preliterate, religion functions as Durkheim suggested: to bring members together and to reaffirm the value of the group. In changing societies with some technology, a growing division of labor, rising social class differences, and increased literacy, religious institutions have contradictory functions: to provide integration for particular groups and individuals, but also to support ideas that may divide segments of the population. In a third type of society, characterized by urbanization, sophisticated technology, advanced scientific understanding, and population diversity, religious institutions have lost many social functions. Many people have no religious affiliation, but those who continue to participate in religious institutions seek personal meaning and integration. In postindustrial societies, then, religion becomes a private conviction rather than a social policy.

As urban populations increase in heterogeneity, churches frequently are pushed together. Many pressures arise to bring religious institutions into a kind of functioning association. Interdenominational service groups, the ecumenical movement, and interfaith services are evidence of these pressures. Together, religious institutions increase their individual resources and offer a religious perspective in public decisions.

The term "religiosity" refers to the measurement of particular forms of religious participation, such as attendance at services, participation in rituals, frequency of prayer, recognition of the teachings of faith, willingness to identify with a denomination, and the frequency of interaction with other members of the church. Researchers are interested in religiosity because it can be empirically documented and verified, although some aspects of religious experience, such as depth of commitment or the intensity of a mystical experience, clearly cannot be quantified. As a result of the quantitative emphasis in religious studies, a substantial body of evidence has been developed demonstrating relationships between social characteristics and religiosity.

For example, members of the same social class and status groups tend to participate in similar religious associations. The middle class participates more actively in churches than the working class, as is true in all forms of voluntary association. At the same time, certain forms of religious participation are distinctively linked to the poor or those who are dissatisfied with the established forms of worship. Sects are particularly attractive to groups rejecting the social environment in which they exist. Females attend church services more often than males; the young and old more often than the middle-aged. There is also a correlation between region and geography and specific denominational memberships. Education, occupation, and income, the components of social status, are correlated to membership in specific religious affiliations. Episcopalians, Jews, and Presbyterians, for example, fall into one category; Methodists, Lutherans, and Roman Catholics into a middle range; and Baptists, both black and white, fall into a lower status grouping according to these criteria. This is not surprising if we consider the urban church as operating similarly to other voluntary associations: people who share the same economic background usually associate with others like themselves.

Table 8-1 shows the extent of religious membership in the United States. These groups are all found in urban areas, with Roman Catholics and Jews dominant in major cities.

One of the most difficult questions to answer is how religion affects behavior. Once again, Max Weber raises this question in his classic, *The Protestant Ethic and the Spirit of Capitalism* (1930). Weber argued that Protestant beliefs reinforced the values of emerging capitalism, so that individuals who supported the puritan work ethic accumulated the capital necessary for success in the economic sphere. The difficulties of interpreting the tie between behavior and belief were illustrated by this thesis. Another example is an examination of anti-Semitism by Glock and Stark (1966). They found a relationship between orthodoxy and prejudice: the more people believe that their religion provides the only true path to salvation, the more likely they are to be hostile toward Jews. Those religious attitudes that reinforce prejudice are usually rigid and dogmatic. However, urban environments can also promote tolerant religious attitudes. A study of Canadian religious practices concluded that "high urbanism is consistently related with high liberalism in beliefs, with tolerance of minority groups, and with approval of centralized public controls over economic activity" (Crysdale, 1976). One difficulty with most studies of religion and social behavior

TABLE 8-1 Specific religious denominations in the United States with memberships in excess of one million

DENOMINATIONS	INCLUSIVE MEMBERSHIP (IN MILLIONS)
Roman Catholic Church	47.9
Southern Baptist Convention	11.5
United Methodist Church	10.8
Jewish Congregations	5.8
National Baptist Convention, U.S.A., Inc.	5.5
Episcopal Church (Protestant Episcopal Church)	3.3
United Presbyterian Church	3.2
Lutheran Church in America	3.1
Lutheran Church—Missouri Synod	2.8
National Baptist Convention of America	2.7
American Lutheran Church	2.6
Churches of Christ	2.4
United Church of Christ	2.0
Church of Jesus Christ of Latter-day Saints (Mormon)	1.9
Greek Orthodox Archdiocese of North and South America	1.9
National Primitive Baptist Convention	1.5
American Baptist Convention	1.5
Christian Church (Disciples of Christ)	1.4
African Methodist Episcopal Church	1.2
Orthodox Church	1.0

SOURCE: Constant H. Jacquet, Jr., ed., *Yearbook of American Churches* (New York: Council Press for the Office of Planning and Program, National Council of Churches, 1971).

is that a cluster of characteristics, rather than a single variable, is present. This means direct causation, or even precise associations, cannot be claimed; what is evident are complex relationships between religion and social factors.

RELIGIOUS STUDIES

Today scholars are trying to interpret religion within a more comprehensive framework of all knowledge systems. Religion is examined as one form of voluntary association; the techniques of persuasion used in presenting religious messages are examined in conjunction with educational messages, advertising, or political propaganda; the patterns of social movement analyzed include religious groups as examples of organized efforts to redefine and change society.

The most important development within this wider intellectual approach has been the emergence of religion as a part of the sociology of knowledge. Sociologists have recognized that ideas have social roots and that they reflect the values of individuals and groups, the historical moment in which the ideas were developed, the cultural issues that dominate the concerns of peoples adopting ideas, and other empirically discernible factors. From this perspective, religion can be viewed as a system of ideas with social origins influenced by social concerns. Incorporating religion within an examination of all ideological belief systems, rather than separating religious ideas from the rest of knowledge, makes possible an understanding of the social significance of religion. It also engenders the study of non–church members, a growing number of people who do not participate in any religious group but who have adopted belief systems that resemble the Judeo-Christian ethic.

This change of direction in scholarship reflects in part the shrinking of church religion (Luckmann, 1967) at a time when there is renewed interest and activity in exploring values and meaning systems. Some of this interest is expressed by such irrational activities as the occult, astrology, or magic, or in changing views toward faith healing and rejection of science. Some sociologists suggest that all societies have mixtures of rationality and irrationality, or that there are cycles in which one emphasis is stronger than the other. The persistence of many forms of irrationality, however, is both fascinating and important in the analysis of social development, and the sociology of knowledge stimulates the investigation of such phenomena.

The student interested in urban religious institutions will find this new approach promising because it may lead to important insight about the processes of personal, social, and intellectual adaptation that have been essential for religious institutional survival during the period of urbanization—both those that occurred in the past and those taking place today. According to Greeley (1972b, p. 363), religious institutions must confront three important areas of change: 1) the need to reinterpret myths that traditionally have justified existence; 2) the recognition that many meaning options exist and believers can choose among competing world views; and 3) the reality of mobility that allows the urban dweller to move among different religious institutions.

Although religious institutions clearly are not the supreme arbiters of knowledge in modern urban societies, nor the most influential social institutions in determining the directions of modern life, these institutions obviously have a large measure of vitality. For many individuals, religion provides meaning and importance to everyday activity and is the source of change in personal behavior. Despite reduced membership in the past decade and a decline in intellectual influence on certain matters, these institutions are unlikely to disappear quickly. According to Greeley, the sacred seems to be too deeply ingrained in the structure of human existence for religion to be replaced by secular knowledge in all aspects of social behavior.

AN ECOSYSTEM ANALYSIS OF URBAN RELIGIOUS INSTITUTIONS

Like all other urban institutions, churches have been confronted with important population changes in recent years. The migration of rural populations to the cities, especially black and Spanish-speaking groups, and the emigration of middle-class white groups to suburban locations outside the central city has led to concern with meeting varied social needs. In central cities the poor, the old, and the black and the Spanish-speaking form the majority of church members, while the more affluent whites belong to suburban churches. In the 1950s and 1960s the rapid growth of suburbia was perceived as a new religious revival in the United States, although the building activity reflected a need for new church facilities more than a spiritual reawakening. Critics of suburban churches charged that the suburban church was more of a social center than a spiritual home and that middle-class religious ideas had turned into secular therapy designed to develop the skills of getting along with others and adjusting to society.

One readily observable response to the demographic changes was church architecture. Economic differences, bold experimental design, changing ethnic tastes in art, and imaginative interpretations of religious themes are expressed in bricks and mortar: Roman Catholic cathedrals became Black Muslim temples and Jewish synagogues were modified for revival meetings. Sometimes unused houses of worship became facilities for dealing with drug addicts or youth groups.

Urban changes, however, affected religious institutions on a much deeper level. Like all social institutions, religious organizations are the established means of meeting social needs: the teachings of established religions provide answers to theological concerns that also are interpreted for social ends. Christianity usually supports conservative messages: people must accept life and bear their cross bravely, accepting life as God's will. Life after death is more rewarding than life on earth. Important exceptions to this generalization are radical sects and religious revisionists. These groups may present a new religious message demanding important changes in this world for salvation in another, or requiring followers to adopt a way of life or religious rule that will bring about changes. Max

The economic and architectural simplicity of the modern suburban church reflects the residential mobility and transiency of its congregation. (David Gold)

Weber (1958) argued that often these radical views are developed by charismatic individuals, who lead by a combination of personality and historical timing. The religious term "prophet" suggests the kind of person Weber had in mind. In time, a radical message becomes more conventional or, in Weber's phrase, the "routinization of charisma" takes place. This process, he argued, explains the transformation of small religious groups into established churches.

On the other hand, because most religious messages are concerned with justice and righteousness, revolutionaries can find religious themes that support social change. Although established churches support the status quo, the seeds of reform lie within the religious traditions and can be uncovered by those who wish to justify social changes.

The tensions between the status quo and demands for change were evident during the Civil Rights movement of the 1960s. Clergy involvement in the struggle, for example, were dramatically exploited by the media. But the record suggests that many religious believers were at best ambiguous about participation, and some actively opposed any participation. In 1965, one study (Hadden & Heimer, 1975) showed that only 7 percent of the Protestant clergy disapproved of the Civil Rights movement (44 percent of the Protestant Assembly disapproved); in 1966 two-thirds of the clergy at the Council of Churches Triennial replied that progress toward integration was not fast enough, whereas two weeks earlier a Harris poll found that 70 percent of all white Americans thought progress was too fast and only 4 percent believed it was not fast enough. This suggests that many religious leaders were ahead of their members in matters of social justice and social action. In the 1970s, religious leadership appeared more restrained in these areas, reflecting in part the pressure from church members.

Interest in social action varies among denominations and in terms of specific issues. For example, many liberal Protestant and Jewish clergy actively supported the movement for legalized abortion before the Supreme Court decision affirmed this policy. At the same time, the official position of the Roman Catholic Church and the aggressive political role of Right to Life groups illustrate reluctance to accept the Court's interpretation.

Discussion about church participation in social issues is probably as old as established religion itself. However, it assumes new urgency in an era of rapid social change and revolution. The demands of Third World nations for political and economic autonomy, the concerns of black Americans, and the redefinition of the position of women in society are three areas that highlight the difficulties of established church practices. All three are particularly critical issues for urban religious institutions.

Throughout the world, massive urbanization has accelerated the same issues that preoccupied American churches between 1880 and 1970: rural migration, poverty, and the challenge to traditional modes of thinking and acting. Churches are asked to help individuals and groups cope with social transformations. One of the major differences between the American and the Third World experience, however, is the rate of change today.

Technology, increasing population, and political and economic changes aggravate the problems further. Traditional religious leaders are seldom prepared to deal with upheavals. International religious bodies and charity movements attempt to administer to some needs, but the scale of the problem is usually larger than their resources.

The struggle of black Americans is a critical issue in American society. Most black people brought their rural church organizations to the industrial centers of the North when they moved. Religious institutions historically provided one of the few available opportunities for self-expression and leadership training, and the Black Church held an important social position. Storefront churches soon dotted the streets of many American cities, and sects that promised special salvation for long-suffering blacks flourished, as did established Negro churches. Some new groups developed, such as the Black Muslims, but at the same time fundamentalist and evangelical movements remain popular.

It was not surprising the Civil Rights leaders such as Martin Luther King, Jr., were deeply rooted in black religious institutions, and that the black clergy played an active role in this movement. Almost inevitably, religious institutions were divided by debates about strategies to achieve social justice. One of the more radical demands was that of black militants. Their Black Manifesto asked for $500,000,000 in reparations from white religious institutions: "Fifteen dollars for every black brother and sister in the United States is only a beginning of the reparations due us as people who have been exploited and degraded, brutalized, killed and persecuted" (Forman, 1973). Some denominations did respond; others intensified their social relief and assistance programs; but others rejected this pressure forcefully, denying that social action had an important place in religious activities.

In one sense the Black Manifesto can be viewed as an example of another struggle within American religious institutions that had particular meaning to urban institutions: the debate about cultural plurality and cultural integration. A few scholars have suggested that American religious institutions have in fact, if not in name, provided a national religion they call "the civil religion" (Herberg, 1955). Basically, this consists of a belief in God, with little clarification of what is meant by God; support for churches, usually those accepted by Catholics, Protestants, and Jews; and a patriotic acceptance of an America that is directed by God toward peace, justice, and virtue—the so-called "American way of life." Many American "sacred" documents, such as the Constitution or presidential inauguration speeches, do lend themselves to this interpretation of a civil religion. These scholars believe that without some kind of civil religion or understanding agreed upon by most of society there would be social chaos. Opponents of a civil religion reply that it is possible to have a great diversity of ideologies and cultures. For example, a Hindu or a Buddhist is not less American because his or her belief does not fit into the Catholic-Protestant-Jew thesis. Whether or not an urban nation has to substitute some form of national agreement on religious themes to promote social harmony and order is not certain.

A third group demanding change in traditional religious views is women. At the current stage of economic and social development in advanced industrialized nations, women find the age-old roles assigned to them as mothers and wives altered. As more women are educated and technological changes have reduced the need for physical strength in jobs, as the number of children in a family decreases, and as life expectancy increases beyond seventy, the possibility of working outside the home grows, and, the degree of involvement in the work processes of modern society increases while the degree of involvement in church-oriented religion decreases. Religious institutions seldom grant women positions of authority or responsibility, and the traditional religious messages are based upon restrictive interpretations of female roles. Bitter debates develop in those denominations in which women have demanded the right to become official religious leaders, such as the struggle of women to become ordained priests in the Episcopalian Church. But other examples of women's demands for recognition of their changed status can be seen in the growing number of women who wish to restructure official church teachings or who challenge religious practices that range from where women sit during a service to how they can be given a stronger voice in determining church social action policies.

Urban churches have struggled to respond to all three groups on both an ideological and an organizational level. One response has been the development of religious specialists who handle both religious and personal problems. Surveys show that people in trouble seek help from religious leaders for many personal problems, including marriage, divorce, child rearing, and health. Religious staff require specialized training in guidance and counseling. In some cases, adjunct social services, such as the Catholic social services or Jewish welfare, have been created to hire and sponsor professional specialists who deliver the kinds of help required.

One problem with the multiplicity of demands made upon religious institutions and leadership is that clergy need allied skills to supplement religious expertise. For example, religious leaders are asked to provide ethical guidelines on difficult issues raised in technological societies. They must also develop political skills to deal effectively in the local struggles over community resources, and the management expertise to run a voluntary organization effectively.

The need for religious involvement in social services to help people and the sophisticated pastoral guidance required in affluent suburban churches are no less important than continued demands for hellfire-and-brimstone preachers and technical media experts who can present religious messages. Modern ideas about personal freedom and changing standards of morality often compound the private lives of religious leaders, as evidenced by rising divorce rates among married clergy and by debates about celibacy in the Catholic Church. Conflicting role expectations about what a religious leader should do and his or her style of life often engender criticism from church members who are either more conservative or more liberal than church officials. As a result, the authority of religious leaders is no longer "given" but must be earned. They need to use all their personal skills to support institutional authority in sermons. In such a situation, role strain and social conflict are common. Many clergy are poorly prepared to deal with these pressures, as Norton (1964, p. 21) describes: "Trapped with an image of man as fundamentally agrarian and indoctrinating its clergy with a view of man's social nature that is based on small-scale society, the church now finds itself without a leadership that can grasp quickly and speak effectively to the new mass society and its problems."

The urban scene is also an arena for many organizational experiments in religion. Partly as a reaction to church bureaucracy, and partly in conjunction with other trends in contemporary society, there is renewed interest in new forms of organization that allow room for spontaneity, personal recognition, and informality. Cults or secret associations proliferate in this situation, as do religious fads including experimentation with drugs and space-age theologies. Prayer groups, charismatic movements that communicate directly with the "spirit," and religious communes are other efforts to build more personal and emotionally satisfying religious contacts. Even well-established denominations have not escaped these trends. Efforts to modernize Roman Catholicism after the Vatican Councils, changing ideas on sexual morality, education and sophistication among the Catholic lay population, and suburban-urban strains and debates about the role of the clergy have caused severe stresses in the rigid Roman Catholic bureaucracy. A dramatic decline in church attendance and fewer men and women electing to serve in religious orders are indications of these problems.

Another response to institutional bureaucracy has been increased specialization among religious institutions. As already noted, class influences have been clearly discernible in church groups: affluent worshippers belong to suburban churches and inner city churches are generally populated by poorer people. Intelligent, sophisticated populations require different religious associations than the uneducated. In contrast, urban strains lead to a growing number of religious believers seeking certainty and reassurance, causing a strong resurgence of fundamentalist and evangelical religion.

Such organizational experimentation is unlikely to cease in the near future. Mainstream churches continue to experiment to find organizational arrangements that satisfy both groups. New ideas or the rediscovery of other traditions from the East will stimulate the growth of special sects. At the same time, fundamentalist approaches to religion, which can promise certainty amidst modern confusion, are likely to continue to appeal to many. A great many individuals will decide to avoid any official religious membership, finding meaning, belonging, and order through participation in other social contexts rather than in the established religious institutional orbit.

ETHICAL PROBLEMS

One of the most difficult tasks of all religious institutions is responding to the problems caused by advanced technological expertise. Biomedical research, for example, has raised perplexing and troubling issues about the control of genes and the manipulation of the unborn child. Medical technology has made death complex because life can be sustained under conditions previously not possible. The rise in population threatens to upset the ecological balance of the world, and resource depletion fuels the tensions between the have and have-not nations. Traditional sexual morality is attacked as emerging life styles reflect modern realities such as contraception, long life, and widespread changes in families. In many areas, technology now or in the near future portends grave moral concerns. Just as war can never again be discussed without considering the reality of the deadly means of destruction available, so human relationships can no longer be interpreted without reference to the technological factors that influence fundamental decisions about living and dying. Religious organizations are challenged in important and dramatic ways to present guidelines on these complicated topics.

Bitter debates about abortion, birth control, overpopulation, and genetic engineering; the moral concerns over war, weapons, and biological and psychological techniques of combat; and interest in revolutionary and nationalistic political movements, particularly in the Third World, are indications of the range and difficulty of the ethical issues religious leaders confront.

Sociologists point out that to a large degree religious institutions have lost the power to define situations. Because the ethical issues are so complex, and because science rather than religious dogma is the prevailing basis of intellectual authority, churches may not be able to have religious interpretations of these issues accepted—or even heard. According to Budd (1973, p. 154), "Perhaps the most important is the loss of control over activities which are now ruled by secular knowledge and values.... A consequence of such changes is that public discussion of social and moral dilemmas now often refers to 'the religious arguments' as a category to be taken into consideration, but not one that is preeminent."

CONCLUSION

Urbanization in the future, as in the past, will accentuate the transformation of religious institutions. However, these institutions will continue to compete against other institutionalized forms providing meaningful systems from a secular perspective. In the competition, religious groups may become special centers in life rather than the center of social life. No one denominational view will become powerful enough to represent diverse urban populations, and continuous religious experimentation, with both belief systems and organizational arrangements, will continue.

In the past, church and family, as well as government and educational institutions, worked together to present a common framework of meaning in life. Today these institutions are more often than not at odds with each other. This does not mean, as has often been predicted, that religious institutions will disappear; it does mean that they will change and redevelop to meet different human concerns.

Such changes will not occur easily: powerful status arrangements, rules that clearly define human relationships, and satisfying answers are not instantly discarded. In a sense, then, the future will be more of the past: the urban church will be called upon to reinterpret daily life for those believers who have faith in a supernatural being or in a code of ethics or political philosophy. At the same time, many will look for meaning in nonreligious activities and will bypass traditional religious institutions.

SELECTED BIBLIOGRAPHY

ALFRED, R. "Religion and Politics." In Roland Robertson, ed., *Sociology of Religion.* London: Penguin, 1971.

ARGYLE, M., and BEIT-HALLAHMI, B. *The Social Psychology of Religion.* London: Routledge & Kegan Paul, 1975.

BELLAH, R. "Civil Religion in America," *Daedalus* (Winter 1967): 1–21.

BERGER, P. *A Rumour of Angels.* New York: Doubleday, 1970.

———. *The Sacred Canopy.* New York: Doubleday, 1969.

BERGER, P., and LUCKMANN, T. *The Social Construction of Reality.* London: Penguin, 1972.

BROTHERS, J. *Religious Institutions.* London: Longman, 1971.

BUDD, S. *Sociologists and Religion.* New York and London: Collier-Macmillan, 1973.

COX, H. *The Secular City.* New York: Macmillan, 1965.

CRYSDALE, S. "Some Problematic Aspects of Religion in Canada," *Sociological Focus* 9 (April 1976): 137–148.

CULLY, K., and HARPER, F., eds. *Will the Churches Lose the City?* New York: World Publishing Co., 1969.

DURKHEIM, E. *The Elementary Forms of Religious Life.* New York: Free Press, 1915.

EISTER, A. "Religious Institutions in Complex Societies: Difficulties in Theoretic Specification of Functions," *American Sociological Review* 22(1957): 387–391.

FORMAN, J. "The Black Manifesto." In Victor Ficker and Herbert Graves, eds., *The Revolution in Religion.* Columbus, Ohio: Charles E. Merrill, 1973.

GALLUP POLL. "Report to Episcopalian Convention." Minneapolis, Minn.: September 1976.

GEERTZ, C. "Religion as a Cultural System." In Michael Banton, ed., *Anthropological Approaches to the Study of Religion.* London: Tavistock, 1968.

GLENN, N., and HYLAND, R. "Religious Preference and Worldly Success: Some Evidence from National Surveys." In Joseph Faulkner, ed., *Religious Influence in Contemporary Society.* Columbus, Ohio: Charles E. Merrill, 1972.

GLOCK, CHARLES and STARK, RODNEY. *Christian Beliefs and Anti-Semitism.* New York: Harper & Row, 1966.

GREELEY, A. *The Denominational Society.* Glenview, Ill.: Scott, Foresman, 1972.

———. *Unsecular Man: The Persistence of Religion.* New York: Delta, 1972.

HADDEN, J., and HEIMER, E. "Empirical Studies in the Sociology of Religion: An Assessment of the Past Ten Years," *Sociological Analysis* 31(1975): 153–171.

HERBERG, W. *Protestant, Catholic and Jew.* New York: Doubleday, 1955.

JACQUET, C., ed. *Yearbook of American Churches.* New York: National Council of Churches Press, 1971.

LUCKMANN, T. *The Invisible Religion.* New York: Macmillan, 1967.

NORTON, P. *Church and Metropolis.* New York: Seabury Press, 1964.

NOTTINGHAM, E. *Religion: A Sociological View.* New York: Random House, 1971.

WEBER, M. *From Max Weber: Essays in Sociology.* Trans. C. Wright Mills and H. Gerth. New York: Oxford University Press, 1958.

————. *The Protestant Ethic and the Spirit of Capitalism.* Trans. Talcott Parsons. New York: Scribner's, 1930.

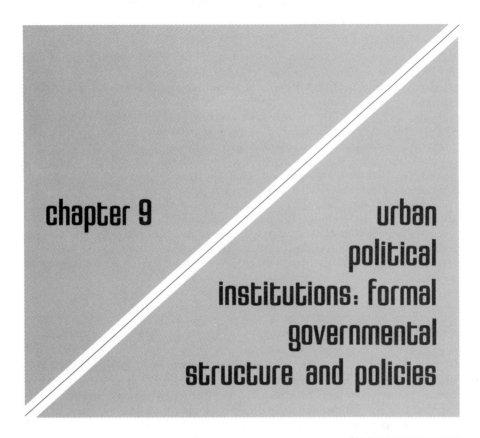

chapter 9

urban political institutions: formal governmental structure and policies

BY DONALD M. LEVIN

As urban areas grow in size and complexity, the problems of governing them and responding to the needs of their inhabitants become increasingly difficult. Growth and accompanying changes prompt added demands on government to shape the urban environment and to provide the public services required by people and institutions for survival. To meet these needs, large numbers of people must be housed and supplied with necessary amenities, goods and persons must be moved, and land and services must be available for industry and commerce. In addition, many people are looking toward local government to solve the overwhelming problems that seem to characterize urban life: racial conflict, rising crime rates, inadequate educational institutions, deteriorating services, congestion, poor housing, environmental neglect, and high unemployment, to name but a few of the most serious ones.

Since no general consensus exists as to how the resources of the urban community should be used to shape this environment and deal with these problems, urban political institutions are constantly bombarded by competing demands and pressures exerted by a changing electorate and social structure. Diverse groups attempt to influence elected officials and community leaders to bring about structural and administrative alterations that will, ostensibly, favor their interests. Thus, we increasingly hear calls for more "law and order" policies, Black Power, community control, decentralization, neighborhood schools, metropolitan government, strict zoning controls, or school integration. Many argue that urban problems are really national in nature and can only be solved by greater federal involvement. Others, fearing the imposition of federal regulations and restrictions, propose different solutions that will ensure local control and autonomy. Still others argue that government at any level is not capable of adequately dealing with these problems and that the only solution is for increased voluntary citizen involvement and initiative.

In this chapter and the one that follows we will examine some of these proposals and, in so doing, discuss the general topic of influence and decision making in urban areas. First, however, we will consider the general nature of urban political institutions with special reference to the historical, structural, functional, and power bases of urban politics and city government.

GOVERNING THE METROPOLIS

The problems just described are mainly the products of the rapid urbanization and metropolitanization of the twentieth century. The governance of urban areas in the earlier days of American society was a more orderly activity and less concerned with the problems of conflict resolution. The American cities of the pre-Civil War period were, for the most part, sparsely populated, compact, and composed of largely self-contained communities. The existing communities of this period were generally separated from one another by wide expanses of rural land and were each, in great measure, self-sufficient in their economic, social, and governmental activities.

As urbanization began to intensify after the Civil War, new pressures were imposed on the existing government pattern. Large-scale immigration, a rapidly growing population, and the impact of the industrial revolution drew huge masses to the cities. During the early years of this period, the local governmental system seemed to be keeping pace with these changes. Many municipalities experienced substantial increases in population and enlarged their territorial size by annexing adjoining land to accommodate the growth. Eventually, however, the various states adopted policies that deliberately made annexation laws more difficult while, at the same time, encouraging the incorporation of new cities. Even though a considerable upsurge in municipal annexation has occurred in the post–World War II years, its usefulness has been confined to the absorption of neighboring unincorporated urban fringe areas. Now most of the largest cities have become locked into geographical space and have found annexation to be of little or no value.

While the problem of governmental jurisdiction within the metropolitan area has emerged as one of the critical issues in urban politics today, it is by no means the only problem facing urban political institutions in their adjustment to the metropolitan age. Social scientists, who traditionally have

Much of the government in early American cities was conducted through the town meeting. (Library of Congress)

tended to concentrate on the formal structure of government, are now increasingly interested in the informal attributes of the local political process. The result is a much greater awareness that the metropolitan area, fragmented as it may be, does constitute a viable social and political system in which interaction takes place among its parts and in which public policy emerges in one fashion or another. Many of the problems identified are interdependent and not easily reduced to simple cause and effect analysis. Governmental balkanization, fiscal and other resource deficiencies, bureaucratic responsiveness, or the conflict produced by competing power and interest groups are among the major problems that emerge.

A Fragmented Governmental System

The failure to develop a cohesive governmental structure flexible enough to keep pace with the expansion of urban areas has resulted in most metropolitan regions having a complexity of distinct political jurisdictions.

While this fragmented system is true of most metropolitan areas, the degree of complexity varies. Chicago is perhaps the most complex area in the country: within its SMSA, two states are represented as well as six counties, forty-nine townships, ten towns, thirty cities, 110 villages, more than 400 school districts, and 235 special tax districts. On the other hand, metropolitan Baltimore, twelfth largest in the country with a population of approximately 2.5 million, contains only twenty three local governments. As a general rule, however, the greater the population of an urban area, the larger the number of local units.

This high degree of fragmentation within an area of great urban density that is economically and socially integrated is not only a confusing and inefficient arrangement but one that also places great burdens on some groups within the population while giving advantages to others. The central city probably suffers the greatest disadvantages, because it is locked in and unable to partake of the affluence that generally accompanies expansion at the periphery. Murphy (1974, p. 520) describes this as follows:

> Characteristically, the older residential and business sections of the city fall into disrepair as residents and business firms move to sites outside the central city, where taxes are lower, transportation not as congested, and parking areas feasible. As the city's tax base declines, the per capita share of government cost increases and falls more heavily on those who remain. At the same time, through the growth of smaller corporate units all around it, the city may be entirely shut off from expansion through annexation which might make possible the further growth of factories and commercial establishments and thus an augmented tax base.

Perhaps the most apparent effect of governmental fragmentation in a metropolitan area reflects the failure to deal with the interdependent nature of such areas. Metropolitanization has created demands requiring areawide action. Certainly this is the case with regional transportation lines needed to carry people from one end of the urban complex to the other. Much of the unemployment problem in urban areas, particularly central cities, can be classified as structural unemployment, where the skills of the labor force do not match the requirements of available jobs in the region. Creating resources that will lessen the geographic isolation of potential employees from job opportunities can only effectively be done on an areawide basis. Other examples of areawide needs include police and fire protection, public and private housing, pollution control, water resources, and recreational services, to name but a few.

A study of any large metropolitan area will reveal numerous service and fiscal inequities. Many small suburban municipalities lack the fiscal and administrative resources to provide services, particularly when population is building up rapidly. As the more affluent citizens leave the central city for the peripheral communities, they are often replaced by low-income residential populations whose needs for health, education, and welfare services put added strains on a fiscal budget just when the city's resources are decreasing. Furthermore, this population displacement also tends to deprive the city of strong civic and political leaders whose talents could be used in various ways.

With many separate governmental units operating independently within an interdependent metropolitan area, a climate of political nonresponsibility also tends to develop. In the absence of some central authority to speak for the area, no policy-making body is held accountable for metropolitan problems and for failure arising from governmental action or inaction. Hence, the diffusion of political responsibility and authority tends to act as a roadblock to coordinated efforts for progress. Walsh (1969, p. 56) sees this as a problem of inertia and wasted energy.

The problems of fragmentation generally are well known and have received attention from public administrators, social scientists, and others. A consideration of how this problem has been and can be dealt with will be presented later in the chapter.

Financial Problems of the Metropolis

While money alone will not solve the various ills of urban America, many of the maladies are tied to economic factors that seem increasingly difficult for cities to deal with. Testifying before the Congressional Joint Economic Committee in 1976, Wallace I. Stecher, Budget Director of the City of Detroit, sounded the alarm by saying, "The basic structure of the local revenue base in America does not allow cities, at least the older core cities,

Public officials speak out on the issues at political rallies. (Marc Anderson)

to cope with the changing socioeconomic conditions in which we live. Very simply, the matter is slipping out of our hands."

What Stecher is referring to is that local governments, for the most part, depend on the property tax as their main source of income. Once an adequate source of revenue for expanding, economically prosperous cities, the property tax base in many large American cities is declining. This decline is due to several factors. The withdrawal of private property for freeway construction, the demolition of a slum area to make room for public housing, or the creation or expansion of urban service facilities such as schools and universities, hospitals, or civic buildings may all be important contributions to the quality and vitality of an urban area, but they also contribute to the demise of the tax base since they convert private (tax-producing) property to public (nontaxable) use. The central cities, where this problem is most acute, are limited in their ability to compensate for this loss by raising the tax rate on the remaining property. First of all, many cities are precluded from raising their rates because of city charter or state constitution restrictions. Second, if the tax rate goes too high there is always the danger that business and individuals may choose to relocate outside the city.

Another and perhaps related problem to the declining tax base crisis is that most of the central cities have been experiencing significant population losses. Between 1960 and 1970, the central cities of metropolitan areas lost 345,000 persons per year through net emigration; between 1970 and 1975 they lost 1,404,000 persons per year, or more than four times as many (Bureau of the Census, 1975). While it might appear on the surface that population loss should result in less pressure for spending, the economic reality is otherwise. Describing this predicament confronted by the older cities, Peterson (1976, p. 44) writes:

> ... few of the costs associated with urban growth are easily reversible into economics of diminution. Once a city's road, sewer, and water networks have been constructed to serve a given population, the costs of maintaining these networks does not decline significantly when population shrinks. On the contrary, as capital infrastructure ages, it becomes more costly to keep in repair. Cities that are losing population actually spend more, per capita, in capital investment than cities that are gaining population, due largely to the necessity (and difficulty) of replacing their antiquated capital stock.

Another problem related to the city's population decline is that the need for public services, such as fire and police protection, does not decline in proportion to the population and, in some cases, may actually increase. To reduce public employment expenses is difficult even under the best of circumstances and is particularly difficult when the city is losing private sector employment outlets, which is generally the case during periods of serious population declines. In addition, population loss is selective, withdrawing the more affluent, younger, and better educated people in the city and leaving behind proportionately higher numbers of the less well-educated, those having lower incomes, the nonwhite, and the elderly. Since these are the population characteristics associated with higher crime rates, lower school achievement scores, and the need for special health and housing services, it becomes obvious that the social composition of the population and not just the actual numbers involved takes on important economic aspects.

Not only are the central cities experiencing financial problems, but cities in general are currently under great financial pressure due to circumstances in addition to those just described. Virtually all cities confront pressure to expand city services, given the emphasis on environmental safeguards, police protection, employment programs, health care, and improved housing. In addition, cities are particularly vulnerable to inflationary pressures, especially labor costs. Labor-related costs, including salaries and provisions for fringe benefits, constitute 70 to 80 percent of most city budgets (Advisory Commission, 1976). Pension and other retirement benefits now account for a significant part of state and local wages. City workers have been demanding parity with workers in the federal and private sectors. Not always able to meet these demands, city administrators have frequently chosen, instead, to make concessions on fringe benefits that, in the long run, have proven to be prohibitively expensive to cities. As indicated in a governmental report, "some municipalities have not yet adopted the practice of fully costing out fringe benefits in dollar-and-cents terms thereby temporarily hiding the full cost of a labor settlement. . . . The net result from the standpoint of the city is an ever-increasing cost in terms of retirement payments, health and hospitalization payments, and decreasing productivity from employees because of longer vacations, more holidays, and generally shortened work weeks" (Advisory Commission, 1976, p. 230).

Several remedies have been proposed to alleviate these financial difficulties. One method would be to extend the central city's authority either to reach the more affluent tax base of the suburbs or to impose local income taxes on suburbanites employed in the city. Cities currently subjecting nonresident workers to income taxation include Baltimore, New York, Cleveland, St. Louis, Detroit, and Philadelphia. This method has not been too successful since the rates have been low (about 1 percent on the average) and industrial and commercial decentralization has shifted many jobs away from the central city (Caraley, 1977, pp. 414–415). Some have advocated greater use of the benefit principle which, in effect, means that people who use facilities or services should pay accordingly; for example, special assessments for sidewalks and sewers or admission charges to parks and museums. As equitable as this arrangement may appear, it soon becomes obvious that most services, such as police and fire protection, street lighting, or education are not divisible or capable of being individualized. Usually, those people who need the services most are the ones least able to pay for them.

Even if these problems did not exist, American cities by the late 1970s were finding themselves victims of a growing public resentment and a mood of irritation about the amount of money they have been required to spend on public needs. Frustrated by accelerating taxes and the squeeze of an inflationary economy, voters were turning to the ballot box to bring relief in one of the few areas over which they have some direct control—local property taxes. Spurred on by the passage of Proposition 13 in California, which limited property taxes in the state to 1 percent of the market value of property and restricted future assessment increases to a maximum of 2 percent per year, the electorate in other states also have voted to limit property taxes or have more directly placed limitations on the annual expenditure growth of state and local governments. Over the long term, the net effect of these moves will be that cities will be forced to seek new alternatives to meet their financial needs. In particular, states with distressed cities are being asked to choose between using their extra resources for urban fiscal relief or for middle-class taxpayer relief.

Facing these problems and struggling to survive the squeeze on their budgets, cities have experimented with such other revenue-producing sources as income taxes, sales and gross receipt taxes, intergovernmental grants, charges and fees, and the sale of public utility services to other communities (Durr, 1971, pp. 126–133). While some of these tactics have proven useful, it is increasingly obvious that the local urban communities, regardless of what methods they use, are limited in the resources they can tap to meet their needs. Many argue that the state and federal governments should assume a larger role in carrying the burden, particularly in such high-cost areas as education and welfare and, in so doing, relieve the local communities so that their own resources could be used to satisfy public service needs.

The question of which level of government within the federal system should be responsible for the urban political issues discussed here is a complex and controversial one that will be treated in the next section.

URBAN POLITICAL ORGANIZATION

Local Governmental Structure

How urban governments are organized and structured varies greatly in the United States. Differences exist in the degree of legal power and responsibility given to the various officials, governmental bodies, and other agencies that constitute the governmental complex. Differences also exist in how each of these political elements relate to one another in terms of legal superiority or subordination. An understanding of influence and decision making in urban areas certainly requires more than knowing the formal governmental structure of a city, such knowledge is important because it helps us to understand the ultimate route through which power and influence are channeled on their mission to effect change.

Basically, urban governments in the United States are organized along one of the following patterns: the mayor-council plan, the council-manager form, or the commission form. Each of these patterns was, in some ways, a response of municipal reformers of the Progressive era who sought to develop new governmental mechanisms to supplant the deficiencies of the weak mayor-council system that dominated urban politics during the last part of the nineteenth century. The weak mayor–strong council system, which emerged after the Civil War, was actually a product of Jacksonian democracy, with its emphasis on government by the average citizen. This political philosophy welcomed the urban masses to share in the function of government, broadened the base of popular participation in elections, and ensured access to government by all without regard to special qualification or prior training. Rotation in office, popular election of numerous officials, and broadbased party organization with its emphasis on the spoils system became standard features of local government during this period.

Instead of resulting in the popular control of municipal government, the Jacksonian ideology actually contributed to the development of boss rule, machine politics, corruption, and a patronage system that produced a cadre of city officials who were totally unprepared to deal with the complex problems of governance. The weak mayor–strong council structure that emerged became the most typical form of city government during the post–Civil War years and provided the opportunity for enterprising politicians to manipulate city affairs to their own advantage. By fragmenting the power of city government, this structure created a "disjointed, leaderless, and uncoordinated local governmental monster with dispersed power centers in local legislatures and the distribution of influence among many independent administrative boards and commissions" (Shank and Conant, 1975, p. 18).

The major Progressive era reorganization plans that attempted to remedy these problems evolved approximately between 1890 and 1915. The strong mayor plan was seen as a means of strengthening executive authority and centralizing control over administration by creating a chief executive with powers of appointment and removal of key department heads. Under this plan the mayor would also have power to submit budget plans, propose legislation, transfer funds as needed, and exercise the veto on legislation passed by the council.

Not all cities today that are organized along the mayor-council plan fall within the strong mayor format. One must really view the mayor-council structure as existing along a continuum, with some cities operating toward the strong mayor pole while others are positioned more toward the strong council end. Detroit, New York, Philadelphia, Cleveland, Boston, and Baltimore are good examples of cities whose governmental structure tends to veer toward the strong mayor pole, while Seattle, Milwaukee, and Los Angeles more closely limit the authority of their mayors.

Unlike the mayor-council system, the commission plan calls for a fusion of governmental responsibilities by providing for the election of a small governing body whose members collectively make legislative policy and individually exercise executive functions over the various city departments. This plan has not been used in cities of over 500,000 population and is currently only being used in three large cities with a population over 250,000—Portland, Oregon; St. Paul, Minnesota; and Tulsa, Oklahoma. While attracting a lot of interest when first started in Galveston, Texas, in

1901, it later became less popular as the council-manager form gained fame. The lack of a central focus of political leadership and the difficulty of reconciling the policy-making and administrative functions have tended to make this plan unappealing to most large cities today. Almost every year sees cities organized along this plan opting for a different type of structure, and there have been practically no new adoptions of this form of government since the 1930s.

In many ways the council-manager structure is similar to the commission plan in that a single body (in this case the council) has both legislative and executive authority. Unlike the commission form, however, the council delegates its administrative function to a professionally trained manager. Based on the desire to introduce efficiency and businesslike managerial skills while at the same time separating politics from administration, this type of organization has been particularly attractive to small and medium-sized cities, and, since World War II, has been used with great frequency by rapidly increasing numbers of suburban communities. It has become and still is the most widely used form of government in cities with populations between 25,000 and 250,000. This plan has not been used more widely in large cities partly because of the political neutrality of the manager and the diffusion of political authority among the council members. Shank and Conant (1975, p. 93) consider this aspect of the plan to be a structural limitation for large, complex cities: ". . . since the council is considered a governing body of coequals, affirmative governmental action cannot be achieved unless there is a fairly high level of consensus on public issues. Thus, the council-manager plan seems more adaptable to communities with relatively homogeneous populations rather than to cities with relatively diverse ethnic groups and considerable cleavage over issues."

Generally speaking, the mayor-council plan, with its concentration of political power in a single office, has become the dominant government structure in the large, heterogeneous, multiproblem central cities of the United States, particularly those located in the northeastern and midwestern sections of the country. These cities, most affected by the problems that have become known as the urban crisis, require strong mayors as agents of mediation because, as one political scientist observes, "there are so many competing interests . . . that a premium is placed on political leadership which can arbitrate the contest for the stakes of power in the city, and be held responsible by the electorate for its success in doing so" (Kessel, 1962, p. 616). The council-manager plan, on the other hand, is found more often in the homogeneous white middle-class suburbs, which tend to have less divisive populations. The commission plan, the least popular of the three, is used most frequently in "declining" communities (Shank and Conant, 1975, p. 94)—cities experiencing a loss in population, low mobility, low educational levels, and low white-collar composition.

State Politics and the Cities

Cities and the political leaders associated with them constantly are being criticized for not coming to grips with and solving the major social, environmental, and economic problems existing within their territorial domains. It is not uncommon for rising political personalities to find their careers disrupted because their inability to "get the city moving again" becomes a personal reflection of their incompetency and ineffectiveness. Such attitudes are caused, in part, by the lack of understanding that exists about the political authority cities actually have. Within the American federal system, cities per se do not enjoy any inherent rights of self-government. They exist as creatures of the states and can only exercise those governmental powers specifically allowed them. Even those municipalities that enjoy the privilege of home rule have a definite and explicit limit on the authority of the local entity to adopt ordinances that conflict with provisions of the state constitution or with state law concerned with matters of general state interest.

This subservience of the local cities to their parent states need not, by itself, be a major problem if the states were more responsive to urban concerns. The real problem arises from a lack of concern and, in some cases, a negative political orientation on the part of the states that has impeded or blocked efforts to deal with contemporary urban issues. Discussing the degree of effort that various levels of government have made in coping with these issues, Campbell and Shalla (1970, pp. 24-25) make the following assessment:

> Students of these matters generally agree that of the various parts of the governmental system, states have performed least well. Local governments, particularly city governments, have vigorously strained their tax bases to meet some of the problems of their areas. Suburban jurisdictions, responding to constituency demands, have concentrated on providing quality educational services. The federal government has initiated many new relevant programs and approaches to urban problems, even though the allocation of resources has been wholly inadequate. Such efforts do not characterize state governments. . . . Governors and legislators have simply found excuses ranging from the constitutional to the political for inaction.

Many reasons are given for the state governments' low level of responsiveness. One problem has been the limiting provisions of most state constitutions. Unlike the federal Constitution, which grants the national government specific powers, state constitutions are instruments of limitations. Since the states are delegated all the powers not granted to the federal government, state constitutions have developed strong limiting provisions as a protection against the fear of excessive government involvement by a political unit holding residual and nonenumerated powers. The result of these restrictions has been a ridigity and inability to respond to changing needs. For example, most states tend to limit the development of strong executive leadership by the governor by allowing for the direct election of various department heads who, as a result of this provision, develop their own constituencies and are not really responsible to the governor. The chief executive of the state, therefore, does not enjoy the strong leadership role many observers believe is needed to resolve urban problems.

Many states are also limited constitutionally in their ability to raise and expend the kinds of revenues needed to deal with these problems. Unlike the federal government, most states must abide by a constitutional tax limit

One of the most imposing state capitols is the Utah State Capitol in Salt Lake City. (Stan Wakefield)

that severely restricts the potential for revenue production tied to property values. For those states that have turned to income taxation as a supplementary source of funding, constitutional provisions frequently require that such taxes be both uniform and equal, thus inhibiting the adoption of a graduated income tax such as that used by the national government. This restriction not only results in a regressive and socially questionable form of taxation but also further limits the states' income-producing potential. On the expenditure side of the picture, states also are limited constitutionally in their freedom to use their resources as the legislature or governor may deem wise. Such limits prohibit some states from directly transferring public funds to municipal corporations regardless of the needs of the local communities. A common constitutional limitation is one that prohibits states from expending state funds for the benefit of private persons, corporations, or nonpublic institutions. In an era of growing emphasis on community action and activities by neighborhood organizations, such restrictions limit groups other than governmental agencies from dealing with urban problems. As one writer observes, ". . . some governmental functions and services could be effectively rendered, and potentially incendiary situations in slum and ghetto areas resolved, by providing the community and neighborhood groups with the means to work on problems of their own" (Grad, 1970, p. 39).

In addition to the limitations the states have imposed upon themselves restricting their capacity to deal with urban problems, the local government's ability to function effectively on its own is directly limited. These limitations include constitutional restrictions on the administrative structure of cities, on the range of powers cities can exercise, and on local fiscal matters dealing with the kinds and limits of taxes that can be imposed and the freedom to spend whatever revenues are collected. A. James Reichley (1970, p. 171) gives examples of the consequences of some of these restrictions:

> If the average mayor sets out to revamp the administrative structure that he heads, he must, as John Lindsay discovered in New York, secure approval for his plans from the state legislature. If he is faced by a riot, he may find himself, like Richard Daley in Chicago in the spring of 1968, without the elementary powers to call a curfew or halt the sale of gasoline. In Boston, the chief of police was appointed until 1962 by the governor of Massachusetts, and the police department of St. Louis is still governed by a board of commissioners appointed by the governor of Missouri.

However, even when not specifically limited in what they can do to aid the cities, many members of state legislatures until recently generally were hostile to meeting urban needs. Outstate legislators tended to dominate the membership of at least one house of every state legislative body even among those states with large urban and industrial constituencies. This domination was possible because of various political devices that guaranteed rural representation according to patterns existing in the nineteenth century when rural populations did represent the majority. Fearful of losing this domination in the face of the rapid growth of cities in the late nineteenth and twentieth centuries, reapportionment legislation was enacted that tended to ignore the significant population shifts that were taking place. As a result of this pattern, an overabundance of nonurban legislators existed who tended to share with their constituents "an anti–big city mentality, regarding the cities as sources of corruption, low morals and boss rule, and populated by alien peoples like Irish-Catholics, later, Italian and eastern European Catholics and Jews, and still later, slum blacks. Furthermore, cities were perceived as the homes of intellectuals, free-thinkers, and radical types of all sorts" (Caraley, 1977, p. 71). A governing body characterized by this type of mentality obviously would not be responsive to diverting funds to meet urban needs nor would it be willing to allow these alien groups to enjoy power within the state political structure proportionate to their numbers.

Beginning in 1962, the Supreme Court issued a series of decisions which, many city representatives and their sympathizers hoped, would establish greater equity in urban representation in the state houses. These decisions required the states to redraw their legislative districts to reflect the "one person, one vote" doctrine and thereby guarantee representation proportionate to the reality of population location. In fact, however, reapportionment has not led to substantial strengthening of the political power of the large cities in the state capitals but has tended, instead, to work to the political advantage of the suburbs. Given increased metropolitanization and the rapid growth of the suburbs, it soon became obvious that the "one person, one vote" principle would increase suburban representation, not necessarily that of the central cities, many of which have actually been losing population since 1960. As a result, large cities currently face resistance from new adversaries—no longer rural members but equally unsympathetic suburban representatives who frequently see the interests of their constituents as being different from those of their neighbors in the large central cities.

The general conclusion that emerges is that the central cities do not now and will not in the foreseeable future have the votes to pass legislation favorable to their interests. This does not mean that the cities are without legislative weapons. Party politics, particularly for the Democratic majorities in the large cities, can be influential as a bargaining tool on the state level, and the use of lobby tactics, especially when they are used by urban business interests, can also be of great benefit. Regardless of what tools are used to influence political behavior on the state level, the truth remains that the states have a number of unique qualifications for playing a leading role in urban affairs. Not only do they have the legal and constitutional authority to do so but they also have greater taxable sources upon which to draw and the capacity to equalize resources and services among their local units. Furthermore, covering the wide geographical areas they do, the states have the latitude to meet needs on an areawide basis that cannot be effectively administered by local communities who are locked into the restricted patterns making up the governmental mosaic of the average metropolitan area.

The Cities and the Federal Government

Under the American federal system as it was originally conceived under the Constitution and later through nearly 200 years of operation, each level of government has its own special function to perform. Having no direct jurisdiction or regulatory control over local government (other than the control inherent in the constitutional provision establishing the laws of the United States to be the "supreme law of the land"), the federal government, until the 1930s, had directed little attention to the problems of individual cities. Beginning in the 1930s and spurred on by the pressing economic demands created by the Depression and the New Deal political philosophy of Franklin D. Roosevelt, a variety of welfare, health, and housing programs were passed by Congress. While the legislation creating these programs was not directly aimed at dealing with urban problems, they did have impact on the nation's cities because many of the Depression era victims lived there. As Roscoe C. Martin (1965, p. 111) describes it, the year 1932 constitutes "a sort of geological fault line in the evolution of the federal government's relationship with large cities."

That relationship, for the most part, has taken the form of various urban-oriented grant programs. Unable to assume direct responsibility for cities, as national governments do in other countries, Washington has chosen instead to involve itself in urban problems by providing resources from the federal treasury to deal with such areas as housing, planning, poverty, income maintenance, health, education, urban renewal, and crime. During the post-World War II period (1946-1960), the major emphasis was on the continuation and expansion of the welfare, health, and housing programs begun in the 1930s with new programs also developing in the fields of education, transportation, and community development. The Housing Act of 1949 was a particularly significant piece of legislation because it not only enlarged the public housing program but also established a continuing slum clearance and redevelopment program that was to be the forerunner of the controversial urban renewal programs that began appearing in the mid-1950s.

Federal involvement in the cities during the decade of the fifties might have been even greater had the national political climate been less ambiguous. The presidency was occupied by Dwight D. Eisenhower (1952-1960) while the Congress was predominantly Democratic. Basically a conservative on domestic economic and social issues, Eisenhower was cautious and reluctant in advocating and supporting various congressional proposals that would establish programs for area redevelopment, broaden social security benefits and unemployment compensation, establish medical care for the aged, or provide federal aid to education, water pollution control, community health facilities, and the like.

The changes in the political climate after 1961 with the election of John F. Kennedy and later with the ascendancy of Lyndon B. Johnson to the presidency brought with them a rapid escalation of the national government's grant programs. Responding to the urban political-interest groups that usually support Democratic politicians, and also motivated by the growing national awareness of the plight of the cities, the Democratic administrations were able to create grant programs in such areas as air pollution (1963), neighborhood youth corps (1964), equal employment opportunity (1964), community action (1964), aid for educationally deprived children (1964), solid waste disposal (1964), water and sewer programs (1965), law enforcement assistance (1965), and model cities (1966). In addition, many other programs were established to deal with the "war on poverty" as well as a wide variety of health services. While most of these programs were not considered to be the manifestation of an urban policy by the national government, they have, for the most part, had their major impact in the large metropolitan areas.

Unlike the earlier programs, many of these newer efforts bypass the states and send aid directly from Washington to local governments, an approach that has come to be known as "direct federalism" (DeGrove, 1970, pp. 145-46). However, regardless of whether the cities receive the money directly or the funds are administered through the individual states, the grant program has affected the large cities in various ways. As previously discussed, the fiscal plight of urban governments made it difficult and, in some cases, impossible for many municipalities to meet their essential obligations let alone to assume additional tasks, desirable as they may be. The support and subsidies available from the national treasury, while not solving this problem, have at least prevented it from becoming even more critical. In the view of one political scientist, grant programs helping to provide "low-cost public housing, urban renewal, community action, and

The U.S. Census, conducted every ten years, provides the government with the information it needs to administer federal programs on the local level. (Irene Springer)

manpower training have stimulated city governments to undertake new programs that the cities lacked the will, imagination, or financial capacity to establish and maintain on their own" (Caraley, 1977, p. 136).

Not everyone, however, has looked favorably on the grant programs. Many of the governors have been especially strong in their objections because they feel that their authority and power have been diminished when local governments and state administrative departments deal directly with federal authorities. Others complain because the recipient city governments are obliged to comply with federal regulations and guidelines that affect hiring procedures, affirmative action, and the maintaining of certain procedural requirements, necessitating a complex and costly reporting system. Still others question whether the negative byproducts of the grants program compensate for its positive accomplishments. The massive interstate highway program, for example, as beneficial as it has been, has contributed to lowering the tax base of many cities by demolishing usable older homes, thereby reducing the city's stock of low-rent housing. Furthermore, the new highways helped to facilitate the flight to the suburbs by the middle-class, affluent, white families, leaving behind less mobile citizens who not only contribute less in taxes but frequently require more in services. This problem is further aggravated because the highway construction has stimulated the use of private automobiles, adding to traffic congestion during commuting hours, and providing less incentive for the development of mass transit systems.

During the Nixon-Ford years the national government began backing away from the direct grant approach in favor of the concept of revenue sharing, which would provide federal funds to the states and local governments to be used at their own discretion according to a complex formula that assigns various weights to population, local tax efforts, and per capita income. This concept was philosophically more appealing to the Republican administration because "it moved public-decision making responsibility away from Washington and seemed to be a way to ease out the narrowly targeted 'categorical' programs of the 1960's, many of which were regarded as alien, ineffective, or mischievous" (Gorham and Glazer, 1976, p. 13). Promoted as an approach that promised to provide the cities with more federal support than they were previously receiving, the special revenue-sharing program (passed into law in 1972) initially provided funding at the same level as the categorical grants they replaced. Once the general concept of revenue sharing was adopted, the federal government began to play a less active role in the resolvement of local urban problems.

Opponents of the revenue-sharing law argue that it not only allows the federal government to be less involved, but that it usually provides resources in greater abundance where they are less needed (the fast-growing affluent suburbs) as opposed to where the greatest needs exist—the older central cities. Zimmerman (1975, p. 467) argues that revenue sharing will also delay the kinds of structural rearrangements that are critically needed to deal with the urban realities of the late twentieth century.

> One implication of federal revenue-sharing is clear. It will help to perpetuate the atomistic government of the metropolis because the shared revenue will enable many small units to survive, perhaps delaying the formation of a metropolitan government. Congress would have chosen a wiser course of action had the enabling act contained a clause providing incentives for the formation of a a two-tier system of local government in metropolitan areas. The upper tier could be either a modernized county government or a new area-wide government.

The current relationship between the federal government and urban communities tends to be cautious and somewhat tenuous as a general conservative mood pervades the national political scene.

MODERNIZING URBAN GOVERNMENT

As must be evident by this time, urban areas in the United States are experiencing problems of growth and management that are frequently greater than the capabilities of the political structure that has been provided to govern these areas. Much experimentation has taken place, resulting in a wide variety of schemes, proposals, and plans directed at the broad issue of metropolitan reorganization. Many of these ideas have not been acted on while others have been successfully implemented. We cannot discuss all these proposals, but we can at least mention some of the more prominent ones so that the reader may be aware of the possibilities involved.

Annexation traditionally has been the most commonly proposed remedy for the problems of urban sprawl and fragmentation. While once an important factor in bringing about orderly urban growth, annexation has been much less viable in recent years, particularly for the older large cities surrounded by fairly affluent suburbs. The suburban communities tend to vote against annexation because of the fear of higher taxes and being controlled by a corrupt and inefficient central city government as well as the desire to be separate from the social constituencies found in many of the central cities.

Another approach somewhat similar to annexation, at least functionally, is the extension of a city's boundaries to make them contiguous with those of the county. City-county consolidation has been accomplished in several ways. In a complete consolidation, a new government is formed by the amalgamation of the county and municipal governments, while a partial-consolidation plan merges most county functions with the city's but still allows the county to perform a few functions unilaterally as required by the state constitution. There has been a lot of experimentation lately in merging a single service or activity being performed separately by a city and county (such as a health or educational service) but for the most part city-county consolidation has not been widely used. Daniel Grant (1970, p. 68) explains the failure of this approach: "Constitutional requirements for county officers, taxes rates, methods of electing officials, debt limits, and many other provisions have either inhibited cities and counties from making the consolidation effort, or have caused countless headaches over court litigation following its adoption."

Other plans commonly proposed but almost never adopted call for the restructuring of local government in urban areas to form metropolitan federations. Modeled after the federal system, this proposal calls for areawide government to perform those functions that transcend municipal boundaries while the city governments perform purely local functions. The state governments generally have not been very supportive of this idea and it has also been resisted by the local communities, which fear the loss of autonomy and diffusion of their power base. The best known examples of metropolitan federation are the governments of Greater London and metropolitan Toronto. In the United States the closest thing to this type of government is the fusion found in Dade County and Miami but, as one political scientist describes it, "in practice, Dade County's metro is more nearly a 'municipalized county' than it is a federation of municipalities, since the cities as such are not represented on the board of commissioners" (Grant, 1970, p. 72).

Metropolitan reorganization schemes have also called for the transfer of functional responsibility to the state, intergovernmental service agreements, the creation of special district governments, and various forms of tax sharing. In recent years, however, new types of organizations have developed to bring about regional planning and coordination short of the actual restructuring of the local governmental system. These plans usually call for the establishment of Councils of Governments (COGs). Stimulated by national legislative requirements that each application for a federal loan or grant be accompanied by evidence indicating that the proposed project is in accord with the goals of regional planning, COGs are voluntary coordinating agencies made up primarily of elected representatives of municipalities and counties within a given urban area. In contrast to proposals calling for governmental restructure, a proposal to create a COG usually encounters little opposition since no threat to "home rule" exists. While there are certainly advantages and disadvantages to voluntary organizations of this nature, whether COGs or other regional counterparts will be able to solve highly controversial issues such as housing and welfare without the authority needed to compel compliance is questionable.

Although there is no shortage of plans and proposals such as those described above, various legal and political considerations continue to work against any meaningful metropolitan reorganization at this time. Speaking about the future possibilities of urban governmental reform, Alan Shank (1973, p. 353) remarks:

> Future metropolitan cooperation must take into account the increasing inability of local governments to cope with areawide problems. Whether the future will bring voluntary interlocal cooperation, integrated metropolitan government, new 'national cities,' 'metropolitan states,' or reformed federal-state-local financial arrangements is difficult to forecast. But one thing is certain: Comprehensive metropolitan solutions will not be possible until new consensus is established to erase city-suburban hostilities and to unite the divergent goals of different political constituencies.

SELECTED BIBLIOGRAPHY

ADVISORY COMMISSION ON INTERGOVERNMENTAL RELATIONS. "City Financial Emergencies." In Alan Shank, ed., *Political Power and the Urban Crisis*, pp. 214–242. 3rd ed. Boston: Holbrook Press, 1976.

BAKER, JOHN H. *Urban Politics in America.* New York: Scribner's, 1971.

BANFIELD, EDWARD C., and WILSON, JAMES Q. *City Politics.* Cambridge, Mass: Harvard University Press, 1965.

BOLLENS, JOHN C., and SCHMANDT, HENRY J. *The Metropolis.* New York: Harper & Row, Pub., 1965.

CAMPBELL, ALAN K., and SHALLA, DONNA E. "Problems Unsolved, Solution Untried: The Urban Crisis." In Alan K. Campbell, ed., *The States and the Urban Crisis*, pp. 4–26. Englewood Cliffs, N.J.: Prentice-Hall, 1970.

CARALEY, DEMETRIOUS. *City Governments and Urban Problems.* Englewood Cliffs, N.J.: Prentice-Hall, 1977.

CLEAVELAND, FREDERIC N. *Congress and Urban Problems.* Washington, D.C.: The Brookings Institution, 1969.

DANIELSON, MICHAEL N., ed. *Metropolitan Politics*. 2nd ed. Boston: Little, Brown, 1971.

DEGROVE, JOHN M. "Help or Hindrance to State Action? The National Government." In Alan K. Campbell, ed., *The States and the Urban Crisis*, pp. 139–168. Englewood Cliffs, N.J.: Prentice-Hall, 1970.

DOWNES, BRYAN T., ed. *Cities and Suburbs*. Belmont, Calif.: Wadsworth, 1971.

DURR, FRED. *The Urban Economy*. San Francisco: Intext Educational Publishers, 1971.

FITCH, LYLE C. "Fiscal and Productive Efficiency in Urban Government Systems." In Amos H. Hawley and Vincent P. Rock, eds., *Metropolitan America in Contemporary Perspective*. New York: John Wiley, 1975.

GOODMAN, PERCIVAL, et al. *Crisis in Urban Government: A Symposium Restructuring Metropolitan Area Government*. Silver Spring, Md.: Thomas Jefferson Publishing Company, 1971.

GORHAM, WILLIAM, and GLAZER, NATHAN, eds. *The Urban Predicament*. Washington, D.C.: The Urban Institute, 1976.

GRAD, FRANK P. "The States' Capacity to Respond to Urban Problems: The State Constitution." In Alan K. Campbell, ed., *The States and the Urban Crisis*, pp. 27–58. Englewood Cliffs, N.J.: Prentice-Hall, 1970.

GRANT, DANIEL R. "Urban Needs and State Response: Local Government Reorganization." In Alan K. Campbell, ed., *The States and the Urban Crisis*, pp. 59–84. Englewood Cliffs, N.J.: Prentice-Hall, 1970.

GREER, SCOTT. *Governing the Metropolis*. New York: John Wiley, 1962.

HADDEN, JEFFREY K., et al., eds. *Metropolis in Crisis*. 2nd ed. Itasca, Ill.: F. E. Peacock Publishers, 1971.

HAWLEY, AMOS, and ROCK, VINCENT, eds. *Metropolitan America in Contemporary Perspective*. New York: John Wiley, 1975.

KESSEL, JOHN H. "Governmental Structure and Political Environment: A Statistical Note About American Cities," *American Political Science Review* 56 (September 1962).

KOTLER, MILTON. *Neighborhood Government*. Indianapolis, Ind.: Bobbs-Merrill, 1969.

LEACH, RICHARD H. *American Federalism*. New York: W. W. Norton & Co., Inc., 1970.

LEMAY, M. C. "The State and Urban Areas: A Comparative Assessment," *National Civic Review* 61 (Dec 1972): 542–548.

LINEBERRY, ROBERT, and SHARKANSKY, IRA. *Urban Politics and Public Policy*. New York: Harper & Row Publishers, 1971.

LOCKARD, DUANE. *The Politics of State and Local Government*. 2nd ed. New York: Macmillan, 1969.

MARANDO, V. L. *Local Government Reorganization: An Overview*. Washington, D.C.: National Academy of Public Administration, 1973.

MARTIN, ROSCOE C. *The Cities and the Federal System*. New York: Atherton Press, 1965.

MOGULOF, MELVIN B. *Governing Metropolitan Areas*. Washington, D.C.: The Urban Institute, 1971.

MURPHY, RAYMOND E. *The American City: An Urban Geography*. New York: McGraw-Hill, 1974.

PALEN, J. JOHN. *The Urban World*. New York: McGraw-Hill, 1975.

PETERSON, GEORGE E. "Finance." In William Gorham and Nathan Glazer, eds., *The Urban Predicament*, pp. 35-118. Washington, D. C.: The Urban Institute, 1976.

PROUDFOOT, MALCOM J. "Chicago's Fragmented Political Structure," *Geographical Revue* 47 (1957): 106-117.

REAGAN, MICHAEL D. *The New Federalism*. New York: Oxford University Press, 1972.

REICHLEY, A. JAMES. "The Political Containment of Cities." In Alan K. Campbell, ed., *The States and the Urban Crisis*, pp. 169-195. Englewood Cliffs, N.J.: Prentice-Hall, 1970.

REUSS, HENRY S. *Revenue-Sharing*. New York: Praeger, 1970.

SHANK, ALAN. *Political Power and the Urban Crisis*. 2nd ed. Boston: Holbrook Press, 1973.

SHANK, ALAN, and CONANT, RALPH W. *Urban Perspective*. Boston: Holbrook Press, 1975.

U.S. BUREAU OF THE CENSUS. *Mobility of the Population of the United States: March 1970-March 1975*. Washington, D.C.: October 1975.

WALSH, ANN MARIE HAUCK. *The Urban Challenge to Government*. New York: Praeger, 1969.

ZIMMERMAN, JOSPEH F. "The Patchwork Approach: Adaptive Responses to Increasing Urbanization." In Amos H. Hawley and Vincent P. Rock, eds., *Metropolitan America in Contemporary Perspective*. New York: John Wiley, 1975.

chapter 10

urban political institutions: informal power structure and local decision makers

BY DONALD M. LEVIN

URBAN POLITICAL INFLUENCES

In the preceding chapter we have concentrated mainly on the formal governmental structure and have examined some of the problems associated with that structure. The question that is frequently raised by sociologists and political scientists is whether or not the formal governmental mechanisms really indicate how community decisions are made, or whether more important informal mechanisms are at work. During the last quarter of a century a good deal of attention has been given to this question, with the result that a large body of studies has emerged focusing on the community power structure. These studies have attempted to answer some of the following questions: 1) Are the power and influence operative in American communities monolithic in nature, or is there instead a series of competing power structures that tend to act as checks and balances against one another? 2) Which groups or individuals actually wield power and in what fashion? 3) Are there differences in the power structure pattern between small cities and large complex cities? 4) Is there any relationship between a city's power structure and that of regional and national power systems? and 5) What effect do population shifts have upon the influence patterns at work?

From these various studies two general schools of thought have emerged. One school holds that decision making operates in a monolithic system with the power concentrated in the hands of a ruling elite who, because of the dominant economic roles they play in the community, are able to wield their influence over political decisions. The opposite view contends that social power in a community is relatively decentralized and, to the extent that power structures exist at all, they tend to be highly pluralistic with elected political officials, economic elites, and various other special-interest groups combining together on various issues to form temporary power groups.

Elitist and Pluralistic Views: Theory and Research

The leading proponent of the "power elite" perspective at the national level was C. Wright Mills (1957, pp. 3–4), who argued that the concentration of power in America has come to rest in the hands of

> men whose positions enable them to transcend the ordinary environments of ordinary men; they are in positions to make decisions having major consequences.... For they are in command of the major hierarchies and organizations of modern society. They rule the big corporations. They run the machinery of the state and claim its prerogatives. They direct the military establishment. They occupy the strategic command posts of the social structure, in which are now centered the effective means of the power and the wealth and the celebrity which they enjoy.

Mills thus sees an "interlocking directorate" of top-ranking military, political, governmental, and business leaders who essentially determine all the major policy decisions.

David Riesman (1953, pp. 246–247), on the other hand, presents the case for those advocating the plurality of power:

> There has been in the last fifty years a change in the configuration of power in America, in which a single hierarchy with a ruling class at its head has been replaced by a number of "veto groups" among which power is dispersed. The shifting nature of the lobby provides us with an important clue as to the difference between the present American political scene and that of the age of McKinley. The ruling class of businessmen could relatively easily decide where their interests lay and what editors, lawyers, and legislators might be paid to advance them. The lobby ministered to the clear leadership, privilege, and imperative of the business ruling class. Today we have substituted for that leadership a series of groups, each of which has struggled for and finally attained a power to stop things conceivably inimical to its interests and, within far narrower limits, to start things.

Unlike Mills, Riesman does not believe that the same group or coalition of groups sets all major policy. To Riesman, many power structures are potentially available to influence policy, but these power groups are fre-

Philadelphia's City Hall is one of America's largest and one of its most notable municipal government buildings. (Philadelphia Chamber of Commerce)

quently dormant on most issues and come to life selectively when their own self-interests are at stake. Given the wide range of policy issues possible, the actual exercise of power tends to be highly diffuse.

One of the early studies that attempted to examine the power structure within a local community was conducted by Floyd Hunter in 1953. Using an investigatory approach known as the "reputational" method, Hunter sought to identify the power leaders in Regional City (a psuedonym for Atlanta, Georgia) by first assembling lists of known civic, governmental, and business leaders and then submitting this list to a panel of knowledgeable judges who were asked to rate them according to their ability to influence decisions. There was a high degree of consensus among the judges as to who the real power leaders were. Drawn mainly from business and industrial circles (the mayor was the only elected official among the top ten leaders), these leaders constituted a small, highly interrelated group in which the members were known to one another. Preferring to remain anonymous, they remained behind the scenes, relying instead on government officials to carry out their wishes. "They are able to enforce their decisions by persuasion, intimidation, coercion, and, if necessary, force" (Hunter, 1953, p. 24).

Using a different methodological approach, Robert Dahl, in his study of New Haven, Connecticut, in 1961, chose to analyze the resolution of various kinds of community issues to determine the dynamics involved in the decision making. Rather than rely on opinions of who the leaders were, Dahl was more interested in studying power in action. He first identified a group of 238 economic notables as well as other potential people of influence (such as elected officials and religious leaders) who did not occupy roles of economic importance. Then, by looking at the specific issues under investigation, he sought to identify those people actually involved in the decisions made. From this investigation Dahl came up with results dramatically different from those of Hunter's study. He concluded that the top leaders were not a monolithic and covert elite but a coalition of public officials and private individuals who reflected the interests and concerns of different segments of the community. As Dahl (1961, p. 72) reports: "The Economic Notables, far from being a ruling group, are simply one of many groups out of which individuals sporadically emerge to influence the politics and acts of city officials."

While the research of Hunter and Dahl is frequently cited as classic examples of community power studies, many other investigations of this issue have also been undertaken. As previously indicated, the results of these studies generally favor either the monolithic elite theory or the pluralist position. On the other hand, some investigators have concluded that power at the local level, be it monolithic or pluralistic, is relatively unimportant since higher levels of government and industry make more and more decisions, reducing local autonomy. Robert Presthus (1964) found in his study that where resources are of local origin (school, hospitals, and new industry) local power still operates; but in other spheres local power is declining because of nationwide centralization in both political and economic decision making.

Given the current state of knowledge on the diffusion of power in local communities, the early tendencies to generalize about all American cities clearly were oversimplified. An understanding of the power structure of a particular city can only be understood in relation to that community's peculiar social, economic, demographic, and governmental characteristics. Lineberry and Sharkansky (1971, p. 159) believe that "each community possesses certain features that make it unique and imperfectly comparable to other communities. . . . what is really important may not be [only] the presence of particular factors but their combination and interaction in a particular setting." For example, these writers propose that a pluralistic power structure is more likely to be the mode with cities that have larger number of inhabitants, a more diversified economic system, strong labor unions, large proportions of absentee-owned enterprises, a socially heterogeneous population, a large number of secondary associations, and competitive party politics. The more complex the community and the more politicized the electoral process, the more likelihood that the political power in the community will be relatively broad.

Besides knowing the degree to which a particular city corresponds to the democratic ideal of broad citizen participation, knowledge about the power structure of a community is essential in understanding how and in what terms public policy will be formulated there. For example, cities with monolithic power structures may offer fewer public services to poor neighborhoods, may emphasize economic development over social welfare policies, may limit acess to public employment, or may tax and spend at lower than average levels. Pluralist communities, on the other hand, may develop policies that are quite varied and diffuse, sometimes favoring one interest and at other times interests of divergent groups.

Comparing the various community power studies of the past two decades, Boskoff (1970, p. 233) concludes that the results of these studies indicate "a diversity that disturbs the quest for therapeutic simplicity of a Hunter or a Mills." Nevertheless, he has managed to synthesize a set of generalizations from these findings that may help to bring some order to the wide range of investigations that have focused on communities of different sizes, varied population mixes, diverse economic foundations, and divergent regional locations. Included among these generalizations are the following:

1. Urban power structures tend to be more clearcut and visible in smaller urban regions, in more isolated urban regions, and in those that are relatively immune from processes of political, technological, and economic changes.

2. In newly developed cities (such as those found in the western United States), public officials normally dominate processes of community decision making. This may occur because the "satellite" elites are not consciously organized or because potentially influential elites are immersed in their business pursuits, have migrated and identified with suburban areas, or are not facing pressure from national corporations for community participation.

3. In complex cities (particularly the largest metropolitan regions in the United States), a great variety of issues and relevant satellite groups in effect serves to limit the influence of such groups. Over time, these groups tend to cancel out their respective strengths. . . .

4. In general, economic elites predominate in smaller, slowly developing cities, in early stages of significant economic growth of larger cities (such as Dallas), and in cities where the governmental structure institutionalizes the diffusion of authority (as in weak mayor systems or the commission form) (Boskoff, 1970, pp. 233–34).

Implicit in the above generalizations and supported through the observations and analyses of other social scientists is the conclusion that the increased complexity and interdependence of urban life has acted to bring a diffusion rather than a concentration of power within the delicately balanced network of groups that make up contemporary urban communities. Reflecting this conclusion after reviewing the extensive literature on community power, William Spinrad (1966, p. 229) writes:

All that has been said tends to substantiate a pluralistic interpretation of American community power. People try to exercise power when a particular decision is salient and/or required. This obviously means that different groups in the community will be more involved in different kinds of decisions. Many groups possess appropriate resources, internal decision-making mechanisms, access to those who make the necessary formal decisions, widely accepted legitimacy and values, means for communicating to and mobilizing large publics. The investigation of power then becomes a study of discrete decision-making processes, with many sectors of the population revealing varying degrees of impact on different type decisions.

COMMUNITY LEADERSHIP—LOCAL DECISION MAKERS

If, as just described, the contemporary American city is truly a pluralistic enterprise with multiple power centers coming to the surface at various times in accordance with their own self-interests, the principal actors who make up these power groups now deserve consideration. Some of these principals operate as official representatives of the governmental structure while others belong to economic, social, religious, or professional organizations that have become "politicized"—they seek regularly or occasionally to further their aims through the institutions of government. Regardless of which power structure theory one subscribes to, there is agreement that power does not always reside with those who are the actual occupants of formal positions. Decisions are ultimately made as a result of the give and take between the various official and unofficial groups that compete within the arena of urban politics. Bollens and Schmandt (1965, p. 184) describe this decision-making process:

> The metropolitan area, feudal and balkanized as it may be, constitutes a viable social and political system in which interaction takes place among its parts and in which public policy emerges in one fashion or another. This policy may be sufficient or inadequate, sound or unsound, in the public interest or against it. Whatever its quality, the final product results from the accumulated effects of many decisions by many autonomous or semi-independent governments, agencies, interest groups, and individuals. So long as an area-wide authority with general governmental powers is absent, public policy-making in the metropolis can be of no other character.

Some of those who participate in this decision-making process will now be discussed according to the several major organizational categories in which they are found.

Mayors

A good deal of attention has been focused on the leadership role of big-city mayors since the 1960s as the nature and extent of the urban crisis has become dramatized throughout the nation. During this period, as never before, the mayors have had to deal with riots, crime, lawlessness, and a growing sense of community fear. Increased racial animosities, blight, unemployment, high taxes, and the low quality of public services has accelerated the middle-class flight to the suburbs. Attempting to deal with these problems, the mayors have come up against bureaucratic unresponsiveness, public employee strikes, and lack of budgetary controls. Big-city mayors face one of the toughest public jobs in America. . . . The men in City

Hall often find it difficult to resolve the conflicting demands of a fragmented, hostile, and politically polarized constituency. Their capacity to develop effective solutions to urban problems depends largely on public support, available resources, and authority to get things done—all of which are frequently lacking.

How then do those who hold the office of mayor respond to this challenge? The approaches are obviously quite varied depending upon the background and personality of the person holding the job and the nature of the community involved. Realizing, that there are many ways to categorize mayorality styles, Duane Lockard (1969, pp. 146-154) groups the mayors as reformers, program politicians, evaders, and stooges.

The "reformer" rides aggressively into town promising to do away with corruption, bossism, special interests, and other varieties of political sin. "Invariably dramatic and often demagogic, always courageous but inclined to moralistic tilting with windmills," the reform mayor is also usually a competent politician who can gather together an effective organization from his or her wide following in the community. While still on the contemporary scene, the old-fashioned political machine's decline has reduced the reformer's opportunities to wage war against "the bad guys" and, consequently, relatively few mayors today display this type of leadership role. Perhaps the best known mayor who would fit this mold was Fiorello LaGuardia of New York, who is described by Lockard as being a "flamboyant egoist, demagogue, driving political master and chief flagellant of the party leaders of New York City."

The "program politician" is the hardworking activist mayor who sees his or her role as similar to that of the chief executive of a large corporation. Committed to the goal of moving the city ahead, this type of leader tends to be innovative and imaginative in presenting new programs and policies and works diligently to promote his or her proposals.

Unlike the types described above, the "evader" category has not produced a cadre of well-known examples, since the careers of such mayors do not commend them to national audiences. Lockard describes this type of politician as one whose style is based on the avoidance of conflict. "To assure their tenure they avoid commitments, seek zealously to placate disputes, and follow the lead set by councilmen or other actors." While this type of mayor may be found in any city, it is more commonly seen in smaller, stable communities relatively free from such serious problems as blight, financial difficulties, or crime. To some extent, the structure of weak-mayor systems also lends itself to developing this type of leadership role.

Finally, the "stooge," who is a figurehead for a political machine or for some other type of covert power structure, appears to be less in evidence today as the power plurality in metropolitan areas expands. Some evidence exists, however, that new types of influence, such as organized crime, may be able to exert control over elected officials today, as indicated by recent indictments and convictions of some mayors. Sometimes after a mayor enters the office as a "stooge," he or she attempts to break away and assert independence. Usually these attempts have not been successful because, as Lockard notes, "if the political conditions of a community are such that an organization has strong enough control over access to office to choose a compliant stooge, then it is likely that the power can be used to squash a rebel."

Regardless of the leadership style adopted, the job of big-city mayor today is precarious. With limited political and economic resources at their disposal and confronted with problems that go beyond the geographical boundaries of their authority, most mayors today do not have the political power needed to deal effectively with the responsibilities and tasks that face them. Dahl's (1961, p. 204) description of the plight of New Haven's mayor illustrates this problem well: "The mayor was not at the peak of a pyramid but rather at the center of intersecting circles. He rarely commanded. He negotiated, cajoled, insisted, demanded, even threatened, but he needed support from other leaders who simply could not be commanded. Because the mayor could not command, he had to bargain."

City Councils

The people who make up the bodies of the city councils in the United States represent a highly heterogeneous group, coming from varying income, educational, occupational, and ethnic backgrounds and having differing views about their jobs, their levels of responsibility to their constituencies, and the powers they should exercise. The actual mix of those who serve as councilmembers in a particular city will depend on several factors. The most important of these factors may be related to the type of election procedures at work. In the ward system, where the city is divided up into small districts with representatives chosen for each district, the net effect will probably differ from what would occur with at-large elections. Ward systems tend to increase the representation of lower socioeconomic groups and minorities since homogeneous districts are assured of representation that might not be possible if candidates from these neighborhoods had to run against other candidates on a citywide basis. Other factors that may influence the types of people chosen for the council are: 1) the degree to which labor unions and ethnic and racial groups are organized and involved in local politics; 2) whether the city pays councilmembers enough to sustain working-class representation on the council; 3) whether the party system facilitates representation of various social groups; and 4) whether a covert power structure recruits or prevents recruitment of certain kinds of candidates (Lineberry and Sharkansky, 1971, p. 153).

The actual roles that councilmembers play will, to a great extent, be determined by some of these factors. Ward councilmembers will more often be concerned with the bread and butter issues of urban government— street paving, police protection, recreational facilities, and civil service opportunities for their residents, while at-large councilmembers can afford to deal with broad social, economic, or political issues since their political futures depend less upon material gains for a limited geographical area. Another factor that may affect the decision-making behavior of a councilmember is the degree to which the person is politically ambitious. Schultze (1974, p. 277), discussing studies conducted in the San

Francisco Bay Area, found that ambitious councilmembers (those who had aspirations for higher political office) had a broader policy outlook than those who were not ambitious. The desire for political mobility seems to motivate this type of individual to look beyond his or her own constituency and to support policies and programs that will affect the total area. Schultze concludes that "we can expect councils dominated by ambitious members will be more receptive to proposals for intergovernmental consideration than those dominated by political amateurs." He goes on to speculate that the failure of regional government perhaps is at least partially explained by the findings of these studies, which revealed that 62 percent of the councilmembers interviewed were not politically ambitious and that only 17 percent were "clearly ambitious."

Studies on political behavior of councilmembers frequently have attempted to differentiate between "trustee" and "delegate" roles. Representatives who see themselves as trustees vote according to their own conscience and best judgement without trying to reflect the prevailing sentiments of their constituencies. Delegate councilmembers, on the other hand, feel bound to vote the interests and concerns of their constituents regardless of their own views. Most studies seem to agree that the dominant pattern in urban politics is for councilmembers to adopt the trustee role and, in so doing, minimize the democratic ideal of citizen participation and legislative responsiveness to the public's desires. The dominance of the trustee orientation may be attributed to several factors. Some writers have suggested that since many councilmembers are amateurs—part-time and receiving low salaries—they do not feel that they must be mirrors of the public mood. Furthermore, many city legislators are not always sure what that mood really is. The electoral results and interest-group activities frequently convey unclear or conflicting pictures of constituency preferences and, consequently, the councilmember may find it easier to use his or her own judgement than to find more accurate information.

The difficulty in obtaining reliable information is a problem that councilmembers as well as other public officials face continually—a problem that may thwart the efforts of even the most dedicated public servants who would prefer to behave in a rational and responsive manner. Decisions frequently are required to be made within a short time frame and often there just is not enough time to accumulate the information, survey all the possible alternatives, and select from among them. Even if time were available, the high cost of obtaining information is also an impediment to the rational process. With limited resources for data collection and interpretation and with little if any trained support staff, councilmembers must face increasingly complex and technical policy issues with only their own wits and political wisdom to guide them.

And, finally, there may be a tendency to exercise a trustee position out of sheer frustration. Many of the political and policy problems that confront urban governments can only be solved, ultimately, at higher levels of government. Lineberry and Sharkansky (1971, p. 156) conclude: "Many of these issues are too broad in scope for the council—or any other city officials—to tackle by themselves. Issues such as air and water pollution and mass transportation involve area wide coordination and a scale of financial resources that make state and federal governments the prime actors, and may reduce city councils to the role of observers."

Bureaucracies

Below the level of the elected policy makers such as mayors and city legislators exists a large-scale bureaucracy charged with carrying out the day-to-day operation of government. Those who occupy positions at this level collectively, and sometimes individually, have a good deal of power at their disposal, which can manifest itself in several ways. Given the complexity of governing and managing a modern city, politicians are increasingly dependent on the knowledge, specialized skills, and advice of professional administrators and technicians. The expertise of the bureaucrat thus can become an important influence on the decision-making process, since elected officials find it more and more difficult to challenge policy advice based on specialized knowledge. Wishing to protect the advantages afforded them because of their positions of expertise, those in managerial positions often attempt to thwart any efforts that could undercut their autonomy, such as maneuvers by elected officials to appoint political or nonprofessional department heads. Another tactic frequently employed by administrators is to use their position as a basis for influencing policy decisions. Thus, police administrators, school officials, and heads of welfare departments may covertly or overtly try to influence legislative and governing boards by using their expertise as the basis for predicting the consequences of a particular action or the lack of a particular action.

Part of the motivation of the bureaucrat to exert influence on decision making must be seen, of course, in terms of self-interest—a motivation no different from that of other power groups. It is to the advantage of a particular bureau, department, or agency to maintain its autonomy and, if possible, expand its programs or operations. Each unit, whether a school district, municipality, or countywide sewer district, has its own entrenched officials and employees and its own protected area of jurisdiction. Groups within these categories often vie with each other to ward off any actions that may threaten their existence. For example, county sheriff and municipal police departments may argue over their respective jurisdictional spheres, fearing possible budget cuts or the loss of personnel if one or the other group becomes more dominant. In this ongoing battle to protect their interests, bureaucrats may seek to align themselves with other interest groups. City planners may seek support from business interests while teachers and educational administrators may attempt to associate themselves with parent-teacher associations, where the focus of their lobbying efforts may be directed toward such socially approved issues as quality education rather than on issues that would appear to be more self-serving.

Finally, and perhaps most importantly, bureaucrats wield tremendous power in terms of the discretion they have to execute policy. Building inspectors, police officers, health officials, or welfare workers, to name but a few, frequently have a great deal of latitude to determine the degree to

Police officers stand guard over a crowd at Madison Square Garden, New York. (Marc Anderson)

which laws or policies are to be enforced or individuals may be favored. According to Sayre and Kaufman (1960, p. 421), "it is in execution that the bureaucrats have their most nearly complete monopoly and their greatest autonomy in affecting policy. They give shape and meaning to the official decisions, and they do so under conditions favorable to them. Here the initiative and discretion lie in their hands; others must influence them." This source of power is what political scientist Theodore Lowi (1967) describes as the "new machines" in urban politics. What he sees is a shift of power from the old party machines, which were characterized by voter mobilization and a material reward exchange system, to an emerging "bureaucratic city-state" organized around specific services and clientele. Those who labor within the "new machine" are insulated from the political battles of the outside and, accordingly, are less responsive to change and innovation.

Political Parties

The political machine, so characteristic of urban political life in the late nineteenth and early twentieth century, has fairly well passed out of existence. Fred Greenstein (1964, p. 3) describes this organization as being structured along the lines of a disciplined party hierarchy led by a single executive or board of directors. By being able effectively to exercise control over who could be nominated to public office, the party was able to control the elected officials, whose political future depended on good party standing. The party leadership seldom held public office themselves and sometimes did not even hold formal party office but, nevertheless, was able to maintain "a cadre of loyal party officials and workers, as well as a core of voters . . . by a mixture of material rewards and nonideological psychic rewards—such as personal and ethnic recognition, comaraderie, and the like."

Several factors can be cited to explain the demise of the machine. Internal factional rivalries began to cut into the disciplined harmony as ambitious politicians within the organization would argue that the leadership was no longer responsive to the needs of the people. With growing affluence among urban voters and an increased sophistication on political issues, the simplistic inducements of boss rule were less appealing. Furthermore, this affluence in turn contributed to residential and occupational mobility, which changed the character of ethnic bloc voting in city elections. By the time the New Deal came around in the 1930s, much of the "helping hand" approach used by the machines was being undercut by the federal government. Also, the complexity of city jobs increased as new technology developed, demanding skilled technicians and professionals who could not be easily recruited from among ward and precinct workers. Finally, the reform movement that began around the turn of the century and the increased dependence on the civil service system increasingly removed middle- and low-level jobs from patronage.

Today, nonpartisan municipal election systems are found in a majority of American cities. Advocated by the reformers to eliminate the excesses of the machine, nonpartisan systems have had an important effect on the nature of the electoral process at the local level. The practice of not relating candidates to a political label has tended to confuse many voters, who are deprived of the benefits of being able to identify candidates with ideological and policy goals that have become associated with particular parties. This insulation from party identity has actually worked to the advantage of Republican candidates, who usually can do better in large city elections where the electorate is normally Democratic. Not having to bear the negative reactions to their party label, these candidates are free to rely on such old standbys as name familiarity and ethnic identification. In addition, without the resources of the party organization, candidates must be more dependent on personal financing or backing from special interest groups in the community—which tends to either exclude the less affluent from politics or create obligations that can limit political independence once the candidate is elected. Nonpartisan elections also seem to limit the number of people who actually go to the polls. Without the party organization and machinery to help "get out the vote," interest and participation is reduced. This effect has been particularly detrimental to the Democrats since those voters who would normally vote that party label are less likely to cast a ballot without the voter mobilizing activities usually provided by the party faithful. Greenstein (1964, p. 12) finds it ironic that nonpartisan elections, rather than eliminating the barrier between citizens and their officials, "often attenuates the citizens connections with the political system."

In those cities where political parties still operate at the local level a new style of partisan politics has emerged. Unlike the old machine, the new party draws its membership from the middle and upper classes where the rewards tend to be more psychological than material. The satisfactions derived from working with their fellows in an ideological cause become important incentives for service. The result of this new membership cadre has been to produce a greater heterogeneity and pluralism within the party structure and leadership. This heterogeneity, in turn, has had its own series of consequences. Individuals can more easily challenge the party leadership and win election on their own and, accordingly, the turnover of leaders is higher than before. In addition, the party organization becomes more dependent upon other groups (such as unions, business associations, and civic groups) to solidify its political influence in the community. The old system was clear-cut and direct while the new structure makes it more difficult for the individual to fix responsibility for action or inaction. While supporting the greater egalitarianism found within the current party structure, political scientist John Baker (1971, p. 136) also is concerned that the political process may become "so complicated as to render any discussion of responsible democratic government meaningless." He would like to see a middle ground somewhere between the two extremes, represented by the old machine and the new politics. Such a structure ideally would allow for the development of "political parties that are centralized enough to be held responsible for government actions, yet heterogeneous and pluralistic enough to admit to the possibility of alternating those actions should the public call for changes. The search for a rational role for political parties in our cities must always be conducted in full awareness of the tension between these competing values."

SPECIAL INTEREST GROUPS

We have been examining the nature and extent of influence exerted on city governmental decisions by elected leaders, appointed officials, and those working within political parties. Certainly these individuals enjoy important power positions in their communities but, given the reality of political life in a democratic, pluralistic society, they do not have a monopoly of power. Many private individuals, groups, and organizations within the community also exert political influence in varying degrees upon political decisions and policy choices. These private, generally voluntary associations of individuals are most often referred to as special interest groups because they are organized for the purpose of influencing public policies through political resources in a manner that would be advantageous to their own interests. While many of these interest groups are the traditional economic groups representing industry, commerce, and labor, there are others whose major motivations are ideological and status protection.

No Nukes demonstrations typify the ecological and environmental concerns of the 1980s. (Marc Anderson)

Caraley (1977, pp. 303–305) describes the major organizational categories in which these groups are found. Occupational and business interests constitute an important focus that joins individuals together in such organizations as trade associations, professional societies, or labor union locals. Some of the interests represented in these organizations are also found in large general affiliations like chambers of commerce or central labor councils. These groups are concerned with preventing the adoption of any legislation or policies that are seen as being detrimental to their work and encouraging policies that would confer special advantages (such as licensing procedures, safety regulations, and taxes). Groups also are organized along specific problem areas or along the lines related to a particular governmental function or program. In this category are found groups such as parent-teacher associations, community service organizations, tenants' councils, consumer groups, or those concerned with ecological and environmental issues. Ethnic interests also have been an important basis of group organization in large urban areas where various racial, religious, or nationality minorities frequently have experienced economic, political, and educational discrimination. These groups may be local in origin and sometimes are of an *ad hoc* nature, responding to a particular problem and disbanding after the resolution of the problem, or they may be local affiliates of such national organizations as the Anti-Defamation League of the B'nai Brith, the Urban League, or the American Civil Liberties Union.

Other interest categories include groups centering around the character and vitality of a particular geographical area. Central business district associations, homeowner groups, and neighborhood associations and block clubs have become important sources of political influence since many of these groups also overlap with racial and ethnic categories. Once the province of those residing in middle-class areas, neighborhood and community organizations have been used increasingly and effectively in low-income areas since the 1960s. In these areas the groups have taken assertive positions and have called for the upgrading of city services, better police protection, or the removal of such irritants as abandoned apartment houses or concentrations of prostitution or drug facilities. Many of these groups have been encouraged and supported by the provisions of the 1964 Economic Opportunity Act, which provided for the development of community action programs.

The methods used by these various groups to exert influence are varied, depending upon the character of the group, its resources, and the emotional investment in the issues involved. Direct lobbying of specific officials through public hearings, letters, phone conversations, and informal meetings are perhaps the most common tactics used. These approaches frequently are supplemented by propaganda or public relations campaigns, which may include the use of press releases, letters to the editor, newspaper advertisements, radio or television interviews, and other like activities designed to stimulate favorable public opinion which, it is hoped, would exert pressure on officials. Many groups also engage in electioneering for or against the election or appointment of specific persons who they believe would be favorable or unfavorable to a particular group. Direct campaigning, the contribution of funds, political endorsements, or providing a favorable forum for the candidates to present their views are all part of the electioneering process. Labor unions in the United States have used this approach frequently, choosing to support candidates for public office from the major political parties rather than create their own party organizations. Finally, an approach that was greatly used in the 1960s, first by so-called radical groups and later by more middle-class associations, involves protest demonstrations or other direct action. This approach includes such practices as marches, boycotts, group picketing, or the threat or actual use of violence as a means of dramatizing the group's demands.

Social scientists disagree about the power of interest groups to influence public policy. On some occasions and in some cities these groups appear to be all-powerful while at other times they seem to have no impact at all and may even create a negative reaction to their interests. Some argue that interest groups, particularly labor and business groups with rather substantial resources at their disposal, work against the democratic process which, theoretically, allows for the equality of political participation. Baker (1971, p. 157) believes that just the opposite effect occurs: ". . . to the extent that interest groups do serve to influence the form and substance of decisions in the public sphere, they increase the channels that are at least in theory available to the citizen who wishes to change governmental decisions. . . . The vague and general mandate of the ballot box can be rendered much more specific by active interest groups which at least purport to speak for their membership as voting citizens."

Ethnic and Racial Influences

The efforts of ethnic and racial groups to bring about social and political change during the last two decades is an important illustration of contemporary urban interest groups at work. Much of the intense political conflict that has come to the surface in our large cities during this period has been associated with issues arising from the demands of various cultural and racial minorities—particularly blacks and Latins—for improvement in their status, and from the resistance of other groups and institutions to these pressures. While many of these groups represent large numbers of people, it has not always been easy for them to convert their numerical resources into effective political power. The traditional democratic weapon—the ballot—was, in the early days of the developmental history of these groups, not very useful. Elections were held at wide time intervals and rarely presented clear-cut issues. Furthermore, most of these groups were poorly organized and did not have much in terms of a communications network to unite the members or organize them for action. The plight of these groups is described by the Fainsteins: "The success of urban political movements requries a combination of favorable historical circumstances and organizational momentum, but such momentum is hard to gain when one's starting point is at the bottom"(Fainstein and Fainstein, 1974, p. 191).

Given this disadvantageous position, the question is how can a group or groups, with limited power, influence the urban decision-making process? The experiences of the black community in many American cities may offer some answers. At least three basic strategies have been used. One approach has been for the minority group to divorce itself from the dominant society and to create its own economic, social, and political systems. The Black Muslims, who have been able to integrate their members through religious doctrine, profess the belief that white people are basically corrupt and unjust and all contact with them must be avoided. This approach, while psychologically satisfying for some, has not proven to be very effective for the group as a whole. The second strategy is to discount the local institutions, officials, and programs because of their bias and take the dispute into a larger arena where, through the machinery of the federal system, states and localities will be coerced to respond to the needs of these groups. Much of the efforts of the civil rights movement of the 1960s was directed toward this strategy, which has found wide support among liberals who advocate federal involvement as the only effective way to resolve problems that local government has either ignored or handled poorly. The third approach is for the minority community to strengthen its organization internally as a means of working within the system or enlarging the system to deal with, bargain with, or force city officials to alter their policies.

This third strategy has many variants. One is the nonviolent civil disobedience approach first used by Martin Luther King in 1955 when he led a black boycott of the local bus system in Montogomery, Alabama, to bring about desegregation of that city's public transportation. Similar activities followed in the years after and, as a result, several important goals were achieved. Many blacks were now motivated to take action for their own interest and thereby apathy was reduced. Southern as well as northern whites were made aware of black grievances and the need for change. Sympathy for the black cause was obtained when the lengths to which whites were prepared to go to keep blacks in "their place" became obvious.

By the mid 1960s, the black protest movement, spurred on by the frustrations imposed by the sometimes subtle discrimination found in the urban ghetto communities, particularly in the North, began to display greater militancy in dealing with the power structure in the white community. This mood of militancy was helped along by the urban riots that first began in the summer of 1964. "Black Power" became the slogan of the new militant leaders, who came to share certain central beliefs in common. One was a desire to mobilize group consciousness and a feeling of identity as a prelude for self-help. "Black is beautiful" was the message being transmitted as a necessary prerequisite for this new awareness to develop. Blacks should not assimilate into the decadent and materialistic white middle-class society but should instead develop their own strengthened institutions and organizations to meet the enemy on an equal footing. As two representatives of this approach, Stokeley Carmichael and Charles Hamilton (1967, p. 40) explain: "the fundamental premise of black power is that before a group can enter the open society, it must first close ranks. . . .Enter coalitions only after you are able to stand on your own."

By the early 1970s this militancy had created a new group of activists who had made the transition from subjugation to self-esteem and independence. Blacks, frustrated and intolerant with what they saw to be only token concessions from their white liberal "friends," now began to demand that they be given control over their own communities and the institutions within those communities. The objectives of the community control movement were direct representation of neighborhood on city councils, boards of education, police commissions, and other important governing agencies; the transfer of as much authority as possible to "neighborhood governments," and the development of black ownership or management of private business activities within the neighborhood. The results of these efforts have been mixed. Increased law enforcement seems to have improved police protection in the black neighborhoods, while effective school decentralization has been hampered by diminishing fiscal resources and an intricate network of entrenched interest groups.

The future of community control is uncertain: its opponents are many and influential. Officials at the city level are not anxious to see a diffusion of their power. Other interest groups, including municipal bureaucracies (such as teachers, police, and welfare workers), are fearful because they see a threat to their own job security and mobility. Many moderate black leaders also oppose it. Bayard Rustin (1970, p. 28), for example, sees "black community [to be] as futile a program as black capitalism." These leaders see integration as the ultimate answer and see community control as regressive. Yet, as the movement has progressed, it has served to develop an effective corps of leadership resources which, unlike the white underclass, tends to remain in the community since the access of these people to suburban mobility is limited. Shank and Conant (1975, pp. 196–197) believe that "community control may be critical to the long-range interests of blacks in some cities where blacks are permanently in a minority position" but in cities with substantial and growing black populations they see "the more profitable course [to be] control of city hall."

As the central cities have become increasingly inhabited by blacks and other minorities their political influence has shifted from protest strategies to actual political control. By the late 1970s, blacks had made substantial progress in winning control of the executive and legislative branches of many urban governments where, only ten years before, they were considered to be radical militants with little respectability outside of their own limited constituencies. These new black political leaders (mayors, councilmembers, police chiefs, judges) are now attempting to establish solid political bases in the central cities they control and from these centers of influence establish coalitions at the state and national levels to bring about greater resources to solve the problems in their communities. Many of these new leaders are finding that merely occupying the formal power positions and controlling the political machinery is not enough. While often more responsive and sympathetic to the needs of their citizens, they are facing even more critical problems than their white predecessors. The growing lack of resources, the fragmentation of political authority, and the problems of the central cities, exacerbated by racial divisiveness and class differences, still impede the qualitative betterment of public services regardless of who controls city hall (See Chapter 14).

THE INFLUENCE OF THE GENERAL PUBLIC

While the expansion of organized interest groups and the greater egalitarianism found within partisan politics has given more people than ever an opportunity to directly participate in the political process, particularly at the local level, voting for most Americans is still the most vigorous type of political activity they are likely to undertake. And yet even this type of activity is engaged in only minimally during municipal and local elections. During off-year elections, when national and state candidates are not on the ballot, only about 31 percent of the adult population turns out to vote (Lineberry and Sharkansky, 1971, p. 53). And it is not uncommon for the voter turnout to drop to as low as one-fourth of the registered electorate, with the usual turnout in school district and other nonmunicipal contests even lower.

To review the extensive literature on local voting patterns and attitudes is impossible here, but some general observations can be made. Most of the studies report a strong positive correlation between voter interest and socioeconomic status. Since high status is correlated with more education, better jobs, and greater income, there are several possible reasons to explain the greater voting interest by those who occupy this status. Such people are likely to be more knowledgeable about public issues and have a greater stake in the outcome of the election. High stakes may be tied to either material or ideological gains or losses that the individual perceives could be affected. Businesspeople, developers, municipal employees, homeowners, or suppliers are examples of those who are more likely than the average person to see local politics as being relevant to their pocketbooks. These people are interested in such issues as urban renewal, zoning, economic development, or property taxes—all issues that are decided on the local level.

Mobility, length of residence, homeownership, age, race, and ethnic affiliation also affect local participation. Generally speaking, the longer a person lives in the same locality, the greater the likelihood he or she will vote in local elections. The long-term resident has probably developed roots and has a vested interest in the community. A similar statement could be said about homeowners, whose investment perhaps gives them a greater sense of permanence and concern about protecting the value of their property. The lower voting record of younger people undoubtedly reflects their stage in the life cycle. Geographically and occupationally more mobile, their residential patterns usually are fluid, and consequently they have not yet settled into the community and neighborhood commitments that are associated with an interest in local public affairs.

The evidence on ethnic or racial membership seems to indicate that ethnic identity and affiliation actually increases political activism. Ethnic groups, particularly in large central cities, have been important targets for politicians since the heyday of the political machine. Since a good deal of attention and energy is still spent to win the ethnic vote, these groups are frequently well politicized. Robert Lane (1959, p. 239), in discussing ethnic voting behavior, has noted: "In a real sense, the seat of ethnic politics is the local community, not the national capital. This is evidenced by the fact that although ethnic groups often vote no more frequently than native white Protestants in national elections (with the Jews excepted) and sometimes less frequently, they usually vote more frequently in local elections." Racial identity, however, is related to voting behavior only to the extent that blacks are disproportionately represented in the lower socioeconomic groups. When such factors as income, education, and occupation are held constant, political activity among blacks does not differ from their white counterparts at the same class level (Bollens and Schmandt, 1965, p. 225).

Both social scientists and politicians have long been concerned with the low degree of political interest shown at the local level, and several explanations have been offered to explain this phenomenon. For many people, the decisions made locally do not generally affect their psychologi-

Public hearings offer opportunities for citizens in a given community to express their views. (Irene Springer)

cal or material well-being. Involved in the day-to-day business of making a living or raising a family, few outside of the slum-ghetto-dwellers feel that they are dependent on local political actions for their ongoing existence. National politics involve such issues as war and peace, civil rights, and Medicare, while local elections more often center around issues such as charter reform, capital improvements, or debt retirement. Not only are these issues lacking in emotional excitement, they also represent problems of a technical nature that many people do not thoroughly understand. Even for those who are aware and concerned about issues at the local level, there has developed, in many cases, a sense of resignation that it probably doesn't matter much who wins. Given such a frame of mind, little incentive exists for any but the most conscientious voter to go to the polls.

Nevertheless, elections are the vehicles by which city officials are chosen and it is through the ballot that the general public is able to exert its greatest influence. As just discussed, not all take advantage of this opportunity and, of those who do, many make their choices on the basis of incomplete information, negative appeals, or a sense of frustration. Outside of its ability to confer legal, decision-making authority on particular individuals, the general public does not seem to have much impact on general city policy or the specifics of major operating decisions. Reflecting a view shared by other social scientists, Caraley (1977, p. 361) offers the following appraisal of the general public's influence on urban politics:

> At times the broader public can express at least a mood about the urgency or complacency with which particular problems or the demands and grievances of particular groups should be addressed. And on rare occasions, it can even

be a directive that some particular thing be done. But on the specifics or details of day-to-day city governmental policies and programs, the general public is normally without direct influence, as city officials and other activists negotiate and bargain-out their settlements in virtual privacy.

SELECTED BIBLIOGRAPHY

ALTSHULER, ALAN. *Community Control.* New York: Pegasus, 1970.

ARKEN, MICHAEL, and MOTT, PAUL E. *The Structure of Community Power.* New York: Random House, 1970.

BAKER, JOHN H. *Urban Politics in America.* New York: Scribner's, 1971.

BANFIELD, EDWARD C., and WILSON, JAMES Q. *City Politics.* Cambridge, Mass.: Harvard University Press, 1965.

BOLLENS, JOHN C., and SCHMANDT, HENRY J. *The Metropolis.* New York: Harper & Row Publishers, 1965.

BOSKOFF, ALVIN. *The Sociology of Urban Regions.* 2nd ed. New York: Appleton-Century-Crofts, 1970.

CAHN, EDGAR S., and PASSETT, BARRY A. *Citizen Participation: Effecting Community Change.* New York: Praeger, 1971.

CARALEY, DEMETRIOUS. *City Governments and Urban Problems.* Englewood Cliffs, N.J.: Prentice-Hall, 1977.

CARMICHAEL, STOKELEY, and HAMILTON, CHARLES V. *Black Power.* New York: Vintage, 1967.

CAPUTO, DAVID A. *Urban America: The Policy Alternatives.* San Francisco: W. H. Freeman & Company Publishers, 1976.

CORNWELL, ELMER E. "Bosses, Machines, and Ethnic Groups," *The Annals* 353 (May 1964).

DAHL, ROBERT A. *Who Governs?* New Haven, Conn.: Yale University Press, 1961.

DYE, THOMAS. *The Politics of Inequality.* Indianapolis, Ind.: Bobbs-Merrill, 1971.

DYE, THOMAS R., and HAWKINS, BRETT W. eds. *Politics in the Metropolis.* 2nd ed. Columbus, Ohio: Charles E. Merrill, 1971.

ERICKSON, ROBERT, and LUTTBERG, NORMAN. *American Public Opinion: Its Origin, Content, and Impact.* New York: John Wiley, 1973.

FAINSTEIN, NORMAN I., and FAINSTEIN, SUSAN S. *Urban Political Movements.* Englewood Cliffs, N.J.: Prentice-Hall, 1974.

GEORGE, ALEXANDER L. "Political Leadership and Social Change in American Cities," *Daedalus* 97 (Fall 1968).

GREENSTEIN, FRED I. "The Changing Pattern of Urban Party Politics," *The Annals of the American Academy of Political and Social Science* 353 (May 1964).

HAHN, HARLAN, ed. *People and Politics in Urban Society.* Beverly Hills, Calif.: Sage Publications, Inc., 1972.

HARRIGAN, JOHN J. *Political Change in the Metropolis.* Boston: Little, Brown, 1976.

HAWLEY, AMOS, and ROCK, VINCENT, eds. *Metropolitan America in Contemporary Perspective.* New York: John Wiley, 1975.

HUNTER, FLOYD. *Community Power Structure.* Chapel Hill: University of North Carolina Press, 1953.

KORNHAUSER, WILLIAM. "Power Elite or Veto Groups?" In Reinhard Bendix and Seymour Lipset, eds., *Class, Status, and Power,* pp. 210–218. New York: Free Press, 1966.

LANE, ROBERT E. *Political Life.* New York: Free Press, 1959.

LINEBERRY, ROBERT, and SHARKANSKY, IRA. *Urban Politics and Public Policy.* New York: Harper & Row, 1971.

LOCKARD, DUANE. *The Politics of State and Local Government.* 2nd ed. New York: Macmillan, 1969.

LOWI, THEODORE J. "Machine Politics—Old and New," *The Public Interest* (fall 1967).

LYNCH, HOLLIS R. *The Urban Black Coalition: A Documentary History, 1866–1871.* New York: Thomas Y. Crowell, 1973.

MARX, KARL. *Capital.* New York: Modern Library, 1936.

MILLS, C. WRIGHT. *The Power Elite.* New York: Oxford University Press, 1957.

PRESTHUS, ROBERT. *Men at the Top: A Study in Community Power.* New York: Oxford University Press, 1964.

REUSS, HENRY S. *Revenue-Sharing.* New York: Praeger, 1970.

RIESMAN, DAVID. *The Lonely Crowd.* New York: Doubleday Anchor Edition, 1953.

ROGERS, DAVID. *The Management of Big Cities.* Beverly Hills, Calif.: Sage Publications, Inc., 1971.

RUCHELMAN, LEONARD J., ed. *Big City Mayors.* Bloomington: Indiana University Press, 1969.

RUSTIN, BAYARD. "The Failure of Black Separatism," *Harpers* (January 1970).

SALISBURY, ROBERT H. "Urban Politics: The New Convegence of Power," *Journal of Politics* 26 (November 1964): 775–797.

SAYRE, WALLACE, and KAUFMAN, HERBERT. *Governing New York City: Politics in the Metropolis.* New York: Russell Sage Foundation, 1960.

SCHULTZE, WILLIAM A. *Urban and Community Politics.* North Scituate, Mass: Duxbury Press, 1974.

SHANK, ALAN, and CONANT, RALPH W. *Urban Perspective.* Boston: Holbrook Press, 1975.

SPINRAD, WILLIAM. "Power in Local Communities." In Reinhard Bendix and Seymour Martin Lipset, eds., *Class, Status, and Power,* pp. 218–231. New York: Free Press, 1966.

WILSON, JAMES Q. "The Mayors vs. the Cities," *The Public Interest* 16 (Summer 1969).

WOLFINGER, RAYMOND E. "The Development and Persistence of Ethnic Voting," *American Political Science* 59 (December 1965).

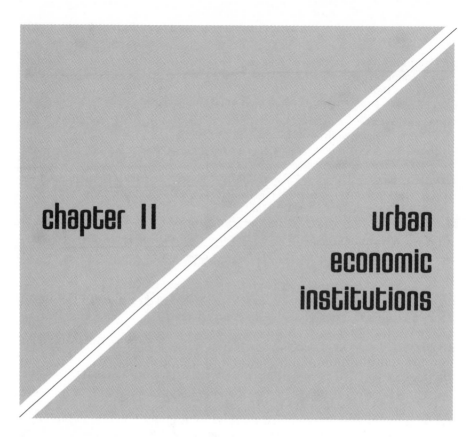

chapter 11

urban economic institutions

In preindustrial societies, the family, religion, and the state have often been the dominant social institutions, and many preindustrial urban communities have been organized totally around these institutions. Of course, all human communities also have been organized around some kind of basic economic activities, which provide the necessary means for survival. But in preindustrial urban communities, such economic activities often have been incorporated into the kinship system, the church, or the sustaining political body. As such, the economy has not necessarily been regarded as a separate entity with its own set of institutional characteristics. In urban-industrial societies, the economy not only becomes a separate institution in its own right, but also becomes a dominant social institution. The economy is so powerful a force that it has the capacity to alter the forms and processes of other institutions rather than the other way around. In this chapter we will review some of the characteristics of economic institutions in urban America. The emphasis will be on the processes of production, distribution, and consumption in the urban marketplace and on the urban world of work.

In our earlier discussion of the impact of the industrial revolution on the development of cities (Chapter Three), we emphasized the emergence of the factory system and those features of capitalism that were conducive to increased levels of productivity within the manufacturing sphere of the economy. To a certain extent, modern manufacturing organizations have solved the problems of production and the emphasis now is on problems of distribution and consumption. In response to the increased scale and complexity of metropolitan development, urban societies increasingly have come to be marked by new patterns of economic organization, including the emergence of corporate bureaucracies; increased centralization in the channels of distribution, such as chain stores and mail order houses; and supplementary economic organizations designed to facilitate the flow of manufactured goods to the consumer, such as advertising agencies, market research agencies, consumer credit facilities, consumer-oriented interest groups, and governmental regulatory agencies designed to regulate the flow of commerce or to protect consumers' interests.

THE CORPORATE BUREAUCRACY

The dominant form of ownership of productive organizations in the early days of the industrial revolution was small individually or family-owned proprietorships and partnerships. While such small businesses still are prevalent in modern urban-industrial communities, much of the productive capacity is now concentrated in much larger units of organization. These larger units, usually corporations, are created by pooling and coordinating the resources, facilities, and skills of many previously competing smaller firms or establishments into an autonomous and impersonal system, which legally separates ownership from the management of such enterprises. The greater efficiency and profit-producing potential of corporations are such that they tend to be always expanding, spreading their influence and control over ever wider sectors of the urban economy.

The growing concentration of industrial power in the hands of a relatively small handful of corporations had become of widespread concern even before the turn of this century. The Sherman Antitrust Act was passed in 1890 and the Clayton Act in 1914 as efforts by the federal government to prevent the monopolization of manufacturing activities. In spite of these and other efforts, however, the concentration of ownership of industry has continued to grow. By the beginning of World War II less than one-twentieth of the total number of corporations owned 93 percent of the corporate assets in the fields of transportation and public utilities. In manufacturing, less than 2 percent of the corporations owned 66 percent of the assets. Even in the construction industry and in agriculture, which still tend to be strongly competitive, a few multimillion dollar corporations own over one-fourth of the total corporate assets. Figure 11-1 illustrates the percentage share of the market held by the top several corporations in each of several major manufacturing industries in the United States at the beginning of the 1970s. As the figure indicates, one, two, three, or four giant corporations control well over half of the total market in each of the industrial areas represented.

The tendency toward "bigness" and concentration of ownership extends not only into manufacturing but into transportation, distribution,

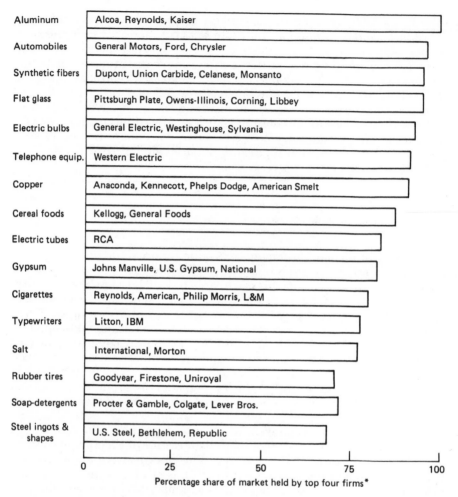

Industry	Firms	
Aluminum	Alcoa, Reynolds, Kaiser	
Automobiles	General Motors, Ford, Chrysler	
Synthetic fibers	Dupont, Union Carbide, Celanese, Monsanto	
Flat glass	Pittsburgh Plate, Owens-Illinois, Corning, Libbey	
Electric bulbs	General Electric, Westinghouse, Sylvania	
Telephone equip.	Western Electric	
Copper	Anaconda, Kennecott, Phelps Dodge, American Smelt	
Cereal foods	Kellogg, General Foods	
Electric tubes	RCA	
Gypsum	Johns Manville, U.S. Gypsum, National	
Cigarettes	Reynolds, American, Philip Morris, L&M	
Typewriters	Litton, IBM	
Salt	International, Morton	
Rubber tires	Goodyear, Firestone, Uniroyal	
Soap-detergents	Procter & Gamble, Colgate, Lever Bros.	
Steel ingots & shapes	U.S. Steel, Bethlehem, Republic	

Percentage share of market held by top four firms*

FIGURE 11-1   Industries dominated by a few big firms.
*Only the names of leading firms in each industry are identified. In some cases there is only a single dominant company; in others there may be two, three, or four.
(Source: From *The American Corporation* by Richard J. Barber. Copyright © 1970 by Richard J. Barber. Reprinted by permission of the publisher, E. P. Dutton.)

and communications industries as well. For example, in the newspaper industry almost half of the daily and Sunday newspaper circulation is concentrated in 386 newspapers owned by seventy owners or chains (Rivers, 1971, p. 277). Between 1909 and 1974, the number of daily newspapers has been reduced from 2,600 to 1,750, although total circulation has more than doubled during the same period. By 1972 only half of all the states of the nation had competing daily newspapers in any of their cities (Horton and Leslie, 1974, p. 483).

Along with the growth of the modern corporation, the complexity and size of the market for manufactured goods has increased enormously. The variety of wants among urbanities who have the purchasing power to pursue these wants in the urban marketplace is almost beyond estimation. As a result, it becomes increasingly difficult for producers accurately to calculate consumer demands and to plan the development of new products or to plan future production schedules to meet anticipated future sales. At first glance, this would seem to suggest that modern business enterprise faces greater risks in the marketplace than in preindustrial economies, in which the relationship between the producer and customer is at a much more personal and intimate level. Yet, according to economists such as Galbraith (1958, pp. 101–102), modern industry is no longer primarily attuned to the rigors of competition in the classical sense, but exhibits instead a comprehensive effort to reduce risk-taking.

INNOVATIONS IN PRODUCTION, DISTRIBUTION, AND CONSUMPTION

In response to the complexities and uncertainties of the urban-industrial market, modern urban societies have developed a number of institutional innovations designed to produce a more efficient and controllable relationship between the production and the purchase or consumption of manufactured products. These innovations include:

Market Research

Modern industry sponsors a good deal of sample survey research designed to measure consumers' preferences, wants, and anticipated future purchases of an extremely wide variety of products, from pantyhose or toothpaste to automobiles, major appliances, or houses. Such research may also pretest the appeal of newly developed products to a selected sample of potential users. Market research not only identifies the potential size of the market for a given product but often will also precisely identify which specific segments of the population are most likely to purchase the product. Thus "demographics," a set of techniques for differentiating the population according to such variables as age, sex, income, life style, place of residence, or purchasing power, is often used in market research to identify target groups of likely consumers.

Product Diversification

To minimize the risk of promoting obsolete products or overdependence on the success of a limited range of products, modern industry attempts to diversify its product or model lineup to satisfy multiple tastes and preferences. For example, the automobile industry has moved from the position in which a given firm would produce one or two basic models (the Model "T" or Model "A" available in black only from the Ford Motor

Market research, production diversification, and advertising are three of the innovations in the urban industrial market. (Marc Anderson, Burke Marketing Services, Inc., and A.T. & T. Co. Photo Center)

Company are examples of concentration on a single product line in the early days of the auto industry), to the present format of offering a relatively wide range of models to suit the varied preferences of a wide assortment of consuming groups. Automobile manufacturers now offer two- and four-door sedans, sport coupes, station wagons, and vans in a variety of sizes and weights, colors, and price ranges, with a still wider variety of available options, such as air conditioning, engines, transmissions, radios, tape players, tires, trim, seats, etc. Moving still further toward greater diversification, automobile manufacturers now produce home appliances and other products not directly related to automobiles. Thus, when these manufacturers miscalculate the demand for any single model or product, they are able to shift their productive resources to other products and models and minimize their potential losses.

Of course, the other side of the coin is that the modern urban consumer grows ever more sophisticated and discriminating in selecting from among the competing products. In this task the consumer is now often aided by a growing number of consumer-oriented interest groups and product-testing organizations. Among the best known of these is the Consumers Union, which publishes the monthly *Consumers Report* of objectively tested competing products, such as cameras, record players, appliances, dehumidifiers, clocks, autos, bedding, processed foods, or television sets, comparing their design, usability, durability, or safety.

Standardization

Paradoxically, the ever increasing diversity of goods offered in the urban marketplace often confuses the consumer, particularly products that are too new or unknown to inspire the consumer's confidence in their quality. Therefore, many manufacturers or distributers will emphasize and promote the "name brand" of their products as standards of quality and reliability. The consumer then comes to rely on standardized name brands as at least an indication that the manufacturers "stand behind" their product and have sufficient resources to honor warranties, supply parts, and make repairs. But often simply the comfortable familiarity with a product name will induce the consumer to purchase a particular brand, as against the uncertainty of purchasing an unlabeled product. In the fast food industry, for example, the golden arch of MacDonalds is assurance of a uniform-quality hamburger, no matter in what neighborhood, city, or region it is purchased and eaten.

Advertising

To the extent that urban economies depend on maintaining high rates of consumption, mass media advertising has become a ubiquitous force in the everyday life of urbanites, as producers attempt to create and maintain a high degree of demand for their products through their constant display of highly visible advertising messages. Through television, radio, magazines, newspapers, circulars, and mailings, advertising daily invades the home of nearly every urbanite. Leaving home provides no escape, as the urbanite is met with lighted signs and posters and billboards along highways, in store fronts, and in buses and trains. Even the sky may present advertising messages carried by aircraft, the Goodyear blimp being a notable example.

A more subtle form of advertising is institutional public relations. In this format, large corporate institutions do not attempt to sell their products directly but attempt instead to create a generally favorable public impression of their corporate enterprises. A giant oil or chemical producer may not directly urge the public to buy its products but will focus instead on its attempts to preserve and enhance the environment or raise the general standard of living. The millions of dollars spent yearly on direct advertising or institutional public relations attest to the efficacy of advertising to generate or maintain consumer demand.

Consumer Credit

Whereas the earliest phases of the industrial revolution were in part made possible by the emergence of standardized monetary and wage labor systems, which place disposable cash in the hands of workers, modern urban economies are sustained to an ever increasing degree on the widespread use of consumer credit. Systems of consumer credit allow people to purchase goods for which they do not presently have sufficient cash on hand and to pay later through an agreed-upon number of installment payments. The use of consumer credit was originally limited to such high-cost purchases as houses, automobiles, large appliances, and furniture. Now credit is widely used for paying for restaurant meals, theater tickets, drugs and notions, and medical bills. Consumer credit may now be used to purchase every conceivable product or service now available in the urban marketplace. One additional convenience to the consumer is the ability to travel or shop without carrying substantial amounts of cash, carrying instead an assortment of credit cards that are almost universally negotiable. That the consumer pays dearly for the use of such credit does not seem to be a deterrent. Far from the values of thrift, savings, and investment that characterized the earliest days of the industrial revolution, today's values promote indebtedness as healthy for the economy. Government economic planners despair when consumers attempt to reduce their indebtedness or save rather than spend their current and anticipated income. Indeed, the failure to raise consumption through the liberal use of consumer credit now almost seems un-American to many business leaders in the current urban scene. On the other hand, to be denied credit as a poor risk may be as stigmatizing today as to have been labeled "idle" or "lazy" at the turn of the century. At the very least, the individual who does not have consumer credit at his or her disposal may be seriously disadvantaged in the everyday aspects of modern urban living.

In many ways, these characteristics of modern urban economic institutions so pervade urban culture that other social institutions are altered to conform to the new exigencies. One can even now find that some aspects of modern religion and formal education have bent to the demands of the marketplace and have adapted forms of survival that are analogous to those used by the corporation. Schools and churches now conduct market research studies to identify relevant target populations, diversify their product in response to the segmentation of their constituents' (customers') needs and wants (schools diversify their curricula, while churches offer social activities for such diverse groups as young people, the aged, married couples, or divorcees), advertise their services or offerings in local media such as newspapers, radio, or television, and offer the option of installment or credit card payments for charitable contributions or tuition fees. In these and many other ways the values and practices of the corporate economy have invaded nearly all aspects of urban living.

THE LOCAL ECONOMY OF CITIES

The discussion so far has focused on the economic processes of urban society. We now turn to these processes in the context of local urban communities. Of course, in the modern world no individual city has a completely self-sufficient economy, since no city can produce all that is consumed by its inhabitants, and no local urban economy produces goods and services for strictly local consumption. Consequently, the economy of any urban community must in some way be linked in exchange relationships with economic units external to it and over which local economic functionaries can have little or no control. The economy of any urban community thus consists of essentially three components: 1) *the export sector,* consisting of those activities primarily oriented toward the export of goods and services to other communities and social entities; 2) *the local sector,* consisting of those activities primarily oriented toward production, distribution, and consumption within the local community; and 3) *the import sector,* consisting of the goods and services that must be obtained from external producers for local consumption.

While economists debate the relative importance of the first two sectors for the growth and viability of a city's economy, Lewis (1973, pp. 62–63) argues that in the absence of convincing evidence to the contrary, neither of the two sectors appears to be preeminent. While export activities bring new wealth into the community's economy, without adequate support from locally oriented activities the industries in the export sector cannot adequately thrive. On the other hand, the need for imports is far less controversial. The more mature and elaborate the local economy, and the greater its ability to produce for local consumption, the less it will need to rely on imports (the one major exception is of course reliance on foodstuffs, which are produced in rural areas). In turn, the lesser the reliance on imports, the greater will be the degree of economic self-sufficiency and autonomy for the local community. However, this latter point cannot be carried to its logical extreme in modern urban economies because complete economic self-sufficiency is probably impossible. For this reason Hawley (1950) refers to all modern urban-industrial communities as "dependent" communities, as opposed to the "independent" communities of the early preindustrial era. At any rate, no such completely self-sufficient local economy has yet been identified in the modern world.

EMPLOYMENT TRENDS

While the twentieth century has been characterized by extraordinary economic growth, this growth has not proceeded evenly among individual sectors of the economy. According to the Bureau of Labor Statistics, the fifty years between the end of World War I and the beginning of the 1970s saw the following changes occur in American industry:

1. A decline by approximately one-half the number of workers employed in mining.
2. A doubling of workers employed in manufacturing.
3. A tripling of employment of construction workers.
4. A relatively insignificant rise in transportation and public utilities employment.
5. More than a tripling of workers employed in buying and selling (trade).
6. A tripling of employment in banking, finance, and insurance.
7. Nearly a fivefold increase in employment in government and service industries.

The major significance of these trends is the increase of employment in the service-producing sectors of the economy, in both absolute terms and in relation to the goods-producing or manufacturing sectors. Until the post–World War II era, goods-producing industries outnumbered the service-producing industries in the number of workers they employed. As of 1947, the proportion of the labor force in service-producing and in goods-producing industries was nearly equal. But by the beginning of the 1970s the service industries had pulled ahead to the point that 62 percent, or more than six out of every ten workers in the American economy employed for wages and salaries (outside of agriculture), worked in the service sector. On the other hand, employment in the goods-producing industries had declined to 38 percent.

Wolfbein (1971, p. 34) suggests that the United States has become the only country in the world that has had such a rapid growth in service employment, to the extent that it has produced a marked service bent to its economic profile. For this reason, a number of observers have begun to refer to the United States as a *postindustrial* society.

OCCUPATIONAL SPECIALIZATION AND THE DIVISION OF LABOR

The emergence of the corporate bureaucracy and other organizational and technical trends in modern industry has produced a highly complex division of labor and an increasingly more elaborate degree of specialization among the jobs available in the urban labor market. Even in manufacturing a product as simple as a straight pin, Adam Smith was able to point out in the early days of the industrial revolution a division of labor so specialized that one worker would draw out the wire, another would straighten it, a third would cut it, a fourth would grind a point at one end of it, a fifth would grind the other end, and two or three others would do the necessary tasks to make the head of the pin. Wilensky and Lebeaux (1958) have identified "cracker breakers," "meringue spreaders," "pie strippers," and "pan dumpers" as occupational specialities at which one can make a living in the baking industry, while in the meat-packing industry one can specialize as a "large stock scalper," "belly shaver," "crotchbuster," "gut snatcher," "gut sorter," "snout puller," "ear cutter," "eyelid remover," "stomach washer," "hindleg toenail puller," "frontleg toenail puller," and "oxtail washer."

No one knows for sure how many such specialized occupations exist in the modern labor force. The *Dictionary of Occupational Titles* lists and describes more than 22,000 distinguishable occupations, but Wilensky and others estimate that there are probably more than 30,000 occupations in the United States. It is interesting to compare this estimate with efforts by the Census Bureau to itemize a complete list of occupations just a little more than a century ago. In 1850 only 323 different occupations could be identified, just a small fraction of the current number of available occupational specialties.

The enormous proliferation of occupations in the United States is by no means confined to manufacturing industries but has occurred throughout the entire occupational hierarchy. Such specialization has divided fields such as medicine, dentistry, social work, law, and the academic disciplines, as well as clerical, sales, and administrative work, into countless subspecialities. A humorous but pointed exaggeration of increased specialization in the medical profession has been provided by Nicholas von Hoffman:

> In medicine, specialization takes the form of coy little ads which read "Sharply P. Ripthroat, M.D., practice limited to diseases of the left eyeball, member, American College of Left Eyeball Surgeons." Years of advanced training permit Dr. Ripthroat to charge larger-than-usual prices for confining himself to blinding you in the left eye. In the old days before scientific research had brought the healing arts to their present pitch of perfection, the same man was permitted to put out your right eye as well, but then he usually charged less and sometimes threw in six free lessons for your seeing-eye dog (*Washington Post*, January 1, 1975, p. C1).

Even in a field such as sociology, it is now virtually impossible for any one individual to master the entire discipline. One specializes in Deviant Behavior, Criminology, the Family, Stratification, Social Psychology, Demography, Methodology and Statistics, Medical Sociology, or any of the many other increasingly wide range of subspecialities within the field.

Several consequences of this elaborate division of labor are that individuals are confronted with a bewildering variety of occupational choices; no one individual will have intimate knowledge of more than a handful of the many occupations available, most of which are "invisible"; likewise, once an individual has chosen an occupation, that occupational role will most likely be obscure to most people with whom one comes in contact. Recent studies of occupational prestige, for example, have generally indicated that most respondents cannot properly identify the kind of work associated with as many as fifty to one hundred different occupational titles with any degree of accuracy.

OCCUPATIONAL GROUPS IN THE LABOR FORCE

Enormous shifts have occurred in the occupational composition of the United States labor force since the turn of the century. Table 1 details the major changes in the eleven major occupational categories of the labor force from 1900 to 1970, with projections estimated to 1980.

Perhaps the most striking change in the American labor force is the

TABLE 11-1   Profile of the American labor force, 1900–1980 (in percent)

MILLIONS OF WORKERS	(29) 1900	(49) 1930	(62) 1950	(67) 1960	(79) 1970	(95) 1980
White Collar						
Professional and technical	4	7	9	11	14	16
Managers and proprietors	6	7	8	11	11	10
Clerical	3	9	12	15	17	18
Sales	5	6	7	6	6	6
Total	18	29	36	43	48	50
Blue-Collar						
Skilled workers	10	13	14	13	13	13
Semiskilled workers	13	16	20	18	18	16
Unskilled workers	13	11	7	6	4	4
Total	36	40	41	37	35	33
Service Workers						
Private household workers	5	4	3	3	2	*
Service workers, other than private household	4	6	8	9	10	*
Total	9	10	11	12	12	14
Farm Workers						
Farmers and farm managers	20	12	7	4	2	*
Farm laborers and foremen	18	9	4	4	2	*
Total	38	21	11	8	4	3

*No figures given.

SOURCES: David L. Kaplan and M. Claire Casey, *Occupational Trends in the United States, 1900 to 1950,* Bureau of the Census, Working Paper No. 5 (Washington, D.C.: U.S. Department of Commerce, 1958); *Statistical Abstract of the United States, 1961,* and *Statistical Abstract of the United States, 1971* (Washington, D.C.: U.S. Government Printing Office); U.S. Department of Labor, Bureau of Manpower Administration, *Manpower Report of the President, 1972* (Washington, D.C.: U.S. Government Printing Office, 1972), p. 259; U.S. Department of Labor, Bureau of Labor Statistics, *The U.S. Economy in 1980* (Washington, D.C.: U.S. Government Printing Office, 1970), Bulletin 1673.

Electronic computer personnel, including interview coders, comprise a group classified as white collar workers. (Courtesy of Burke Marketing Services, Inc.)

remarkable decline in the number of people who works on farms or in farm-related activities. In Table 11-1 we see that the proportion of *farmers* and *farm managers* has dropped from 20 percent in 1900 to about 2 percent in 1970, while the proportion of *farm laborers* and *foremen* has declined from 18 percent to 2 percent in the same period. In all, farm workers constituted only 4 percent of the labor force in 1970 and are expected to decline to about 3 percent by 1980. This further documents the degree to which America has moved from being an agrarian society to being an urban society in which the vast bulk of the labor force is employed in nonagricultural work.

In the following sections we shall discuss in some detail the major occupational trends in the urban or nonfarm segments of the labor force.

White-Collar Workers

Clerical workers and those in related occupations amounted to only 3 percent of the labor force in 1900. Since then, the increase in numbers and proportions of clerical workers has exceeded that of all others. By 1980 this category will have increased sixfold, to about 18 percent of the labor force. The number of those working in these occupations will continue to grow to about twenty million workers in 1985 and will widen its lead over its nearest competing occupational category (Ritzer, 1977, p. 17). The largest single group within the clerical work force is composed of secretaries and stenographers; together with typists and receptionists, they now number well above the three million mark. Included also are electronic computer personnel and other office machine operators. Bookkeepers, bank tellers, telephone operators, and shipping and receiving clerks account for most of the rest of the workers in this category.

A major reason for the massive growth in clerical work is the proliferation of large-scale bureaucracies in industry and government. Such large-scale organizations require innumerable clerical workers to handle the paperwork that is their lifeblood. In addition to increasing the numbers of people employed in this category, bureaucratization has also radically altered the nature of white-collar work. Whereas white-collar clerical work formerly brought with it higher status than blue-collar work, the growing "factory life" structure of many bureaucracies has reduced the status of much white-collar clerical work by making it virtually indistinguishable from blue-collar factory work (Ritzer, 1977, p. 18). Another factor in the growth of many of the occupations in this category is technological change. The development of the typewriter, dictating machine, copying machines, and related office equipment has triggered the rise in the number of secretaries and typists. The development of the computer is a more recent technological advance that has had a spectacular impact on the nature of white-collar clerical work. In 1960, for example, there were less than 2,000 operators of computers and related equipment. But by 1970 that number had grown to almost 120,000 workers (Ritzer, 1977, p. 18). In the decade of the 1960s, over 100,000 new jobs as keypunch operators were created. Wolfbein (1971, p. 46) suggests that the demand for clerical workers will continue almost without end, as technological and bureaucratic changes continue to expand occupational opportunities in the clerical categories.

Professional and *technical* workers have increased from 4 percent of the labor force in 1900 to 14 percent in 1970. This tremendous increase was exceeded only by that of clerical workers. Taken together (and a significant proportion does work together), professional and clerical personnel now account for about one out of every three employed workers in this country.

The increasing need for professional and highly trained technical expertise has led to the expansion of professional and technical careers such as teaching at all levels; engineers and draftsmen; the health fields, including doctors, nurses, nurses' aids, dentists and dental technicians, pharmacists, veterinarians, dietitians, nutritionists, medical and X-ray technicians; and the scientists' group, including physicists, mathematicians, chemists, biologists, geologists, metallurgists, and astronomers. In the so-called helping professions, therapists, counselors, social workers, personnel workers, psychologists, and librarians are members of growing areas, while in business and government, accountants, city planners, economists, and programmers are on the list of expanded occupations, as are architects, lawyers, and clergy.

Because the professional and technical fields are so varied, no single factor can fully explain the growth of the many different kinds of occupations in this category. Likewise, the use of the concept "profession" to describe some of the occupations in this category is somewhat misleading, for sociologists may have something quite different in mind when assessing the question of whether or not a given occupation has earned professional status than the far more arbitrary criteria used by the government for classifying labor force statistics into occupational categories. Professionalization is a process in urban societies that has significance in its own right, independent of the problems of labor force classification schemes. Nevertheless, several factors leading to growth of professional and technical occupations can be tentatively identified. One factor is the increasing sophistication of knowledge, techniques, and machinery, which has led to a burgeoning demand for highly trained people to handle these areas. Almost by definition, the professional occupations most affected by technological changes are those of scientists, as virtually all technological changes are now derived from basic and applied scientific research. In turn, each new scientific discovery that leads to technological change raises a host of new scientific questions (effects on health, safety, the environment, climate) that require still more scientific research. As both a cause and a result of technological change, the number of doctorates in science rose from 60 in 1885 to about 16,000 in 1969 (Zuckerman and Merton, 1973). It has been estimated that 90 percent of the scientists who have ever lived are alive today (Price, 1965). In a similar way, growth in engineering and related technological fields has proceeded at a rapid rate from the late 1800s to the present, creating not only an increase in the total number of engineers (over one million in 1970) but also an increase in the number of engineering specialties, such as civil, mining, metallurgical, mechanical, electrical, chemical, aeronautical, automotive, nuclear, and medical. Many new kinds of technical occupations now exist that were not even heard of just a few decades ago. For example, the occupation of computer programmer is now common, but was not even listed in the 1949 edition of the *Dictionary of Occupational Titles.*

The increased wealth and sophistication of the American consumer has led to an increased demand for the services of professional occupations, such as psychoanalyst, psychologist, marriage counselor, tax accountant, divorce lawyer, architect, and interior decorator, and many mass media publications advise their readers as to the desirability of employing these and other professions to help solve their problems. The helping professions themselves attempt to generate increased demands for their services by informing the public of their value. In these and many other ways the urban public is increasingly dependent on a growing core of professional workers. In turn, the professions have become among the most attractive career alternatives to a growing number of young people who have the necessary prerequisites; mainly, the appropriate amount and type of higher education. Thus, the increase in the number of professional workers in the United States is directly related to the increased portions of the population seeking the sort of credentials provided by attending institutions of higher learning, such as colleges and universities.

The category labeled *proprietors and managers* in Table 1 is composed of two quite distinct groups insofar as employment trends are concerned. About 75 percent of the group is made up of salaried managers and officials of business enterprises, and their numbers have been increasing substantially as they have become the prime workers in the corporate economy. All in all, they have increased by almost 60 percent during the decade of the 1960s. New types of managerial occupations have been created by technological changes. A good example is the manager of computer services, an important kind of new position in industry, government, and medical service facilities such as hospitals and clinics. In a similar way, a substantial number of traditional management positions have been modified by social and technological change. The manager of the accounting department in many organizations has been forced to deal with and manage the many new kinds of technologically advanced electronic data processing services, and therefore has been forced to learn the theory and functioning of electronic computers. The manager of the personnel department has been forced to deal with a wide range of new demands imposed by workers or the government with respect to pension plans, health insurance plans, and other "fringe" benefits, workmen's compensation laws, and affirmative action programs. In fact, many new occupational subspecialities within the ranks of personnel work have recently been created to deal with demands such as these.

The remaining 25 percent of the proprietors and managers category is composed of the independent proprietors of small businesses—gas stations, grocery stores, and retail specialty stores of all kinds—that have been condescendingly referred to at times by government officials as "mom and pop" stores. Also in this category are small machine shops and manufacturing facilities, beauty and barber shops, restaurants, and repair and maintenance service centers that are individually owned and operated. The number of these small businesses has declined rapidly in recent decades as part of the long-run shift to larger corporate-type business organizations, reducing the total number of people who earn their living as self-employed business proprietors. During the 1960s total employment in this category declined by almost 25 percent, and the decline has been continuing throughout the 1970s. As a result, total employment in the proprietor and management category is expected to have declined slightly by 1980 as a portion of the total labor force. Growth in the managerial segment is not expected to be sufficient to offset the losses in the proprietor segment.

The final category in the white-collar segment of the labor force is *sales workers.* More than 50 percent of all sales workers are employed in retail outlets of one kind or another. Also included, however, are real estate agents, insurance agents, and manufacturers' representatives. This segment of the labor force has just about kept pace with the growth in overall employment during this century and has maintained a relatively constant 6 percent share of the total overall employment over the past four or five decades. To a certain extent, the shift in retailing toward large branches of chain stores with their growing emphasis on self-service and check-out counters has somewhat depersonalized sales transactions and limited the potential growth in the number of retail salespersons in favor of cashiers, security guards and store detectives, stock handlers, price markers, inventory clerks, and other personnel who are included in other more rapidly growing segments of the labor force.

Blue-Collar Workers

Blue-collar work is classified by the skill levels associated with the jobs in this category. At the top of the skill ladder among blue-collar workers are the *craftsmen*. This group is a varied one and includes tool and die makers, auto mechanics, locomotive engineers, bakers, typesetters, supervisors, instrument repairers, and a range of construction skills including carpenters, plumbers, electricians, bricklayers, masons, and painters. The skilled worker category generally implies a period of prescribed training or apprenticeship anywhere from several months to several years as a prerequisite to entry. Back in 1900 there were six recognized skilled trades—engravers, locomotive engineers, brick masons, blacksmiths, metal molders, and shoemakers—which together represented 20 percent of all the skilled craftsmen. In the 1970s they represented only 5 percent of that group. In 1900 another six trades—carpenters, mechanics and repairmen, cranemen and stationary engineers, plumbers, electricians, and telephone linemen—together represented less than 40 percent of the skilled craftsmen. But now they include close to 70 percent (Wolfbein, 1971, p. 49). Thus, within this group quite different trends of growth or decline of employment opportunities have developed. Overall, however, this segment of the labor force has increased slightly during this century, from 10 percent of the total in 1900 to 13 percent in 1970. Skilled craftsmen are the elite of the blue-collar world, whose income often exceeds that of many white-collar workers. In terms of income or prestige, in fact, social scientists often have difficulty in deciding whether to classify these workers as members of the lower or working classes or as having achieved middle-class status. At any rate, a substantial portion of skilled blue-collar workers now reside in suburban communities that are generally characterized as middle class (see Chapter Four).

The *semiskilled* operative group makes up the largest segment of the blue-collar labor force. It is typified by the operator of a production machine on the assembly line of a factory. Such specialties are semiskilled in the sense that it may take several days or several weeks of supervision to train a worker to use and maintain such a machine properly. Another important semiskilled operative group comprises the workers who make their living as drivers or delivery persons, including long-distance truck drivers, taxicab and bus drivers, and those who deliver bread, milk, or retail packages. The mechanization of industry and the growth of the automobile and truck as principal means of transportation and the movement of goods grew rapidly in the first half of this century, and the semiskilled went from 13 percent of the labor force in 1900 to 20 percent in 1950. This was largely at the expense of unskilled work, which was often upgraded to the semiskilled level as the machine began to displace unskilled manual labor. Since 1950,

Construction work is one of the many occupations classified as blue collar work. (Marc Anderson)

the proportion of semiskilled workers in the labor force has begun to decline and is expected to be down to about 16 percent of the labor force in 1980. This is due in part to the increased efficiency of production because of innovations in engineering, science, and management, which have raised the productivity of the American industrial worker. For example, the average amount of goods and services produced by a worker in an hour of work *doubled* between 1949 and 1969 (Wolfbein, 1971, p. 37).

At least part of the reason for increased productivity also has been the mechanization of control of the production process, commonly referred to as automation. There is a great deal of controversy regarding the eventual effects of automation. Those who view the effects of automation as positive, in creating more jobs as well as more wealth, tend to see these as long-run rather than short-run gains. On the other hand, those who view automation with alarm are equally concerned with its more immediate consequences: those that will affect the current labor force and perhaps the children of this generation. Since the impact of rapid technological change is already taking its toll among significant numbers of workers whose skills have been rendered obsolete or whose jobs have been seriously altered or eliminated, automation and related technological changes tend to generate feelings of insecurity among both semiskilled and unskilled workers.

At the turn of the century, *unskilled* laborers constituted the largest segment of the blue-collar labor force (13 percent). Unskilled manual jobs were the ticket of entry into the urban economy for millions of migrants from domestic and foreign rural regions. Literacy was not an imperative for obtaining unskilled jobs and they could be learned in minutes, hours, or days. In fact, most unskilled workers at the turn of the century were functionally illiterate; they had no formal education beyond the fourth-grade level. Even as recently as 1949, 10 percent of the labor force was still functionally illiterate, and more than half (54 percent) never went beyond elementary school. But for all the reasons discussed above, opportunities to obtain employment as an unskilled blue-collar worker have been steadily shrinking over every decade of this century compared to other segments of the labor force. Unskilled workers now constitute only about 4 percent of the total. Among this segment of the labor force functional illiteracy and unemployment have remained consistently the highest in recent decades. The largest unemployed pool of unskilled workers in American society now tends to be concentrated in large American cities, where it is now most difficult to gain accessibility to other segments of the labor force because they have become more geographically decentralized, and where educational resources are inadequate for the task of training more literate and skilled workers (see Chapter Ten) to meet changing job demands and opportunities. This is widely perceived as one of the most important urban social problems of American life. Current newcomers to urban living can no longer expect to rely on unskilled manual labor as a way to obtain secure positions in the urban labor market.

HOW CHANGES IN THE LABOR MARKET TAKE PLACE

In the previous sections, shifts from agricultural occupations, from manual labor to skilled blue-collar occupations, and from all other categories to the professions (where higher education becomes the intervening variable) were described as among the major changes occurring in the urban labor market of the United States during this century. Some of these shifts have been gradual, but others have been abrupt and dramatic, producing sharp imbalances between the supply and demand for certain skills at any given time. Thus, in the 1960s and 1970s there were critical shortages of workers in professional, scientific, educational, and social service areas, while at the same time there was a surplus of workers in the manual labor categories. In the 1970s public school teaching moved from a shortage occupation to a surplus occupation virtually overnight. Continuous changes in the occupational composition of the labor force are ubiquitous in all modern urban societies. The questions that the resultant imbalances in the supply and demand for labor raise are: 1) How do shifts in the labor force take place? 2) What are the mechanisms through which segments of the population move from one part of the labor force to another? and 3) What is likely to happen to workers who are displaced from one segment of the labor force as they attempt to find employment or new career opportunities in other occupational areas?

BASIC ASSUMPTIONS OF A FREE LABOR MARKET

In American urban society the assumption is usually made that people make job changes within the framework of a free or laissez-faire labor market. The basic assumptions of a free labor market are well known to all Americans. They also have traditionally formed the foundation of the work of labor economists. These common assumptions can be restated as follows: 1) all individuals are free to seek the work of their choice; 2) individual occupational choices are rational; they are based on the maximization of individual self-interests and involve the selection of the best occupational arrangement from among the various opportunities available; 3) all individuals are free to compete for available occupational opportunities, and all available jobs are open to free competition; 4) all individuals will compete for the most desirable positions (those offering the greatest rewards), and the most skilled and motivated competitors will win the most desirable jobs or positions; 5) the incentives for occupational competition—the rewards—are primarily economic. These consist of the wages, salaries, or earnings available in exchange for one's work.

In effect, the free labor market system just described is supposed to work something like this: as each individual finds his or her own occupational level or niche, the needs and the requirements of the society are somehow met. The free labor market is expected to ensure that there will always be an appropriate distribution of skills throughout the labor market, and that the society's needs for labor are therefore best met through the free play of the labor market. In a free labor market, it is anticipated, the labor force will automatically adjust itself to the needs for labor existing at any given time, preventing serious imbalances between the supply and demand for workers.

BARRIERS TO CAREER CHANGES IN THE LABOR MARKET

In actuality, while this model is useful for conceptual purposes, it is not an entirely accurate representation of current reality. One would be hard pressed to find empirical examples of a completely open labor market, even in a free society such as the United States. There are many barriers or impediments to the free movement of workers from one segment of the labor market to another, and such movements do not take place automatically. Relatively high rates of unemployment in periods of relatively high general prosperity in recent decades testify to the existence of forces that make it difficult if not impossible for many workers to readily shift their occupational roles from one area to another. These barriers affect not only unskilled workers but highly skilled specialists as well. It is possible tentatively to identify what some of these barriers are. Some of them are the personal characteristics that the workers themselves bring into the labor market, but many of them are barriers that are imposed by employers in their recruitment or selection of workers.

Workers may resist shifting occupation when such shifts also require geographic mobility or a willingness to relocate. Although the number of people who migrate any given year is quite high (more than thirty-five million people move their place of residence across county lines each year), a majority of the working population resists such moves. Professional and technical personnel were the only workers whose migration rates were greater than 50 percent over a recent five-year period (Wolfbein, 1971, p. 64). Clerical workers, service workers, and skilled and unskilled blue-collar workers all had a migration rate of less than 30 percent during the same five-year period. Age is another important factor affecting the willingness or ability of workers to migrate from one region to another to secure or enhance their occupational status. Young workers between ages twenty and twenty-nine have the highest rates of migration. Thereafter, the migration rates drop off sharply from thirty to sixty-five years of age. Clearly, the older worker may have more invested or more at stake in resisting job change requiring a geographic move. It is also clear that the geographic preference of workers who migrate does not necessarily coincide with the availability of job opportunities. For example, sun-belt cities or coastal cities such as San Francisco continue to attract migrants in numbers well beyond their capacity to be absorbed easily into the local labor markets, while communities considered undesirable places to live may have difficulties in attracting enough workers to fill available positions.

A lack of knowledge of available opportunities may restrict movement in the labor market, and many new kinds of occupations tend to be "invisible" to potential recruits. The process of looking for work or choosing a career may be one of the most difficult and complex tasks faced by urban dwellers. Also, the task is made more difficult because many job opportunities are not announced or made available to the general public and are filled instead through personal contacts or word of mouth. Many graduating university seniors do not have the slightest notion of how to go about obtaining employment, which suggests that the lack of such information is by no means limited to unskilled or poorly trained individuals, although these groups may experience far more difficulty in obtaining secure employment.

Other barriers to free movement in the labor market that may be attributes of workers themselves are: having skills so specialized that they are not readily transferable to new areas; having a degree of investment in a current job, such as seniority, pensions and retirement benefits, loyalty to employer, or attachment to coworkers; resistance to change (cultural lag) or an unwillingness to take risks because of fears of an uncertain future. People may also have different levels of motivation or aspiration, inasmuch as not everyone necessarily wishes to compete for the most rewarding or prestigious positions available.

Employers, in setting up criteria of any kind for the recruitment and selection of workers, are, in effect, at the same time establishing barriers that may exclude certain segments of the labor force from consideration as prospective employees. Of course, this serves as a barrier to free movement in the labor market for the job seekers so excluded. Many such barriers are legitimate in that they pertain directly to the skills required to perform the jobs that are available. But employers may also consciously or not introduce biases or procedures in the recruiting process that may be incidental to the task of finding individuals who are best qualified to perform the necessary work tasks. These practices run contrary to the expectations of the free labor market. For example, some employers may engage in the kind of recruiting where having attended the "right" schools, coming from the "right" families or social circles, or having the "appropriate" social values is substituted for skill as a criterion for selection. There may also be biases about physical characteristics, such as weight, height, physical attractiveness, hair style, and style of dress. More invidious, of course, are biases having to do with the racial, ethnic, religious, age, or sexual characteristics of potential employees. The latter are now generally discouraged or forbidden by fair employment legislation, but by no means have they been completely eliminated.

In response to the difficulties of moving about freely and flexibly, modern urban society has evolved a number of innovative institutional devices. Public and private employment agencies, vocational guidance counseling, retraining programs, systems of unemployment compensation, university placement offices, detailed governmental studies and projections of labor market trends, and affirmative action programs are all designed to encourage free and open movement in the urban labor market. More recently, the mass media have been increasingly used to disseminate occupational information to the general public. In turn, all of these activities have helped to create a number of new occupational specialties, such as employment interviewers or counselors, job development specialists, trainers, affirmative action investigators, and human resource development workers.

ORGANIC SOLIDARITY AND ECOLOGICAL INTERDEPENDENCE IN THE LABOR MARKET

In the early seminal work *The Division of Labor in Society,* Emile Durkheim (1947) saw preindustrial societies characterized by what he called "mechanical solidarity," in which social unity stemmed from the fact that everyone did essentially the same kind of work. As the nature of work becomes more differentiated and specialized within the more complex division of labor of modern urban industrial societies, mechanical solidarity becomes gradually displaced by what he called "organic solidarity." Organic solidarity refers to the social integration of society based on the recognition that individuals in highly specialized occupational roles are highly dependent on other individuals in other highly specialized but unlike roles to supply goods and services that they cannot supply themselves. In modern ecological terms, the interdependent interactions among individuals who occupy specialized roles that are different from one another are called "symbiotic" relationships (Hawley, 1950). Durkheim argued that organic solidarity requires an ethical or moral system that emphasizes the need for a high degree of conscious cooperation and understanding among unlike segments of the labor force. However, Durkheim also recognized that organic solidarity did not come about automatically, and that social integration of societies characterized by an increasing division of labor was threatened by the following possibilities: 1) anomie, or a sense of normlessness or isolation, may increase with the division of labor; 2) individuals may be reluctantly forced to perform tasks that are not in line with their character or to conform with a division of labor that may not be of their own choosing; and 3) the division of labor may be so minute that any given work task does not seem to be meaningful or relevant. Yet, the degree of interdependence among all segments of the modern urban industrial labor force is so great that the entire economic system may be seriously disrupted when any one group of highly specialized workers for whatever reason withholds its services from the labor market.

Thus, in recent years, work stoppages by workers such as firefighters and policeofficers, truck drivers or bus drivers, dairyworkers, school teachers, television performers or technicians, public sanitation workers, lithograph and press operators (employed by daily newspapers), gasoline station attendants, nurses and other health workers, longshoremen, telephone operators, supermarket cashiers, social workers, and countless other urban service workers have threatened to disrupt the daily flow of activities that urbanites routinely depend on for their survival or well-being. Urbanites tend to take these occupational activities for granted until they are inconvenienced by strikes, walkouts, picketing, and other work stoppages by workers who might not always be visible, but who are nevertheless essential to the daily rhythm of the urban economy. But when the daily newspaper fails to appear, a house burns down with firefighters standing idly by, or someone is robbed while policeofficers are home with the "blue flu" due to labor problems, or when one cannot routinely shop at the local supermarket because delivery men are on strike and the shelves are bare, the typical urbanite will respond with frustration, anger, or miscomprehension at what is happening to him or her.

Urban workers increasingly have become formally organized as labor unions or are willing to use strategies invented by labor unions to further their occupational self-interests. Once thought to be characteristic only of production workers in industrial work organizations, labor unions are now common among all segments of the urban work force, including white-collar and professional workers. One can now find university professors, physicians, and clergy organized into labor unions, although just a few decades ago it was widely believed that the values of such professionals would prevent their considering unionization as an acceptable alternative for furthering their occupational goals (Lipset, 1967). Even self-employed agricultural workers were recently considering withholding from planting their crops as a national protest against prevailing federal agricultural policies, which illustrates the degree to which urban behavior patterns penetrate rural areas in a society that is highly urbanized (see Chapter Four).

In the broadest sense, labor unions, trade unions, professional associations, and business associations may be described as *categoric* units of social organization. A categoric unit, according to Hawley (1950, p. 218), is one made up of members occupying a single status category who unite in a collective attempt to meet common external threats or to maintain the status quo:

> Categoric units emerge only in those occupations that have been confronted by challenges, which, if unattended, might impair or eliminate the sustenance base of the individuals involved. These are usually the most highly skilled occupations which are often so specialized that the individuals committed to them cannot readily shift to other occupations. The medieval guild and modern professional association are illustrative of highly developed categoric units.

Thus, whenever their occupational aspirations appear to be threatened or frustrated in any way, the members of an occupation will collectively demand that their representative organization, be it a union, professional association, or trade association, provide a solution to the problem. Very often the problem concerns job security and advancement or increased control over the conditions of work, as well as a desire for higher income. When lobbying, public relations, or attempts at negotiations fail, strikes, work stoppages, picketing, and other devices pioneered by trade unions to protect their interests increasingly are used by workers.

This trend can be seen most clearly among public service workers in local government. Until the mid-1930s, municipal workers conceived of themselves primarily as "public servants" or as professional or quasiprofessional workers and had not yet begun to affiliate with labor unions. But by the mid-1960s, municipal unions such as the American Federation of State, County, and Municipal Employees were among the fastest growing segment of the labor union movement. Today roughly half of the eleven million public employees (including public school teachers) are now organized into unions, compared with only 20 to 25 percent of the workers in the private sector (Williams, 1977).

Power struggles between public employees' unions and the city governments for which their members work are now a common occurrence in American cities, and there is no end to these in immediate sight. Without debating the merits of the arguments on each side of the struggle, one can reasonably conclude that disruptive labor disputes are often a detriment to the solution of communitywide problems that require cooperative effort by municipal officials and municipal workers as well as by the public at large. Yet municipal employees' potential to exercise power has been so recently recognized that it has been largely ignored in community power structure studies. Most studies of decision-making processes in local communities focus on broad segments of the community (public officials, business elites) or on individuals occupying key community positions. Rarely do they isolate the various technical occupations employed by municipalities for more concrete analysis (see Chapter Ten).

SELECTED BIBLIOGRAPHY

DURKHEIM, EMILE. *The Division of Labor in Society.* New York: Free Press, 1947.

GALBRAITH, JOHN K. *The Affluent Society.* Boston: Houghton Mifflin, 1958.

HALL, RICHARD H. *Occupations and the Social Structure.* 2nd ed. Englewood Cliffs, N.J.: Prentice-Hall, 1975.

HAWLEY, AMOS H. *Human Ecology.* New York: Ronald Press, 1950.

HORTON, PAUL B., and LESLIE, GERALD R. *The Sociology of Social Problems.* 5th ed. Englewood Cliffs, N.J.: Prentice-Hall, 1974.

LEWIS, MICHAEL. *Urban America: Institutions and Experience.* New York: John Wiley, 1973.

LIPSET, SEYMOUR M. "White Collar Workers and Professionals: Their Attitudes and Behavior Toward Unions." In William A. Faunce, ed., *Readings in Industrial Sociology,* pp. 525–548. New York: Appleton-Century-Crofts, 1967.

MONTAGNA, PAUL. *Occupations and Society.* New York: John Wiley, 1977.

PRICE, DON K. *The Scientific Estate.* Cambridge, Mass.: Harvard University Press, 1965.

RITZER, GEORGE. *Working: Conflict and Change.* 2nd ed. Englewood Cliffs, N.J.: Prentice-Hall, 1977.

RIVERS, WILLIAM L., et al. *The Mass Media and Modern Society.* San Francisco: Rinehart Press, 1971.

WILENSKY, HAROLD L., and LEBEAUX, CHARLES N. *Industrial Society and Social Welfare.* New York: Russell Sage, 1958.

WILLIAMS, ROGER. "The Clamor over Municipal Unions," *Saturday Review* (March 5, 1977).

WOLFBEIN, SEYMOUR. *Work in American Society.* Glenview, Ill.: Scott, Foresman, 1971.

ZUCKERMAN, HARRIET, and MERTON, R. K. "Age, Aging and Age Structure." In R. K. Merton, *The Sociology of Science.* Chicago: University of Chicago Press, 1973.

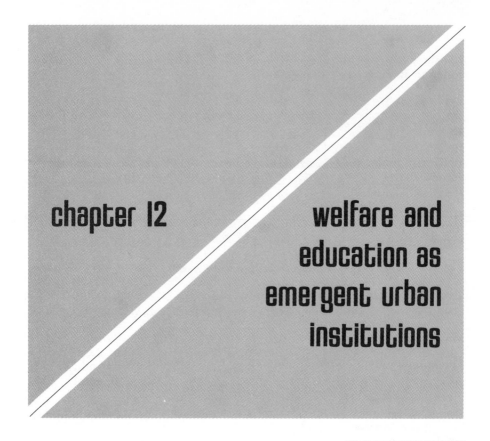

chapter 12

welfare and education as emergent urban institutions

BY JACQUELINE SCHERER

The quality of life in any urban area depends, to a large degree, on the functioning of social institutions concerned with health, education, and welfare. The idea that society has a social responsibility to help individuals and families with problems by maintaining medical facilities or operating free public schools is a relatively recent idea in human history. Traditionally, the family and the tribe provided all personal services; later, voluntary efforts by churches and philanthropic groups assisted small local programs. Today, however, in most parts of the developed world, central governments have superceded the original voluntary and local institutional care givers.

The changeover from individual to social responsibility has not been smooth or even: urban institutions ostensibly provided help only in response to urgent needs, operating inadequate programs grudgingly funded. Critics have charged that public services have reduced the influence and authority of the family and have fostered dependence on the government, thereby reducing personal responsibility and concern for helping others. On the other hand, the demands for assistance have continued to increase in response to the difficulties that human beings encounter as they try to survive the changes in everyday life brought about by urbanization, industrialization, and rapid technological and social events.

Service institutions may be thought of as "social inventions that seek to meet the needs of modern man in his interrelationships and roles, much as technical innovation is a response to the physical requirements of modern living" (Kahn, 1970, p. 1). Urban institutions developed gradually as existing social structures proved inadequate to serve the human needs in the total environment: older institutions gradually became powerless, and newer, more dynamic social approaches became established.

THE EVOLUTION OF AMERICAN WELFARE

The term "welfare" is used loosely to include many different activities, such as providing money for poor families or administering adoption centers for orphans. In many industrial countries, social welfare is thought of as an institution comprising "all those policies and programs by which government guarantees a defined minimum of social services, money and consumption rights, through the employment of access or distribution criteria other than those of the market place and through demand management of the economy" (Kahn, 1970, p. 24). The system includes poor and affluent alike, and contains programs dealing with health, education, employment services, child care, housing, and income maintenance.

In the United States, welfare has largely been used to refer to income maintenance programs for specific categories of recipients, such as the elderly, disabled, or children under eighteen. A clear distinction has been made between services for the needy and poor ("welfare") and those services provided for all citizens as a right, such as education, veterans' payments, or social security benefits. American resistance to coordinated human services as a "right" accorded to all citizens can be explained by a complex fusion of cultural, historical, and social attitudes. The belief in individual self-reliance, a puritanical attitude toward work and leisure, a foundation in the Judeo-Christian ethical code, the rise of capitalism and industrialization, and historical "timing" are some of these elements. The right to free education, for example, developed much earlier in the United States than did the "right" to free health care, nor is it likely that most Americans today accept the "right" to guaranteed annual income or some other form of financial support. In many European cultures, in contrast, the right to health care and income maintenance has been established longer than the "right" to free education. When a social good is perceived as a right, rather than a form of special assistance, there is a social guarantee that the institution will receive public resources. T. H. Marshall (1964) argues that the history of citizenship may be viewed as the extension of rights from fundamental social rights in the 1700s, to political rights in the 1800s, to economic rights in the 1900s. This is simply stated by Romanyshan (1971) as a movement from "charity to justice."

To understand the development of American urban welfare institutions it is important to recognize the strong English influence on American institutions. The early colonists brought the English pattern of social services to America and this pattern dominated welfare until the late nineteenth century. Two dimensions of the English tradition were critical: the belief that welfare was the responsibility of local government rather than the national government, and the belief that the poor were morally inferior, especially if they were able to work and did not do so. These beliefs were articulated in the English Poor Law of 1601. Although it is hard to understand today, the original law was a reform effort concerned with the problems of pauperism. When the English economy changed from farming to grazing, the small plots of land that supported marginal farmers were "enclosed" and hundreds of laborers were displaced.

The key provisions of this important law included: 1) appointing overseers from the local community annually; 2) requiring all ablebodied persons to work; 3) taxing all householders for funds to support the program; 4) binding out poor children as apprentices; 5) requiring parents to support children and children to support indigent parents; 6) building workhouses on wastelands; and 7) committing those persons who would not work to the House of Correction. Another feature of the Poor Law was the policy of helping only the worthy poor: orphans, the elderly, the disabled, or those who could not work. Others either worked and were paid for services, or were "unworthy" to receive assistance. Those who were unworthy also suffered a grave moral stigma; it was their own fault for not succeeding. Such views combined puritan theology stressing the value of hard work for salvation and the dominant belief in the power of the individual to shape his or her own destiny.

As a result of the emphasis on local responsibility and the moral inferiority of the unworthy poor, American villages and towns developed various strategies to deal with the needy. Those unable to work were sent to the "poorhouse" or "almshouse." These were often unpleasant homes on farms where assistance was meager and the idle or lazy were punished. By the mid-nineteenth century, the idea of "outdoor relief" became popular. As explained in one account: "Worthy indigent persons should, if possible, be kept from the degradation of the poor house, by reasonable supplies of provisions, bedding, and other absolute necessaries, at their own homes" (Komisar, 1974). The worthy poor were generally widows with small children, the old and ill unable to live with relatives, and the disabled unable to work. But pauperism, considered a weakness of character in others, continued to be treated with spiritual and moral advice rather than money. Health care was viewed as one part of the overall relief program and "a responsibility assumed by individuals or by private organizations" (Hyman, 1975, p. 1). Education was a luxury for the wealthy, or forced upon the poor as part of their religious education.

Emerging Welfare Institutions

Cities gradually built a few specialized health institutions locally supported and controlled. For example, the first American hospital was established in Philadelphia in 1732 and another in New York City in 1760. Port cities adopted public health measures to protect residents from the threat of plague and other epidemics associated with trade. There were also a few colleges on the eastern seacoast that trained wealthy young men in the ministry and established professions.

During the 1840s a brief reform era led to the establishment of state mental health hospitals after Dorothea Dix, a humane crusader, helped to arouse public indignation about the terrible conditions that existed for the mentally ill. The reform efforts, however, were short-lived because the influential concepts of local welfare, individual responsibility, and moral inferiority dominated the thinking of the day.

After the Civil War, charity organizations that combined a moral zeal to improve the character of the urban poor with the humanitarian goal of relieving their suffering increased in number. In both England and the United States, charity organizations tried to coordinate voluntary efforts for reasons of "economy, efficiency, and uniform service standards" (Lubove, 1973, p. 220). By 1892 America had ninety-two Charity Organization Societies that directed voluntary efforts. The "undeserving" poor were still scorned by these groups, and only those who were found worthy of aid were given assistance.

The late nineteenth century was dominated philosophically by the doctrine of "survival of the fittest" applied to human behavior. This was a harsh view of the human condition, asserting that only those who could successfully compete in life would survive its rigors and struggles. It also implied that those who were successful "deserved" to be rewarded. In response to this powerful theme the doctrine of a social gospel also developed. This taught that the wealthy had a religious duty to save the souls of the urban poor from wickedness and sin. Organizations such as the Salvation Army, the YMCA, and the YWCA were maintained by voluntary contributions to assist in this work in urban areas.

The Immigrant Problem

By 1890, the number of foreign-born Americans in the major cities of the country had become critical. The personal problems faced by many of these people were often overwhelming: poverty, inability to communicate in English, loneliness for a faraway homeland, separation from family members, frustration in adjusting to the developing industrial society, unhealthy working conditions, poor education, and political powerlessness (see Chapter Three). The existing urban welfare institutions had few resources that could be used to assist the large numbers of needy immigrants seeking assistance. As the problems became clear, many reformers tried to bring about changes in public welfare. Between 1890 and 1910 significant gains were made. The United States Children's Bureau, for example, was developed in 1912, the Public Education Association of Philadelphia in 1881, the Juvenile Courts of Denver and Chicago in 1895, and a growing number of charitable trust funds developed, such as the Rockefeller and Carnegie Foundations.

One of the most interesting reforms was the settlement house movement. The most famous of these, Hull House, was founded by Jane Addams in Chicago. Settlement workers helped the poor to find work, obtain job skills, learn about health care, how to use community resources, and to improve their lives in many ways. Most importantly, the settlement workers were eager to apply the new ideas of medical and social science to their work, laying the foundations for a new occupation: professional social work.

The National Welfare Program, 1930-1960

Local and voluntary charitable organizations still dominated the welfare environment when the Great Depression of the 1930s took place. Cities were soon bankrupt and private charity inadequate to meet the needs of the many unemployed and poor living in the cities. Clearly there was an urgent need to develop some form of national welfare to respond to the problems.

After several unsuccessful efforts and considerable experimentation, Congress passed the Social Security Act in 1935. In many ways this was a remarkable act. For the first time there was a public recognition that the local units of government could not manage the human problems created by the economic system and that "welfare" was a national concern. In addition, the new law provided for grants of money rather than goods. New categories of aid were established for the aged, for children under the age of eighteen living with a parent (Aid to Dependent Children), and for the disabled. Old Age and Survivors Disability Insurance programs insured that families could receive some support if the head of the family, or the bread-winner, was injured or killed.

But even in 1935 some elements of the Elizabethan Poor Law remained. The concept of "categorical" aid given to people who fell into specific categories of need was kept, as was the requirement that recipients had to be residents of a particular locality. Even financing was based on the idea of local involvement. The federal government provided a portion of the funds, the state another portion, and the local government a third share.

Those persons not eligible for assistance because they did not fit into the categories of need, or because they were not residents of the locality, could still apply for General Assistance. These were county and local programs held over from the established local traditions and did not provide the benefits or protection of the new Social Security programs, such as cash payments.

Shared financial arrangements for welfare was to become a controversial issue in the 1960s and 1970s. The original formula for Washington's share favored rural areas and assumed that the wealthy cities could pay a substantial share of the costs of welfare. When cities were no longer able to do this in the late sixties and seventies because of a decline in revenues and a heightened demand for welfare assistance, appeals to Washington for changes fell on deaf ears. It was not until 1971 that the Supreme Court declared the residency requirements illegal, and the local basis of welfare that had been an inherent part of the American system since its inception was disbanded.

National Response to Urban Poverty, 1960

The Social Security Act established a national system of welfare, but, as noted, because of the local participation in funding it was to develop some critical problems during the 1960s. From 1940 onward there had been a steady migration of poor people from the South to the North and from farms to cities in search of better jobs. Opportunities for jobs in factories continued throughout the fifties. At the same time, increased mechanization of agriculture forced marginal farmers from their small holdings. It is sobering to realize that at the time of the Great Depression in 1930 over one-third of the working population was rural. By 1970 the proportion of the working force engaged in agriculture had shrunk to slightly more than 4 percent. It is not an exaggeration to state that we had undergone an economic revolution. One result of this was the large-scale migration of poor workers into established cities. At the same time, many affluent workers moved out of the central cities to suburban communities surrounding the city borders for more attractive housing. As the poor moved into the cities and the middle-class moved out to the suburbs, the urban population of cities changed radically. Many of the newcomers were black Americans, who faced some of the problems that immigrants arriving in America at the turn of the century had also faced. They were predominantly rural, often poor and unprepared for industrial occupations, not well educated or skilled. Unlike the immigrants of an earlier day, however, black Americans gradually encountered a shortage of unskilled jobs. Automation and other technological changes began to alter the industrial sector rapidly (see Chapter Fourteen). International and national markets dictated economic decisions; highways and new communication arrangements enabled industrial firms to relocate outside of the central city areas; railroads grew obsolescent and mass transportation no longer dominated economic decisions.

The results of these economic trends meant that the urban populations, particularly within central cities, were increasingly poor and in need of welfare assistance. These demands for help came at the same time that cities had reduced tax revenues from which welfare funds could be generated. Moreover, the black population of American cities challenged the political arrangements that reduced their opportunities to fully participate in American society. The Civil Rights movement expressed their frustration and led to demands for national assistance with urban problems.

By 1965 the federal government responded to the urban problems of poverty with several innovative programs. The "War on Poverty" that President Johnson announced included such programs as Model Cities Assistance, Head Start programs in schools, neighborhood assistance, and community development grants. Many of these programs were extraordinarily naïve, assuming that poverty was a simple problem that could easily be changed. Most depended upon some form of training, although the serious problem of developing new jobs for the trained workers was never addressed. In addition, the war in Vietnam consumed greater amounts of the federal budget and many promising programs were dropped or funding reduced just at the point when they showed some promise. Growing disenchantment with Washington led to a major redirection in welfare programming through a state and federal partnership. Revenue sharing provided the national funds for state programs, and cities had to compete with the politically powerful suburban districts in the state for these funds.

Federal initiatives to deal with urban poverty gradually withered away. The national welfare system, with its inequities in funding, continued intact despite almost unanimous agreement that changes were necessary.

The experience of the last twenty years illustrates how difficult it has been to shift away from the old English tradition of local responsibility. National economic and social problems have been neglected in a structural arrangement developed for rural societies. As metropolitan welfare problems become increasingly complex and interdependent, federal responsibility for dealing with these issues will again be tried. In the meantime, the urban poor have to survive within the present confusing pattern of assistance.

Urban Poverty

Poverty remains the most serious problem in social welfare, aggravating other conditions. Although it is true that if everyone had adequate money to provide a reasonable standard of living, problems of health, unhappiness, educational failure, and crime would still occur, it is equally true that the absence of an adequate income aggravates each of these conditions. For example, the number of poor people to be found in prisons, mental institutions, and hospitals is higher than that of middle-income individuals. There is a strong correlation between poverty and educational failure, marital instability, child abuse, and juvenile delinquency. This does not mean that poverty causes any of these conditions, but rather that poverty makes it harder for an individual to overcome difficulties and to make reasonable progress. It is not a coincidence that public opinion surveys consistently find that poor people are less satisfied with the quality of their lives than those who are more affluent. The poor have more problems, fewer chances at happiness, and require more welfare assistance than any other population category. For this reason any discussion of modern welfare must begin with an analysis of poverty.

Poverty continues to be one of the most serious problems affecting cities in America, as well as in the rest of the world. (Marc Anderson)

Poverty and Urban Immigration

To be poor is not to be able to "buy" what is needed for basic needs. But basic needs is a subjective concept. For a time, someone could live on bread and water, but no one would claim that it is an adequate diet. Poverty is *relative*: it depends upon social context. Once we move away from basic survival, it is difficult to ascertain the level of adequacy required. Policy makers, however, require a statistical unit to develop programs of income maintenance. This usually is based on the costs of food for a minimal diet with an austere clothing and housing allowance. Determining this level is a complex and controversial process. It is estimated, on the basis of the federal government standard, that 12 percent of the United States' population was poor in 1975. But the kinds of poverty affecting individuals and groups, and its location within the country, varies considerably. For example, like the European and Asian immigrants at the turn of the century, urban migrants are generally poor. Black Americans and Hispanic Americans, particularly Mexicans and Puerto Ricans, have faced some of the same problems of adjustment from rural to urban environments (see Chapter Fourteen). Mexican immigrants who have entered the country illegally often face additional problems when they seek assistance.

Other minorities found in the city include native American Indians who have left the reservations, Chinese immigrants from Hong Kong who have come to America within the last decade, and displaced citizens from all over the world who are caught in the complex swirls of international political struggles.

On occasion one hears a statement that the urban poor have flocked to the cities because of generous welfare benefits. The evidence does not support this, however. Between 1950 and 1960 when the majority of black Americans moved to cities, welfare rolls were low. Most of them found the jobs they sought in migrating. The 108 percent increase in welfare took place in the mid-1960s after the peak of black migration. The majority of urban poor receiving assistance today were born and raised in the cities and are not new migrants from rural areas.

Poverty and Sex Discrimination

Another group subject to discrimination in American society and concentrated in urban areas is females, particularly those who support families. A recent study of welfare concluded:

> Probably the largest factor underlying the changes in economic status is change in family composition. Divorce, new children and other such domestic changes often result in dramatic shifts in well-being, particularly for women and children in the sample. For example, a third of the women who were divorced and not remarried fell below the poverty line. . . . (New York Times, 1977)

Since 70.9 percent of all fully employed women earned less than $7,000 in 1972, or approximately 60 percent of what males earned at equivalent jobs, their earning potential is lower, and often their family responsibilities include child care. Of the 20.5 million women employed, over two-thirds are at jobs paying little more than the minimum wage. The rise in female heads of families during the last few years portends an increase in urban poverty.

Other groups of poor located in cities are the elderly, former mental patients, and other "stigmatized" groups who must find inexpensive housing to survive. Since suburban homes are often expensive and designed for single families, central city apartments and rooming houses provide the main attraction for these people to remain.

Although the city continues to play its historical role as a center for those seeking a new life, at the same time impressive obstacles for fulfilling this dream exist for those who are poor.

The Welfare Crisis

The differences in local costs for welfare contributions vary considerably throughout the United States. New York City, for example, pays a larger share of the welfare burden than any other metropolitan area in the United States, whereas eleven other cities pay no welfare bills. Cost of living differences also vary throughout the United States. In 1975, for instance, a woman with no means of support and several children would receive a maximum benefit of $194 for rent in New York City, $168 in Cleveland, and $116 in Houston because of differences in rentals available.

It is difficult to compare the proportion of an urban population receiving aid from city to city because some cities put all federal programs together, but rough estimates for those members in one program, Aid to Dependent Children, are: 13 percent of New York City's population, 17 percent in Detroit, 3 percent in Seattle, 16 percent in Philadelphia, 10 percent in Los Angeles, 18 percent in Denver, Chicago, and Kansas City, 4 percent in Atlanta, and 2 percent in Dallas. This does not mean that Denver and Detroit have a higher proportion of poverty than Atlanta; it might mean that they are trying harder to assist the poor, making it easier for those eligible to receive the aid to which they are legally entitled.

Routinely, city governments have appealed to Washington to make all welfare programs national in scope. Mayors argue that the poor are affected by national economic conditions; by not assisting cities with financing welfare programs, the national government is placing an intolerable burden on municipal budgets.

Another serious problem with existing welfare arrangements is the growing bureaucratic nightmare that encompasses the system. Mistakes by workers, client misinformation and cheating, delays in reporting and receiving assistance have made the existing programs inefficient and costly. This contributes to the negative attitudes surrounding welfare and the poor. As late as 1972 an opinion poll showed that the majority of Americans believed that poor people themselves are to be blamed for poverty. Over 80 percent agreed that "there are too many people receiving welfare who are not honest about their need" (Faegin, 1972). According to innumerable studies and statistical analyses, however, the vast majority of those receiving aid are either unemployable or cannot find jobs. Experts believe that the number of ineligible recipients of welfare is probably no higher than those who cheat on income tax or expense accounts, but the stereotype of shiftless welfare cheats remains dominant, frustrating urban efforts to help with the problems of poverty. Receiving welfare is still regarded as an indication of personal failure and a cause of shame for many Americans.

Other strategies suggested to eliminate urban poverty reflect these American attitudes: they include programs to train people for the labor market; efforts to change the local labor market so that it reduces poverty; and aid to depressed urban areas to develop employment opportunities. None of these strategies deals directly with the economic transformations affecting urban areas and which cause the loss of employment opportunities for the poor. Other urban societies (such as Germany, Japan, England, Sweden, and Denmark) have tried to develop national programs so that the issue is viewed not as a city problem but as a national concern. In the United States, however, the national focus is still relatively weak.

Other Public Assistance Programs

Most social agencies have a variety of other programs in addition to income maintenance to deal with social needs in urban society. Assistance with child care includes work with adoptions, foster care, counseling, juvenile delinquency, battered children, and recreation. Assisting troubled families is the goal of family agencies and social services and includes a wide variety of activities: homemaking services, marriage counseling, sheltering abused wives and children, training programs, and family planning, to name but a few. Working with the aged has expanded significantly during the past decade and many social agencies have a full complement of services for this group. The needs of the handicapped are met in rehabilitation centers, special recreation programs, and medical services.

Changing Style of Service Delivery

Another transformation paralleled the economic changes in American society—a shift from personal, small-scale, and unskilled service delivery to bureaucratic and large-scale professional arrangements. When social service responsibilities rested on local governmental units, the care-givers were usually prominent local citizens or professionals in a very general sense. There were, for example, local doctors in the American colonies, but the state of medical science was not advanced and a young boy could learn the essentials of medicine with a small amount of formal scientific education through an apprenticeship with an older, experienced doctor. Elementary teachers had only to read and write reasonably well to qualify for teaching children, and even at the university level any "educated" adult who was reasonably well read in a particular field was qualified to teach it. The idea that it was necessary to study the poor or to develop specific skills in assisting the less fortunate would have been ridiculed.

Initially, municipal services reflected this generalist approach to service delivery. After the Civil War, specialized bodies of information, particularly in medicine, became important in the training of doctors and nurses. But the degree of specialization was limited and the apprenticeship model of learning, sometimes in an institutional setting, dominated. By the turn of the century, however, the increase in knowledge considered important in health, education, and welfare led to demands for professional training. Regulations regarding licensing, training, and professional responsibilities emerged in the medical field; teachers attended "normal" schools to absorb the growing body of social scientific knowledge about child development, psychological growth, and teaching methods. Volunteers and philanthropists were replaced by professional social workers who tried to combine scientific knowledge about human behavior with the problems of poverty in the rapidly growing cities of an industrialized nation.

Since professional care-givers found technological aids useful in providing services, urban hospitals, schools, and welfare agencies became central locations for housing material resources and for administering services. Organizational structures were necessary to raise money and to account for the ways in which funds were allocated. Administrators and clerks, as well as employees in many subsidiary capacities, became essential parts of the organization. New types of social workers developed: liaison experts, program coordinators, public relations specialists, volunteer leaders, federal grant administrators, and employee relations workers, to name but a few. New departments were created, rules and procedures codified, and organizational complexity accelerated.

This transformation from personal to bureaucratic service delivery enabled urban institutions to provide more care for more people. The kind of care received also changed as individual specialists applied an expanded body of knowledge and developed particular skills to work with special problems. Often this specialization bewildered the person seeking help. The institutional aura surrounding service centers was a poor substitute for the warm and loving personal care received from friends and family in an earlier age. The gap between poor clients and professional, usually middle-class care-givers impeded easy communication.

In the late 1960s, complaints against professional care-givers and service delivery styles were a major factor in the federal government's efforts to devise new social welfare policies. One example of this concern was the provision for Model City programs in poor neighborhoods, whereby local residents and paraprofessionals were encouraged to play important roles. Neighborhood mothers, for example, were paid to serve as teaching aides, and local clinics, staffed by neighborhood residents and supplemented by professionals, experimented with providing health care. Other examples were crisis hotlines, manned by volunteers, who worked on problems of suicide, loneliness, or personal unhappiness; neighborhood service centers that ran food cooperatives assisting the poor in buying food in bulk quantity to save money, or providing free legal advice for those in trouble. Many of these newer organizations could not survive because of financial problems, the resistance of established professional care-givers and organizations, or the loss of volunteer support. But many have become firmly established in cities and have made lasting changes in service delivery.

The tensions between professional expertise and local control efforts will probably result in conflicts for many years to come. For example, professional educators fought against community control of schools when it meant that local residents could hire and fire school staffs directly. Medical professionals have demanded stringent regulations specifying who can provide medical services and who is not qualified to do this. Social workers have developed licensing and training procedures to control entry into these fields. At the same time, the use of citizen review boards, new professionals, and paraprofessionals in many areas of social service has increased.

Another social phenomenon that may have an important impact on service delivery is the consumer movement. The basis of consumerism is the belief that those receiving a service or a product have a right to redress if the service or product does not meet a reasonable standard of usefulness. In addition, consumers argue that the government has an obligation to protect citizens against abuses and to specify minimum standards of service and quality. The rising number of malpractice suits brought against doctors and the interest in competency examinations for graduating high school students are two examples of the techniques consumers employ to bring about their goals.

The Relationship Between Urbanization and Welfare

Do welfare institutions help resolve the problems of urban poverty or do they contribute to these problems by controlling urban populations with bandaid treatments? This question has become a crucial issue in the last part of the twentieth century as poverty, increased demand for social services, unemployment, and rising costs stubbornly refused to go away. Rural poverty is also a persistent issue in the world, but the concentration of poverty within central cities dramatizes and highlights urban poverty. Many believe that the city actually is the cause of the problem. Others believe that urbanization has simply intensified the problems of modern life.

But even if one concedes that urbanization initially may have only intensified basic human problems, clearly urbanization gradually has altered the ways in which people perceive their environment and how they earn a living. Inevitably, the personal and individual ties of responsibility traditionally binding people together shifted to large-scale, bureaucratic institutional arrangements. New organizational ties supported by voluntary contributions or public tax money, staffed by specialists and officials, and, increasingly, based upon scientific and technological knowledge replaced ties based on love and affection. Such institutional arrangements can operate efficiently in many areas and contribute significantly to a better quality of life for most urban dwellers. At the same time, these structures sometimes are incapable of absorbing the changing populations entering urban areas: they can be inflexible and rigid when the diverse needs of people require different and original responses.

Some critics of American urban welfare argue that the function of welfare is not to help the poor as much as it is to perserve order in the cities. According to Piven and Cloward (1971, p. 347):

> ... large-scale work relief—unlike direct relief which merely mutes the worst outbursts of discontent—tends to stabilize lower-class occupational, family and communal life, and by doing so diminishes the proclivities toward disruptive behavior which gave rise to the expansion of relief in the first place. Once order is restored in this more profound sense relief-giving can be virtually abolished. . . .

Whatever the analyses of welfare functions, all observers tend to agree that the complex, bureaucratic agencies working on separate programs cannot provide the services that will substantially reduce poverty. New approaches to the problems of welfare are badly needed.

The emphasis on the moral foundations of poverty and on individualism made the United States "more reluctant than any rich democratic country to make a welfare effort appropriate to its affluence" (Wilensky and Lebeaux, 1965, p. xvii). Wilensky and Lebeaux suggest that other nations have moved faster to accept national social policies dealing with health, education, and welfare because they entered the industrial era later than the United States and could not avoid the implications of interdependence for national social policies. Urbanization demands higher standards of service, now thought of as citizen rights, and has placed powerful pressures upon national governments. In older urban contexts, welfare developed gradually and expectations were lower and more simply satisfied. Social welfare institutions, like all urban institutions, must respond to the needs of individuals in a constant process of adaptation, renewal, and redefinition, reflecting changes and generated changes at the same time.

EDUCATION: HISTORICAL ANTECEDENTS

In America, education is a unique welfare institution because it is not viewed as serving the poor but rather as a path of upward mobility: self-improvement, better jobs, and economic opportunities. This link between education and occupational success was not always strong. In preindustrial America schools were justified for two reasons: to insure that every child could read the Bible for salvation; and to make sure that voters in a democracy were literate enough to read about political issues. Both of these objectives could be obtained in elementary schools or village centers where young children could learn the essentials of reading and writing in a short period of time. Further education was restricted to the wealthy.

These two justifications of public education were the foundation of a national debate over "common schools" that took place from 1820 through 1850. Charity schools, it was argued, had no place in a democracy because all citizens should have an equal opportunity for a common education, which would in turn provide the cultural cement to bind Americans together. Horace Mann, leader of the public school movement, proclaimed three essentials for American education: 1) public schools should be tax-supported and controlled by the public; 2) they should be free; and 3) attendance should be compulsory. In 1852 Massachusetts enacted the first compulsory attendance law. New York City experimented with infant schools to educate and train very small children. Even in the South, the common school idea was received enthusiastically, although by the 1850s the movement was discredited as a dangerous northern view (Taylor, 1973). European cities also had instituted forms of common school education, with English and Prussian systems held up to America as examples. The early schools stressed strict discipline, memorization, and moral character development. Not all were pleased with the emphasis on morality taught in common schools, particularly Catholic immigrants. By 1840 Catholics began to build separate parochial schools, free from "Protestant" teachings. Others did not welcome the end of elitism, and maintained private schools. These alternatives to the common school have remained in urban areas throughout American history, influencing thousands of students.

By the late 1800s urban schools concentrated on a different goal: Americanization. Immigrant children, whose parents came to America to find work in the growing industrial economy, were to be socialized and the "melting pot" theory accepted as "the American way." Basically, this assumed that children from many different cultures could be taught together and in the process become American; their differences "melted" away, so that all left school with one culture (see Chapter Fourteen). Support for expanding free public education can be traced back to this pressure for citizenship training. It was fueled also by the writings of educational reformers such as the famous John Dewey, who saw the school as the institution in American urban society that could replace the family, the church, and the small community as an agent of socialization. Dewey argued that schools should deal with "the whole child": teachers should assist in learning reading and writing, but also should teach democracy. Students could "learn by doing," and gain experience in all spheres of life, accumulating both cultural understanding and practical knowledge, especially scientific skills. This influential educator caused a revolutionary shift in American thinking about schools. Instead of schools being viewed as short-term centers for basic instruction, they became pivotal social institutions for the training of youth and the preservation of democracy. Americans have tended to romanticize the common school movement, and believe that the common school successfully accomplished the many tasks it undertook. Recent historical investigation, however, suggests that failures occurred as well as successes. Indeed, there never has been a complete melting pot; some groups remained outside the idealized English view of American culture altogether. The costs of melting, even when successful, were high; abandonment of native language and culture, isolation from family, and often only minimal acceptance. Thus, many Polish and Italian children had to give up speaking their native language; German culture became something one was ashamed of rather than proud to share; Catholicism was a suspect religion, as was Judaism; and black Americans were almost totally excluded from educational rewards.

Furthermore, urban schools did not successfully accomplish many learning tasks. "In virtually every study undertaken since that made in the Chicago schools in 1898, more children have failed in school than have succeeded, both in absolute and relative numbers" (Greer, 1972, p. 108). Greer calls "the triumph of the public schools" an article of "popular faith" and a "canon of historical scholarship" (p. 116), but unreal if one examines the actual evidence. Schools did succeed in improving the quality of life for many, but they also failed with many kinds of students, particularly those who did not fit easily into the rigid organization of the institution.

Reformers sought to change schools by standardizing teaching methods and by adopting testing devices. Large city schools developed elaborate bureaucratic organizations copied from business models: the Board of Education (Board of Directors), administrators (business managers) and teachers (workers) "produced" the product of educated students. This product could be counted, measured, and standardized. The advantage of educational bureaucracies, as in most bureaucratic arrangements, is that the division of labor and economics of scale make it possible to service many students. However, the usual disadvantages of bureaucracy— impersonality, red tape, reluctance to change, and concern with organization for its own sake—also resulted. Other educational responses to urban needs were the extension of the school year and the growth of the secondary schools. Compulsory attendance laws were modeled after the Massachusetts law, and the Supreme Court's Kalamazoo Decision of 1872 enabled school districts to use tax funds to provide free secondary education. Within forty years, the concept of twelve grades was firmly entrenched in the United States and the last southern states established free public high schools.

Higher Education

The recognition that modern industrial society and Americanization required more than basic reading and writing skills justified the expansion of public high schools, just as it was to justify the expansion of urban institutions of higher education. In 1900 only four out of the ten largest cities in the United States had university enrollments of over 2,000, but by 1924 145 urban institutions (or 15 percent of the total number of universities) enrolled 40 percent of all students. For example, the City College of New York had 1,294 students in 1900, but by 1930 the number had increased to 35,189. Most of the growth in urban institutions took place between 1920 and 1930, and again in the post–World War II era.

The earliest urban institutions of higher education were either pri-

Urban universities, such as the University of Mexico, reflect the urban transformation of their particular country. (Mexican National Tourist Council)

vately owned or municipally supported. Unlike small religious colleges, urban universities reflected the urban transformation of American society, just as many famous European universities reflected urban environments through the centuries. A new form of higher education that developed at the turn of the century was the technical institute. Institutions such as Rensselaer Polytechnic Institute, the Massachusetts Institute of Technology, and the Carnegie Institute of Technology taught students the skills required in a technical society.

Equality of Opportunity

It is important to acknowledge the myth of the success of the urban school in the Americanization process to understand the debates about a second myth concerning urban education that has received considerable attention since the 1960s—that the schools can provide equality of educational opportunity and thereby equal opportunity for success in society. This relationship between economic well-being and education has involved educational institutions in the welfare debates as a strategy to eliminate poverty and reduce racial inequalities.

Historically, urbanization and industrialization occurred together in the United States. Immigrants arriving at the turn of the century were absorbed in the expanding and dynamic industrial economy. As industrial growth became more sophisticated, technologies such as computers, marketing, and communications grew in importance. After 1940 the need for educated workers was almost insatiable. The G. I. Bill, for example, provided free college education for returning soldiers after World War II. The purpose of this legislation was to avoid unemployment among returning veterans as the economy shifted from wartime to peacetime production. Its effect, however, was to enlarge the pool of skilled and educated workers. The simultaneous development of the tie between education and occupational success that most Americans accept without question appeared to be solid. Limitations on opportunities for sound education were perceived as economic limitations. As in the case of social services, local financing for education meant that cities had insufficient tax revenues to meet the costs of schools. Noted educators such as James Conant (1961) denounced the growing disparity between suburban education and urban school decline, warning that the United States was developing "social dynamite" in the cities.

The demand for improved urban schools encouraged the federal government to sponsor new programs. The 1965 Elementary and Secondary Education Act, particularly Title I designed to assist poor children in cities, marked a significant turning point in school federal financing. Levine and Bane (1976, pp. 3–4) summarize the tie between education and economic opportunity:

> The explicit idea of education as a weapon against poverty is a recent development. It has strong roots in the traditional conception of education as the key to social integration and mobility, a notion apparently justified by the assimilation of successive waves of immigrants through the schools. It was

Field trips for urban school children form an approach to education for city life. (Harry Gold)

reinforced after World War II by the theorists of human capital, who showed that investments in schooling yielded ample returns in the form of lifetime earnings streams. And it had inherent attractions because of its very indirectness. Publicly supported education, it seemed, could give the poor the tools they needed to escape from poverty by dint of their own efforts.

The Act authorized federal monies to be spent on public education, particularly for poor and minority children. Although federal money had been used in America to encourage higher education through the land grant colleges, and state money had been used to support municipal colleges when cities could no longer maintain these institutions, federal support to basic education was limited.

By the mid-1970s American faith in education as the social means of providing equality of opportunity was under severe attack. A profound disillusionment replaced the idealistic romanticism of the previous decade, and urban schools faced public indifference as well as the serious problem of teaching growing numbers of poor children. One scholar has described the differences in issues confronting urban educational institutions as two separate crises: "The 'old crisis' is the persistence of gross inequalities in educational resources which derive from the local organizational format of public education and the absence of minimal national standards. If the traditions of American public education have been adapted to the social, cultural, regional and religious diversity of the United States, this advantage has been purchased at the cost of highly uneven minimum performance." In contrast, the "new crisis" is linked to "the transformation and

organization of the labor market under advanced industrialization"
(Janowitz, 1969, p. 7).

Desegregation of Urban Schools

Perhaps no single welfare policy has been more controversial than the
desegregation policies developed in urban education. As discussed, most
Americans do not even think of education as a welfare program although
they clearly understand that schools do serve the common good. This is
partly because the benefits of good education—personal enrichment and
higher-paying jobs—are thought to be individual benefits and not social
goods. Also, the term "welfare" has been clearly identified with income
maintenance programs or those policies related to the handicapped or
special groups of individuals. Yet, from an economic and social perspective,
education is one form of social welfare.

The demands of black Americans for civil rights in the early 1960s
were soon extended to the educational institutions that had increasingly
become linked with the occupational sphere by providing the necessary
credentials for high-paying jobs. In 1952 the Supreme Court rendered a
historic decision in the case of *Brown vs. Topeka* (Kansas) by stating that
segregated schools were unconstitutional. The Court decided unanimously
that separation implied inferiority and required that all public schools become desegregated with deliberate speed. By the early 1960s very little had
changed. Urban schools reflected the residential patterns of urban areas
that remained clearly segregated. School boards actually fostered this
segregation by developing artificial boundaries and by administrative decisions. Finally, federal courts announced that if a school district was found
guilty of deliberately segregating students, corrections had to be made.
Given the established residential patterns in urban areas, this usually took
the form of busing students to different schools.

Busing is a highly controversial method of achieving desegregation in
public education. Less drastic strategies include voluntary desegregation,
open school enrollments, creating magnet schools, and mixing teaching
staffs. The courts ordered busing only when other strategies failed and
when the school districts were found to be clearly guilty of promoting
segregation. Busing was never mandated beyond district boundaries or in
cases where school authorities had not developed segregation policies.
Even so, incidents of violence and wide-scale protest followed court orders
for desegregation programs.

Research has been mixed concerning the effects of desegregation.
Many were disappointed that these programs did not immediately raise the
educational achievement scores of students participating in the new programs. Once again there was a naïve assumption that simply mixing together students of different races would lead to change. One factor that
complicated measurement was the concentration of poor children—both
white and black—in the urban school systems. Educational researchers had
long observed a clear correlation between family income and educational
achievement regardless of race. Children from more affluent middle-class

homes, with educated parents, have historically been more successful with academic tasks than poorer children. Major structural and attitudinal changes in education are required to assist poor children in learning tasks, and a strong commitment to these pupils would be required at all levels in society. Without this commitment and these changes, the probability of changing educational achievement levels is remote.

Current Realities in Urban Education

The present reality is that educational systems are drastically split between serving poor children in the inner city and affluent children in the suburbs. The gigantic urban school systems, once perceived as avenues of mobility enabling poor children to rise from the ghettos, and believed to be the foundation of the American way of life, appear incapable of doing so. School achievement scores in large cities are below national averages; crime and violence are familiar in many schools; resistance to judicial orders to end desegregation has torn apart school systems in Boston and other places; teachers have become increasingly militant and defensive, with strikes occuring regularly in large cities; and most urban school districts are in desperate financial condition. The following facts illustrate the present reality:

> In 15 of the largest U.S. cities, 31 percent of the children who complete the 9th grade fail to achieve their high school diploma as compared to 24 percent nationally. The rate of unemployment for male school leavers 16–21 is higher (as high as 15 percent) than the rate for high school graduates. Six percent of children who start fifth grade in big cities never start tenth grade. In Cook County, 88.4 percent of applicants for general assistance in a six-week period had not completed high school, and this pattern has been found elsewhere as well (Sizer, 1977, p. 206).

The solutions suggested for these problems are legion, ranging from designing more relevant curriculum for city students to national financing of education to provide more equitable distribution of resources. Reform efforts have included school decentralization (breaking up the large system into smaller units), compensatory education (special instruction for weak students), and alternate schools, but the success of these innovations is difficult to assess.

URBAN SOCIAL SERVICES: POLICY ISSUES

In modern society human beings depend on institutional resources for assistance throughout their lives. The family is unable to provide the bulk of this assistance as it has done in the past. Nor has the local community the resources or technical skills to provide the kinds of specialized assistance that are expected, given the present state of knowledge in helping fields.

Individual helplessness is further aggravated by international and national factors that affect individual lives but that are almost unaffected by individuals working independently.

In addition, the pace of social change requires constant learning and adaptation to new conditions. Because of the mobility and temporary nature of many social relationships, individuals require institutional support for many kinds of services. Some writers speak of the constant need for therapy to help heal the scars of confusion and loneliness encountered in many life situations. Such assistance was given in the past by a close friend or clergyman. Today, crisis centers, telephone hot-lines, and a multitude of drop-in centers try to achieve the same ends.

The paradox of social welfare and urbanization is that urban centers make possible the high degree of specialization that leads to impressive expertise in areas of welfare and education. The concentration of population makes it feasible to establish central locations where technological assistance can be used. Thus, urban hospitals, libraries, cultural centers, and other essential facilities enable professional care-givers to deliver many kinds of assistance to those seeking help. The irony, however, is that the political structures that sustain these centers, as well as the social attitudes that persistently look down upon those seeking help, appear to freeze efforts at delivering such services more effectively. Poverty remains a stubborn and serious social problem that affects all areas of life. Critical issues about justice and equity remain. Social services can no longer be regarded as the area of the pathological or the isolated but increasingly must be seen as a right and social good that every citizen should receive. Unfortunately, the local arrangements are inadequate for meeting these needs.

Institutional building in urban areas is a never-ending process. Urban welfare institutions face grave economic and political challenges as they struggle to assist people with problems of poverty, unemployment, and poor health. The old structures that provided funding for urban institutions are inadequate: the old concepts of moral inferiority are no longer useful. The challenge now is to create new institutional foundations that can serve human concerns more effectively.

SELECTED BIBLIOGRAPHY

AMERICAN ASSOCIATION OF SCHOOL ADMINISTRATORS. *Imperatives in Education.* Washington, D.C.: National Education Association, 1966.

ANDERSON, O. *The Uneasy Equilibrium: Public and Private Financing of Health Services in the U.S. 1876–1965.* New Haven, Conn.: Yale University Press, 1968.

BOOTH, C. *Life and Labor of the People of London.* Vol. I. New York: Macmillan, 1892.

CONANT, J. *Slums and Suburbs.* New York: Signet, 1961.

COOK, L. "How Welfare Benefits Vary Across the Nation," Detroit News, October 16, 1975.

CREMIN, L. *The Genius of American Education and the Transformation of the School.* New York: Vintage, 1965.

CURTI, M. *The Growth of American Thought.* 2nd ed. New York: Harper & Row, Pub., 1951.

EMERSON, H. *Local Health Units for the Nation.* New York: Public Health Association Committee on Administration, Commonwealth Fund, 1945.

FAEGIN, J. "God Helps Those Who Help Themselves," *Psychology Today* 6 (November 1972): 101–110, 129.

GREER, V. *The Great School Legend.* New York: Basic Books, 1972.

GRISCOM, J. *The Sanitary Conditions of the Laboring Population of New York with Suggestions for Improvements.* New York: Harper & Row, Pub., 1845.

HANDLIN, O. "John Dewey's Contribution to Education." In J. Barnard and D. Burner, eds., *The American Experience in Education.* New York: Franklin Watts, 1973.

HOCHMAN, H. *The Urban Economy.* New York: W. W. Norton & Co., Inc., 1976.

HYMAN, H. *Health Planning: A Systematic Approach.* Germantown, Md.: Aspen Systems, 1975.

JANOWITZ, M. Institution Building in Urban Education. New York: Russell Sage Foundation, 1969.

KAHN, A. J. *Social Policy and Social Services.* New York: Random House, 1970.

KOMISAR, L. *Down and Out in the U.S.A.* New York: Franklin Watts, 1974.

LEVINE, D., and BANE, M. J. *The Inequality Controversy: Schooling and Distributive Justice.* New York: Basic Books, 1976.

LUBOVE, R. *The Professional Altruist.* New York: Atheneum, 1973.

MARSHALL, T. H. *Class and Citizenship.* New York: Doubleday, 1964.

PIVEN, F., and CLOWARD, R. *Regulating the Poor.* New York: Random House, 1971.

REINHOLD, R. "Poverty Is Found Less Persistent But More Widespread Than Thought," New York Times, July 17, 1977.

ROMANYSHAN, J. *Social Welfare: From Charity to Justice.* New York: Random House, 1971.

SHATTUCK, L. *Report of a General Plan for the Promotion of Public and Personal Health Relating to a Sanitary Survey of the State.* Boston: Harvard University Press, 1850 (reprinted 1948).

SIZER, T. "The Schools in the City." In L. Lowenstein, ed., *Urban Studies.* 2nd ed. New York: Free Press, 1977.

STRONG, J. *Our Country and Its Possible Future and Its Present Crisis.* New York: 1885.

TAYLOR, W. R. "The Patrician South and the Common Schools." In John Barnard and David Burner, eds., *The American Experience in Education.* New York: Franklin Watts, 1973.

WILENSKY, H., and LEBEAUX, CHARLES N. *Industrial Society and Social Welfare.* 2nd ed. New York: Free Press, 1965.

WOODROFF, KATHLEEN. *From Charity to Social Work in England and the U.S.* Toronto and Buffalo: University of Toronto Press, 1971.

PART IV

PERSISTENT URBAN SOCIAL PROBLEMS: URBAN PLANNING AND SOCIAL POLICY

chapter 13

urban crime, unrest, and social control

Virtually all contemporary social problems have in one way or another been associated with the process of urbanization. A large number of these have been alluded to or implied throughout this book, although we have not intended to suggest that urbanization can best be understood in the context of the problems or crises it is alleged to generate. The relationship between a very broad and general social process such as urbanization and the much more concrete examples of social problems such as those that are commonly classified within the framework of social disorganization, deviant behavior, or value conflict are very difficult to observe directly, and there is a very complex and indirect chain of events by which these two levels of social behavior can be said to be even remotely connected. The purpose of this and the following chapters is to review some of the general theoretical perspectives within which the link between urbanization and social problems can be better explained and to follow this more general discussion with a review of two commonly recognized urban social problems—crime, and race and ethnic conflict. These problems have been touched upon in a variety of contexts in many chapters of this book. Here and in the following chapter they become the main objects of our attention.

Urbanization and the related industrial or technological forces that accompany it are often referred to as major sources of disruption in Western society. While there is some truth in this judgment, it is not the city or metropolis as such, any more than it is technology, that directly causes such problems as racial tensions, crime, or poverty. Problems such as these are aberrations of a process that on the whole produces more in the way of stable and constructive changes than the reverse. Inherently there is no more reason for urbanism to be associated with social disorganization or personal pathologies than there is for rural life. As discussed in Chapter Five, studies have concluded that rural environments are as prone to manifestations of social and personal disorganization as are cities and the metropolis.

But even though the physical facts of urbanization and industrialization are not themselves necessarily involved in creating social problems, certain historically related social processes definitely can be implicated. Nisbet (Merton and Nisbet, 1966) has identified four such processes that are particularly significant for our discussion here: 1) conflict of institutions; 2) social mobility; 3) individuation; and 4) anomie. Although these processes are rarely found in isolated, distinct forms, they will be discussed separately for clarification.

Conflict of Institutions

What has emerged in modern urban society is a plurality of social institutions, each with its own authority and functions, each limited or constrained by the presence of others, with all forming together the larger patterns of authority, functions, and allegiances by which a society comes to be known. Such pluralism has certainly been a major feature of American urban society, and one of the major tasks of this book has been to outline the major characteristics of some of the major institutions of our urban society. We have described kinship and religion as dominant institutions that probably wielded the greatest influence on the lives of people in preindustrial urban communities. Since the advent of industrialization, economic, political, and social service oriented institutions have separated from kinship or religious groupings to become competing institutions in their own right. Self-contained local communities or neighborhoods have become engulfed and transformed by larger, more complex, and more elaborately differentiated forms of urban organization.

Institutional pluralism cannot be overlooked as a background to modern urban social problems, for it is frequently at the bottom of the conflicts and dislocations forming the substance of many kinds of deviant behavior. The resultant conflict of institutions is deeply involved in the migration of peoples from the old world to the new; in the passage of American society from rural to urban; in the changed position of the generations and the sexes to one another; and in the rise of such new institutions as the corporate bureaucracy, public education and welfare, mass communications, political parties, labor unions, and the suburban complex. This pluralism is characterized by a wide range of competition and social strain, leading to an almost endless conflict of goals and behavior patterns.

Nowhere has such conflict been more vivid and agonizing than in the transplanting of peoples from Europe, Africa, or Asia to the United States, or from rural to metropolitan areas. These dislocations are often reflected in the minds and personalities of the people concerned, sometimes in epic and compulsive degree as they react to changes involving intrusions into, or alterations of, their social and physical environment. The conflict between established habits and new values, between old and new allegiances, often becomes incorporated in people's personalities and thus comes to exert confusing or ambivalent influence on their behavior.

Social Mobility

With the advent of modern democracy and legal egalitarianism and a general rise in humanitarianism in advanced urban-industrial societies, rigidly fixed social status has been supplanted by a high degree of geographic mobility and vertical social mobility for thousands of groups. Geographic mobility has released many groups from social and cultural isolation, as have the newer forms of mass communications. Throughout history there has been a striking tendency for religions, ethnic groups, social classes, and other social groups to maintain privacy from one another and to guard their respective cultures from externally produced changes. In rapidly growing urban communities, such previously isolated groups often find themselves in direct competition for living space or for access to the rewards and amenities of urban living. As groups having different backgrounds converge on the same neighborhoods or areas of the metropolis, misunderstandings, suspicion, and hostility often develop among them. Whereas assimilation or integration of racially, religiously, or ethnically distinct groups previously may have been forbidden by law or custom, new and uncertain rules or understandings must be worked out by trial and error. In this process, the legal, economic, and social positions of ethnic and racial groups have been altered; relationships of social classes have been profoundly changed; and patterns of influence, prestige, power, or wealth have been transformed or sharply modified. These changes have afforded a relatively high degree of vertical social mobility for countless numbers of individuals, but not without a real or threatened loss of social status and influence for countless others.

With the blurring of traditional social class lines and the removal of the more flagrant legal and economic privileges of certain classes, a marked change has occurred in the whole status structure of modern urban society. As fixed social status is displaced by emphasis on upward mobility and the ethic of "success," intensive striving for status naturally becomes an obsession for large numbers of people, not all of whom are successful.

Singapore, like other cities, has undergone change in the status structure of its urban society. (United Nations)

Individuation

One of the fundamental characteristics of urban society is the relatively high degree of people's legal and moral autonomy. Tönnies, Durkheim, and Simmel were among the first sociologists to foresee a decline or a weakening of the individual's ties to such social groups as the extended family, neighborhood, guild, or parish, and the maximization of the autonomous individual and the impersonal, atomistic, and mechanical relations of contract or of the marketplace. While it has meant greater freedom of personal choice, detachment from the traditional forms of association has also led to loneliness, depersonalization, and alienation for many. As people seek new identities, statuses, or affiliations of their own choosing from among the wide variety of new social forms available in urban communities, which are in themselves not necessarily deviant or pathological, many will fail to make stable social ties and will succumb to patterns of alcoholism, drug abuse, mental illness, or other patterns of illegitimate or delinquent behavior. While it would be easy to exaggerate the extent of excessive detachment from meaningful social groups or its negative consequences (see Chapters Five, Six, and Seven), it is nevertheless true that such estrangement is not uncommon in modern urban communities and is regarded as problematic.

Anomie

All human behavior is normative. It is directed to goals or values, and draws its meaning and importance in terms of those values. When moral values are widely accepted in a society, they form the basis on which the society achieves consensus and integration. Such values are also essential to the integrity and success of individual personality. When values become confused, when they are in conflict with one another, or when they lose their immediacy to human beings, the resultant condition can be referred to as a state of normlessness, or *anomie*.

Much of the history of modern urban society is the history of the breaking up of traditional values. The rise of capitalism, religious individualism, and democracy have inevitably affected the traditional values of church and kinship, and such urban-industrial doctrines as critical rationalism, utilitarianism, and science also have challenged traditionally sacred value systems. The conflict between the old and the new or the sacred and the secular are just a few of the many value conflict arenas. Anomie, with its implicit tensions of moral conflict, alienation, and meaninglessness, is a notable and persistent aspect of modern urban societies and contributes to the creation of their widely recognized social problems.

What is common to the major social processes discussed above is that all imply rapid and massive change. Largely unplanned and unanticipated, such change moves unevenly through society, affecting some parts differently than others. The speed and unevenness of social change rather than urbanization per se underlies most of the social problems commonly identified as characteristics of modern urban living. Even the most stable and unchanging societies could never be completely problem free, since any particular type of social structure tends to generate its own particular type of social problems. But we would expect the problems to be far different from those that have been generated in our own rapidly urbanizing society. While the problems of crime and racial or ethnic conflict to be discussed in this and the following chapter are complex and have a multiplicity of causes, we can understand them at least partly in the context of the tumultuous social changes that have accompanied the urbanization process in our own society.

URBAN CRIME

Any discussion of crime as a social problem must begin with an agreed-upon definition of the nature of the problem, for crime is apt to mean many different things to different people. Strictly speaking, any act that violates the law of the political jurisdiction in which it takes place and that is punishable by that political jurisdiction in a legally prescribed manner is a crime. Under this definition, any act meeting the above criteria is a crime, no matter how innocent, innocuous, or abhorrent that act may appear to interested parties. Such an act is a crime whether or not an arrest or conviction has been made, or whether or not the act has been observed by legally reliable witnesses or reported to the police. This definition is objectively the most usable because it gives us the best basis for estimates of the actual amount of crime committed, independent of the subjective impressions of how extensive different people with different standards *think* crime is. Public perceptions of crime as a social problem may vary drastically from its actual incidence. This is a phenomenon we will discuss later.

THE EXTENT OF CRIME IN AMERICA

The Uniform Crime Reports, based on statistics collected by the Federal Bureau of Investigation from local police departments, are the most widely cited attempts to measure the incidence of crime yearly in the United States. The data represent crime reported to the police in a relatively small handful of major crimes selected by the FBI for inclusion in the report. This source has reported a 158 percent increase in the number of crimes reported to the police between 1960 and 1975. Provisional data for the late 1970's indicate a leveling off or potential decline from the previous year for the first time since the late 1950s (UPI, December 16, 1977). The crime rates are standardized to a base of every 100,000 persons. In no case does the incidence of the crimes reported in the FBI Uniform Crime Reports exceed about several hundred reported crimes per 100,000 population.

But there are several important reasons why data on crimes reported to the police cannot give an accurate measure of the amount of crime actually committed. First, most crime is never reported to the police and therefore never appears in the official crime statistics. Second, some crimes reported to the police are not officially recorded and included in crime statistics. Third, the conditions under which local police departments receive information about crime and officially report it may vary drastically. Fourth, the FBI Uniform Crime Reports classify only certain types of crimes which the FBI thinks important, and the types included are only a tiny segment of the total range of crimes. White collar crimes, for example, which we will discuss later, are routinely excluded from the Uniform Crime Reports.

Likewise, arrest and conviction statistics represent even a smaller portion of total crimes committed and are even less reliable than data on reported crime as a measure of total crime. In 1970, of each 100 offenses known to the police, only twenty led to arrest and only five actually led to a conviction. In one case, the police in a given city arrested over 1,500 persons but in the end issued only forty warrants (Horton and Leslie, 1974, p. 123). Wholesale arrests such as these probably have more to do with law enforcement practices than with crime itself and may make the local arrest rate meaningless as a measure of crime.

For these reasons, it is impossible to determine the exact amount of crime actually committed by tabulating reported crimes, arrests, or convictions. The truth is that nobody really knows for sure how much crime there is. Yet most experts agree that the commission of crimes is far more common than most people would care to admit. Some studies and estimates would go so far as to suggest that virtually no one in American society is above violating the law at some time or another under certain circumstances. In one classic study, of a sample of nearly 2,000 adults from a relatively affluent upper-middle-class suburban county, 99 percent admitted having committed one or more felonies carrying prison sentences of one year or more at some time in their lives. The men in the sample admitted to an average of eighteen felonies in their lifetime, while the women, somewhat more law abiding, admitted an average of eleven felonies (Wallerstein and Whyle, 1947). Yet most of the crimes committed by this sample, who would normally be considered among the more law-abiding segments of American society, were never reported to the police and of course never resulted in arrest or conviction. Later studies similarly conclude that of the various crimes committed by or known to various sample groups, only a small portion ever shows up in officially recorded crime statistics (Horton and Leslie, 1974, p. 122).

The same reasons that make measuring the amount of crime at any given point in time nearly impossible also make knowing whether crime has been on the increase in recent years uncertain. Recorded crime rates, as just indicated, certainly have increased dramatically since the 1960s. But police efficiency and the methods of detection have also improved over the same period, as have techniques for reporting and recording crime, in response to official demands. Therefore, reported increases in crime may be due to these factors rather than to an actual increase in crime. Mass media reporting of crime probably has intensified, and this too may have a bearing on the public's greater willingness to report crime to the police. Most reported crime has indicated that youthful age groups are more crime prone than other segments of the population. If this is actually true, then the recent upsurge in the proportion of young people in the population would seem to support the notion that crime has been increasing. But even more recent reductions in the birth rate would, by the same reasoning, suggest that crime should begin to level off or decline in the very near future, which may already be happening according to the provisional data reported above.

But without more reliable data for both the past and the present, criminologists are divided over whether crime actually is increasing. Some suspect that, even though recorded rates have been increasing, actual crime is not on the rise. According to them, American society has always been crime-ridden and has always had a high degree of tolerance for lawlessness (Bell, 1960, p. 137). Thus, there is no reason to suspect that crime is any more widespread now than it has always been. Others, however, believe that there actually has been a substantial increase in the commission of crime and will point to what are to them logical reasons why this is so. But there is as yet no consensus among social scientists on this question.

CRIME ON THE STREETS

Another difficulty in assessing crime as a social problem is that there are many different types of crime, each with different causes and consequences, and each of which differs in the degree to which the public perceives it to be serious enough to warrant drastic efforts at solution. For the

Police presence is designed to alleviate fears of crime in the city, as well as to serve as a crime deterrent. (Marc Anderson)

most part, it is the so-called "street" crimes such as murder, armed robbery, assault, and rape that the public is most likely to identify as *the* crime problem. These kinds of crimes crowd newspaper front pages and often are highly dramatized on television and radio news broadcasts. Such reporting makes the amount of street crime seem vastly exaggerated to those who rely exclusively on the mass media for their information, no matter how extensive street crimes are in reality.

In the city of Detroit, for example, approximately seven hundred homicides were reported to the police in a recent year (Detroit Free Press, September 28, 1976:A1). For this relatively high incidence of homicide, Detroit often has been luridly labeled in the media as "the Murder Capital" of the United States. To the Detroit area resident addicted to watching the daily televised local news, the description may seem apt, for the viewer sees an average of about two homicides reported on every single day of the year! The broadcast usually opens with extended visual stories on murder, transmitted by a reporter at the scene of the crime, and these reports often include pictures of the victims or their distraught families and neighbors. This immediate intimacy, of course, has a dramatic impact on the viewer.

Although two homicides daily in a population of approximately 1.3 million makes the probability of any given individual becoming a murder victim on any given day rather remote, this cold statistic does not seem to lessen the average viewer's fears. For the typical Detroit suburbanite traveling to the city on any given day for shopping, legitimate business, or entertainment, the probability of becoming a homicide victim is even less (over 70 percent of the Detroit homicides involve offenders and victims who are related or are intimately known to one another and are likely to be involved in some sort of personal quarrel at the time of the crime). In fact, the risk that the same Detroit suburbanite will be killed in an automobile accident on his or her way to or from the city is at least several times greater than the risk of being murdered by a stranger while in the city. The pattern is probably similar in many other large American cities.

Horton and Leslie (1974) aptly suggest that violent, dramatic street crime of the type we have described should not really be considered as *the* main crime problem. Instead, they conclude that the less dramatic and less publicized types of crime may be more costly and disruptive to the general public overall than the more widely feared violent street crimes:

> For every woman killed by a "sex fiend," several are slaughtered by their husbands; but the sex crimes attract more interest and arouse far greater anxiety. For every person murdered in calculated detective story fashion, dozens are killed by drunken and reckless drivers (negligent homicide, if it can be proved). For every dollar taken in armed robbery, hundreds or thousands are taken by gamblers, racketeers, and white-collar criminals. The corruption of police and government officials by organized and white-collar crime wreaks an injury to public life and public morals beside which the depredations of pickpockets, shoplifters and bank robbers are of minor importance. Yet these crimes rate the headlines. It would be only slightly exaggerated to say that the genuine social destructiveness and financial cost of a form of crime varies *inversely* with the publicity it receives and the public concern it arouses (Horton and Leslie, 1974, p. 139).

But whatever the arguments of objective social scientists or statistics to the contrary, the fear of violent crime among the population rose dramatically during the late 1960s and early 1970s. During the same period a widespread and almost hysterical demand for greater "law and order" was also a very potent political issue, which was successfully exploited by the Nixon administration throughout its first term in office and during the 1968 and 1972 national election campaigns. A 1971 Harris Survey reported that 55 percent of the population was more worried over violence and safety in the streets than they were a year earlier, compared to only 5 percent who were less worried. This anxiety had been increasing steadily between 1966 and 1971 (Harris Poll, July 5, 1971). According to a 1975 Gallup Poll, 50 percent of Americans thought that crime had risen in their own neighborhood during the previous year. Nineteen percent of the respondents said that they were fearful in their own home at night. Even more revealing is that in the "recession" year of 1975, 21 percent of the residents of large cities with a population of 500,000 or more listed crime as their city's worst problem by a two to one margin over unemployment (11 percent) and by a four to one margin over the high cost of living (5 percent). Further, the percentage naming crime as their city's top problem had increased more than fivefold since 1949 (Gallup Poll, July 27, 1975). There was also a long upward trend in the percentage of respondents who said that there were places in their neighborhood where they would be afraid to walk alone at night.

These surveys seem to indicate that concern over crime and safety in the streets had reached acute proportions by the mid-1970s. However, a more recent Gallup Poll (December 18, 1977) indicated that for the first time in the 1970s public concern with the dangers of crime appeared to be subsiding or leveling off. The percentage of Americans who thought crime in their own neighborhood had risen or who were fearful in their own home at night had declined by 6 or 7 percent between 1975 and 1977, while the percentage who were afraid to walk alone at night in their own neighborhood leveled off. Americans also now seem to support the observations of some crime experts that crime is beginning to move into the suburbs and may be increasing there at a more rapid rate than in the cities. In fact, the same survey indicated that residents of small cities and rural areas were far more likely to report increased crime in their communities than were those living in the largest of medium-sized cities.

Not included in the above surveys are public responses to several other major crime categories alluded to earlier—white collar crime, organized crime, and professional crime. Evidently the public has more tolerance, or at least less concern, for these crimes. But since any realistic, objective discussion of crime as a social problem should deal with all types of crime, a brief discussion of each of these is in order here.

WHITE-COLLAR CRIME

White-collar crime was originally thought of as crime committed by business and professional people in the course of their occupation (Sutherland, 1949). In current usage, the concept has been loosely broadened to include nearly all nonviolent illegal acts committed by "respectable" persons having community standing and status. Thus, middle- or upper-class individuals or businesspeople who cheat on their taxes, make false claims for their products, fix prices, embezzle their company's funds or misappropriate its property, or bribe public officials would be committing white-collar crimes (as would also the public officials receiving the bribes).

The public does not become as aroused by these types of crimes because they probably do not see them as direct and immediate threats to their safety or security. Such acts nevertheless are criminal if they violate the criminal law. While some authorities believe that such white-collar crimes as consumer fraud or antitrust violations are not as serious as street crimes, others believe that the extent and costs of white-collar crime are tremendous and are probably several times as great as the costs of all the crimes against property generally perceived of as street crimes. For example, the President's Commission on Law Enforcement and the Administration of Justice has estimated that the cost of such white-collar crimes as fraud, embezzlement, tax evasion, and forgery was roughly three times greater than the combined cost of burglary, larceny, auto theft, and robbery (*Congressional Quarterly*, May 7, 1971, p. 1048).

Concern about crime is often popularly expressed in terms of "we," the good, respectable, law-abiding majority, versus "they," the bad, disrespectable, law-violating minority. This view tends to see crime as caused by a small antisocial criminal "class." Those who hold this view often respond with disbelief when they discover that even prominent business leaders or top governmental officials and law-enforcement personnel are themselves not above occasionally committing crimes, usually of the white-collar variety, when it suits their purposes. For example, John Mitchell, the Attorney General of the United States from 1968 to 1972, was later convicted of a felony and sent to prison for criminal acts associated with the "Watergate" affair. More fortunate was former Vice-President Spiro T. Agnew, who escaped indictment on fifty criminal charges, including accepting bribes while Vice President, by pleading no contest to one minor charge of tax evasion. Former President Nixon, of course, escaped possible criminal indictment and conviction for Watergate-related offenses by resigning the presidency and by being pardoned by his successor. Yet all of these men were among the strongest advocates of strict law enforcement and had publicly criticized those who were "soft" on law violators or who favored "coddling" the "criminal class." This obvious double standard is not uncommon in the United States and is one of the reasons that it is so difficult to deal with crime as a social problem. Those who demand the suspension of traditional Bill of Rights protections afforded the so-called criminal class nevertheless are quick to demand these same rights for themselves when they are similarly suspected of violations of the criminal law.

At a lower level, a number of major cities have experienced widespread exposure of corruption within local police departments. In New York City, the Knapp Commission uncovered the involvement of hundreds of police officers in criminal protection rackets involving gambling, drug trafficking, and prostitution. In Chicago, widespread police involvement in extortion and burglary was uncovered in certain police districts, and a small group of police officers was indicted for dealing in drugs and even murdering several people to protect their activities (Scarpitti, 1977, p. 485). Recent indictments and public hearings suggest that some officials of high-ranking national law-enforcement and investigative agencies such as the FBI and the CIA have been implicated in violations of the criminal law in the conduct of their official duties.

ORGANIZED CRIME

Organized crime is crime conducted by large, organized groups of criminals who operate in more or less clearly defined territories and maintain constant connections with law-enforcement officials, without whose connivance such criminal organizations probably could not sustain themselves. Organized crime is distinguished from other types of crime by its hierarchical organizational structure, its dependence on the threat of force and violence to maintain a monopoly over its area of criminal activity, and its immunity from the law through the corruption of law-enforcement officials. The activities of organized crime involve traditionally illicit services, such as gambling, narcotics, loan sharking, and prostitution. Racketeering—which involves the regular extortion of money from legitimate businesses—was once a major organized crime activity, but is probably on the decline because of the relatively low yields and high risks. More and more, organized crime is beginning to infiltrate legitimate businesses by reinvesting its illegal earnings into enterprises that it then attempts to manage or control. Hotels and motels, night clubs, restaurants, liquor and cigarette distributors, vending machine distributors, real estate syndicates, and linen supply services are businesses that have been infiltrated by organized crime in many large cities. Some labor unions and banks or loan agencies also are controlled by organized crime interests, which now attempt to profit from the less risky and violent areas of white-collar crime. Organized crime is big business and is estimated to cost the national economy about $15 billion a year (Palen, 1977, p. 186).

The success of organized crime seems to rest on supplying illegal goods and services to supposedly honest, ordinary people who want and will gladly pay for them. Many people, for example, are eager to buy such stolen merchandise as autos, jewelry, bicycles, or television sets at bargain prices as long as they can expect to get away without being caught. Likewise, those who wish to gamble or use alcohol and drugs under illegal conditions are not deterred, especially if wholesale evasions of existing laws are widely condoned or tolerated by the general public as well as by law-enforcement officials.

The people who use the services of organized crime may themselves be engaging in what Horton and Leslie (1974, p. 142) refer to as *institutionalized* crime. This refers to criminal acts that are repeated so often that they become a part of the normal behavior of a group, yet are so perfectly rationalized that they are not defined as crime by those committing them. The compliance of otherwise honest law-enforcement officials may also fall in this category, especially when they do not wish to be criticized for "harassing" the public by disrupting what they know to be widely accepted patterns of community behavior, no matter how criminal these may be according to the law.

CAREER CRIMINALS

Career criminals include safecrackers, bank robbers, jewel thieves, pickpockets, check forgers, counterfeiters, con men, and the like. What these types have in common is that they all define themselves as criminals and consciously organize their lives around a criminal career. They are sometimes referred to as "professionals," but perhaps the only work traits they share with well-established, legitimate professions such as medicine or law is that they are highly skilled and take great pride in their competence or craftsmanship. They tend to be contemptuous of amateur criminals, and they take pride in maintaining their reputation as professionals among others of their own "calling." Career criminals rarely get caught, for to do so brings humiliation because it implies incompetence. But if caught, the career criminal will use expert lawyers and a wide variety of legal devices designed to lessen the possibility of imprisonment. Incarceration rarely reforms career criminals because of their lifelong commitment to an illegitimate career. Imprisonment, if it does occur, is regarded as merely a temporary nuisance, inconvenience, or embarrassment.

While the professional career criminal frequently is portrayed in the mass media as a sympathetic and sometimes heroic figure (as the aristocrats of the criminal world, they rarely commit acts of violence and are contemptuous of ordinary street criminals), a very tiny fraction of all crimes committed involve professional career criminals, who are something of a rarity today, if indeed they ever were very common.

URBANIZATION AND CRIME

Having briefly discussed several categories of crime that many experts contend are overall more damaging and costly than the types of street crimes routinely measured by the FBI Uniform Crime Reports, we must now come back to street crime because it is still the type of crime most closely linked in the public mind to city life and urbanization. So far, we have not yet dealt with the question of the spatial distribution of street crime and the degree to which it is more characteristic of big cities or small towns and rural areas. Unfortunately, there is no clearcut answer to the above question because of the inadequacies of recorded crime statistics discussed previously.

The recorded data do clearly indicate that rates of crime known to the police historically have been higher in urban areas than in rural areas and higher in metropolitan areas than in smaller urban areas. The 1975 FBI Uniform Crime Reports indicated that the rates of serious crime were 15.9 per thousand population in rural areas, 36.1 per thousand in the suburbs, and 52.1 per thousand in central cities. Many of the large cities reported even higher rates, sometimes more than 100 reported crimes per thousand population (*U.S. News and World Report,* April 5, 1976). The National Commission on the Causes and Prevention of Violence reported earlier (1969) that the average rate of major violent offenses in cities of over 250,000 inhabitants was eleven times greater than in rural areas and eight times greater than in suburban areas. However, a breakdown of data in the FBI Uniform Crime Reports for 1973 showed that rates of murder and forcible rape were higher in rural areas than in metropolitan areas.

Although street crime still is higher in cities than in suburban or rural areas, provisional data from the 1977 Uniform Crime Reports indicated that crime known to the police was decreasing for the first time in several decades and that it was decreasing more rapidly in cities than in other areas. During 1977 it decreased by 7 percent in urban areas, 5 percent in suburban areas, and 3 percent in rural areas (Detroit Free Press, December 16, 1977). The Attorney General of the United States, in releasing the data, attributed these improvements to better law enforcement (the implication being that law enforcement was improving more rapidly in the cities than in suburban or rural areas).

Most experts conclude that the available data support the notion that the "true" rate of crime is probably directly related to the degree of urbanization. After observing that crime rates rise consistently with city size, Wolfgang (1969) has suggested that the regularity and consistency of the data lead to the conclusion that "criminogenic" forces were probably greater in the city than in less urbanized areas. Palen (1977) has concluded that even with the serious biases and problems of obtaining reliable crime data, the national problem of crime is clearly an urban problem to a disproportionate degree. Gist and Fava (1974, p. 524) also conclude that even after allowing generously for inadequacies of incomplete data, the differences in crime rates between rural areas or small towns and the larger metropolitan areas are quite impressive.

However, not all observers are equally convinced that the actual rate of crime is clearly greater in the city than elsewhere. For example, Horton and Leslie (1974, p. 126) make the following qualifications:

> Cities show higher crime rates than rural areas, but it is probable that rural crime is less fully reported. The city also attracts people intending to commit crimes, as it provides more opportunities for crime and provides greater anonymity for those seeking an unconventional mode of life. But there is no evidence that country-reared persons are conspicuously less criminal than their city-reared compatriots.

THE CRIMINOGENIC FORCES OF THE CITY

While it is not entirely certain to what degree the actual rate of crime is greater in cities than in less urbanized places, a number of social and physical characteristics of cities may very well generate the kinds of conditions conducive to violations of the law. Here again, speculation is widespread, but convincing proof is in short supply. Nevertheless, it is useful to review some of the more commonly held views on the criminogenic forces of the city. The following is a typical summation of these forces:

> Urban areas with mass populations, greater wealth, more commercial establishments and more products of our technology also provide more frequent opportunities for theft. Victims are impersonalized, property is insured, consumer goods are in greater abundance, they are more vividly displayed, and they are more portable. Urban life is commonly characterized by population density, social mobility, class and ethnic heterogeneity, reduced family functions, and . . . greater anonymity. . . . When these traits are found in high degree, and when they are combined with poverty, physical deterioration, low education, residence in industrial and commercial centers, unemployment, unskilled labor, economic dependency, marital instability, etc., and a cultural minority status of inferiority, it is generally assumed that deviance is more likely to emerge (Wolfgang, 1969, p. 31).

Because of the very fact that cities are characterized by a wide variety of subcultures, each of which has a certain degree of freedom from constraints and controls by the larger society, it should be no surprise that at least some subcultures will adopt values and behavior patterns that are at variance with those of the larger community. Lacking strong external controls or strong motivations to conform, such subcultural groups at least have the potential to develop traditions of lawlessness or delinquency when it serves their purposes. The urban gang would be a good case in point. Ever since 1936, when Thrasher (1964) identified over 1,300 distinguishable gangs in the city of Chicago, the conditions conducive to the formation and persistence of gangs in big cities have been well described and understood. Big city consolidated schools bring large numbers of age-segregated young people together, further freed from the direct control of their parents and kinship groups by the separation of work from the place of residence. In between school and home, the opportunities for congregation, free from the direct surveillance of either school officials, families, or other formal agents of control such as the church or the police, readily abound. Under such conditions, the rise of the gang is almost inevitable. With the appropriate frustrations or motivations, the opportunity to innovate or experiment in lawless behavior are easily available to the urban gang. And as Thrasher found, the gang is an important factor in the organization of crime in big cities:

> The younger adolescent gangs were shown to be responsible for the bulk of minor delinquencies. The older gangs were for the most part engaged in delinquent enterprises, and gang clubs, likewise, were often semi-criminal groups. The serious crime of the city was largely carried on by young adult gangs, including many adolescents in their membership, usually made up of a criminal residue, the result of a process of social selection. These older gangs were often affiliated with rings and syndicates which they abetted by performing tasks requiring action and strong arm work (Thrasher, 1964, pp. 657–658).

In recent decades, youthful gangs have also developed in suburbs and small towns as well as big cities. Whereas the street corners, vacant lots, or alleys of local neighborhoods are the natural habitat of the big city gang, the easy access to the private automobile or motorcycle provides greater geographic mobility and even greater freedom from adult surveillance or social control for suburban and small town gangs. For these groups, auto thefts may become a major temptation, and it is no wonder that rates of auto theft tend to be relatively high in the suburban areas of the metropolis. The blue-collar areas of suburban Warren, for example, are reported to have higher auto theft rates than the central city of Detroit within the Detroit metropolitan area.

With greater urbanization, formal legal controls, based on rules that are explicit and that have special machinery for enforcement, become more prominent; informal mores and folkways become less so. In the city, a wide range of formal social control specialists arise, including the police, department store and hotel detectives, security officers and guards for such private organizations as apartment houses, manufacturing plants, or warehouses, electronic surveillance devices and alarm systems, and communications devices such as the short wave radio or telephone. All of these make the reporting of crime more efficient and instantaneous. In big cities, the formal and more bureaucratic agents of social control are more likely to report committed crimes in official bodies of crime statistics, whereas minor law violations in small towns or rural areas are more likely to be handled without resort to official police action. Thus, the very presence of the more formal and secondary kinds of social control agents is more likely to produce higher recorded crime rates in the city than in the country. Yet, as the following sections suggest, the existence of more formal and bureaucratic agents of social control, such as the police, does not necessarily serve as a greater deterrent to the commission of crime than the more informal and primary group-like controls associated with villages and rural areas.

INTRAURBAN VARIATIONS IN CRIME RATES

A large body of research exists on the variation in crime rates within metropolitan areas. The basic assumption that the extent and kinds of crime will differ markedly from one part of the community to another tends to be generally supported by this research. One of the earliest studies was that of Shaw (1929), who was among the first to report that delinquency rates decline from the central business district to the outlying areas of the city. He also found that the same pattern held for adult crime, and that rates of recidivism were also highest in the inner zones of the city and declined toward the peripheral areas. Shaw's original study was confined to the city of Chicago. But in a later comparative study of twenty-one cities in the United States and Canada, Shaw and McKay (1969) confirmed that reported crime and delinquency rates were similarly higher in inner zones and slums. Lander (1954) found similar results for Baltimore, as did Schmidt (1960a) for Seattle. Although Schmidt's more detailed analysis found that the central business district, skid row, and contiguous areas had the highest crime rates, it also concluded that each of these areas produced different kinds of crime. The central business district, for example, was characterized by high rates of shoplifting, check fraud, residential burglary (this is possible only in cities having a large residential population in the central business district, as was the case in Seattle), automobile theft, and attempted suicide. On the other hand, the skid row areas were characterized by high rates of fighting, robbery, nonresidential burglary, and disorderly conduct.

In searching for explanations for the spatial patterning of crime, a number of experts have argued that the important factor is not the location or distance from the central business district but rather the social and physical characteristics of the areas in which the crime occurs, or, equally important, in which the offender resides (offenders do not always confine their illegal activities to the areas in which they live). From this perspective, such variables as poverty, unemployment, poor housing, family status,

The social and physical characteristics of an area often provide the environment for crime. (Marc Anderson)

anomie, segregation, social rank, ethnic composition, and degree of urbanization have been associated in one degree or another with the incidence of crime (see Butler, 1976, pp. 109–120; Boggs, 1965; Schmidt, 1960b; Schuessler, 1962; Clark and Wenninger, 1962). However, there is little agreement among studies such as these as to which of the many variables they identify best explain the tendency for higher recorded rates of crime to occur near the center of the metropolis.

URBAN RIOTS

The late 1960s was a period of massive unrest in many large American cities. In 1967 alone, approximately 160 riots of varying intensity and magnitude occurred in cities of different sizes in the United States. Riots, as we are discussing them here, should not be confused with other forms of civil disorder or civil disobedience, such as insurrections or revolutions designed to overthrow a government or to seize state power. Such planned and organized activities are best categorized as political events and are beyond the scope of this discussion. While riots may very well be directed against alleged perpetrators of injustice or gross misusers of political power, they usually have no premeditated purpose, plan, or direction. They are spontaneous and disorganized outbursts of group violence, characterized by excitement and mixed with rage (Conant, 1973, pp. 21–

40). Once a riot is underway, systematic looting, arson, and attacks on persons may occur, and criminal elements may expand their routine activities in the wake of the chaos produced by a riot.

The 1960 riots in American cities have been widely characterized as racial in context, and as the result of the shared anger and rage felt by blacks in the urban ghettos in response to discriminatory practices that frustrated their access to social, economic, and political opportunities. They have also been characterized as a response to specific grievances directed against oppressive police and political practices, unemployment, housing, educational and recreational inadequacies, and against exploitative practices in the white-dominated urban economy (see Conant, 1973; Downs, 1976; *Report of the National Advisory Commission*, 1968). Although riots dramatically subsided in the 1970s, many observers believe that the conditions that produced them still exist in many large cities and that the probability of future riots cannot be safely discounted (Mazur, 1972).

The causes of riots are very complex and are not well understood. Detailed knowledge about the origins of riots is still very limited and many of the most basic questions remain unanswered. There have been many attempts to explain empirically the precipitating causes, but many of these investigations have been at the micro level. Lieberson and Silverman (1965), for example, have focused on the immediate events precipitating riots, such as interracial fights, murders, shootings, or rapes, specific violations of civil liberties, disputes over the use of public facilities, and responses to police practices. Other investigators have focused on the socioeconomic characteristics of the rioters (Oberschall, 1968), the demographic or racial composition of the cities in which riots have occurred (Butler, 1974), or the ecological characteristics of the local areas within cities in which riots have occurred (Grimshaw, 1960; Abadu, 1972; Schulman, 1968). Warren (1969) has attempted to link rioting to structural characteristics of neighborhoods, such as patterns of neighborhood visiting or the kinds of commitments local residents may have to their neighborhood.

But other observers are inclined to doubt that the specific characteristics or conditions of specific neighborhoods, communities, or cities are sufficient to cause riots in themselves and that the racial disorders of the 1960s were necessarily responses to community characteristics in local cities. Spilerman (1970), for example, argues that local conditions do not differ significantly enough by city or community for them to overcome blacks' exposure to the various stimuli that lead them as individuals to develop black solidarity and to foster a conscious identity that transcends geographic and social class boundaries. The only variation among cities that is significant, according to Spilerman, is that cities with large black populations are more prone to racial disorders than cities with smaller black populations. Butler (1976, p. 430) reasonably concludes that "events that make up riots are patterned, and the severity of riots is linked to certain characteristics of cities. But further specification is needed before the generalizations arising from this research can be wholeheartedly accepted."

Urban riots did not begin in the 1960s, of course, and intermittent outbreaks of violent riots can be identified throughout American urban history. Also, not all of the previous riots were racial in nature, and it is misleading to assume that all riots are necessarily related to racial antagonisms and conflicts. Indeed, there have been extended periods in American history in which racial tensions and antagonisms were extensive but did not lead to the outbreak of riots. For these reasons, riots have been discussed in this chapter on crime and unrest, rather than in the following chapter on race and ethnic relations.

In lieu of more convincing evidence, the best general explanations for riots still seem to rest within the theoretical framework of the major social processes spelled out at the beginning of this chapter (conflict of institutions, social mobility, individuation, and anomie). In this respect, it is interesting to notice that almost all of the major urban riots that have taken place in American cities have occurred during periods when the nation was at war. Riots took place during the Civil War, the Spanish-American War, World War I, World War II, and of course during the undeclared Vietnamese war of the middle and late 1960s. The general unrest and massive dislocations of people that took place during these periods, along with the general climate of violence associated with war, were probably factors contributing to the violence of the urban riots of these periods. While this association is largely speculative, it represents conditions that curiously are overlooked in most attempts to analyze the causes of major urban riots.

THE URBAN POLICE

Urban police departments occupy the front line in the urban community's day-to-day efforts to protect its citizens from the actual damages and fears produced by crime and the threat of crime. Urban residents look to the police for personal safety and for the freedom to walk the streets or to be secure in their homes. Stang (1973) has identified the three broad areas of responsibility the police ordinarily are called upon to fulfill. First, they are called upon to "keep the peace." This peace-keeping duty is a mandate involving the protection of life and rights, ranging from handling street-corner brawls to the settlement of violent family disputes. Second, the police have a duty to provide services ranging from bestowing menial courtesies to the protection of public and private property. This responsibility is one that many police officers complain about as most demeaning but that they are nevertheless called upon to perform most frequently. As Wilson (1968) notes, a police officer is expected to recover stolen property, direct traffic, provide emergency medical aid, get cats out of trees, check on the homes of families on vacation, find lost children, and help people who have locked themselves out of their apartments. The preponderance of such services is illustrated by a study showing that only 16 percent of all telephone calls received by the Detroit Police Department were related to predatory crime (Bercal, 1970). The third and widely considered the most important responsibility of the police is that of combating crime by enforcing the rule of law. This responsibility involves a variety of police operations, such as stakeouts, investigations, and arrests.

But there are many reasons why the police have been widely perceived as a rather weak link in the chain of institutional arrangements that constitutes the urban criminal justice system. Law enforcement carries stresses for the police because the assignment of "social service" duties may produce role conflict in such situations as family disputes, tavern brawls, disorderly loitering in the streets, and quarrels between neighbors. In these kinds of situations, one or another of the parties involved is likely to feel harassed, outraged, or neglected, and the police officer—who quite frequently has no clear legal standard to apply—must devise a solution based almost entirely on his or her own discretion and judgment, which may please none of the parties involved.

In our society the democratic emphasis on civil rights also places the police in an awkward position when they are under strong pressure from many groups to suppress crime at all costs. They are expected to maintain order in the dynamic and complex environment of the streets and to enforce the law as gatekeepers for the courts. The identification of the police with strong demands to maintain "law and order" makes them favorite targets of criticism whenever the real or perceived incidence of crime and lawlessness exceeds tolerable limits. But at the same time, the police may be viewed with hostility and suspicion as unfair, brutal, or suppressive by minorities, nonconforming life-style groups, or political protest groups whenever they have been targeted as the objects of police operations.

In many cases, police officers have been recruited from those segments of the community that have had little direct day-to-day experience with the minority and nonconformist groups they are expected to "keep in line." For example, young police officers who are recruited from a lower-middle-class conservative white community and are assigned to a minority ghetto community may have grown up without any significant contact with that minority and may experience "cultural shock" when brought into contact with what to them may be an alien way of life. Their latently negative attitudes thus may be reinforced by the aggressive and militant hostility that greets them, even when they are attempting to perform, to the best of their ability, a community service or order maintenance function in a minority community, or when they are attempting to apprehend a criminal whose victim is a member of the minority community.

For these and similar reasons, the urban police may be faced not only with inconsistent public expectations and public reactions but also inner conflict growing out of the interaction of their values and background with their intimate experience of what they perceive to be the "criminal element" of the population. The police live on the grinding edge of social conflict without a well-defined, well-understood notion of what they are supposed to be doing. They often occupy what they perceive as a "damned if they do, damned if they don't" status in the eyes of the public. This often leads to a state of frustration and low morale among police officers, which in turn lowers the efficiency of the law-enforcement process.

The police are, of course, only one of the components of the urban criminal justice system, which also includes prosecutors, courts, juries, and correctional institutions, such as jails, prisons, and probation agencies. However, to conceive of the combination of these components as a "system" in the literal sense is somewhat misleading, because they do not always interact in harmonious or anticipated ways. The expected sequence of procedures handled by the various agents who administer the work of criminal justice (arrest, police booking, detention, preliminary court hearings, arraignment, sentencing, imprisonment, and granting of parole) is fraught with many inconsistencies, conflicts, and strains, which render the so-called criminal justice system less effective, efficient, or fair than ideally desired.

The work of the police would be greatly simplified if they were completely free to collect evidence, apprehend suspects, and obtain confessions according to the necessities of efficient law enforcement only. However, the courts also have a keen interest in their law-enforcement procedures of acquisition of evidence, interrogation, arrest, and detention. These procedures must conform to the rules of law and to the principles of civil rights guaranteed by the Constitution. If this were not so, the specter of a police state would undoubtedly become apparent. Thus, the work of the police and the courts is often at cross purposes.

But the courts in turn breed their own discrepancies between what is considered ideal and the practical realities of law enforcement in a democratic society. One major problem is that the greater population concentrations and increased reliance on formal legal controls in urban society have imposed greater work loads on the courts and have aggravated perennial problems of delay, disparities in sentences or dispositions of cases, and in differential justice for different classes of defendants.

Court dockets become so clogged that trials may be delayed for many years, while the jails become overcrowded with persons awaiting the disposition of their cases. One expediency adopted by the court system in response to these conditions is disposition without trial, to reduce the work load through more rapid processing of cases and to divert offenders from correctional facilities. Johnson (1973, p. 423) reports that somewhere between one-third and one-half of all cases initiated by arrest are dismissed by the police, prosecutor, or judge. Of the cases prosecuted, as many as 90 percent of all convictions circumvent trial through a plea of guilty by the accused. One frequently used device to circumvent trial is commonly referred to as "plea bargaining." Under this procedure a defendant may plead guilty in exchange for a lighter penalty, through reduction of the original charge. The rationale for this questionable but expedient procedure can be summarized as follows:

> By pleading guilty he [the defendant] avoids the publicity of a trial and the greater social visibility of his transgressions as a blow to his reputation. When the victim of the crime is reluctant to testify, or the available evidence may not

convince a jury, the prosecution may accept a guilty plea to gain assurance that some punishment will ensue. Finally, the bargain may induce the defendant to provide information essential to the solution of other crimes (Johnson, 1973, p. 424).

One major criticism of plea bargaining is that the principle of justice may not be well served, since the intent of the law is circumvented. Another important criticism is that plea bargaining may produce large disparities in sentencing and thus violate the principle of equality before the law, which requires identical disposition of all persons convicted of the same crime. Extensive plea bargaining may also undermine the morale of the police, who may perceive that their efforts to enforce the law are being subverted.

THE SEARCH FOR SOLUTIONS TO THE URBAN CRIME PROBLEM

For decades, hundreds of policies and proposals have been suggested to reduce crime in American cities and to reduce the impact of the image of the city as dangerous or unsafe. Some of these recommendations are:

1. Decriminalize victimless crimes such as marijuana possession, prostitution, or gambling, while providing information and treatment programs for drug addicts. Many experts believe that this revision in the criminal law would reduce crime more than any other single remedy.
2. Institute a full-employment policy to lessen the appeal of crime as a way of making a living.
3. Promote tough gun control legislation, with mandatory punishment for gun possession.
4. Improve police–community relations.
5. Recruit minorities for police forces, to make the police more representative of minority communities.
6. Reform police departments to eliminate corruption, and retrain police to function as ombudsmen, counselors, and quasi–social workers operating out of neighborhood precinct offices. This, of course, would require much better educated police officers.
7. Establish a system of early screening and treatment of potential juvenile criminals, along with foster homes and community-based facilities.
8. Establish stiff, mandatory, equalized, and more certain sentences for violent crimes.
9. Disperse or coopt juvenile gangs.
10. Redesign building construction and site planning in urban redevelopment areas to minimize opportunities for crime (better lighting, fewer blind areas, better opportunities for surveillance).
11. Issue grants to neighborhoods and block associations to employ their own security guards (Levin, 1977, pp. 253-254).

While some of these recommendations seem more promising than others, and while some are already being undertaken in some American

Off track betting in New York provides a legal outlet for one form of gambling. (Marc Anderson)

cities, it is highly unlikely that the actual incidence of crime can ever be drastically reduced without drastically overhauling some of the major values and structural characteristics of American society, which would require major sacrifices on the part of nearly everyone. Also, no consensus yet exists as to the basic causes of crime, the methods best suited to reduce crime, the target groups against whom efforts at crime eradication should be directed, or who should pay the enormous social and economic costs of a radically revamped criminal justice system. For these reasons, it is fair to conclude that some form of urban crime will be with us for the foreseeable future.

Dentler (1977, p. 364) succinctly identifies another significant barrier to the eradication of crime, which is to a large extent consistent with the drift of our own discussion regarding the relative significance of street crime:

> Even in American cities that have become relatively saturated with felonious offenses in recent years, the distributive odds are such that most residents go unaffected or are only occasionally and lightly victimized. Hence, criminality, except in its sensational and politically or socially pornographic projections through the mass media, remains an isolated network of subsurface phenomena. In principle in an open urban society, crime and justice are everybody's business; but in social fact, the degree of separation and specialization is extreme. . . . [A] social problem must be widely and commonly identified as such in order to be treated.

Thus, changing public perceptions of and reactions to crime as a problem may be a more significant factor in the impact that crime has on urban society than the actual incidence of crime itself. If past patterns of public response, as measured by public opinion polls over the last several decades, are any clue, the recent high level of public concern and anxiety over urban crime may have been another public opinion "fad" that will diminish (or increase), regardless of actual crime trends.

SELECTED BIBLIOGRAPHY

ABADU, MARGARET J. G., et al. "Black Ghetto Violence," *Social Problems* (Winter 1972): 408–426.

BELL, DANIEL. *The End of Ideology.* New York: Free Press, 1960.

BERCAL, THOMAS E. "Calls for Police Assistance," *American Behavioral Science* (July-August 1970): 682.

BOGGS, SARA L. "Urban Crime Patterns," *American Sociological Review* 30 (December 1965): 899–908.

BUTLER, EDGAR. *Urban Sociology.* New York: Harper & Row, Pub., 1976.

————. *The Urban Crisis: Problems and Prospects in America.* Santa Monica, Calif.: Goodyear, 1977.

BUTLER, GERALD E. *Residential Segregation and Race Riots in the 1960's.* Los Angeles: University of Southern California Press, 1974.

CLARK, J. P., and WENNINGER, E. P. "Socio-Economic Correlates of Illegal Behavior among Juveniles," *American Sociological Review* 27 (December 1962): 826–834.

CONANT, RALPH W. "Patterns of Civil Protest: Ghetto Riots." In Alan Shank, ed., *Political Power and the Urban Crisis,* pp. 445–459. 2nd ed. Boston: Holbrook Press, 1973.

DENTLER, ROBERT A. *Urban Problems: Perspectives and Solutions.* Skokie, Ill.: Rand McNally, 1977.

DOWNS, ANTHONY. *Urban Problems and Prospects.* 2nd ed. Skokie, Ill.: Rand McNally, 1976.

GIST, NOEL P., and FAVA, SYLVIA F. *Urban Society.* 6th ed. New York: Thomas Y. Crowell, 1974.

GRIMSHAW, ALLEN D. "Urban Racial Violence in the United States," *American Journal of Sociology* 66 (September 1960): 109–119.

HORTON, PAUL, and LESLIE, GERALD. *The Sociology of Social Problems.* 5th ed. Englewood Cliffs, N.J.: Prentice-Hall, 1974.

JOHNSON, ELMER HUGH. *Social Problems of Urban Man.* Homewood, Ill.: Dorsey Press, 1973.

LANDER, BERNARD. *Toward an Understanding of Juvenile Delinquency.* New York: Columbia University Press, 1954.

LEVIN, MELVIN R. *The Urban Prospect.* North Scituate, Mass.: Duxbury Press, 1977.

LIEBERSON, STANLEY, and SILVERMAN, ARNOLD P. "The Precipitants and Underlying Conditions of Race Riots," *American Sociological Review* 30 (December 1965): 887–898.

MAZUR, ALLAN. "The Causes of Black Riots," *American Sociological Review* 37 (August 1972): 490–493.

MERTON, ROBERT K., and NISBET, ROBERT A. *Contemporary Social Problems*. 2nd ed. New York: Harcourt Brace Jovanovich, 1966.

OBERSCHALL, ANTHONY. "The Los Angeles Riot of August 1965," *Social Problems* (Winter 1968): 322–341.

PALEN, J. JOHN. *City Scenes: Problems and Prospects*. Boston: Little, Brown, 1977.

Report of the National Advisory Commission on Civil Disorders. New York: Bantam Books, 1968.

SCARPITTI, FRANK R. *Social Problems*. 2nd ed. Hinsdale, Ill.: Dryden Press, 1977.

SCHMIDT, CALVIN F. "Urban Crime Areas: Part I," *American Sociological Review* 25 (August 1960)(a): 555–578.

⸺. "Urban Crime Areas: Part II," *American Sociological Review* 25 (October 1960)(b): 655–678.

SCHUESSLER, KARL. "Components of Variations in City Crime Rates," *Social Problems* (Spring 1962): 314–323.

SCHULMAN, JAY. "Ghetto Area Residence, Political Alienation, and Riot Orientation." In L. H. Massotti and D. R. Bowen, eds., *Riots and Rebellion*, pp. 261–284. Beverly Hills, Calif.: Sage Publications, Inc., 1968.

SHAW, CLIFFORD. *Delinquency Areas*. Chicago: University of Chicago Press, 1929.

⸺, and MCKAY, H. D. *Juvenile Delinquency and Urban Areas*. rev. ed. Chicago: University of Chicago Press, 1969.

SPILERMAN, SEYMOUR. "The Causes of Racial Disturbances," *American Sociological Review* 35 (August 1970): 627–649.

STANG, DAVID P. "The Police and Their Problems." In Alan Shank, ed., *Political Power and the Urban Crisis*, pp. 460–485. 2nd ed. Boston: Holbrook Press, 1973.

SUTHERLAND, EDWIN H. *White Collar Crime*. New York: Dryden Press, 1949.

THRASHER, FREDRICK M. "The Gang: A Study of 1,313 Gangs in Chicago." In E. W. Burgess and D. J. Bogue, eds., *Contributions to Urban Sociology*, pp. 655–659. Chicago: University of Chicago Press, 1964.

WALLERSTEIN, JAMES S., and WHYLE, CLEMENT J. "Our Law Abiding Law Breakers," *Probation* (April 1947): 107–112.

WARREN, DONALD I. "Neighborhood Structure and Riot Behavior in Detroit," *Social Problems* (Spring 1969): 464–484.

WILSON, JAMES Q. *Varieties of Police Behavior*. Cambridge, Mass.: Harvard University Press, 1968.

WOLFGANG, MARVIN E. "Crime in Urban America." In the 1967-68 E. Paul Dupont Lectures, *The Threat of Crime in America*. Newark: University of Delaware Press, 1969.

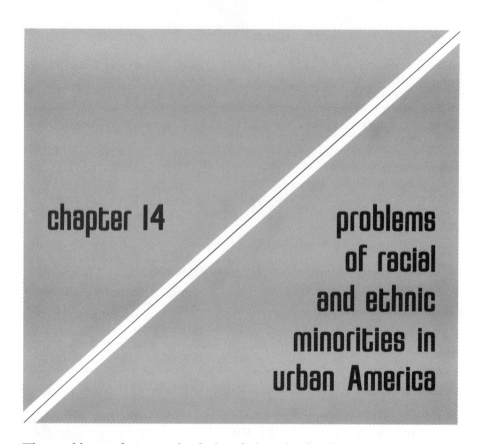

chapter 14

problems of racial and ethnic minorities in urban America

The problems of race and ethnic relations in the United States may be identified or defined in a number of ways. They may be viewed as aspects of a far more general tendency for all humans to separate themselves into groups in which members are linked to one another by feelings of solidarity and a common identity. Such groups, which may vary in size from a single family to an entire community, have been labeled "in-groups" by sociologists. In turn, such groups almost universally tend to develop unfavorable prejudices against "out-groups" consisting perhaps of all groups other than their own. This tendency, which applies to groups of all types, whenever they are differentiated by religion, race, ethnicity, economic status, or any other significant cultural difference, is also referred to as "ethnocentrism" (Gold and Scarpitti, 1967).

American cities have always been characterized by a wide range of ethnic, religious, and cultural diversity as waves and waves of immigrants have poured into them in search of new opportunities. A traditional American myth is that these groups easily assimilated or melted into a single, united American way of life, as the population "melting pot" hypothesis suggests. But with few exceptions, the successive waves of immigrants that have infused American cities have tended to establish their own ethnically homogeneous neighborhoods and social institutions adjacent to those already established by other groups. For the most part, the melting has been restricted to those ethnic groups already having the social and cultural characteristics most similar to those of the dominant established groups, which have been primarily of Protestant Anglo-Saxon origins. In turn, the tendency for dominant majorities in a given society to control or restrict the behavior of minority groups within that society discrimina-tory ways has often become a source of tension and hostility. In American urban centers, relations between the white Protestant majority and the racial, ethnic, and religious minorities such as Blacks, American Indians, Puerto Ricans, Mexicans, Jews, Poles, Orientals, Catholics, Irish, French-Canadians, and almost every other ethnic group have been characterized at various times by in-group/out-group hostilities ranging in intensity from verbal rejection and systematic discrimination to overt physical attacks and violence, including riots, bombings, lynchings, and other kinds of murder. Such strains have not been limited to relations between dominant groups and subjected minorities, but have occurred from time to time between competing minority groups as well.

Of course, it is also possible to characterize ethnic diversity as a posi-tive aspect of urban living, as did Wirth (1938), who saw such diversity as an essential characteristic of cities. He saw unlike groups drawn to one another because they are useful to one another, and he saw ethnic pluralism as contributing to the "spice of life" in urban communities. To a certain ex-tent, cities and metropolitan areas can be described as ethnic "mosaics," which implies an almost esthetic quality to the spatial patterning of ethnic settlements within a metropolitan context. As Dentler (1977, p. 274) so aptly puts it:

> Two or more ethnic groups do not automatically conflict when their members meet along a new frontier. They may cooperate or compete in some ways and merge or assimilate in others. Or, they make contact but for a time remain wholly independent of one another. Conflict is most likely to become the form of the relations between ethnic groups when one of the contacting groups is dominant in size, technology, or resources and when the subordinate group has something that is coveted by the dominant group.

While recognizing the positive aspects of ethnic diversity, we intend to focus on those aspects that have proven to be problematic both in the past and today. We will focus primarily on problems of black-white relations, primarily because blacks are by far the largest minority group in the United States to which the more extreme manifestations of prejudice have been most consistently directed. Also, the majority-minority group problem is the most widely recognized as having the most significant consequences today for the United States as a whole and about which there is the greatest concern and uncertainty in its implications for the future. Secondary em-phasis will be placed on Hispanic Americans and white ethnics of Southern and Eastern European descent. These emphases are not intended to minimize the seriousness of the problems of such other minority groups as Orientals or Indians, but merely represent the practical limitations of this chapter.

The twentieth-century history of black Americans most pertinent to our analysis is one of migration out of rural southern areas into the urban-industrial North. In 1910, 91 percent of the nation's blacks lived in the South. They were predominantly rural, with 73 percent living in rural areas or in small communities of less than 2,500 persons. But by 1970 the proportion of blacks living in the South had dropped to less than 55 percent, and about 70 percent of all blacks now lived in metropolitan areas. A relatively slow but steady outmigration of blacks from the South occurred during each of the first three decades of this century, with some acceleration during World War I, when floods and boll weevils hurt farming in the South and the industrial demands of the war created thousands of new jobs for unskilled workers in the northern cities. The outmigration reached its peak between 1940 and 1960, when approximately three million blacks migrated from the South to the North. World War II and the postwar reconstruction industrial boom were accelerating factors during this period.

By 1970 nearly one-half of the entire black population of the United States was concentrated in the central cities of the nation's fifteen largest metropolitan areas. Six of these cities had black majorities and another eight already had populations that were nearly 50 percent black by 1970. Less than one-third of all black Americans continued to live in the five states of the Deep South, most of them in rural areas (although the trend in the South has also been one of rural to urban migration). Today more blacks live in the Chicago metropolitan area than in Mississippi, and more blacks reside in the New York metropolitan area than in any of the southern states (Pettigrew, 1971, p. 3). By late 1977 the public school enrollment in the city of Detroit was more than 80 percent black (Detroit Free Press, January 8, 1978).

But during the 1970s, black migration from southern areas to northern cities all but ended. Today northern black populations are increasing because of natural growth (more births than deaths) rather than rural to urban migration. According to Tauber (1975), the period of massive migration of blacks from the South to the North is now history.

THE RESIDENTIAL SEGREGATION OF URBAN BLACKS

The early pattern of black settlement within each metropolitan area followed that of earlier white immigrant groups. The earlier migrants converged on the older sections of the central city because the lowest-cost housing was there, the jobs were there, and the older neighborhoods then often had good public transportation. Friends and relatives were also more likely to be there, and the neighborhoods also offered ethnic-oriented churches, businesses, voluntary associations, and service institutions that could provide support in times of need and could serve as a comforting bulwark against the impersonal forces of the larger urban world. As the earlier white immigrants were eventually absorbed by the larger society, many left their predominantly ethnic neighborhoods and moved to outlying areas to obtain newer housing and better schools. Some scattered randomly over the suburban area, while others established new ethnic clusters in the suburbs. For these groups, living in ethnic or assimilated neighborhoods, either in the cities or suburbs, is now largely a question of personal choice.

But the later phases of black settlement and expansion in metropolitan areas diverge sharply from those typical of the white ethnic groups. Nowhere has the expansion of America's black metropolitan population followed the pattern of dispersal open to the earlier white immigrants. Many black families have attained incomes, living standards, and cultural levels matching or surpassing those of many whites who have "assimilated." Yet most black families have remained within predominantly black neighborhoods primarily because they have been effectively excluded from white residential areas. Their exclusion has been accomplished through various discriminatory practices, some obvious and overt, others hidden by subtle "gentlemen's agreements." Deliberate efforts have sometimes been made to discourage black families from purchasing or renting homes in all-white neighborhoods. Intimidation and threats of violence have ranged from throwing garbage on lawns and making threatening phone calls to burning crosses in yards and even dynamiting property (*Report of the National Advisory Commission on Civil Disorders*, 1968, p. 244). Such actions do not require the participation of a majority of whites, many of whom are probably shocked, to effectively discourage black families from seeking housing in all-white neighborhoods. More often, real estate agents simply refuse to show homes in all-white neighborhoods to potential black purchasers, although this practice now violates the ban on discrimination in the sale or rental of private housing that was signed into federal law in 1968. (This practice is another example of white-collar crime referred to earlier in this chapter.) Banks and mortgage loan agencies allegedly "redline" neighborhoods, an attempt to maintain neighborhoods as predominantly white or predominantly black through various mortgage allocation and approval procedures that deny mortgage loans to blacks who wish to purchase homes in predominantly white areas, or to whites who wish to purchase homes in racially mixed areas. All of these practices create an atmosphere in which it is not worth the psychological and sociological efforts or costs to try to move into white neighborhoods for blacks who can economically afford to do so.

White flight from racially changing neighborhoods, and from cities containing high proportions of blacks, is another condition faced uniquely by black Americans. Racial transition in central city neighborhoods has been at least one reason that millions of whites have moved out of central cities into all-white suburban areas. Although by no means are all such moves racially inspired, the results are nevertheless the same—an increase in the pattern of residential segregation that has existed for decades. A study by the Taubers (1965) demonstrated that this pattern characterizes every large city in America. The authors devised an index to measure the degree of residential segregation. The index indicated for each city the percentage of blacks who would have to move from the blocks where they now lived to other blocks to provide a perfectly proportional, unsegregated distribution of the population. According to their findings, the average segregation index for 207 of the largest United States cities was 86.2. This means that an average of over 86 percent of all blacks would have to move to a different block to create an unsegregated population distribution. Studies by Farley (1970), and Kantrowitz (1973), which use different measures and methodologies, support the contention that blacks are becoming more segregated in most urban complexes.

The 1970 U.S. Census showed that blacks were becoming more suburbanized. But this is misleading and should not be construed to mean that they were also becoming less segregated. Suburbanizing blacks for the most part moved into predominantly black suburban areas that were just as segregated as the central city areas from which they moved. Also, they were moving into older suburban areas with declining neighborhoods and deteriorating housing much like that available to them in the central cities (Tauber, 1975). Residential segregation actually varies little between central cities and suburbs. In 1970, as in 1960, the suburbs remained more than 95 percent white, and the 1980 Census is not expected to show a significant change from this firmly established pattern. Clearly, the term "ghetto" applies more aptly to involuntarily segregated urban black communities than to any other similarly urbanized ethnic group.

POVERTY AND UNEMPLOYMENT IN THE BLACK GHETTO

Residential segregation and de facto school segregation still are major barriers to full equality for blacks, and the feelings of despair, apathy, or bitterness and resentment still afflict many blacks caught in the poverty of the racial ghettos in most large American cities. Within many black ghettos, discrimination and the "culture" of poverty have effectively destroyed many people's incentives for acquiring the skills, knowledge, and attitudes necessary to take advantage of the opportunities for educational, occupational, and economic advancement increasingly available to blacks as a result of current civil rights legislation. Many such blacks have also become cynical and disillusioned by past efforts of middle-class liberal outsiders from various "helping" agencies to modify their behavior, especially when these fragmentary efforts did not sufficiently alter the social and economic restrictions that traditionally had been imposed by the larger society.

The changing nature of the American economy has made it far more difficult for blacks to escape from the insecurities of poverty and unemployment like the European immigrants before them. When the European immigrants were arriving in large numbers, America was in the process of becoming an urban-industrial society. To build its major cities and industries, the country needed great pools of unskilled labor (see Chapter Eleven). The immigrants provided the labor, gained an economic foothold, and thereby enabled their children and grandchildren to move up to skilled, white-collar, and professional employment. But now unskilled labor is far less essential than before, and blue-collar jobs of all kinds are decreasing in numbers and importance as a source of new employment. The blacks who migrated to the urban centers for the most part lacked the newer kinds of skills essential to the postindustrial economy, and the ghetto schools have been unable to provide the education that can qualify them for decent jobs (see Chapter Ten). The black migrants, unlike the earlier European immigrants, found little opportunity in the city; they had arrived too late, and the unskilled labor they had to offer was no longer in great demand.

Compounding the problem of black employment opportunity is that whatever industrial growth and development has occurred in the last several decades has not taken place in the cities, which have leveled off or declined in economic growth. Such growth has been confined largely to the outlying parts of the suburban belts surrounding metropolitan areas. The new jobs that have been created as a result of the dispersal of industry and commerce to the suburbs are often beyond the geographic reach of the inner city worker. The lack of effective public transportation between central cities and outlying areas and the high costs of private automobile transportation make it virtually impossible for low-income inner-city residents to seek work and to commute to the areas in which jobs potentially are more available. The growing entry of married women into the labor force also compounds the employment problems of blacks because many women are

Employment opportunities for blacks in the cities are limited because of lack of urban industrial growth. (Marc Anderson)

now directly competing for jobs with both male adult and teenage black workers.

As a result of these factors, plus the persistence of some of the traditional forms of racial discrimination in America, blacks suffer much more unemployment than do white Americans. The official unemployment rate for male adult blacks is more than twice as high as for male adult whites. For black teenagers in search of work, the problem is even worse. In 1978, the estimated official unemployment rate for this group was over 37 percent, almost six times greater than the national average! Many employment experts (Montagna, 1977; Ritzer, 1977) believe that the actual unemployment rate for young blacks in the urban ghettos is even higher. Official unemployment rates include only those who actively have been seeking work. Many black teenagers, however, have lost hope of working in the foreseeable future and have given up the search. This group is not included in official labor force statistics and therefore is not included among the "officially" unemployed. This condition is a source of continuous frustration and unrest among young urban blacks, and the resulting potential for crime and violence has been referred to by some observers as "social dynamite."

THE GROWING BLACK MIDDLE CLASS

To focus entirely on the poor and unemployed black is somewhat misleading and condescending, for, as Palen (1975, p. 219) and others suggest, two somewhat separate and distinct black social classes now exist. One of these is the one we have been describing, which has the grim potential for settling in as a semipermanent urban "under-class." The other is one that is becoming increasingly middle class by most conventional standards. Many changes have been taking place as a result of the civil rights revolution that have meant positive social and economic gains for the middle-class segment of the black minority. Also, some measurable differences between blacks and whites reflecting past restrictions imposed by racial discrimination are beginning to diminish, such as differences in life expectancy, income, education, occupation, and political participation.

According to the 1970 Census, the income of all blacks outside the South was only 74 percent of that of all whites outside the South. But black families outside the South consisting of a husband and wife had an income level of 88 percent of white income. For younger (under age thirty-five) black husband and wife families, income differentials had all but disappeared by 1970. Income for these younger black families had increased from 78 percent of white income in 1960 to an almost equal 96 percent of white income in 1970. When young families in which both husband and wife work are compared, black families outside the South earned 104 percent of what comparable white families earned, the main difference being that black wives were more likely to work full time than white wives (Wattenberg and Scammon, 1973).

In the past decade there has been steady increase of middle class blacks in white collar jobs. (VISTA)

Similar gains for middle-class blacks can be seen in the occupational arena. Whereas only 9.1 percent of the nonwhite labor force held white-collar jobs in 1948, over 31 percent held such jobs in 1973. Over the same time period, the portion of nonwhite workers in the professional and technical job categories went from 2.4 percent to 9.9 percent and from 2.3 percent to 4.1 percent in the managers and proprietors categories. But the greatest gains for blacks were in white-collar clerical work. Only 3.3 percent of all nonwhite workers were employed as clerical workers in 1948, but by 1973 the proportion had increased almost fivefold to 14.9 percent (Montagna, 1977, pp. 100–101).

Many of these economic and occupational gains were directly related to educational gains for blacks over the past several decades, as attained educational level differences between blacks and whites have begun to diminish. An increasing proportion of urban blacks now completes secondary education, college, and postgraduate professional training. The attained educational levels for some portions of the black middle class are now higher than for comparable white populations—black female professional workers have attained a higher educational level than white female professional workers.

Within the central cities of northern metropolitan areas, some residential segregation between lower-class and middle-class blacks is now beginning to occur, with middle-class blacks moving into newer, formerly white neighborhoods on the periphery of the city, while the lower "under classes" remain in the older portions of the inner city (Marston, 1969). But this should not obscure the fact that even middle-class blacks still remain almost completely segregated from their white suburban counterparts. A study of fifteen representative large cities indicated that white upper- and middle-class families were far more segregated from black upper- and middle-class families than they were from white lower-class families (*Report of the National Advisory Commission on Civil Disorders*, 1968, p. 247).

Thus, economic gains for middle-class blacks have not meant assimilation into larger middle-class white society. In this area, various forms of racial prejudice and social discrimination still persist. As a result, when many responsible whites and blacks of similar social status attempt to interact socially in today's changing and uncertain racial climate, a great deal of mutual distrust, suspicion, and misunderstanding still occurs. An unpublished study by Reynolds Farley (Detroit Free Press, December 15, 1977), for example, indicated that a large majority of the white respondents and a smaller but still significant minority of blacks would feel "uncomfortable" living in a racially balanced community that was 50 percent white and 50 percent black. What Arnold Rose said some years earlier is apparently still true: "Members of racial minorities and of the white majority do not know how to associate with each other; they are excessively formal and sensitive in interpersonal relations" (Merton and Nisbet, 1966, p. 474).

BLACK POLITICAL REPRESENTATION AND COMMUNITY CONTROL

During the peak of the civil rights revolution in the late 1960s, one of the most persuasive and justified grievances within the black community was the lack of adequate political representation and influence. The concept of "black power" became a significant and widely repeated symbol of this concern during that period.

With respect to community power and control, the experience of blacks in the urban ghettos had also been different from that of the earlier European ethnic minorities. The report of the National Advisory Commission on Civil Disorders (1968, pp. 279–280) suggests that this difference is one important factor in explaining why blacks have been unable to escape from poverty and the ghetto to the same extent as the white ethnic groups. The white immigrants had settled for the most part in rapidly growing cities that had at the time powerful and expanding political machines, which gave them economic favors in exchange for political support. The political machines were decentralized among the various ethnic wards of the cities, and ward-level grievance machinery enabled the immigrants to make their voice heard and their power felt. The immigrants were also able to enter politics directly by joining the machines as ward "heelers" and in other positions. Since the local political organization exercised considerable influence over the construction of public buildings and roads in the cities, they provided employment in construction jobs for their immigrant voters. Ethnic groups as public employees often were able to dominate one or more of the municipal services, such as the police and fire departments, municipal welfare departments, public transportation and sanitation departments, and sometimes even local public school systems.

But by the time the blacks had arrived, the situation had altered dramatically. The wave of public construction projects had greatly diminished and the political machines were no longer so powerful or so well equipped to provide jobs, political appointments, and other favors. In many cities the political machines succumbed to reform movements that in many ways provided needed improvements in the political management of cities. The reform groups promised greater efficiency; elimination of the "spoils" system that had fostered nepotism, cronyism, graft, and corruption; and cleaner and more fair elections. The reform groups also were nominally more liberal on race issues. But in actuality they often were dominated by middle-class business, professional, and church groups that were unskilled or uncomfortable with minorities and believed that coalitions with any low-income groups, white or black, were too unsavory or unbecoming to their reform objectives.

As a result, blacks were effectively excluded from patronage jobs, political appointments based on recognition of blacks as a legitimate interest group, and were strongly underrepresented on city councils or on the governing boards of vital city agencies. Interestingly, cities such as Chicago and New York, with some form of political machines with strong links to the ghetto wards still persisting into the late 1960s, were able to avoid the civil disturbances and riots that had occurred in the black ghettos of many other large American cities. While there are many other valid explanations for this complex phenomenon, it is fair to conclude that the political officials in these two cities were probably more skillful, better informed, and more responsive in dealing with grievances, unrest, and provocative incidents than cities without such machines, such as Detroit, Cincinnati, or Tampa (see *Report of the National Advisory Commission on Civil Disorders,* 1968, pp. 42–52, 84–108).

The 1970s have seen the gradual movement of blacks into municipal jobs and into key decision-making positions in local government. Cities such as Atlanta, Detroit, Newark, Gary, and Los Angeles now have black mayors, as did Cleveland as early as the 1960s. Many cities now have strong black representation on city councils and on the governing boards of many vital community service agencies. Detroit, for example, now has not only a black mayor, but a black majority on the city council, a black school superintendent and a black-dominated school board, a black police commissioner, and many black judges. Much of this change, which now often goes far beyond the mere "tokenism" of the past, has come about as a result of the increasing proportion of blacks in big city populations. But it is also a result of blacks' greater political awareness, sophistication, and participation, as well as improved black political organization. In some cases, black politicians have gained elected political office with significant support from white voters, as in the case of Mayor Bradley of Los Angeles, where white voters are still the large majority of the total, former Senator Brooke of Massachusetts, and Richard Austin, the Michigan Secretary of State. The "black caucus" is a group of increasingly visible blacks who have been elected to the United States Congress, and as of late 1980 a sprinkling of blacks were in top federally appointed positions, including one Supreme Court Justice, the United States ambassador to the United Nations, the Solicitor General of the United States, a member of the Federal Reserve Board, and the Secretary of Housing and Urban Development in the President's cabinet.

For the first time the black population has become a potent force in American political life at the local, state, and national levels, and at least some politicians and lawmakers at all levels of government have become increasingly responsive to black interests. This has helped lead to increased dignity and self-respect among many black groups, as well as to rising hopes for further social, economic, and political gains in the future.

SOME POLICY ALTERNATIVES FOR BLACK AMERICA

While current trends indicate that blacks are gaining in jobs, education, and local political influence, they have by no means achieved parity with whites. It is also apparent that they are becoming more residentially and socially separated from white American society. In 1968 the basic conclusion of the National Advisory Commission on Civil Disorders was that "our nation is moving toward two societies, one black, one white—separate and unequal." A year later, the Urban Coalition and Urban America, Inc., jointly published a study entitled *One Year After* (New York Times, March 2, 1969), which concluded that "we are a year closer to being two societies, black and white, increasingly separate and unequal."

While these conclusions may not be still valid descriptions of reality, the continuation of some racial *separation* remains a very real alternative for the foreseeable future. Involuntary separatism is, of course, the alternative that has long been favored by white segregationists, but separatism also has been advocated in different forms by some black groups. The late Marcus Garvey, for example, led a back-to-Africa movement that had thousands of black followers earlier in this century. More recently, some groups of young black nationalists have argued for a separate black state within the boundaries of the continental United States. But most blacks have rejected racial separatism (Pettigrew, 1971, p. 259) as a real solution to America's racial problems, as have a large majority of America's social scientists. Horton and Leslie (1974, p. 435) doubt that separation carries much prospect of racial peace, and conclude that "intensified prejudice, growing hostility, and prolonged guerilla warfare are the more likely outcomes." Scarpitti (1977, p. 341) adds that separatism can never lead to the conditions necessary for a harmonious society because it avoids confronting the divisive issues. Grodzins (1967) had earlier described racial separatism as totally negative and fraught with many evils in its social, economic, and political consequences.

Pluralism is a more subtle and complex alternative that has increasingly been advocated by some social scientists, particularly those of a "neoconservative" persuasion (see *U.S. News and World Report,* October 31, 1977; *Newsweek,* November 7, 1977, for reports on conservative political trends in the U.S.). Pluralism is a condition wherein each ethnic group maintains its distinctive identification and a degree of autonomy. Such autonomy implies that ethnic and racial groups also would choose to live in ethnically homogeneous neighborhoods and maintain distinctive ethnic cultural patterns. A key element of pluralism is the idea of choice, for pluralists differ from segregationists in that they advocate voluntary rather than involuntary patterns of ethnic and racial distinctiveness and homogeneity, and they argue that pluralism need not produce inequality in the status of or the relationships between various majority and minority ethnic and racial groupings.

The pluralistic alternative may be romantically attractive to a variety of American ethnics, particularly those who are seeking to establish a positive sense of their ethnic "roots." Whitney M. Young, Jr. (1969, p. 152), a prominent black leader, has stated this ideal as it would apply to blacks: "In the context of positive pluralism, black people would enter the dominant white society with a sense of roots. By now, we ought to see the fatal flaw of the old melting-pot theory, which sought to strip people of culture and traditions in order to transform everyone into middle class, white Anglo-Saxons." Andrew Greeley (1971, pp. 15–16), a social scientist who writes from a white ethnic Catholic perspective, has stated the ideal of pluralism for white ethnic groups in a similar way. But he rightly qualifies his support for pluralism by raising the possibilities that the tensions and diversities of pluralism could lead to a "narrow, frightened and suspicious society" rather than a "richer, fuller human society" if pluralism is not properly directed.

Integration has been the alternative most often advocated by most blacks, most social scientists, and most white civil rights proponents. It is also the alternative that is closest to the American ideal, if not the current American reality. The main areas of disagreement among those who advocate racial integration have been how fast the process of integration should proceed, how complete it should be, the degree to which it should be facilitated by planned social change, and the degree to which it should be forced by legislation and direct governmental intervention. For example, Grodzins (1962, p. 132) has proposed several ways of planning to reduce residential segregation, including controlled migration of blacks into white neighborhoods, returning white populations to central cities, the suburbanization of blacks, and moving blacks out of the big cities into smaller cities, where they are now underrepresented. But Grodzins did not sufficiently identify the mechanisms through which such massive redistribution of both white and black populations could be accomplished, nor did he suggest specific ways in which much expected bitter opposition to such measures could be placated.

Pettigrew (1971, pp. 325–328) strongly supports a course of action directed toward integration as advocated by Grodzins and many others, but he also recognizes that, given the magnitude of the problem and the degree of potential resistance, such an alternative, even if it were eventually successful, cannot possibly alleviate the existing problems of the large black ghettos in the immediate future. Also, at least some blacks will probably prefer to remain in predominantly black inner city neighborhoods, if given a perfectly free choice. Therefore, in addition to maintaining a major effort toward racial integration, he also advocates a simultaneous effort to enrich the existing ghettos. Such enrichment would include restructuring the economics of the ghetto, especially by developing urban cooperatives. Effective job training programs and some reordering of big city public school systems so that blacks have a greater input into their programs and policies are also among the enrichment programs he recommends. However, he cautions that such enrichment programs must contain safeguards to insure that they will not become counterproductive and hinder later dispersal and integration. To Pettigrew's alternatives, which we regard as the most supportable of those discussed here, we would add that the costs of such enrichment would probably have to be borne by the general public through direct federal financial assistance to the ghetto-ridden and debt-ridden cities. But it is not clear at the present time just how willing the American public is to incur these costs, nor is it clear what the priorities of the federal government will be in providing a high level of financial assistance to enrich the urban ghettos.

HISPANIC AMERICANS

In 1970 approximately 10.6 million United States residents were of Spanish-speaking descent. Of these, approximately eight million were raised by a Spanish-speaking mother, and approximately eight million identified themselves with a Hispanic group (U.S. Census, PC (2)1C, 1973). The Census Bureau estimates that the largest Spanish-speaking group is of Mexican descent. Of the 6.3 million Mexicans residing in the United States, six out of seven reside in the southwestern states. This is the largest concentration of people of Latin American ancestry outside of Latin America itself (Pettigrew, 1976). The second largest group consists of over 1.5 million Puerto Ricans, concentrated largely in New York City and the surrounding region. Since their urban experiences differ markedly, each of these groups will be discussed separately.

Mexican Americans

Labeling for this group varies extensively: in New Mexico, "Spanish American" is preferred; in Los Angeles, "Mexican" or "Mexican American" is the most common label; while in San Antonio, the term "Latin American" is frequently used. "Chicano" is now a widely used label among young and more militant Americans of Mexican descent. This lack of agreement on an appropriate label is indicative of the unresolved struggle within this group for an acceptable common identity. The difficulty can be further illustrated

A Mexican-American VISTA volunteer is serving her ethnic community by helping to bring bicultural programming to radio and TV. (VISTA)

by the fact that two major Mexican American political groups, one based in California and the other in Texas, were unable to form one regional group, largely because of disagreement over the label (Moore, 1970, p. 148). In the following discussion, we will use the term "Mexican American" for consistency.

The concentration of Mexican Americans in the southwestern states derives from a complex history that began more than four centuries ago, when Texas, California, and the other states of the region were territories that were colonized by Spain via Mexico. Through frequent military conflict throughout the nineteenth century, this region was ultimately acquired and dominated by the United States. There was a rapid influx of Anglo-American (non-Mexican) settlers during this period, and by 1900 anglos were a majority in every southwestern state except New Mexico, where Mexican Americans remained a majority until about 1950. However, Mexicans have continued to migrate to the United States throughout the present century, for a variety of reasons. For example, the Mexican revolution, which began in 1909, forced hundreds of thousands of peons from agricultural lands to seek employment elsewhere. At the same time, agriculture was expanding rapidly in the United States border states, where a large labor force was now needed. Massive Mexican immigration to the southwestern states was thus triggered, and most of the Mexican American population today derives from this twentieth-century movement. While recorded Mexican immigration for the first decade of the century was less than 25,000, it expanded rapidly to 174,000 between 1910 and 1919, and to almost half a million in the 1920s. It declined sharply during the depression decade of the 1930s and the war years of the 1940s, but began to rise again in the early 1950s. It has averaged out at 40,000 a year ever since (Grebler, 1970). Estimates of illegal immigration are much harder to come by, but the figure is extremely large and may be as high as one million a year.

The depression and the following war hit Mexican Americans especially hard, and many more than before were driven to the cities in search of better opportunities. Roughly 80 percent of the Mexican American population is now urban, and cities such as Los Angeles, San Antonio, or Albuquerque have rapidly growing Mexican American populations. Los Angeles probably contains in its "barrios" (a Spanish word for "neighborhood") more people of Mexican ancestry than any Mexican city except Mexico City and Guadalajara. No one knows for certain, but barrio leaders claim that from 800,000 to one million Mexican Americans live in Los Angeles (Steiner, 1970).

Although generalities about the urban living conditions of Mexican Americans are made hazardous by the group's diversity, the available literature reveals that Mexican Americans tend to be concentrated in low-skilled, poorly paid work. They earn more money with less education than blacks throughout the Southwest, but because of a preponderance of young, large families with a high birth rate, the income per person tends to be less than that of blacks (Pettigrew, 1976). These problems are made worse by public education that is often segregated, inferior, and culturally intolerant of Mexican Americans. Housing is typically described as segregated, old, and overcrowded. According to the 1970 Census of Housing (Vol. 1, 1972), the percentage of families with Spanish surnames living in housing units built before 1940 surpassed that of blacks, while almost twice as many Spanish-surnamed households occupied overcrowded dwelling units as did blacks. Mexican Americans have suffered from the impact of prejudice and discrimination, and frequently have been stereotyped as lazy, dirty, and irresponsible. While not as spatially or socially segregated as blacks, patterns of housing discrimination allegedly do exist. For example, a study of the renting practices of twenty-five apartment houses in one area of Los Angeles, which involved black, Mexican American, and white applicants, revealed that black couples were discriminated against in some fashion on 75 percent of their visits; Mexican Americans were similarly victimized in 50 percent of their visits, while only 17 percent of the Anglos experienced any form of discrimination. One common experience for the two minorities was to be told that no apartment was available, although vacancies had been advertised the day before. Another was to be quoted higher rents and fees than those quoted to the white applicants (Johnson, 1971). For thirty-five southwestern cities, indices of residential segregation have indicated that Mexican Americans are about equally separated from both blacks and whites, and that this separation is about two-thirds of the degree to which blacks are residentially separated from whites (Grebler, 1970).

Relations between Mexican Americans and the larger majority have often been strained, and the widely publicized "zoot-suit" riots between young Chicanos and sailors in the Los Angeles area during World War II first focused national attention on this conflict and on the growing presence of a "new" minority. Conflicts and tensions between Mexican Americans and the police or other agents of social control often have been as great as those experienced by blacks, and violence has sometimes occurred as a result of the less than satisfactory relationships between Mexican American workers and their employers, especially in agriculture or agriculture-related industries.

Among Mexican Americans there is considerable public debate and private ambiguity as to what their group identity really is or ought to be. Pettigrew (1976) concludes that many Mexican Americans occupy a marginal position in American society for the following reasons: 1) the great diversity of the group across region, age, and social class; 2) the accessibility of the Mexican–United States border, which allows new immigrants to move easily back and forth between Mexican and American society; 3) the recency and extent of the group's massive migration to the city; 4) the difficulty in having to deal with anglo authorities, particularly after a long history of bruising encounters with the Border Patrol, the Texas Rangers, and local police; 5) being the largest minority in the United States with an actively maintained world language (Spanish) other than English; and finally 6) the conflict between "making it," or assimilating in an anglo-dominated society, and retaining a distinctive culture.

Yet there is growing ethnic awareness, consciousness, and pride among Mexican Americans, which is reflected in various ways. The land protests in New Mexico, the farm labor protests of Cesar Chaves, and the student-inspired Chicano movement are efforts to solve problems of marginality and to produce positive social and economic gains through collective action, cultural pride, or greater militancy. Like blacks, Mexican Americans have become more sophisticated and active in the political arena. An increasing number have been elected or appointed to political office at the local, state, and national levels, and Mexican Americans have recently been appointed as members of the National Committee of the Democratic Party. These developments indicate the probable future direction of the Mexican American minority in its efforts to win more complete acceptance in American society on its own cultural terms.

Puerto Ricans

Puerto Ricans are the second largest but the most economically depressed Spanish-speaking community in urban America. Of the more than 1.5 million Puerto Ricans in the United States, nearly one million are concentrated within the New York metropolitan region, with large concentrations in East Harlem ("Spanish Harlem"), the South Bronx, Bedford-Stuyvesant, and Brownsville. But the urban Puerto Rican has been geographically mobile, and movement to other cities, such as Philadelphia, Boston, or Chicago, has become increasingly more common.

In New York City, Puerto Ricans are worse off than blacks in many respects. The proportion of Puerto Rican adults with no schooling or limited grade school education far exceeds blacks, and a higher proportion of blacks are high school or college graduates. The proportion of blacks in

In order to make their demands for greater justice and better treatment, Puerto Ricans have developed a strong sense of political identity. (Puerto Rican Community Development Project, Inc.)

professions and technical or managerial occupations is four times that of Puerto Ricans, while greater proportions of Puerto Ricans are in lower paid blue-collar work. Puerto Ricans in mainland cities have experienced many of the same kinds of prejudice and discrimination faced by urban blacks. Their social heritage has been similar to that of blacks in that Puerto Rico had been a colonial outpost of Spain for many centuries and that slavery and its associated institutions of racism formed the nucleus of colonial plantation society.

Because they share a common tradition and the current disadvantages of minority status, one might have expected a joint effort between Puerto Ricans and blacks in the struggle to improve their common lot (Padilla, 1972). In some instances Puerto Ricans actually have joined in a common cause with black political and community organizations. But these Puerto Rican–black coalitions have been based for the most part on single issues and have been generally short lived (Padilla, 1972). Puerto Ricans tend to identify strongly with their Spanish heritage, a condition that overrides racial considerations. Also, they have an expressed preference for "looking white" and greater opportunities for bypassing oppression and achieving social mobility, factors that may serve strongly to limit a stronger association with blacks. On the other hand, lack of experience with English as a native tongue is a barrier not shared in the same way or to the same extent by urban blacks.

Another important difference between blacks and Puerto Ricans is that Puerto Ricans are able to move back and forth between the home island and the mainland of the United States with ease and frequency. This option broadens the opportunities available to Puerto Ricans, and reverse migration from New York to Puerto Rico has become commonplace in recent decades. But this has tended to create a problem for the Puerto Rican communities in New York, because it is the professionally, technically, and managerially trained "elites" who produce a loss of leadership potential and a "brain drain" by their disproportionate representation among the out migrants. The in migrants, on the other hand, are usually among the most impoverished, inexperienced, and undereducated segments of the Puerto Rican population, and these characteristics tend to heighten the usual adjustment problems of the migrants and to strain the social service capacity of the receiving community.

However, mainland Puerto Ricans, like blacks and many other disadvantaged minorities, began in the 1960s to express more conscious dissatisfaction and unrest and to develop a much stronger sense of political identity. They have more aggressively entered the political arena of the cities and states in which they reside in large numbers to make their demands for greater justice and better treatment. These political efforts have now begun to reach to the national levels of Congress and the federal bureaucracy.

WHITE ETHNICITY

The greatest wave of immigration of white ethnic groups from Europe to America occurred during the nineteenth and early twentieth centuries. With some exceptions, most of the European migrants traditionally have settled in cities, thereby helping to produce distinct ethnic enclaves and subcultures. Thus, white ethnic identification has played an important role in American urban development. The early wave of migration, from about 1820 to 1880, consisted largely of immigrants from northern and western European countries, and their descendants are no longer widely regarded as "ethnics." The later major wave of migration, from about 1880 to 1920, was primarily from southern and eastern Europe (see Chapter Three). Many of these immigrants not only settled in cities but usually settled in neighborhoods where there were already people of the same cultural extraction. As a result, many big cities became mosaics of ethnically distinct "natural areas" in which ethnic cultural traditions and roots were maintained. The second, third, and fourth generation descendants of the later wave of migration from eastern and southern Europe are now commonly identified as "white ethnics," and it is these groups to which the following discussion primarily refers.

The popular "melting pot" hypothesis traditionally has suggested that the distinctive cultural characteristics of each of these migrant groups would ultimately disappear, as the migrants were assimilated economically, politically, and socially into established American society. To a certain extent this has happened, particularly in the case of many of those migrants of English, German, Scottish, or Scandinavian heritage who arrived in the early wave of migration and who were culturally the most similar to those groups already identified as "native Americans" (American Indians, of course, were in the past widely excluded from this designation!) To a lesser extent, this has also happened to many of the third or fourth generation descendants of the Italian, Greek, Polish, Slovak, Czech, Hungarian, Romanian, Russian, and other European nationalities of more recent migration status. This melting pot concept of assimilation has been a common cliché in American society and was earlier expressed by Robert Park (1967, p. 120): "By the process of assimilation . . . we may conceive alien peoples to be incorporated with, and made part of, the community or state. Ordinarily assimilation goes on silently and unconsciously, and only forces itself into popular conscience when there is some interruption or disturbance of the process."

Refining this perspective, Guest (1977, p. 303) has divided the process of assimilation of white ethnics into four stages: 1) arrival in the United States with low socioeconomic status and low degree of acculturation; 2) the formation of separate residential communities because low status relegates the group to certain areas of the city and discrimination forces the group to band together; 3) a gradual upward movement in social status and the breakdown of the ethnic community; and 4) the complete integration of the group into American society.

In reality, assimilation has proceeded unevenly, and a growing number of observers doubt that the assimilation process was ever as smooth, automatic, or complete as the melting pot hypothesis suggested, and there is greater awareness that ethnicity has remained a very significant aspect of urban life (see Gordon, 1964; Glazer, 1969; Parenti, 1967; Femminella, 1973; Novack, 1978). The heavy ethnic character of many larger older cities of the Northeast and Middle West is still one of their dominant characteristics. While many of these cities are rapidly gaining black and Spanish-speaking residents as a larger portion of their total population, the overwhelming proportion of the remaining whites in the older northern cities and in the older established suburbs of these cities now tend to be second, third, or fourth generation southern and eastern Europeans and white Appalachian migrants, rather than the more assimilated whites who were much earlier established in American society.

Residential separation between whites of different ethnic origins still remains relatively high in many American cities, although not as great as for blacks and Spanish Americans. For example, if one sought to desegregate such white ethnic groups as Italian Americans, Irish Americans, Russian Americans, or other groups of eastern or southern European heritage, approximately 45 to 50 percent or more would have to be relocated from the residential blocks they now inhabit (Kantrowitz, 1973). By the same measure, even Norwegians and Swedes in New York City are relatively segregated in ethnic enclaves, since 45 percent of these groups would also have to be relocated to achieve complete residential desegregation.

In the past decade or so, many observers have noted a growing sense of positive pride and reidentification with their "roots" or heritage among many white ethnics. Novack (1978) labels this new tendency toward greater ethnic self-awareness as the "new ethnicity." In a series of articles, Novack (1971, 1972, 1973, 1978) variously attributes the new ethnicity as a reaction to the growing consciousness and militancy of blacks; to the emergence of scholars, writers, and artists who display ethnic themes in their work for the mass media; a decline in trust or respect for American leadership provided by the "WASP elite," which has been discredited by its handling of the Vietnam War or its mismanagement of domestic racial tensions (the older image of the truly cultured American of WASP descent is no longer compelling to many white ethnics, who are thrown back upon their own resources); and finally, the disdain for white ethnics displayed among the attitudes of "liberal, enlightened commentators on the crises of the cities," which heap contempt and ridicule upon the white ethnics for their supposed ignorance, uncouth life styles, or racism, as portrayed in "Archie Bunker."

Many white ethnics, with a past history of grinding poverty, exclusion from education, and denial of civil liberties, have a heritage that Novack suggests comes closest of any white Americans to the kinds of prejudice, discrimination, and oppression experienced by blacks. Yet a relatively common stereotype has emerged of white ethnics as racists who have produced a backlash of bitterness and resentment against the gains blacks have made in their struggle for greater social, political, and economic equity. Novack convincingly argues that this stereotype is unearned. He suggests instead that the white ethnic's real resentment is toward the established upper classes who are now asking the white ethnics to psychologically and economically pay for the historical injustices of slavery, the Indian wars, and other past patterns of racial and ethnic prejudice that were perpetrated long before the southern and eastern European groups arrived on these shores. As Novack puts it, "It has not gone without notice that the same elites that once called white ethnics Polacks, Hunkies, Micks and Guineas now call them racists, fascists, and pigs." Novack notes that in terms of racial attitudes, white ethnics are probably far less racist than WASPs in similarly sized communities. He points out studies purporting to show that the white ethnics are more likely to live in racially integrated neighborhoods, less likely to support racially segregated schools, less likely to have voted for George Wallace in presidential primary elections, and more likely to vote liberal in other respects (1973, pp. 18–25).

Novack represents those who strongly advocate the preservation of ethnic identification and diversity, so that a liberal democracy can evolve without submerging different ideas, cultures, and attitudes into an undifferentiated and powerless mass. He envisages a new kind of ethnic politics that would revive such groups from the status that others have called "forgotten Americans." The agenda for the new ethnic politics would focus on a strategy of social awards relevant to the ethnic neighborhoods in the large metropolis. These might include better garbage pickup, better financed and more orderly schools, long-range guarantees on home mortgages, and easier access to federally insured home improvement loans. But more crucial to this discussion is his proposal to provide special financing and help for ethnic neighborhoods that are beginning to integrate blacks:

> As a neighborhood moves from, say, a 10 percent population of blacks to 20 percent or more, integration should be regulated so that long-range community stability is guaranteed. It is better long-range policy to have a large number of neighborhoods integrated up to 20 percent or 30 percent than to encourage—even by inadvertance—a series of sudden flights and virtually total migrations. Institutional racism is a reality; the massive migration of blacks into a neighborhood does not bring with it social rewards but, almost exclusively, punishments (Novack, 1978, p. 272).

But Novack does not deal sufficiently with the strategies for bringing such residential racial balance about, nor does he satisfy those, including many white ethnics and blacks, who consider any sort of racial or ethnic quota system, or any other special treatment for racial or ethnic groups, to be totally unacceptable.

The new ethnicity is not universally advocated or admired, and there are those who doubt its intensity or staying power. Greer (1977), for example, suggests that the disturbing aspect of the new ethnicity among whites is that it represents a tribal kind of ethnocentrism based on the naïve belief that one's own kind are at the center of the world. Such tribalism is a dangerous toll for differentiating among a population and hating or persecuting those who are not liked because of their national origins or religion. But Greer (1977, pp. 156–157) also suggests that "the revival of ethnic tribalism seems largely a figment of the imagination of a few writers, themselves closer to the ethnic past than average, whether because of religion or recency of immigration. It is doubtful that they speak for, or even accurately of, the great mass of the American population." As is usually the case, the current status and identification of white ethnic Americans probably lies somewhere between the extremes presented by such writers as Novack and Greer.

In this chapter we have focused on those aspects of race and ethnicity that have been considered problematic for American urban centers. But to provide a more balanced perspective to this discussion, we will conclude with a lengthy statement by Charles Tilly (1970, p. 157), which is a remarkably useful summary of both the problems that have been fostered by past patterns of racial and ethnic migration to the cities and some of the policy potentials for alleviating those problems and maximizing the contributions that minorities add to the quality of urban life:

> As for the problems directly produced by migration ... they have been seriously misunderstood and exaggerated. Migrants as a group do not notably disturb public order, their arrival does not lower the quality of the city's population, they place no extraordinary demands on public services, and they

do not arrive exceptionally burdened with personal problems. These things happen to them later. The difficulties faced by inhabitants of ghettos and by cities containing them are not to any large degree products merely of migration.

Yet, in two ways the migrant *does* present a challenge to public policy. First, moving over long distance often imposes hardships and confusion on families at the same time as it cuts them off from the agencies that might be able to help them; instead of recognizing the special problems of people on the move, American public services tend to discriminate against them. Second, the newcomer—already by definition an innovator, having an advantage in age, education, and skill, bound to the old ways of his new city by fewer commitments and routines—is in an extraordinarily good position to take advantage of programs breaking down racial barriers, if only they are open to him. The challenge is to make maximum use of the migrant's talents, give him the greatest possible access to the rewards the city has to offer, make sure he can get past the personal crises almost all big moves involve without breaking down, and assure that he has attractive alternatives to the social and geographic isolation of the ghetto.

SELECTED BIBLIOGRAPHY

DENTLER, ROBERT A. *Urban Problems: Perspectives and Solutions.* Skokie, Ill.: Rand McNally, 1977.

FARLEY, REYNOLDS. "The Changing Distribution of Negroes within Metropolitan Areas," *American Journal of Sociology* 76 (January 1970): 512–529.

FEMMINELLA, FRANCIS X. "The Immigrant and the Urban Melting Pot." In Melvin I. Urofsky, ed., *Perspectives on Urban America.* New York: Anchor Press, 1973.

GLAZER, NATHAN. "A New Look at the Melting Pot," *Public Interest* (Summer 1969): 180–187.

GOLD, HARRY, and SCARPITTI, FRANK, eds. *Combatting Social Problems: Techniques of Intervention.* New York: Holt, Rinehart and Winston, 1967.

GORDON, MILTON. *Assimilation in American Life.* Oxford: Oxford University Press, 1964.

GREBLER, LEO, et al. *The Mexican American People: The Nation's Second Largest Minority.* New York: Free Press, 1970.

GREELEY, ANDREW M. *Why Can't They Be Like Us?* New York: Dutton, 1971.

GREER, SCOTT. "The Faces of Ethnicity." In J. John Palen, ed., *City Scenes.* Boston: Little, Brown, 1977.

GRODZINS, MORTON. "The Metropolitan Area as a Racial Problem." In Harry Gold and Frank Scarpitti, eds., *Combatting Social Problems: Techniques of Intervention.* New York: Holt, Rinehart and Winston, 1967.

GUEST, AVERY M. "Residential Segregation in Urban Areas." In Kent P. Schwerian, et al., *Contemporary Topics in Urban Sociology.* Morristown, N.J.: General Learning Press, 1977.

HORTON, PAUL B., and LESLIE, GERALD R. *The Sociology of Social Problems.* 5th ed. Englewood Cliffs, N.J.: Prentice-Hall, 1974.

JOHNSON, D. A., et al. "Racial Discrimination in Rental Apartments," *Journal of Applied Psychology* 1 (1971): 363–377.

KANTROWITZ, NATHAN. *Ethnic and Racial Segregation in the New York Metropolis.* New York: Praeger, 1973.

MARSTON, WILFRED G. "Socio-Economic Forces within Negro Areas of American Cities," *Social Forces* (December 1969): 665-676.

MERTON, ROBERT K., and NISBET, ROBERT, eds. *Contemporary Social Problems.* 2nd ed. New York: Harcourt Brace Jovanovich, 1966.

MONTAGNA, PAUL D. *Occupations and Society: Toward a Sociology of the Labor Market.* New York: John Wiley, 1977.

MOORE, JOAN W. *Mexican Americans.* Englewood Cliffs, N.J.: Prentice-Hall, 1970.

NOVACK, MICHAEL. "Further Thoughts on Ethnicity," *Christian Century,* January 10, 1973.

―――. "The New Ethnicity." In John and Erna Perry, eds., *Social Problems in Today's World.* Boston: Little, Brown, 1978.

―――. *The Rise of the Unmeltable Ethnics.* New York: Macmillan, 1971.

―――. "What the Melting Pot Didn't Melt," *Christian Century* (April 19, 1972).

PADILLA, ELENA. "Race Relations: A Puerto Rican View." In Robert K. Yin, ed., *The City in the Seventies.* Itasca, Ill.: F. E. Peacock, 1972.

PALEN, J. JOHN. *The Urban World.* New York: McGraw-Hill, 1975.

PARENTI, MICHAEL. "Ethnic Politics and the Persistence of Ethnic Identification," *American Political Science Review* (September 1967): 717-726.

PARK, ROBERT E. *On Social Control and Collective Behavior.* Chicago: University of Chicago Press, 1967.

PETTIGREW, THOMAS F. "Race and Intergroup Relations." In R. K. Merton and R. Nisbet, eds., *Contemporary Social Problems.* 4th ed. New York: Harcourt Brace Jovanovich, 1976.

―――. *Racially Separate or Together?* New York: McGraw-Hill, 1971.

Report of the National Advisory Commission on Civil Disorders. New York: Bantam Books, 1968.

RITZER, GEORGE. *Working: Conflict and Change.* 2nd ed. Englewood Cliffs, N.J.: Prentice-Hall, 1977.

SCARPITTI, FRANK R. *Social Problems.* New York: Holt, Rinehart & Winston, 1977.

STEINER, STAN. *Raza: The Mexican-Americans.* New York: Harper & Row, Pub., 1970.

TAUBER, KARL E. "Racial Segregation: The Persisting Dilemma," *The Annals* (November 1975): 87-96.

―――, and TAUBER, ALMA F. *Negroes in Cities.* Chicago: Aldine, 1965.

TILLY, CHARLES. "Race and Migration to the American City." In (Wilson, 1970), pp. 144-169.

WILSON, J. Q., JR., ed. *The Metropolitan Enigma.* Garden City, N.Y.: Doubleday, 1970.

WIRTH, LOUIS. "Urbanism as a Way of Life," *American Journal of Sociology* 44 (July 1938), 3-24.

YOUNG, WHITNEY M., JR. *Beyond Racism: Building an Open Society.* New York: McGraw-Hill, 1969.

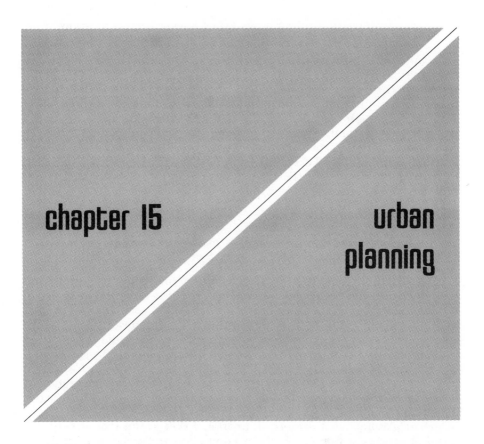

chapter 15

urban planning

The planning of cities is regarded variously as an ivory-tower vision, a practical and necessary program for development, or an undesirable interference with the citizen's freedom to do as he wishes with his own property. Some citizens see planning as a dictatorial force compelling people to do as the government directs. Planners see themselves as servants of the people who are trying to make the city a better place in which to live but who are circumscribed by legal and political restrictions. The truth lies somewhere between these extremes.

—Thomlinson, 1969

David Riesman (1956) has described the city planner hopefully, as a new Renaissance man who ultimately would have great positive influence in shaping the quality of life in modern urban society. But Jane Jacobs (1961) sharply criticized urban planning in her popular book, which opens with the sentence, "This book is an attack on current city planning and rebuilding."

As this suggests, urban planning is a very controversial and complex field. Many of the recent controversies and debates revolving around urban planning efforts such as urban renewal and slum clearance, economic redevelopment of central business districts, housing, and suburban land use controls have arisen because urban planning has emerged as a potential source for producing visible changes in the current urban scene.

In general, urban planning is primarily concerned with the most direct physical, social, and economic consequences of urban growth and development, as reflected in the general pattern and character of land use, the location of physical structures and facilities, the design of street, transit, and transportation systems, and the nature of and distribution of other physical facilities and services considered necessary or desirable for the economic betterment, comfort, convenience, and the general welfare of life in urban communities. Taken by themselves, the problems associated with urban planning are of sufficient magnitude and complexity to warrant separate consideration in this chapter.

THE EMERGENCE AND EARLY DEVELOPMENT OF URBAN PLANNING

We will begin our discussion by reviewing the emergence of urban planning in its own concrete sociohistorical context. It is very difficult to establish the theoretical relationship between a broad and general social process such as urbanization and major institutional responses such as the emergence of new organizational structures and occupations associated with urban planning. The emergence of urban planning in the United States can best be understood in the context of a series of at least three historically related and intertwined developments: 1) the emergence of planning as a social movement; 2) the emergence of planning as a legitimate and continuing function of local government; and 3) the emergence of urban planners as a distinct occupational skill group that attempts to apply in practice a specified body of knowledge and techniques, and that occupies a more or less specific set of role positions in the structure of local government.

Planning cities is not a new development, of course, and examples of planned cities go back several thousand years in history (see Chapter Two). Even in the United States, planned cities were a part of its early history: William Penn laid out a planned street system for Philadelphia in 1682; a plan was made for the fire-swept city of Detroit in 1807; an important plan was prepared for Manhattan Island in 1811; and the original plan for Washington, D.C., was prepared in 1802. Nevertheless, these were examples of fragmentary, isolated efforts and did not in themselves generate a full-scale social movement.

The origins of city planning as a modern social movement can most accurately be traced back to the demands for social reform in both England and the United States near the middle of the nineteenth century. These demands were a response to some of the conditions associated with the industrial revolution, which brought extremely large numbers of people to the cities and helped create urban slums and blight, overcongestion, and a variety of related health and sanitation problems. The concentration of large numbers of people in relatively small land areas made itself felt in intolerable living conditions and in repeated epidemics of major proportions (see Chapter Three). As early as 1834, a sanitary report from New

York City called attention to bad housing as a cause of disease, and a second report, submitted in 1842, was even more detailed and insistent in pointing out the relation between the two. The first tangible result of these studies and of agitation for improvement was the creation of a New York City Health Department in 1866 and the passage of the first tenement house law in 1867. In 1879 a law was passed prohibiting the building of rooms without windows, and in the latter part of the nineteenth century New York and many other large cities began making adequate provisions for the disposal of sewage (Gold, 1965).

A more indirect and somewhat separate attack on the emerging problems of urban overcrowding and congestion was the recreation movement of the latter part of the nineteenth century, which concerned itself with the development of large urban parks, the preservation of scenic resources in and around the larger cities, and the development of playgrounds in the more congested urban areas. Under the direction of leading figures of this movement, such as Frederick Law Olmsted, the city of New York laid out Central Park in 1857, and before 1900 park plans had been prepared for many of the larger cities. Many of the early parks were landscape developments designed primarily to preserve natural scenery and provide passive relaxation. But the need for more active recreation was soon recognized, and a demand rose for a comprehensive park system that would supplement large parks with readily accessible neighborhood recreation areas. In 1893 a study of Boston's park requirements stressed the need for such a program and led to legislation creating the Metropolitan Park Commission. This and the similar park program being carried to completion by Kansas City about the same time set a new pattern of comprehensive park planning (Walker, 1950).

However, the fragmentary and isolated efforts being made to ameliorate problems of urban congestion, poor housing, inadequate facilities for transportation, sanitation, and a host of other needed services were inadequate, and around the turn of the century recognition grew that

The Boston Public Gardens located in the middle of the city are an example of the urban parks development to preserve scenic beauty within the inner city. (Boston Chamber of Commerce)

a more comprehensive approach to solving these problems was needed. Those interested began to realize that all of the problems were highly interrelated. It has been suggested that this realization, along with a growing awareness of the necessity of mapping long-range programs and of anticipating future developments, as contrasted with piecemeal corrective measures, produced the mainspring of modern urban planning (Gold, 1965).

In England these same concerns gave rise to the town planning or "garden city" movement. Led by such men as Patrick Geddes, this movement called for the creation of new self-sufficient and self-contained garden cities decentralized from the existing urban centers. It was based for the most part on utopian concepts envisaging a return to the less complex organization and physical appearance of smaller preindustrial communities of the past (Mairet, 1957; Leggitt, 1964).

The garden city movement was influential in the development of numerous experimental communities in England, Europe, and the United States in the early part of the twentieth century, but was not particularly influential in the later development of urban planning in the United States, where the planning of new cities has been limited to a few notable examples which we will discuss later. For the most part, American planning activities have been focused on replanning communities that have already been built. Thus, the main American experience has been a distinct departure from the earlier examples of planned cities and from the garden city movement.

Another important aspect of the early phases of the modern city planning movement in the United States was certain civic improvement organizations' growing concern with improving the appearance of their communities. Beginning in the last part of the nineteenth century and lasting roughly until World War I, this phase has been identified as the "City Beautiful" movement (Perloff, 1957). Partially inspired by the garden city movement, the major emphasis was on the esthetic appearance of the city, as reflected in civic centers, parks, streets, and landscapes. Much of the inspiration for this movement was drawn from the Chicago World's Fair of 1893. Returning visitors, impressed by the architectural splendor of the exhibits, stimulated popular interest in civic esthetics.

One of the first major results of this movement was the appointment in 1900 of a committee consisting of three architects and a sculptor, all of whom had been associated with the Chicago Fair, to restudy the plan of Washington, D.C. This was the first of a long series of similar plan reports and city plans, each prepared as a unit by professional consultants drawn from the fields of architecture, landscape architecture, and from the earlier developed field of park planning.

Real estate boards, private builders, and bankers were among the private civic groups influencing this phase of the planning movement, and while they may have viewed the ugliness, crowding, and lack of public facilities as among the worst features of urbanization, they probably were also seeking symbols of their own status and achievement through the creation of urban "monuments" to enhance the physical image of their own cities (Perloff, 1957).

Save only a few notable exceptions, the plans advocated and prepared by the earlier protagonists of planning received no official or legal status and usually were never implemented. Most of them have been characterized as little more than broad outlines of future possibilities designed to arouse public enthusiasm (Walker, 1950). Also, the actual producers of the plans, usually architects or landscape architects hired by the private civic groups on a consultant basis, usually had no official affiliation with the municipalities their plans involved.

The next phase of the planning movement, which dated roughly from the Burnham plan for the city of Chicago of 1909 to the late 1920s, began to focus on the efficient functioning of cities and the rational coordination of municipal services. Perloff (1957) has labeled this phase of the planning movement the "City Practical." It provided a set of goals that could be more easily incorporated into the ongoing process of city government, such as zoning and subdivision controls, public works, and other activities that could be justified on the basis of engineering and financial considerations. Also, the preservation and increase of property values associated with sound zoning practices most certainly were predominant factors in the early promotion of zoning as a necessary function of local government.

During the 1920s, the rapid acceptance and use of the automobile increased the importance of the control of traffic and the development of efficient street plans as major goals of the "practical" phase of the planning movement. The economic boom also greatly expanded the construction of mass housing, which in turn increased the concern for building, safety, and environmental standards.

The evolution of structural steel has created new urban skylines in Dallas and the rest of the world. (Squire Haskins Photography, Inc.)

The 1930s saw the planning movement continuing cumulatively to broaden the scope of its goals and activities into a more comprehensive attack on urban problems. The disorganizing effects of the depression were instrumental in focusing heightened attention on such economic and social problems as slums, poverty, inadequate housing, disease, and others that had been glossed over in many of the architectural or engineering-oriented activities of the planning movement during the 1920s. The 1930s also were characterized by the planning movement's increased interest in the administration and organization of planning as an integral part of local government (Walker, 1950). Closely related was the growing concern with intergovernmental relations and with planning for a wider variety of geographic and governmental units, such as counties, metropolitan areas, regions, and states, leaving the boundaries of the units for which planning is done open to almost all possibilities. This trend probably led to the use of the more generic term "urban" planning to describe the movement instead of the more restrictive concept of "city" planning, although these terms now tend to be used interchangeably (Gold, 1976). In fact, city planning, urban planning, regional planning, town planning, comprehensive planning, physical planning, and land use planning are now among the labels intermittently used by the agencies and professionals involved in planning for the orderly growth and development of urban communities.

As mentioned earlier, the initial activities of the planning movement in the United States largely were carried out by civic improvement associations promoted and financed mostly by a small handful of philanthropic and civic-minded individuals who had begun to turn their attention to the esthetic and physical problems of the urban community. A subsequent organizational development was the emergence of private or lay city planning committees, which eventually replaced the efforts of the initial civic improvement groups. These committees were also unofficial, and they were led mainly by business and professional groups interested in protecting and increasing property values in their communities through street improvements, zoning, and the like. These unofficial committees laid the groundwork for the public acceptance of planning and led in the establishment of official city planning commissions, which ultimately replaced the earlier private organizations.

In 1907, some decades after the emergence of city planning as a social movement, the first official planning commission in the United States was created in Hartford, Connecticut. The major functions of the first planning commissions included the preparation of zoning ordinances and long-range "master" plans for community development. Initially, the planning commissions had little or no formal authority, and they functioned primarily as separate advisory boards to the executive and legislative branches of local government, to be consulted largely at the discretion of the mayor or city council. In theory, the planning commissions were supposed to represent a broad cross section of community interests, but in practice they usually were heavily overrepresented by realtors, architects, engineers, and lawyers. This was often justified on the grounds that appropriate technical knowledge or professional training contributed the most desirable qualification for membership on a planning commission

(Webster, 1958). Such disproportionate representation continues to the present, now more of a carry-over of an earlier pattern rather than a functionally sound prerequisite. At any rate, the particular occupational composition of the earlier planning commissions was crucial in spelling out their activities and technical focus until a distinct planning occupational skill group, with its own alleged body of knowledge and techniques, actually emerged.

The breadth and limitations of the technical scope of planning in its early days as a new function for local government can best be illustrated by a summary of the contents of the major plans of that period. An extended survey of plans prepared in the late 1920s reported that they typically were restricted to the following range of topics:

> A commonly used classification divides a comprehensive city plan into six main elements: zoning, streets, transit, transportation (rail, water, and air), public recreation, and civic art or civic appearance. Taken together, street planning, land subdivision regulations, and zoning are counted on to motivate the types of land development and housing which the city plan aims to secure, so that in many plans housing does not appear as a separate element (Gold, 1965, p. 34).

During the depression era of the 1930s, expenditure was somewhat cut back for many local physical improvement programs with which city planners were closely identified, a minor setback in the development of city planning programs and agencies at the local level. Instead, federal agencies such as the WPA, NRA, FHA, and the newly created National Planning Board were created and made funds available for dealing with a wide range of economic and social problems of human welfare on a national scale.

But despite some of the advances in its technical scope and its acceptance as a legitimate function of local government, on the whole urban planning had not made any significantly visible impact on the urban scene in the United States before World War II. Planning activities were few, planning commissions had little or no power to effect changes in the structure and processes of urban areas, and the movement itself was little more than a handful of individuals attempting to advance the cause of planning, while at the same time accomplishing little more than preparing master plans, which were usually ignored, discarded, or filed away for some indefinite or vaguely defined future use.

Since the end of the war, however, the picture has changed markedly. The postwar population explosion, the boom in housing and transportation, the rapidly growing suburbs, the declining central cities, the increased social and geographic mobility of the population, and the resultant demands for higher standards in all phases of urban living led to the dramatic postwar expansion of the planning field. Many of the current controversies and debates surrounding planning efforts in such areas as urban renewal and slum clearance, mass transportation, suburban housing and development policies, recreation facilities and other public facilities arise because urban planning has begun to be recognized as a visible agent of change on the current urban scene.

The current scope of urban planning is so broad and varied that at times it seems to defy description. Unfortunately, no comprehensive and systematic survey of the technical scope of planning activities in the United States has been undertaken recently enough to be of any value here. However, a number of qualified observers have in somewhat more general and impressionistic terms attempted to spell out the focus and boundaries of contemporary urban planning activities, and their descriptions can be presented with the assurance that they illustrate the scope of the planning process well enough for our purpose.

Planning Objectives

Webster (1958), for example, has suggested that the scope of urban planning is almost as broad as the entire range of municipal activities. A summary of the scope and methods of urban planning by the faculty of the Massachusetts Institute of Technology School of City and Regional Planning suggests that the determination of planning objectives is the most important part of the planning process, and these have been summarized as follows:

> *Economic:* efficiency of land use and circulation patterns; preservation or enhancement of the economic base. *Social:* adequate provision for human needs; work, home, play; maximum choice of living environment; congenial social contacts; educational and cultural opportunities within easy reach. *Physical:* sound land use planning (types, quantities, and relationships); proper distribution and density of population (present and projected); efficient circulation and services; preservation of scenic and historic areas and other amenities (Gold, 1976, p. 846).

The range of techniques required to achieve these goals includes two- and three-dimensional physical design, social and economic analysis, research techniques and survey methods, and the varied techniques of law and public administration. These techniques extend the planning process from the preliminary survey through the formulation of a comprehensive master plan to its ultimate implementation.

Comprehensive Planning

The American Institute of Planners suggests that the practice of urban planning has as its central focus "the planning of unified development as expressed through the determination of the comprehensive arrangement of land uses and land occupancy and the regulation thereof" (Gold, 1976, p. 846). Goals of unified development are usually expressed through the determination of the desired comprehensive arrangement of land use and stated in a document variously referred to as a general plan, comprehensive plan, master plan, or other terminology as determined by the local enabling legislation and practice. This plan presents proposals for long-range unified development of the area of its jurisdiction. The plan considers individual functional elements of the community and the basic interrelationships among them, as, for example, the relationship of highways and transportation facilities to traffic generators such as commercial and industrial areas. The process of locating schools and growing residential areas so that children would not have to cross traffic hazards going to and from school would also involve considerations of the relationships among residential areas, the schools, and the transportation and highway systems.

The comprehensive plan usually is based upon analyses of current conditions and predictions of expected population changes, land capability, land use, transportation, geography, and governmental and political factors as influences on urban development. These analyses attempt to indicate which developmental alternatives might be most realistic and desirable. In its final preparation, the comprehensive plan may include maps, diagrams, charts, and symbolic design sketches. The plan usually includes recommendations on density, space, and location standards for private development, programs of public improvements, and public policies necessary to achieve a coordinated development of the community. The purpose of these plans is to present general policy proposals for desirable urban forms and processes.

Planners also are often engaged to do special studies of specific small areas within a larger containing community to determine their influence on other adjacent small areas within the community. These planning studies, when properly designed, are extensions of comprehensive community-wide planning concepts into smaller areas. In studies of smaller areas, the planner's function is to investigate the general character of the area in relationship to overall community considerations and to produce a design or program for improvement of the area. This is both a test of, and an implementation of, concepts in the comprehensive plan. However, the urban planner still deals with the concept of the small area in terms of overall community form and function and not merely with plans for specific buildings and construction projects.

Other planning activities may include developing standards for such governmental activities as subdivision regulations, the substantive provision of a zoning ordinance, a capital improvements program, and other public functions; the designation of certain areas for redevelopment, along with preliminary proposals for new land use; proposals for new thoroughfares; and identification of trends of land development that may create a need for new or expanded public and private facilities.

Finally, urban planning has continued to extend its boundaries from its already broad technical base by borrowing from newer techniques, which themselves have been expanding at a rapidly accelerating pace in other fields—mathematics and systems analysis, electronic data processing, aerial photography and photogrammetry, social work, community development, and community organization.

It follows from the discussion so far that the boundaries of urban planning lack a high degree of "functional specificity." The failure to provide a clearer notion of where the boundaries of the field are is at least partially due to the elaborate and complex division of labor associated with the planning function in local government. In the larger communities a staff of many persons with many different specializations typically is required, and these specialized skills are usually organized into as few as six or more than twenty functionally separate divisions within the planning agency. Thus, the planning activities undertaken by at least the larger planning agencies are extremely comprehensive in their technical scope and require a wide variety of technical skills.

URBAN PLANNING AS A CAREER

Most of the earliest technical tasks of planning were performed by part-time consultants, predominantly trained as architects or engineers and in some cases as lawyers or social scientists, none of whom were actually trained in the techniques of city planning as such. The first formal university training in city planning was introduced in 1909 in the form of a few separate courses given at the Harvard School of Landscape Architecture. Harvard also created the first graduate program in planning in 1923, but very few of the planning practitioners employed on the staffs of city planning agencies were actually trained in the city planning specialty before the end of the 1920s.

Nevertheless, by 1917 a small group of planning consultants had emerged who were trained initially in the fields mentioned earlier, but who conceived of themselves primarily as professional city planners, and in that year twenty-four of them met to form the American City Planning Institute. One of the stated primary functions of this new organization, now known as the American Institute of Planners, was to provide "a forum for the consideration of technical details of the new science of city planning." This event signalled the initial recognition of urban planners as a separate occupational skill group, distinct from the existing occupational groups from which they stemmed.

The current acceptance of urban planning in the United States can be measured in part by the fact that the American Institute of Planners now has more than 5,000 members nationally. Since the 1960s, over 96 percent of all cities over 10,000 population have had official planning commissions or boards, and approximately one-third of these employ their own full- or part-time professional planning staffs. Nearly one-half of them also employ the services of outside planning consultants (Gold, 1976).

Until the early 1950s, planning offices were staffed primarily by engineers, draftsmen, and architects, and the nucleus of the planning agency staff was the "planning engineer." More recently, economists, sociologists, social workers, statisticians, geographers, and people trained as public administrators have been employed by planning agencies in increasing numbers. But more and more, planning agencies are coming to be staffed by those who have been professionally trained as urban planners. A master's degree in city, regional, or urban planning, usually requiring two years of specialized study beyond the baccalaureate, is increasingly becoming the recommended ticket of entry to the profession.

One of the greatest areas of frustration in a planning career that is not always anticipated in advance is that planning goals are so very difficult to achieve, or take so long to achieve in actual practice. In its guidance litera-ture, the profession attempts to warn new recruits in this way:

> Perhaps the greatest drawback to many people is the fact that often you will not see the completion of a project to which you have devoted a great deal of time and effort. Many large-scale projects may take many years to get under way, and sometimes planning proposals are rejected by the public. This of course can be frustrating; but the planner must be able to withstand such pressures and continue to work toward desirable new goals even though he may often be exposed to sharp opposition from ill-informed or selfish interest groups within the community (AIP Vocational Guidance Brochure).

Yet another AIP policy statement suggests that a successful and satis-fying career in urban planning is a realistic possibility for one "who pos-sesses foresight; social consciousness; ability to analyze broad situations, and to synthesize multitudinous details in order to grasp common ele-ments; the broadest sort of imagination and interests; and the ability to engage in constructive and creative efforts involving relationships between the problems and factors of modern living" (Gold, 1965).

THE ATTITUDES AND VALUES OF URBAN PLANNERS

The diversity of backgrounds of people currently engaged in urban plan-ning would suggest that there is no common occupational frame of refer-ence among them. Thus, the goals of the various occupations that have been represented on the staffs of planning agencies tend to resemble their own previously existing job territories, as follows:

> A planner with a civil engineering background tends to emphasize drainage, sewer and water extensions, street-widening, elimination of grade crossings and street-car track removal; a planner with an architectural background tends to emphasize civic centers, monumental buildings, harmonious ex-teriors and quality of design; a planner with a landscape architectural back-ground emphasizes scenic vistas; a planner with a background in geography tends to emphasize topography, climate, weather, water resources, soil condi-tions, and land forms; a planner with a background in sociology tends to emphasize family and communal relationships, social interaction, physical influences on group and individual behavior and the social effects of planned as against unplanned environments; the planner with a background in public administration tends to emphasize the management functions of the chief

executive, capital budget programming, smoother relationships with the planning commission, the city council chain of command, and inter-departmental relationships; the planner with a background in law tends to ... (Gold, 1976, p. 847).

Many urban planners stress the idea of planning as a continuous process rather than an activity with definitely fixed outcomes, and they would argue that the planning process does not necessarily ensure that planners engaged in the process will necessarily share the same goals and objectives. Nevertheless, certain biases tend to occur among planning practitioners, and they can be roughly summarized as follows:

1. Planners generally view the highly decentralized, dispersed, or scattered pattern of development around existing metropolitan centers as inherently undesirable. Such scatteration supposedly reduces open space; leads to longer and more energy consuming journeys to work; minimizes the efficiency of providing community facilities; reduces choices in housing types and residential location, shopping, and access to community facilities; uses far more land than is necessary for urban growth; usurps land that should be retained in agriculture; destroys the countryside; and is somehow "undemocratic."

2. A nearly universal planners' bias is one in favor of the preservation of open space. This view is derived mostly from the middle-class suburban background of many planners, which associates the country and rural life with virtue and rectitude, and the city with sin and evil. According to this bias, if open space can be preserved and if people will but go see it, their lives will somehow be elevated.

3. Planners traditionally favor the maintenance of a strong central business district and the preservation of the density pattern of past cities. They assume that the city must have a high-density core, containing a large proportion of the area's shopping, banking, commercial, managerial, civic, public, educational, and cultural functions. Because central business districts have in the past provided for a large proportion of the cities' tax revenue, planners argue that they must do so in the future.

4. Planners often feel strongly that the journey to work should be reduced by shortening the distance between places of residence and places of employment. They assume that people desire to economize in travel time, distance, and cost.

5. Jane Jacobs (1961) has argued that planners have been traditionally biased toward rigid separation of housing and commercial land uses by zoning such various activities into distinct areas. However, that most planners do indeed share this bias is not certain, and many of them would probably support her own preferences for a more diversified mixture of residence, work, and places of entertainment in more densely concentrated city neighborhoods, such as are characterized by Jacobs's favorite example: Greenwich Village in New York City (Mumford, 1962). At least, it is fair to suggest that much of the suburban zoning legislation designed to protect residential areas from commercial or other mixed land use intrusions comes as much from the interests of the suburban residents and their

elected officials as it does from the recommendations of professional urban planners.

If these values are truly representative of American urban planners, they appear not to have been particularly successful in achieving the goals indicated, since most recent urban growth and development have been in a contrary direction. Metropolitan communities actually have become more dispersed and decentralized, open space within the metropolitan areas tends to get developed, the central business districts of many metropolitan centers have been declining in density and economic activity, and the journey to work may be increasing for many workers as the network of freeways emanating outward from and around the central cities makes this more and more feasible.

Some critics of urban planning (Erber, 1970) suggest that these trends represent the preferences of the general public as they participate in the free marketplace, and that it would be arrogant or undemocratic for "elitist" planners to interfere with "natural" economic and social processes. But many planners would argue that the public has not been sufficiently informed or provided with other alternatives, and that urban planning should supply such alternatives to the public for their consideration. Whatever the merits of these arguments, many of the planning goals specified above remain more as possibilities than actually realized accomplishments.

URBAN RENEWAL, NEW TOWNS, AND REGIONAL PLANNING

The 1950s and most of the 1960s saw widespread recognition of many of the problems of the cities and the burgeoning suburbs, as discussed in this and previous chapters. Many initiatives were undertaken at local, regional, and national levels to alleviate these through a variety of urban planning and public policy efforts. Although many of the programs and proposals were controversial, urban planners and public officials were optimistic that urban problems could be minimized or alleviated through the concerted and cooperative efforts of various levels of government, civic groups, and the private economy. But by the early 1970s many of these efforts had been abandoned as apparent failures, set aside for some vague future consideration, cut short before they were given sufficient opportunity to demonstrate their effectiveness, or blocked from implementation as too controversial by public opinion or organized interest groups. At this time, the possibility of massive public intervention in the affairs of American cities seems too cloudy to predict for the immediate future (although speculation on the future of urban life in general will be the topic of the following and last chapter). But since the quality of life in urban America is of continuing concern, and since the possibility does exist for a renewal of interest in federal governmental intervention or private investment and other public efforts to improve the urban environment, it is useful to examine some of the most significant urban improvement efforts of the recent past for the insights they might provide for the near future.

Urban renewal has become in recent years one of the most controversial and misunderstood aspects of planned urban redevelopment. Technically speaking, urban renewal is not necessarily an integral part of long-range comprehensive planning, as described in earlier sections of this chapter, because many comprehensive community master plans do not contain specific provisions for urban renewal and because some local urban renewal projects have been undertaken without reference to the guiding framework of a comprehensive community plan. In many communities, planning agencies and urban renewal agencies are independent, autonomous, and sometimes competing departments of local government.

The political, legal, and financial impetus for urban renewal in American cities was the Housing Act of 1949, as amended in 1954. Under this legislation, local communities were empowered to condemn, buy, clear, and redevelop inner city land that was considered substandard or was underused with respect to its potential value. The program was aimed at the clearance of areas designated as slums or likely to become slums in the near future. A major goal was the redevelopment by private developers of such land for new residential, commercial, or industrial uses that would be expected to enhance the value and desirability of the land, presumably for the benefit of the entire community. Financing of the program involved matching funds from the local community and the federal government, with two-thirds of the costs to be borne by the federal government. Control of the urban renewal projects was to remain in local hands, provided that certain federal criteria were met. To qualify for federal funding, the local community generally had to go through the following procedures:

1. The submission and approval of a Survey and Planning Application to develop an urban renewal project.
2. The undertaking of the necessary surveys to provide the data essential for programming the project and developing the urban renewal plan.
3. The submission and approval of project plans (application for a loan and grant to carry out the project).
4. The acquisition of properties.
5. The relocation of all families and businesses.
6. Demolition of existing structures.
7. The rehabilitation of any structures determined to be economically feasible for such treatment and permitted by the plan.
8. The installation of all public improvements such as roads, sidewalks, utilities, schools, parking lots, and parks.
9. The resale or other disposition of the cleared land to developers who have agreed to build in accordance with the provisions of the urban renewal plan.
10. Finally, the completion of the new construction (Palen, 1975).

The most relevant criticisms of those urban renewal projects that have actually been undertaken and completed have to do with their impact on low-income housing. Contrary to the original goals of the federally sponsored urban renewal program, many critics maintain that urban renewal to date has materially *reduced* the supply of housing available to low-income groups in American cities by replacing bulldozed slum housing with new luxury housing for higher-income groups or replacing housing with more economically profitable nonresidential commercial development, from which the investors and other commercially oriented groups have profited. Much criticism (Greer, 1965; Gans, 1968) points out that not only have emotional burdens been imposed on low-income groups (predominantly blacks or other ethnic minorities) by involuntarily relocating them from their established neighborhoods but also that urban renewal has not always adequately compensated the relocated groups for their losses—it has not necessarily provided them with better housing or neighborhood facilities than those from which they have been evicted. Of course, this is not so much a criticism of the general concept of urban renewal itself as it is of the particular uses to which urban renewal has been put. Many such critics would probably support urban renewal if it were used to provide more and better low-cost housing for low-income groups, and if relocation problems could be minimized or handled in more helpful and humane ways than they have been in the past.

At the same time, efforts to improve the economic vitality of cities through the redevelopment of commercial and industrial areas remain legitimate goals of the urban renewal process if cities are expected to provide adequate occupational opportunities for their residents or to provide an adequate level of public services. That urban renewal programs have had some notable successes (Palen, 1975) in visibly improving some local areas in the inner cities does suggest that urban renewal does continue as a valuable approach for redeveloping economically and socially declining areas in many cities. Therefore, to understand its potential as well as its past mistakes becomes increasingly important so that future urban renewal undertakings are better understood and planned than heretofore.

NEW TOWNS

The original conception of the new town or garden city movement, as indicated earlier in this chapter, called for the creation of new self-sufficient and self-contained cities decentralized from existing urban centers. The new towns were to differ sharply from the more conventional patterns of urban sprawl in that they were to provide much more in the way of city amenities than commonly associated with "bedroom" or "commuting" suburbs. The new towns were envisaged by their advocates as providing a balanced mix of economic, commercial, civic, educational, and leisure-oriented functions adequate to meet the daily needs of their resi-

Urban planners have to choose between restoring old buildings or tearing them down to rebuild modern structures. (Harry Gold)

dents. Estimates of the minimum population needed to support this range of functions vary anywhere from 30,000 to 100,000 inhabitants, with some running up to a maximum of approximately 250,000 inhabitants. The new towns, to be designed from scratch, would avoid the worst aspects of existing urban centers by rational planning and would be kept separated from these existing centers by rural "green belts." The green belts would maximize a desirable balance between city and countryside and preserve

the natural and agricultural amenities directly accessible to the residents of the new towns for their convenience and enjoyment. The new towns would provide a heterogeneous variety of housing types to accommodate people of various socioeconomic levels or at various stages of their life cycle, and they would decrease the pressures on the burgeoning cities by absorbing some of their surplus populations.

In the United States, the federal government experimented with a program of new towns in the early 1930s. Three such garden cities actually were built: Greenbelt, Maryland; Greendale, Wisconsin; and Green Mills, Ohio. However, they were never fully completed, as the federal government eventually withdrew support because of a shortage of funds and the intrusion of World War II. These experiments did produce what are still considered attractive commuter suburbs, but the new-town vision of supplying jobs to its residents through the development of self-sufficient local industries was never fully realized. Also, the green belts that were supposed to surround these towns gradually succumbed to other uses, as nearby cities extended their suburban development radius. Thus, these experimental new towns have become nearly indistinguishable from the sprawling suburban subdivisions now surrounding them.

After World War II, interest in the new-town movement revived, this time most of them financed and sponsored by private investors. In the 1960s President Johnson called new towns the communities of the future. To many architects and planners, they were a blueprint for easing the ills of the inner city and the sprawl of suburbia. New towns would be carefully planned to meet the housing, recreational, and commercial needs of millions of people, rich and poor, black and white. There would be lakes and parks, townhouses and high rises. Shoppers would be able to walk to malls in town centers, while workers would walk to jobs in landscaped industrial parks. The federal government, through the newly created Department of Housing and Urban Development, was to assist by helping some of the developers secure government-guaranteed loans or subsidies. In all, approximately sixty-four new communities were undertaken or completed between World War II and 1970 (*Newsweek,* November 29, 1976). But whether most of these actually met the conception or criteria of a new town is doubtful, since most of them were primarily large-scale residential tracts or retirement communities for the elderly.

The best-known new towns probably coming closest to their original concept are Reston, Virginia, and Columbia, Maryland, both in the vicinity of Washington, D.C. A newer example is Park Forest South, near Chicago. While Columbia does contain some federally subsidized moderate-income housing units, all three communities have been extremely costly to develop, and the available housing has been affordable mainly by upper-middle-class income groups. However, they have been moderately successful in achieving some racial balance through positive policies of racial integration. For example, it is estimated that 15 to 18 percent of Columbia's population is black (Palen, 1975). In most respects Park Forest South may be the best single example of successful new-town development. It has successfully integrated a minority population of 25 percent, attracted a new state university, and built an industrial park that provides a ratio of one job for every housing unit (*Newsweek,* November 29, 1976).

But while tens of thousands of people now live happily in new towns from coast to coast, and while several of these have drawn praise for their beauty and amenities, nearly all of them are financial flops. The new towns were an inherently risky financial venture for their backers from the start. To plan and develop a town completely can easily take twenty years or more. But before they can attract paying residents, the developers must spend heavily on "front end costs" to assemble the land and install the facilities, while paying taxes and interest at the same time. Even Reston and Columbia, among the most successful of the new towns, have not earned their developers a profit and are still in the red. As a result, most of the developers of existing new towns have indicated they will not build any more of them, and additional investors are not in sight for the near future. Just about everyone who has been involved in developing new towns agrees that ways must be found to cushion the heavy start-up costs, most likely involving federal subsidies of one sort or another. At the time of this writing, such aid from the federal government does not appear to be a top priority.

In addition, not all observers agree that new towns should be a top priority, with some, such as Downs (1976), arguing that any policies supporting them should be part of a balanced program that also recognizes the need to improve older core areas and to upgrade traditional forms of urban growth that are still likely to dominate the future.

Clearly, the new towns are no panacea for solving all existing urban problems, although they do afford opportunities for improving the quality of urban life for some segments of the population. But without changes in current public policy, the Restons and Columbias will merely remain showplaces or monuments to an idea that for the time being is not likely to develop on a large scale.

REGIONAL PLANNING AND REGIONAL GOVERNMENT

Large metropolitan regions in the United States are characterized by their extreme fragmentation into many separate and autonomous local political units (see Chapter Four). This political fragmentation seems to occur because technological advances in transportation and communications, which have permitted and encouraged the physical and economic integration of increasingly larger geographic areas, have not been accompanied by any real increase in government integration. The populations moving outward from the central cities have resisted annexation and have incorporated themselves into small residential enclaves, variously called cities, townships, or villages. The lack of fit between ecological and political boundaries has important consequences for the decision-making structure of the metropolitan regions. It means that no local government decisions applying to all parts of the metropolitan area are possible. Yet many of the social problems of urban areas can only be effectively controlled by an areawide political system. As some public officials note, air or water pollution does not recognize existing political boundaries, nor does crime, urban blight, epidemics, poverty, or traffic congestion. Governmental fragmentation, if it has not actually caused these problems, has nevertheless served to make their solutions more difficult. Perhaps this helps to explain the growing interest in the need for regional planning in recent decades.

Regional planning is a term generally applied to areawide or metropolitan planning efforts that are set up on a multijurisdictional basis. Such regional planning commissions have been multiplying in recent years, and it has been estimated that more than 560 regional planning commissions now exist in the United States (Bollens and Schmandt, 1975). These have been set up to serve units of two or more counties, several municipalities, a combination of counties and municipalities, or a city and county jointly.

In most metropolitan communities, the regional planning commission is not an integral part of any of the local political entities, but serves instead an extragovernmental educational, promotional, or advisory function. An alternative form of intraregional cooperation among adjacent political units is a Council of Governments. This is a voluntary association of local governments that can provide an indirect means of integrating the planning functions more closely with the operating governmental units. Supporters of extragovernmental regional planning bodies see such agencies playing an "adjunctive" role in which they would serve as brokers among interdependent decision-making organizations, act as a regional lobby or a catalyst for action, and mobilize resources to achieve the appropriate regional goals. This view assumes that harmony will be achieved by bringing the realities of urban development and its accompanying problems into proper focus and by providing a framework within which local governments can cooperate with their neighbors while at the same time pursuing their own individual goals.

But many critics are skeptical of these approaches, arguing that nothing short of the complete integration of regional planning into the framework of a strong areawide or regional government will make such planning an effective force for sound regional development (Bollens and Schmandt, 1975). According to them, too much detachment is a serious weakness because it divorces planning from the program and decision-making processes of an ongoing public body with implementing powers.

According to Bollens and Schmandt (1975), the most desirable structural arrangement for regional planning is when the planning function is the responsibility of an areawide metropolitan government. But working examples of metropolitan government are still rare in North America, where resistance to the surrender of autonomy by local municipalities is still great. One notable exception is Toronto, where the metropolitan planning board is a component unit of a government possessing jurisdiction over an impressive array of areawide functions. Dade County and Jacksonville–Duvall County (Florida), and Nashville–Davidson County (Tennessee) are instances where the county government serves as the metropolitan government. But beyond these few instances, there is no clear evidence that American metropolitan communities are making the governmental and planning adjustments necessary to come face to face with the realities of metropolitan growth and dispersion. It is fair to conclude that the full potentials of regional planning and government cannot be adequately evaluated until they have been more widely implemented than they have been so far.

SELECTED BIBLIOGRAPHY

BARR, DONALD. "The Professional Urban Planner," *JAIP* 38 (1972).

BOLLENS, JOHN C., AND SCHMANDT, HENRY J. *The Metropolis*, Chapter 9. 3rd ed. New York: Harper & Row, Pub., 1975.

BUTLER, EDGAR W. *Urban Sociology: A Systematic Approach*, Chapter 21. New York: Harper & Row, Pub., 1976.

CAPUTO, DAVID. *Urban America: The Policy Alternatives.* San Francisco: W. H. Freeman & Company Publishers, 1976.

DAKIN, JOHN. "The Evaluation of Plans," *Town Planning Review* 44 (1973).

DOWNS, ANTHONY. *Urban Problems and Prospects.* 2nd ed. Skokie, Ill.: Rand McNally, 1976.

ERBER, ERNEST, ed. *Urban Planning in Transition.* New York: Grossman, 1970.

GANS, HERBERT. *People and Plans.* New York: Basic Books, 1968.

GOLD, HARRY. "The Professionalization of Urban Planning." Ph.D. dissertation, University of Michigan, 1965.

————. "Urban Change and Development: The Planning Approach." In Harry Gold and Frank Scarpitti, eds., *Combatting Social Problems: Techniques of Intervention.* New York: Holt, Rinehart & Winston, 1967.

————. "The Dynamics of Professionalization: The Case of Urban Planning." In George K. Zollschan and Walter Hirsch, eds., *Social Change: Explorations, Diagnoses, and Conjectures.* New York: John Wiley, 1976.

GREER, SCOTT. *Urban Renewal and American Cities.* Indianapolis, Ind.: Bobbs-Merrill, 1965.

HUBBARD, H. V., AND MEHINICK, H. K. "City Planning as a Professional Career," *Journal of The American Institute of Planners* (1942).

JACOBS, JANE. *The Death and Decline of American Cities.* New York: Random House, 1961.

LANSING, JOHN B., and MARANS, ROBERT W. *Planned Residential Environments.* Ann Arbor, Mich.: Institute of Survey Research, Survey Research Center, 1970.

LEGGITT, CAROL. *Social Values and Urban Form.* New Brunswick, N.J.: Urban Studies Center, Rutgers University, 1964.

MAIRET, PHILIP. *Pioneer of Sociology.* London: Lund Humphries, 1957.

MICHELSON, WILLIAM. "Planning and Amelioration of Urban Problems." In Kent P. Schwerian et al., *Contemporary Topics in Urban Sociology.* Morristown, N.J.: General Learning Press, 1977.

MOYNIHAN, DANIEL P. *Toward a National Urban Policy.* New York: Basic Books, 1970.

MUMFORD, LEWIS. "The Sky Line: Mother Jacobs' Home Remedies," *The New Yorker* 38 (1962): 168.

PALEN, JOHN J. *The Urban World*, Chapters 10 and 12. New York: McGraw-Hill, 1975.

PERLOFF, HARVEY S. *Education for Planning: City, State, Regional.* Baltimore, Md.: Johns Hopkins University Press, 1957.

————, ed. *Planning and the Urban Community.* Pittsburgh, Pa.: University of Pittsburgh Press, 1961.

RIESMAN, DAVID. *The Lonely Crowd.* New York: Doubleday, 1956.

SCOTT, MEL. *American City Planning Since 1980.* Berkeley: University of California Press, 1969.

THOMLINSON, RALPH. *Urban Structure,* Chapter 11. New York: Random House, 1969.

WALKER, ROBERT A. *The Planning Function in Urban Government.* Chicago: University of Chicago Press, 1950.

WEBSTER, DONALD H. *Urban Planning and Municipal Public Policy.* New York: Harper & Row, Pub., 1958.

WILSON, JAMES Q., JR. *Urban Renewal: The Record and the Controversy.* Cambridge, Mass.: MIT Press, 1966.

chapter 16

social policy and the future of urban life

BY JACQUELINE SCHERER AND HARRY GOLD

Throughout this book, the focus has been primarily on past and current trends in the process of urbanization. Much of what has been said here about urban life suggests that it is a complex and ever changing phenomenon. By the time we have begun to understand some of the forces that have been shaping the urban present, the even less well-understood forces that will shape the urban future are already underway. Predictions about the urban future by philosophers, scientists, planners, and ordinary citizens abound, ranging all the way from optimistic projections of a problem-free brave new urban world to the most pessimistic prophesies of doom for urban civilization as we now know it. Of course, nothing is absolutely certain about the direction of the urban future. But since current human activity is to a large extent based on anticipation of the future, it is important to look at some of the social, economic, and political trends of the present that seem most likely to extend into and shape the future, thus providing the key contexts in which the opportunities and problems of urban life are likely to unfold in the decades ahead.

Actually, the study of the urban future is old in many ways. Since ancient times, people have speculated about the future and have tried to visualize what was ahead. These speculations were more imaginative and fanciful than scientific, usually designed by philosophers who were concerned with the "good" community or the ideal state. Later science fiction provided a more realistic note to future dreams, particularly when actual scientists such as Leonardo da Vinci tried to imagine flying machines and other technical inventions. Some of the best science fiction today presents brilliant glimpses of the future. As one writer notes:

> One of the functions of science fiction is to serve as an early warning system. In fact, the very act of description may prevent some futures, by a kind of exclusion principle. Far from predicting the future, science fiction often exorcises it. At the very least, it makes us ask ourselves: What kind of future do we really want? No other type of literature poses such fundamental questions, at any rate explicitly (Clarke, 1977).

Artistic expressions of the urban future may also be found in abstract paintings and sculpture that also conceive of the world of tomorrow subjectively interpreted by the creator.

Social scientists have approached the study of the future with different methods, using empirical and logical techniques of analysis rather than original speculation. The study of social change, for example, has been at the heart of sociology since its inception, although what was traditionally and basically examined was the history of changes in social arrangement that had already taken place or were in the process. However, in the past several decades a branch of social science known as "futurology" has grown in importance. Futurologists are concerned with examining the future systematically, either by projecting current trends into the future or by projecting alternative future scenerios developed from contemporary situations.

The principal futurist argument (Gabor, 1964; de Jouvenal, 1963) is that the future is contained within a domain of alternative possibilities that may be specified by logical means and laid out in balance sheets that facilitate rational selection among the alternatives. Once this is done, policies to bring about the desired alternatives may be more effectively formulated.

In recent years, the methods for forecasting the future have expanded almost immeasurably in many different directions, and it has become much clearer that the particular vision of the future that is achieved will differ according to the method used. For example, Berry and Kasarda (1977, p. 426) have drawn up the following list of forecasting methods that have appeared in futurist literature:

1. Genius forecasting: a process of individual intuition and judgment.
2. Trend extrapolation: the concept that the historical changes and forces of change will continue into at least the near future.

The Mitchell Park Conservatory in Milwaukee, built between 1959 and 1967, exemplifies an artistic expression of the urban future. (Communications Division, Metropolitan Milwaukee Association of Commerce)

3. Modeling and simulation techniques: a conceptual image depicting the interrelationship of several parameters involved in a particular process or subsystem.
4. Historical analogy: the study of historical events and circumstances surrounding certain periods of change in an effort to generalize about what might happen under similar circumstances in the future.
5. Morphological analysis: all of the variables of a particular problem are defined and combined in all possible ways. The less promising combinations are weeded out, and goals or potential courses of action are selected from among the remaining alternatives.
6. Cross-impact matrix techniques: an attempt to assess the relationships between future policies and likely socioeconomic developments. Using questions of relationship and their impact on one another, an estimate of probabilities is derived of the items being considered with one another.
7. Delphi: an interactive survey process whereby group intuitive judgment is the basis for plausibility ratings for future developments.
8. Scenario writing: a process that demonstrates the possibility of future developments by exhibiting a chain of events that might lead them, and the interaction of complex factors in this chain.

The study of urban futures has led to the analysis of future patterns of urbanization and has spurred the collection of data in many different contexts. Demographers, urban planners, social policy analysts, and scholars in all of the fields concerned with urbanism and urbanization have become interested in projecting aspects of the future that seem both plausible and probable if particular conditions are present. There is general agreement that the future for the United States and for most of the world will be an urban one, since the historical processes contributing to the growth of urban societies are not likely to reverse the process. Further, most projections of future population growth trends suggest that the demands for shelter, food, and other basic essentials of living will require the kinds of complex social and economic organization that are characteristic of urban societies. However, within the broad range of these generalizations, much less agreement exists on the particulars of future urban life.

SOME HAZARDS OF FORECASTING THE FUTURE

Projecting the future throughout most of history was probably less risky a task than it is today. True, the unexpected always has occurred, and it would have been difficult even in the past to have imagined the social impact of many natural disasters, such as earthquakes, epidemics, floods, or volcanic eruptions, or the unusual circumstances that influence the outcome of a particular battle, war, or struggle for political power. Although predictable in some ways, the causes of plagues and epidemics were little understood. Until several centuries ago, however, the rates of social and technological change were probably more gradual and slow than they are now. Technology did not yet have as powerful grasp upon the daily lives of people, and the kinds of rapid technological transformations implied in terms like the "industrial revolution" or "urban revolution" had not yet occurred. In today's urban world, by contrast, the rate of change has so accelerated and its impact has become so severe that events now often outrun our understanding of what is actually happening.

Another "new" feature of the study of the future is the gradual recognition that purposes and goals—either clearly articulated or unconsciously pursued—will shape many of the crucial future developments. After more than a century of rapid technological change and a growing sophistication about the way social policies may influence and promote the direction of urban growth and development, appreciation for the powerful role of human purposes in shaping the future is growing. According to one scientist:

> ... man is now technologically capable of vetoing the continued evolution of his species. He can exercise that veto by the nuclear destruction of the race and the radioactive poisoning of his total environment. Or he can, by neglecting the development of food production and material resources, produce starvation. His ingenuity and capacity are such that he may reach out for the other planets, but his species as such must survive on the surface of this earth, subsist from nine inches which feeds, shelters or clothes him or from the seas, which cover seven-tenths of this small planet and from which he emerged all those hundreds of millions of years ago (Lord Richie-Calder, 1972).

In addition to an ever accelerating rate of change and to the growing realization that human purposes affect what areas of life will develop and grow, another complexity is produced by humanity's intellectual development and its capacity to foresee the future in a growing variety of ways, as suggested earlier. For example, sociologists have produced a competing number of theories of social change. One prominent sociological perspective concerning social change is the *structural-functional* perspective, in which social systems are viewed as having a strong tendency to reach a state of "equilibrium" between the different parts of the system. According to this perspective, if change occurs in one part of the system, it places strains on all the other parts, causing the entire system to develop mechanisms that will lead to equilibrium. But *conflict* theory has also emerged as a competing sociological perspective regarding social change. This perspective (Dahrendorf, 1959) argues that social conflict is a permanent condition of all human societies, and that one can find a constant struggle between different groups in a society trying to maximize their relative positions of wealth, prestige, or power. Relationships to the means of production or to the prevailing hierarchy of power and authority are among the alterative bases for social change. Given the nature of the struggles, social change inevitably is the result of such social conflict.

The debates among the proponents of the various theories of social change (see Zollschan and Hirsch, 1976) have not been resolved, although a good deal of historical analysis has been employed in the attempt. One's perspective on the urban future may very well depend on the particular perspective one has on the sources and nature of social change.

Finally, the complexity of even well-planned social change may render prediction difficult because of unintended or unanticipated social consequences. The invention and widespread adaption of the telephone as an instrument of communication is a case in point. When the telephone was first invented, many observers thought that it would lead to the end of urban congestion, enabling people to live at great distances from each other. Instead, as John Carty, the chief engineer of AT&T said in 1908:

> It may sound ridiculous to say that Bell and his successors were the fathers of ... the skyscraper.... Suppose that there were no telephones and every message had to be carried by a personal messenger. How much room do you think the necessary elevators would leave for offices? Such structures would be an economic impossibility (Weisner, 1977).

But such a judgment involved hindsight that was not available to an earlier forecaster:

> In 1877 the Chief Engineer of the British Post Office was asked if the newly invented telephone would be of any practical value. He replied, "No sir, the Americans have need of the telephone, but we do not. We have plenty of messenger boys" (Weisner, 1977).

Ithiel de Sola Pool (1977) has pointed out that the telephone also helped to build suburbia. It also has helped police catch criminals and criminals evade the police. It invades our privacy, but at the same time it can also protect our privacy. He concludes that the telephone is a facilitator that allows people to do more easily whatever it is they want to do. In these and many other ways, the telephone is just one of many possible examples of both an invention and a cultural adaptation that has and still is producing many unanticipated consequences.

With these kinds of forecasting hazards in mind, we shall now move ahead to review some of the major kinds of forecasts that have been made about the future of urban America. These involve some utopian as well as some decidedly nonutopian views.

SOME UTOPIAN VISIONS OF THE URBAN FUTURE

People have long searched for the ideal city. The forms of their conception of the ideal have varied from century to century. In the fourteenth century, for example, the English statesman and writer Sir Thomas More envisaged

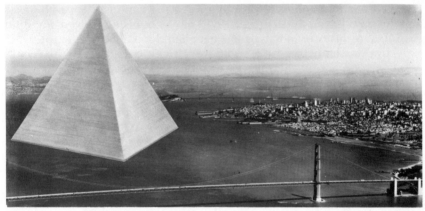

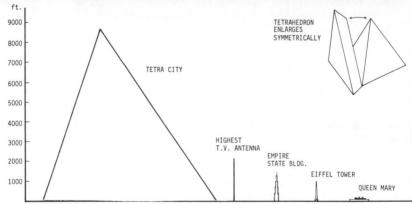

Future urban planning might include the "tetrahedronal city," shown here in an artist's rendering, which would accomodate one million people in a most efficient way. (R. B. Fuller)

an ideal society, which he called utopia in a major book of the same name. More presented a vision of a community where all sociopolitical ills had been eliminated and the entire social order was rationally reformed to benefit the community as a whole. Since the initial success of this work, the label *utopia* has been applied to all kinds of portrayals of the problem-free ideal community, no matter how impractical such fantasized projections may seem. From the rational scientific perspectives that have dominated the twentieth century, utopian visions of future cities usually have been described as fantasies too grandiose for a practical world and as representing the abandonment of all reason.

Yet utopian thought regarding the city seems to have experienced some revival during the past several decades, and utopian thinking has been defended by responsible social scientists as a useful tool for anticipating or planning the urban future. Meyerson (1961) has suggested that planners ought to recognize the value of utopian formulations in the depicting of the community as it might be seen through alternative normative lenses, while Dahl and Lindblom (1953, p. 73) suggested earlier that "as models, utopias . . . indicate directions in which alternatives to existing reality might be looked for, . . . help one to focus on long-run goals, . . . function as aids to motivation."

Eldredge (1974) has ably summarized some of the more extreme utopian visions of the possible urban future:

A. Megastructures or minicities.   These are commonly represented by Paolo Soleri's concept for giant supraterrestrial human "hives" housing up to hundreds of thousands of persons, or by Moshe Safdie's design for a "plug in, clip on" megastructure, which he called *Habitat,* and which was on display at Expo 1967 at Montreal. These concepts involve miniaturizing cities and building them so that they can be compactly arranged within a single, giant, enclosed megastructure, or within a close web of physically interconnected structures. Such cities would supposedly reduce time and space obstacles to human activity and would be the means for bringing "beauty, harmony, efficiency, and spaciousness" to cities. Dantzig and Saaty (1973) have prepared a detailed plan for a compact city that incorporates the ideas of the influential architect Le Corbusier and the city planning critic Jane Jacobs as well as those of Soleri. Their city would include a population base of 250,000 people residing in a compact area of approximately 2.2 square miles. The city would have a circular radius of 3,000 feet, which would be exactly eighteen times its height. Its core would contain shops, churches, and hotels; its core edge would serve as a parking area and would contain ramps for ascending and descending to various levels, as well as a promenade with small parks and recreation areas. The city would also have an inner residential area, a midplaza, and an outer residential area. Each part of the city would be interconnected by roadways featuring electrically powered automobiles, but only a very limited number of such vehicles would be necessary, because of the compactness of the city. Most movement of people would be on foot. In 1966, Governor Rockefeller of New York proposed a similar type of megastructure development for the lower tip of Manhattan. It was to consist of massive towers, high connecting bridges, dozens of highrise apartment houses with an elevated pedestrian mall surrounded by other physically interconnected dwellings housing thousands of people. The entire project, if ever undertaken, was to be developed on a large land fill totaling approximately ninety acres.

B. Water cities. These involve large scale "futuristic" designs for enormous activity nodes standing on stilts in shallow coastal waters. They would include Buckminster Fuller's concept of floating communities of 30,000 persons in up to twenty-story-high structures sitting on ferro-concrete platforms, which could be built in shipyards and towed to usable places just offshore of existing coastal cities and anchored in water up to twenty or thirty feet in depth. There have been similar proposals for Tokyo Bay and for Baltimore Harbor, and some advocates conclude that floating settlements on the oceans would be considerably less costly than settlements on difficult to develop land formations (mountains, swamps, deserts, frozen soil) within the next century or so.

C. Underwater, underground, or space cities. Jacques Cousteau has collaborated in the design of a floating island in which ". . . more comfortable dwelling quarters may be floating stably a hundred feet or so below the surface where any wave motion is so damped as to be unnoticeable" (Eldredge, 1974). Huge salt mine caverns have been proposed for underground experimental cities that could have community temperature and atmospheric controls, which would be especially desirable in hot desert areas or subarctic regions. All of these kinds of proposals have been widely illustrated in countless science fiction novels and films, and not uncommon, of course, are the science fiction-like proposals to ease the environmental burden of the planet earth by developing extraterrestrial space communities and opening up the solar system to human settlement.

D. The Wired City. Here, the city becomes a nonterritorial, high-intensity participatory community fitted to a national cable/microwave grid of metropolitan multichannel informational networks, reinforced or supplanted by satellite connections and lasers. Computers serving both as storage facilities and as analysts with display capabilities would be at the center of this technology, based on the infinite possibilities of multichannel electronic communications and interaction. In the wired city, every dwelling would have a typewriterlike keyboard with printout capabilities and a display screen located in a home recreation, information, or business center. Communications would become a substitute for outmoded and costly transportation systems, which would become less necessary. Distance, which is an important consideration in transportation, would become almost irrelevent in the wired city.

E. Communes. Communes are in a sense one of the most concrete expressions of utopian goals. They are experimental attempts to create new and appealing life styles as alternatives to the traditional features of modern urban-industrial life. Generally seeking "freedom," "love," or "escape," thousands of groups have been seeking to create such innovative communities in the United States during the past and present centuries. Some of the better known nineteenth-century efforts include the celibate New England Shakers, the Owenites at New Harmony, Indiana, or the Oneida community of New York State. More recently, the counterculture of the so-called hippie youth movements and the religious-political cults such as the Manson Cult or the People's Temple, for better or worse, have created a wide diversity of experimental communelike alternative life styles. Despite the murderous and dehumanized results of a very small number of these innovative communes, Eldredge (1974, p. 34) argues that "such exotics must not be crushed." As he further states, "The affluent West affords millions of the idle rich, non-producing youngsters, idling oldsters and millions of unemployed; it most certainly can afford a few tens of thousands of experimenters seeking a better life on earth. They might even have something!"

The list of utopian designs for the urban future could go on and on. But the major criticisms that can be made about such utopian images of the urban future is the oversimplicity of many of the alternatives represented. Although imaginative, usually in terms of a reordered physical or technological environment, most of them do not involve the social, economic, or political dimensions essential for dealing with the complexities of a new kind of urban world. Sociologists, aware of the complexity of contemporary social arrangements, and anthropologists, recognizing that everyday realities in all cultures rest upon a complicated web of assumptions, values, and adaptive behaviors, are acutely aware of how limited is our understanding of such social complexities. Likewise, political scientists and economists are equally aware of the danger of projecting the kind of technological determinism that is often reflected in the physical designs for projected utopian communities. With these cautions in mind, several nonutopian visions of the urban future will be reviewed. They are more limited in scope and more tied to an empirical assessment of the realistic constraints that make it highly unlikely that perfection is ever achievable in the social and physical arrangements of human communities.

SOME NONUTOPIAN VISIONS OF THE URBAN FUTURE

Some of the most common types of forecasts of the urban future by social scientists are based on the extrapolation of trends that are currently underway and extend into the near future. Chinoy (1972), for example, forecasts continued metropolitan growth, greater growth in the suburbs than in the cities, continued white migration out of central cities, central cities becoming proportionately more black in population composition, less densely populated cities, fewer jobs available in cities for their residents, and more unplanned growth. Cohen (1976) has listed some of the problem areas that will remain difficult to manage in an urban future that arises from the "more of the same" that is forecasted: 1) the changing size of the metropolitan cities; 2) the increasing bureaucratization and professionalization of

Detroit's newly constructed Renaissance Center has not only added to the city's revitalization but has also expanded its tourist industry. (Renaissance Center)

municipal services; 3) the growing distance between the centralization of decision making and the points of impact; 4) the explosion in public demands and expectations; 5) the growing complexities of federal-state-local interdependence; 6) the increasing breakdown of formal political machinery at the local level; 7) the scale and character of future migration patterns; 8) the interdependency of urban living; 9) the metropolitanization of many urban problems; 10) the inadequacy of the political arrangements for mayoral leadership; 11) the inability to adequately renew older sections of the city; and 12) more generally the pervasive mood of alienation and powerlessness alleged to be characteristic of urban life.

Projections such as these tend to imply a continued drift in the existence of already recognized urban social problems and a growing dissatisfaction with the quality of urban life. They also anticipate that there will be little motivation or initiative to make the radical changes required to redesign the urban future, so that, almost by default, a continuation of current social arrangements is likely to characterize the urban future.

One problem with these forecasts is that they tend to ramble over a diversity of unrelated issues in somewhat of a "shotgun" approach. But a potentially more coherent framework for anticipating the urban future in a more orderly way is the ecosystem approach mentioned in the introductory chapter. Using the ecosystem components of population, technology, environment, and social organization, the following discussion speculates on some possible future developments for urban America in each of these areas.

Population

To determine future population size, assumptions must be made along three dimensions: 1) fertility—how many children each woman will bear; 2) mortality—how many people will die, and at what age; and 3) migration—will people move, and, if so, to what new locations? Uncertainties about future trends in immigration and mortality are obvious, and to make responsible assumptions about the future course of fertility in projecting the population of the United States is even more difficult. Based on alternative assumptions developed by the Census Bureau, the projected population would range between 251 million and 300 million persons in the year 2000, and anywhere between 265 million and 392 million in the year 2020. (U.S. Census, Current Population Reports, Series P-25, no. 493, December 1972). These estimates assume that migration to the United States will remain at its current low levels, so that most of the increase in population size would then be due to natural increase—a surplus of births over deaths. But even the lowest and most conservative of these estimates forecasts sizable and continuing population growth for the United States in the near future. Just where that increased population will live is a major issue that must still be confronted.

If massive migration from rural areas to urban areas has just about leveled off, and no unexpected massive migration occurs from urban areas to rural areas (although a slight trend in this latter direction has been detected in the late 1970s), most of the population increases probably will take place in the existing metropolitan areas of the United States, or within daily commuting distance of these areas (see Chapter Four). What is not so certain is how the future metropolitan populations will be distributed among central cities and their suburban belts. If current trends continue, the large central cities will continue at their present population levels or lose population to the suburbs, which would continue to grow. If, on the other hand, a newer trend toward people moving back to the cities from the suburbs, which is now quite small, significantly accelerates, the cities might begin to again gain parity with the suburbs in their relative population size.

Of course, each of these sets of circumstances would pose different consequences for urban society. Political reapportionment and changes in the relative political power of cities and suburbs, and the resultant priorities of the federal government in aiding either cities or suburbs in spending and tax policies would be among the areas expected to be affected by changes in the relative distribution of the future United States population among cities, suburbs, and their surrounding regions.

The changing age structure of the United States is also another factor to be considered in assessing the urban future. In recent decades, due to declining fertility rates and improvements in longevity, the population has been aging, with larger proportions of elderly and retired people. This has been reflected in the changing priorities of the federal government. In 1969, the elderly were getting about 23 percent of the national budget in federal programs and benefits. In fiscal 1979, they got about 40 percent of the national budget, which was more in dollars than the entire federal budget for 1969 (Detroit Free Press, January 24, 1978, p. A1)! If fertility rates remain at their current levels or decline still further, and mortality continues to improve at its present rate, the elderly are expected to be an even larger proportion of the population in the future, and they will be an even more potent political force in demanding services and expenditures from the federal government (while at the same time demanding cutbacks in other programs not directly related to their own needs, such as schools and day care centers). If the elderly choose to reside primarily in cities, this can mean pressure for additional federal aid and appropriations to the cities. But if they choose to live elsewhere, the cities may be bypassed in favor of the more pressing priorities of the elderly elsewhere.

If the United States population continues to consume energy, raw materials, and manufactured goods at its current per capita levels, then expected population growth will most certainly create additional demands against the finite supplies of these resources. If new and cheaper sources of energy and raw materials are not found or developed, the rising costs and shortages expected are very likely to force consumption rates down, thus potentially lowering the American material standard of living. In anticipation of these problem developments the country is attempting to develop a national energy policy that will bring about these changes gradually and predictably, to ease the burden somewhat.

A growing population is also expected to increase the costs of land for housing as the available homesites in and around the major metropolitan centers are gradually used up. The increased costs of housing in the recent past has made single family home ownership increasingly impossible for a growing portion of the American population, and nothing is now in sight that is likely to alleviate this trend in the near future. This too will have a significant impact on the future standards of living and life styles in the United States.

Technology

Americans have always had a high degree of faith that science and technology could be used effectively to solve critical problems and to enhance the quality of life. Technology undoubtedly has contributed in many ways to the relatively high general health levels of the nation and to much more material comfort for the average individual than in prescientific eras. Many urban and social planners have seen future advances in social engineering and in communications and transportation as technological arenas for continuing to improve the workability and livability of urban communities. Adherents of advanced technology believe that it will eventually be able to provide an unlimited supply of energy from nuclear power, solar conversion, water, wind, or geothermal power, or from still other as yet undiscovered sources. According to them, science and technology can be relied upon to control the growth of the population, to solve problems of food shortages by increasing the food supply, and even to control climatic extremes.

But not all observers are so optimistic about the role of technology in shaping human life and values. Marcuse (1964) has argued that technological society is essentially enslaving, limiting human existence to one narrow dimension. As technology introduces itself into more and more spheres of daily living, it produces profound changes in the values and institutional structures of modern society. Slater (1971) argues that a technology-based value system is fundamentally antihumanistic, as it takes precedence over alternative human values, which increasingly become subordinate to the demands of technology. But not only philosophers and technological experts have increasing doubts about an excessive reliance on technology. Heilbroner (1974) asserts that recent years have witnessed a more general loss of faith in scientific progress and a reduction in the belief that movement toward a better state of affairs is inevitable. Many people now have become increasingly aware of the finite limitations on their ability to engineer social change and that many pressing problems tend to defy technological solutions. Also, more are aware that many well-intentioned technological improvements may yield unanticipated negative consequences that may far outweigh their benefits. As a result, many "watchdog" groups have arisen that seek to monitor the potential hazards of technological innovations and to resist those technological changes that rightly or wrongly are perceived to threaten the quality of life. Well-organized resistance to the deployment of nuclear power generating facilities in many regions of the country is one good case in point. The increasingly active role of the federal Food and Drug Administration in monitoring new drugs and medical procedures is another good example.

If such trends continue, we probably will not as blindly subscribe to technological solutions to social problems as we have in the past. Whether or not this will alter the degree to which technology will continue to exert its influence on the social values and institutions of the future remains to be seen. Certainly, no major technological panacea for the general problems of urban living is in sight for the foreseeable future.

Environment

In early 1978, the midwestern regions of the United States were digging out of one of the worst snowstorms in many decades. The entire transportation system was brought to almost a complete standstill, as major highways, local roads, local transit systems, railroads, and many airports were closed by the storm. Many deaths and injuries were attributable to the storm, and most business, governmental, educational, and social activities were severely curtailed for days. This is just a reminder that weather and climatic conditions still are capable of severely disrupting the daily rhythm of urban life, no matter how extensively technology has been employed to minimize such disruptions. Floods, droughts, hurricanes, tornadoes, earthquakes, landslides, forest fires, and other natural disasters also continue to occur often enough to remind us that human beings have not completely mastered the natural environment, even in the most technically advanced urban centers. Any reasonable prognosis suggests that natural environmental conditions will continue to intrude into the lives of both urban and rural dwellers for the knowable future.

In the United States, there has been an aggregate movement of people in the last several decades from the Northeast and Midwest to the South and West. The movement is also from the interior of the country to the peripheral coastal regions. There are many possible explanations for this movement, the one most appropriate here being a desire of many people and industries to relocate in the more moderate climate of the coastal regions and the "sunbelt." At the same time, the widespread adaption of central air conditioning has somewhat neutralized some of the more unpleasant aspects of the hot and humid summers of some of the southern areas now enjoying relatively high rates of industrialization and inmigration.

The environment of urban communities has been receiving heightened attention in recent years, as the negative effects of pollution, smog, and the depletion of natural resources on health and the quality of life have become increasingly more visible. While air pollution has long been recognized as a problem for urban centers, the chemical pollution of food supplies brought about by industrial wastes and insecticides has more recently come to the forefront of attention. As a result of certain public programs and policies, air pollution is now being contained or reduced in many American cities. As more is understood about chemical contaminants of food supplies, there is at least the hope that this problem can also be reasonably contained in the future.

But according to Meier (1974), the most difficult environmental problem of all will be ensuring adequate water supplies for metropolitan areas. In his survey of a variety of metropolitan crises during the 1960s, he found that problems of maintaining an adequate supply of clean water surpassed other natural disasters, energy failures, accidents, and even revolution, rebellion, or war as the crisis potentially most disturbing to large metropolitan areas over one million in population. The severe restrictions on water usage due to periodic droughts in areas of California is a good illustration.

In general, the future well-being of urban centers will rely extensively

Pollution is one of the environmental concerns that is affecting the quality of life in cities. (*Dallas Morning News*)

on the degree to which they can be brought in better balance with environmental and physical considerations. Nevertheless, these have been among the dimensions of urbanization most neglected by sociologists.

Social Organization

In the introductory chapter, urban social organization was described as a complex web of relationships among social units of increasing size and complexity. These units include individuals, primary groups, neighborhoods, social networks, voluntary associations, bureaucracy, and finally, at the largest and most abstract levels, major social institutions. Many of these units have been reviewed in the context of the territorially based local community, while it was also recognized that the larger and more complex units of social organization were beginning to take on national forms and no longer were limited to the boundaries of the local community.

Many observers project this trend into the future by suggesting that we are passing through a revolution that is "unhitching the social processes of urbanization from the locationally fixed local city or region to a scale of organization that is at least as wide as national urban society and may in fact be world wide in scope." Webber (1968) refers to this movement "from ancestral localism toward the unbounded realms of the cosmopolites" as an inevitable form of urban social organization he calls *high scale society*. Coleman (1976) further suggests that local communities are becoming less and less the building blocks of which society is composed, with a greater freeing of individuals from local community bonds, a trend that destroys local community organization. Of increasing importance, according to Coleman, are occupational groups, religious groups, political groups, and various other life-style groups, all of which may be organized on an extraterritorial basis.

Another long-term trend allegedly destructive of community organization is the growth of the mass media and the consequent invasion of the community by values, norms, and attractions from the outside world of national society. Coupled with these changes has been the transition from local decision making and attentiveness to problems of the local community to central decisions that destroy local community organization. Coleman suggests that this trend is very likely to continue, decreasing the capability of cities to develop strong and stable local organizational structures. In the view of Coleman, Webber, and others, all of these kinds of changes have important implications for the treatment of modern social problems, which no longer can be understood or treated in the local community context. Thus, problems such as crime, poverty, unemployment, broken families, race riots, drug addiction, mental illness, or juvenile delinquency no longer have their roots in the local communities in which they occur but are now national or supranational in origin. As Webber (1968 p. 1091) states: "We cannot hope to invent local treatments for conditions whose origins are not local in character, nor can we expect territorially defined governments to deal effectively with problems whose causes are unrelated to territory or geography."

There is no doubt that the United States has become a national urban society, and that much of modern urban life can best be understood at this scale of size and complexity. But it has been correctly pointed out by those who are more cautious that this does not necessarily mean that the smaller social units at the local community level will have disappeared or can be safely ignored:

> The city may indeed be finished . . . but someone apparently forgot to tell the inhabitants. For over fifty years sociologists have been predicting the imminent disappearance of localized ethnic and racial urban communities. . . . But the working-class ethnics and minorities who live in these neighborhoods have not yet heard that their life-styles represent a pre-industrial past and thus must inevitably fade away. The significance and strength of territoriality and ethnicity tend to be consistently underestimated . . . (Palen, 1977, p. 287).

Social institutions were described in the introductory chapter as representing groping trial and error adjustments to the complexities of urban living. It was further asserted that the survival and well-being of modern urban civilization are to a large extent dependent on how successful urban social institutions respond to the challenges confronting them. Throughout the book, challenges currently facing such institutions as the family, organized religion, government, the economy, social welfare, education, and urban planning have been discussed, along with some of the prospects for these institutions in the near future. The prospects for rational attempts at institution "building" were also introduced as relevant to at least some of these institutions (see Chapter Twelve). Increasingly, social observers and social planners emphasize the strategic importance of viewing these institutions on a national scale and as amenable to rational guidance. But here again, our working definition of social institutions (Chapter One) involves a complex web of relationships among relatively small and simple to relatively large and complex social units, many of which continue to manifest themselves at local or territorial levels of urban social organization. Thus, to assume that basic social institutions can be easily or directly modified by centralized social planning would be a mistake. It is far more likely that social institutions will continue to change from the bottom and middle levels as well as from the top, largely as a result of grass roots changes in the values and life styles of their members. These more or less spontaneous changes cannot be easily foreseen, anticipated, or guided by agents of planned social change. Paul Ylvisaker (Chinoy, 1972), for example, forecasts an urban way of life so intricate in its design and interdependencies that it will be extremely resistant and in some respects immune to frontal efforts to plan and order. He also fears that "urban culture, like amoeba, will be capable of infinite reproduction and will spread on its own volition."

Yet, keeping abreast of institutional proliferation and change may provide at least some opportunities for directing these changes toward socially useful purposes. "Alternative" institutions, for example, may be creative efforts to bring people together in ways that are more psychologically satisfying. According to Kanter (1972), the goals of alternative institutions are to "make work more meaningful, integrate life activities, distribute power more equitably, offer experiences of community and shared ownership, and replace stale myths with concepts that revitalize spiritual life." She adds that new values are being developed that challenge the traditional Western view of life, and she describes the alternative institutions as bringing a new sense of institutional boundaries that are more open, fluent, and subject to penetration and modification than the traditional social institutions.

Recent psychological investigations of personal coping mechanisms, the effects of stress upon health and well-being, and the impact of changing environments on personal development will probably provide some of the directions for building these new institutions (see Chapter Six). But Bennis (1968, p. 124) has described the future of these new alternative institutions as temporary and as characterized by "non-permanent relationships, turbulence, uprootedness, unconnectedness, mobility, and above all, unexampled social change." In even less flattering terms, Toffler (1970) speaks of "future shock" as a psychological condition with serious personal consequences. He suggests the development of a "transience index" that could disclose the rate at which people are making and breaking relationships with the things, places, people, organizations, and information structures that comprise the urban environment, as well as other indicators of measurable social change, so that such changes could be more effectively guided and regulated.

Michael (1968) has presented a view of the urban future based upon three critical factors. The first is increased complexity, which will be brought about by population increases, the expansion of urban areas, an expanded demand for human support services, the need to ease race tensions, a dramatic increase in the number of events that will occur, and an increase in the amount of available information and knowledge. The second factor will be increased turmoil, brought about by malfunctions in the social and physical environment, accidents, and incomplete or faulty information. The third factor will be scarcities of all kinds—not only physical resources, but scarcities of time and skill as well. As a result, Michael concludes that the technological ability to change the urban world will vastly exceed the ability to anticipate whether or not the urban world is being used wisely or well. This means that not only old institutions must be radically changed and new ones created, but that systems of checks and balances to control institutions and to keep them in harmony with one another must also be found or created. He suggests that these trends will lead to a much more extensive use of long-range planning, even though urban society is ill-prepared institutionally, methodologically, or in other ways to do it well. The implications for future urban policy making and implementation, of course, pose some enormous issues and challenges that will be most difficult to resolve.

SOME MAJOR URBAN POLICY CONSIDERATIONS

There are several fundamental issues to address in any serious consideration of future urban social policies. One very basic issue is whether or not to do long-range planning at all. If so, how much planning is acceptable? For example, are plans to be as complete as early Russian five-year development plans, or are they to be simply loosely defined guidelines to be considered when making choices? Most of the urban past was not a result of rational and deliberate planning, but rather the result of many separate factors occurring spontaneously. The few occasions when either physical designs shaped building programs or social policies actively directed social change in predictable directions are probably the exception rather than the rule. Also, there are those who strongly believe in a laissez faire system in which the best results are those that are left to the free play of the marketplace. To the extent that planning disrupts these "natural" forces, it is seen by some as highly undesirable. The advocates of inclusive, strictly defined plans argue that they are necessary to make it possible to impose a pattern or order on circumstances. But urban and social planning might not be flexible enough to incorporate new ideas, or might be too frozen to permit necessary adaptation to changing circumstances.

If there is some agreement that planning should occur, one major issue is who would do the planning, and for what time periods should plans be made? Should there be ways to "veto" plans by dissident groups, and what, if anything, should be done to encourage active participation in the planning process by interest groups and the public at large? It has often been alleged that too often in the past planning has consisted of technical or physical schemes devised by technological elites, implemented by a narrow power structure, and imposed on the powerless masses. But broad citizen participation, on the other hand, has not been easy to establish. Numerous experiments in community development projects have demonstrated how difficult it is to obtain participation by a majority of the affected population. To combine political values of citizen participation with the kinds of expertise required to anticipate and plan for complex future environments is a formidable task.

Another important related issue is within what boundaries or political jurisdictions should planning take place? Should planning be done at the national, state, regional, or strictly local levels? One of the main difficulties is the lack of fit between the ecological, political, and social communities that make up American urban society, which has important consequences for the decision-making structure of the urban community, particularly for metropolitan regions. It means that no local government decisions applying to all parts of the metropolitan area are possible because of social and political fragmentation into many autonomous, competing units. Yet many of the social problems of urban areas can only be controlled by an areawide political system, which has the support of the many diverse groups of people scattered throughout the area.

If governmental and social fragmentation has not actually caused such problems as traffic congestion, pollution, and urban blight, it has nevertheless made solving these kinds of problems much more difficult. Perhaps, at least in part, this helps to explain the increasing involvement of the federal government in the many problems of metropolitan areas. But national urban planning remains highly controversial in the United States and is strongly resisted by those who argue for stronger local self-sufficiency and social control. Because of its history and tradition of states' rights and local autonomy, the United States has had more difficulty in resolving this issue than most of the other technologically advanced countries of the world.

If conditions are established to deal with these issues, the next series of issues revolves around values and priorities. For example, by what criteria will alternative policies be established? What are the most important and least important goals for urban development? Since values will determine the priorities established for future policies, it is essential to make clear what these values are and to assess how widely they are shared. For example, to what extent is there consensus that existing gaps between the rich and the poor be reduced or eliminated, and to what extent should social policy insure that a uniform quality of life be made available to all, regardless of their ability to pay?

Gans (1973), for instance, argues for a detailed policy for redistributing wealth and political power, to produce not only equality of opportunity, but also what might be termed equality of results. He advocates new policies to promote equality in the areas of income, political power, education, and the social worth of jobs. To Gans's goals of equity, one could easily add proposals to provide greater economic parity between cities and suburbs. If, for example, the mix of low-, middle-, and high-income groups were the same for both city and suburbs, regardless of individual differences in the distribution of wealth, individuals and families would have greater freedom to choose between city and suburban living. Likewise, if cities and suburbs contained similar mixes of socioeconomic groupings, some of the current strains and conflicts between cities and suburbs conceivably could be minimized. With greater equity, Gans (1973, p. 23) more generally argues, internal political antagonisms would decline because "conflicts can best be compromised fairly if the society is more egalitarian, if differences of self-interest that result from sharp inequality of income and power can be reduced."

But there are a number of reasons why egalitarian goals are extremely difficult to achieve in American society. First, the vested interests that profit from the status quo are highly likely to resist any policies that threaten their present advantages. Moreover, the individualistic ethic and the striving for individual economic advancement in competition with others are deeply ingrained in the American value system. More generally, any conscious effort to produce major changes in the institutional structure of the society, including changes in the current system for distributing economic rewards, must contend with institutional inertia as well as consciously organized opposition. For all these reasons, the possibility of a smooth transition to a system of greater equality, no matter how desirable, is highly unlikely. But these are still issues that must be confronted before future urban policy can be established.

Finally, how can urban policies be part of a comprehensive plan, and yet be so constituted that they may be changed with relative speed and ease when it is prudent to make these changes? In summary, how can there be the desirable combinations of order and flexibility; long-range visions and short-range strategies; freedom and social control; elaborately designed futures and open-ended tomorrows?

These largely unanswered questions illustrate just a few of the fundamental difficulties faced by policy makers and social planners as a prelude to the pursuit of any given policy or particular issue. The obvious difficulty of the task, however, does not mean that it is impossible. Caplow (1975) for example, notes:

> The improvement of society is not a forlorn hope—because many societies have deliberately improved before; nor is it an apocalyptic triumph to be accomplished once and for all—human nature being what it is. But it is not a matter out of our control, since modernization can proceed under a variety of institutional arrangements, and seems to be compatible with both despotism and freedom.

He accompanies this optimistic appraisal of prospects for controlling the urban future with a fairly common model for the policy-making process, which includes the following steps: 1) an accurate description of the existing condition to be changed; 2) a careful and honest description of the end condition to be achieved; 3) a division of the project into successive stages and a description of the conditions to be achieved at each stage; 4) practical methods for getting from each stage to the next; 5) estimates of the time, personnel, material resources, and information required to get from each stage to the next; 6) procedures for measuring goal attainment at each stage; and 7) procedures for detecting unanticipated results at each stage. The problem of implementing alternative future policies, according to Schneider (1968, p. 264), is not as difficult as other parts of future development. Instead, ". . . the enormity of our task in world development is inspiration and conception, not achievement."

THE FUTURE OF URBAN SOCIOLOGY

Serious students of urban sociology sometimes ask what future lies ahead for this challenging field of study. It seems appropriate to close with some reflections on this topic. First, it is clear that urban sociology will continue to develop and change, both as a disciplinary subspecialty within the academic arena and as a field with potentially important contributions to make in the social policy arena. Moreover, the boundaries of the field have always been loosely defined and interdisciplinary in character, and probably will remain so because of the complexity and scope of the phenomena studies. Urban sociology also has become part of a larger interdisciplinary effort, commonly referred to as the field of *urban studies*. All of the social sciences, for example, are central to the examination of urban structure and processes. History, economics, political science, anthropology, and psychology, as well as sociology, all have made and will continue to make important contributions to our understanding of the many human dimensions of urban society. Physical sciences of all kinds—biology, chemistry, physics, zoology, geology, and geography—are becoming increasingly concerned with the interrelationships between social and physical structures and are likely to become involved in more collaborative research efforts with social scientists. Engineering, architecture, and landscape architecture have long focused on improving the urban environment and have continuously expanded their horizons to incorporate knowledge and ideas acquired from the social and physical sciences. Urban planning, social work, journalism, and public administration, among some of the newer practicing professions that focus on dealing with some of the social problems associated with urbanization, and the social sciences and applied fields have been and will continue to instruct one another. Psychiatry and law are among the better established practicing professions that have expanded their focus to include urban concerns.

In short, the study of urban societies will require much more comprehensive and intensive disciplinary research, and will at the same time require academic specialists to work closely together with scholars from other disciplines and to keep abreast of information being developed across a number of fields. Both of these ends will be greatly facilitated in the future by more frequent use of computer technology and newer methods of information retrieval and data manipulation, by more rapid dissemination of information through newer means of communication, and by new forms of academic organization that encourage more direct interaction and exchanges between scholars among the various participating disciplines.

Second, urban sociology and urban studies can flourish only if sufficient funds are available to support and encourage research and scholarship. In the past, much urban research has been characterized by small-scale and narrowly defined problem areas, uncoordinated projects on related topics, and sporadic funding. Without a serious investment of money, skill, and energy, the field cannot grow as rapidly or rationally as desired. Urban scholars, on the other hand, must find new modes of adapting to political demands for assistance in attacking well-recognized social problems and for contributing directly to the design of social policies. More and more, professionally trained sociologists and other scholars are finding employment on the staffs of various public and private agencies directly involved in developing and applying social policies to the solution of real problems. But this may be extremely difficult to do without compromising research integrity or scholarly independence, and young scholars employed by policy-making agencies outside academia are forced to create new occupational self-images or mixed roles in efforts to avoid the traumas of intense role conflict.

The relationship between policy and disciplinary research must be better defined. It must be understood that policy research is significantly different from disciplinary research in at least the following respects:

> Its object is to provide information immediately useful to policy makers in grappling with the problems they face. It begins outside a discipline with a

social problem defined by a decision maker. The pace of the research is forced by the policy maker's need to make a decision dictated by nondisciplinary imperatives. The intended audience is the decision maker, to whom it must be made intelligible and convincing if it is to be useful. Generally, little time is available to collect new data or to engage in prolonged analysis (Berry and Kasarda, 1977, p. 427).

Third, it will become increasingly important in the near future to pay a considerable amount of attention to translating for various audiences what sociologists and other scholars have learned about urban life and urban communities to date. The social policies and alternative futures considered for urban communities will affect virtually everyone, so it has become important to raise the level of knowledge and sophistication of the ordinary citizen high enough so that he or she can appreciate the consequences of the choices that will have to be made. Too often, popular discussions of urbanization are short-sighted, overly dramatic or sensational, lack historical perspectives, or oversimplify very complex factors. Even more important is the more general purpose of providing a better understanding of the urban world in which most of us live and must function, as a tool for a more satisfactory adaption to the many daily demands and opportunities of urban living. It is essential that well-written, interesting, and clearly presented syntheses of urban processes be available for many more people than those seriously committed to becoming urban scholars or professional practitioners, and it was partially with this goal in mind that the present volume has been prepared.

Finally, ethical concerns will become critical considerations in undertaking urban studies. This does not mean necessarily continuing the "do good" attitude that has often sparked past urban reform movements with both beneficial and negative results, but rather a greater commitment to examine urban conditions with an overall concern for enhancing the quality of urban life, rather than a concern with manipulation or social control. The destructive impact of the atom bomb has demolished the previous myths of scientific purity and isolation. It is now much clearer that knowledge may indeed be a source of power and can be put to both constructive and destructive political uses. Although social scientists, as well as other scientists, have a common commitment to work as objectively as possible, the essence of humanity guarantees that one can never be totally objective or value free, so that no human being can forever escape making ethical choices. Many of the ethical issues in urban studies have been difficult, painful, and confusing. Those who professionally continue the examination or control of urbanization in the years ahead may well find this task the most overwhelming of all.

SELECTED BIBLIOGRAPHY

BENNIS, WARREN G., and SLATER, PHILIP E. *Temporary Society*. New York: Harper & Row, Pub., 1968.

BERRY, BRIAN J. L., and KASARDA, JOHN D. *Contemporary Urban Ecology*. New York: Macmillan, 1977.

CAPLOW, THEODORE. *Toward Social Hope.* New York: Basic Books, 1975.

CHINOY, ELI, ed. *The Urban Future.* New York: Leiber-Atherton, 1972.

CLARKE, ARTHUR. "Communications in the Second Century of the Telephone." In A. Bolger, ed., *The Telephone's First Century and Beyond.* New York: Thomas Y. Crowell, 1977.

COHEN, HENRY. "Governing Megacentropolis: The Constraints." In Paul Meadows and Ephriam Mizruchi, eds., *Urbanism, Urbanization and Change: Comparative Perspectives.* 2nd ed. Reading, Mass.: Addison-Wesley, 1976.

COLEMAN, JAMES S. "Community Disorganization and Community Problems." In R. K. Merton and R. Nisbet, eds., *Contemporary Social Problems.* 4th ed. New York: Harcourt Brace Jovanovich, 1976.

DAHL, ROBERT, and LINDBLOM, CHARLES. *Politics, Economics, and Welfare.* New York: Harper & Row, Pub., 1953.

DAHRENDORF, RALF. *Class and Class Conflict in Industrial Society.* Stanford, Calif.: Stanford University Press, 1959.

DANTZIG, GEORGE B., and SAATY, THOMAS L. *Compact City: A Plan for a Livable Urban Environment.* San Francisco: W. H. Freeman & Company Publishers, 1973.

ELDREDGE, H. WENTWORTH. "Alternative Possible Urban Futures," *Futures* (February 1974): 26–41.

GABOR, DENNIS. *Inventing the Future.* New York: Knopf, 1964.

GANS, HERBERT. *More Equality.* New York: Random House, 1973.

GREER, SCOTT. *The Emerging City.* New York: Free Press, 1962.

HEILBRONER, ROBERT L. *An Inquiry into the Human Prospect.* New York: W. W. Norton & Co., Inc., 1974.

DE JOUVENAL, BERTRAND, ed. *Futurables: I and II.* Geneva: Droz, 1963.

KANTER, R. M. *Commitment and Community.* Cambridge, Mass.: Harvard University Press, 1972.

KENNISTON, KENNETH. "Does Human Nature Change?" In R. Eells and C. Walton, eds., *Man in the City of the Future.* New York: Macmillan, 1968.

MARCUSE, HERBERT. *One Dimensional Man.* Boston: Beacon Press, 1964.

MEIER, RICHARD. *Planning for the Urban World.* Boston: MIT Press, 1974.

MEYERSON, MARTIN. "Utopian Predictions and the Planning of Cities," *Daedalus* 90 (Winter 1961):180–193.

MICHAEL, D. N. *The Unprepared Society.* New York: Basic Books, 1968.

PALEN, J. JOHN, ed. *City Scenes.* Boston: Little, Brown, 1977.

RICHIE-CALDER, LORD. "Technology in Focus: The Emerging Nations." In M. Kransberg and E. Davenport, eds., *Technology and Culture.* New York: Meridian, 1972.

SCHNEIDER, K. *Destiny of Change.* New York: Holt, Rinehart and Winston, 1968.

SLATER, PHILIP E. *The Pursuit of Loneliness: American Culture at the Breaking Point.* Boston: Beacon Press, 1971.

DE SOLA POOL, ITHIEL. "The Social Effects of the Telephone." In Bolger (1977).

TOFFLER, ALVIN. *Future Shock.* New York: Random House, 1970.

WEBBER, MELVIN M. "The Post-City Age," *Daedalus* 97 (Fall 1968): 1091–1110.

WEISNER, JEROME. "Technology and the Telephone." In Bolger (1977).

ZOLLSCHAN, GEORGE K., and HIRSCH, WALTER, eds. *Social Change: Explorations, Diagnoses, and Conjectures.* New York: John Wiley, 1976.

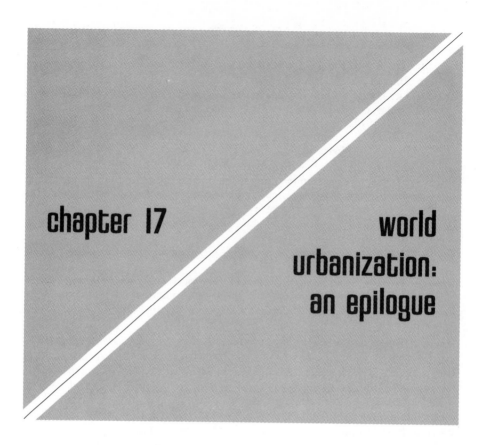

chapter 17

world
urbanization:
an epilogue

This book has focused almost entirely on North American urbanization and urban life. It has long been the author's view that it is not possible to adequately deal in detail with all of the topics contained in this book in a comparative way for all other parts of the world, and at the same time do justice to North America, in a single volume or even a single course. Fava (1968, p. vii) recognized the problem succinctly in her statement that "teachers of urban sociology and related courses may be pardoned if they sometimes believe that emergence from the ethnocentric cocoon in studying the city is more a bane than a blessing."

It is also increasingly true that the theoretical frames of reference for the study of urbanization that have commonly been used for the North American experience may not be useful or valid for the analysis of urbanization in other parts of the world. Along these lines, Berry (1973, p. xii) has made the following observations:

> The opportunity to compare a variety of circumstance around the world in rapid succession also convinced me that despite certain broad commonalities, there was not one but several paths being taken by twentieth-century urbanization, and that both the causes and consequences differed along these paths. ... I ... disavow the view that urbanization is a universal process, a consequence of modernization that involves the same sequence of events in different countries and that produces progressive convergence of forms.

While Berry's observations have led him to emphasize a comparative approach, they have only served to reinforce this author's position, derived from nearly two decades of teaching urban sociology at the undergraduate level, that such comparative urban analysis, involving so many divergent perspectives, is simply much too much to handle in an introduction to urban sociology.

But our focus on North America should not obscure the fact that urbanization is indeed a worldwide phenomenon, which could have an important bearing on the future development and well-being of American urban society. Modern transportation and communications technology make the world's cities closer and more interdependent than ever before. In the modern world, New York, Chicago, or Washington, D.C. in many ways may be more directly affected by what happens in London, Paris, Moscow, Tokyo, or Teheran than what may be taking place at the same time in Omaha, Phoenix, or St. Louis. The volume of travelers and commuters between New York and London or San Francisco and Tokyo may exceed that between various pairings of American cities. It is common to think of these interdependencies in terms of trade and commerce, but world peace and stability also may be affected by the outcomes of transactions between the world's principal cities. Moreover, urban developments in other parts of the world may provide useful models for planning or guiding our own urban future, helping us to improve our urban communities as well as to avoid the mistakes that have been made elsewhere. Therefore, it is fitting to close this book with a brief glance at urban trends in other parts of the world. Because of space limitations, attention will be focused on population and metropolitan growth trends, land use or physical development trends, emerging urban problems, and efforts to contain these problems through urban and social planning policies.

WORLD POPULATION GROWTH

Any discussion of world urbanization must be seen in the context of unprecedented growth in the size of the world population in recent centuries and especially in recent decades. At the time reliable data on world population first began to be available around A.D. 1650, the world population was estimated at about 500 million people. Assuming that the first human being appeared well over a million years ago, it took all of this time in human history to achieve a population of this size. Ehrlich (1970) estimates, for example, that it took at least 1,500 years for the population to double during the period from about 8000 B.C. to A.D. 1650.

But during the next 200 years—1650 to 1850—the world population doubled again to one billion people. This was just the beginning of a revolutionary increase in growth. In the eighty years between 1850 and 1930, the population again doubled to a total of two billion people. Between 1930 and 1975, a period of only forty-five years, it doubled still again to about four billion people. As of July 1977, world population had grown to over

4.25 billion people, and it was growing at a rate of 1.9 percent a year (see Table 17-1). At this rate, the time required to double the world population had shrunk to just over thirty-five years (see Table 17-2).

If this rate of increase continues, the world population will number over eight million people by the second decade of the next century. At the 1977 growth rate, the world was adding to its population more than 200,000 people a day, or about eighty million persons a year (U.S. Census, 1978)!

The reasons for this unprecedented growth in the world population are obvious. Only three demographic factors can produce population changes: 1) fertility; 2) mortality; 3) migration. Since migration is not a factor for the world as a whole, only fertility and mortality need be considered in explaining the past and present world population trends. Historically, industrialization, modernization, and urbanization have produced a gradual decline in birth rates in those parts of the world where these processes have occurred. But the same processes, along with resultant improvements in preventive and curative medicine, agriculture, and transportation, have raised the standard of living and have produced an even more rapid and dramatic drop in the mortality rates. As these processes have spread to all parts of the world, they have produced a large proportion of births over deaths, and the result has been the rapid explosion of the world population.

Demographers Freedman and Berelson (1974) argue that the rate of growth that currently characterizes the human population as a whole is just a temporary deviation from the annual growth rates that prevailed during most of humanity's history. This projection is based on the concept of a demographic "transition," which has taken place in the industrialized regions of the world during the past century or two. In these regions the first phase of the transition was characterized by high birth rates plus high death rates, which equaled low growth rates. The next phase was characterized by slowly declining births plus very rapidly declining death rates, which equaled high growth rates. The final stage is characterized by both low birth and death rates, which again produce low growth rates. These demographers argue that not only is low growth anticipated, it must prevail again in the future if the population is not to exceed the earth's carrying capacity.

Thus, future birth rates will have to be significantly lower than they are now or the much less desirable specter of significant increases in the death rate will likely prevail. For example, some futurists have predicted that the major crises most likely to affect the world by the end of this century are directly related to problems of the growth and distribution of population. These crises include severe food shortages, deterioration of the biosphere, materials and energy shortages, nuclear war, and imbalances in the worldwide distribution of wealth:

> The issue is human survival. The world population is growing faster than its ability to produce food. Increased numbers are damaging the ecological system and absorbing resources at an ever quickening pace. The gap between

TABLE 17-1 World population and average annual rates of growth, by continent and development category: 1950 to 1977

Region	MIDYEAR POPULATION (THOUSANDS)						
	1977	1975	1970	1965	1960	1955	1950
World	4,257,655	4,100,271	3,721,518	3,371,239	3,057,737	2,769,606	2,525,852
More developed	1,154,439	1,137,410	1,087,279	1,036,567	975,288	913,389	855,150
Less developed	3,103,216	2,962,861	2,634,239	2,334,672	2,082,449	1,856,217	1,670,702
Africa[1]	430,757	407,368	356,384	313,369	277,011	247,032	222,039
Asia	2,486,045	2,382,246	2,132,872	1,902,520	1,710,322	1,533,925	1,386,861
More developed	159,870	155,561	143,256	133,187	124,306	115,944	106,305
Less developed	2,326,175	2,226,685	1,989,616	1,769,333	1,586,016	1,417,981	1,280,556
Latin America[1]	341,599	324,341	284,295	248,501	216,389	188,539	165,764
North America[2]	240,258	236,409	226,308	214,075	198,661	181,740	166,075
Europe and Soviet Union[2]	737,096	728,566	702,217	675,129	639,540	604,249	572,577
Oceania	21,900	21,341	19,442	17,645	15,814	14,121	12,536
More developed	17,215	16,874	15,498	14,176	12,781	11,456	10,193
Less developed	4,685	4,467	3,944	3,469	3,033	2,665	2,343
Excluding the People's Republic of China:							
World	3,275,124	3,157,234	2,874,938	2,617,222	2,374,662	2,159,386	1,978,488
Less developed	2,120,685	2,019,824	1,787,659	1,580,655	1,399,374	1,245,997	1,123,338
Asia	1,503,514	1,439,209	1,286,292	1,148,503	1,027,247	923,705	839,497
Less developed	1,343,644	1,283,648	1,143,036	1,015,316	902,941	807,761	733,192

	AVERAGE ANNUAL RATE OF GROWTH (PERCENT)					
	1975–77	1970–75	1965–70	1960–65	1955–60	1950–55
World	1.9	1.9	2.0	2.0	2.0	1.8
More developed	0.7	0.9	1.0	1.2	1.3	1.3
Less developed	2.3	2.4	2.4	2.3	2.3	2.1
Africa[1]	2.8	2.7	2.6	2.5	2.3	2.1
Asia	2.1	2.2	2.3	2.1	2.2	2.0
More developed	1.4	1.6	1.5	1.4	1.4	1.7
Less developed	2.2	2.3	2.3	2.2	2.2	2.0
Latin America[1]	2.6	2.6	2.7	2.8	2.8	2.6
North America[2]	0.8	0.9	1.1	1.5	1.8	1.8
Europe and Soviet Union[2]	0.6	0.7	0.8	1.1	1.1	1.1
Oceania	1.3	1.9	1.9	2.2	2.3	2.4
More developed	1.0	1.7	1.8	2.1	2.2	2.3
Less developed	2.4	2.5	2.6	2.7	2.6	2.6
Excluding the People's Republic of China:						
World	1.8	1.9	1.9	1.9	1.9	1.7
Less developed	2.4	2.4	2.5	2.4	2.3	2.1
Asia	2.2	2.2	2.3	2.2	2.1	1.9
Less developed	2.3	2.3	2.4	2.3	2.2	1.9

[1] Less developed.

[2] More developed.

SOURCE: U.S. Bureau of the Census, 1978, *World Population: 1977 –Recent Demographic Estimates for the Countries and Regions of the World* (Washington, D.C.: U.S. Government Printing Office, 1978).

TABLE 17-2   Doubling Times

DATE	ESTIMATED WORLD POPULATION	TIME FOR POPULATION TO DOUBLE
8000 B.C.	5 million	1,500 years
1650 A.D.	500 million	200 years
1850 A.D.	1,000 million (1 billion)	80 years
1930 A.D.	2,000 million (2 billion)	45 years
1975 A.D.	4,000 million (4 billion)	
	Computed doubling time around 1970	35–37 years

SOURCE: Paul R. Ehrlich and Anne H. Ehrlich, *Population; Resources; Environment: Issues in Human Ecology.* 2nd ed. (San Francisco: W. H. Freeman & Company Publishers, 1972), p. 6.

the *have* nations and the *have nots* continues to widen. These consequences of population growth create social unrest and economic and political upheavals; they increase the possibility of nuclear warfare, not because of ideologies but more likely because of desperation brought on by the exhaustion of a nation's capacity to feed its people and supply them the materials for survival (Eitzen, 1980, p. 279).

World population problems are compounded because the distribution of the world population, as well as its rate of growth, varies considerably from country to country or region to region. Of every ten people in the world today, four live in either China or India. Add the Soviet Union and the United States, and one-half of the world population is covered. The other half of the world's people are distributed unevenly among the remaining 196 countries.

Asia by far is the most populous continent and contains roughly 2.5 billion people, or 58 percent of the world total. Although the rate of increase is lower in Asia than in such continents as Africa or Latin America, the actual net gain in population surpasses that of any other continent, due to the sheer size of the existing population base. For example, two-thirds of the world population growth in 1976 and 1977 took place in Asia alone (U.S. Census, 1978). Figure 17-1 illustrates the distribution of world population by region, while Table 17-3 illustrates the total population, rates of annual population increase, and other vital population data for selected countries around the world. These materials support the idea that while population growth for the entire world is of explosive dimensions, by no means is this phenomenon of equal size or impact for the various countries and regions of the world.

DEVELOPED AND DEVELOPING COUNTRIES

A glance at the data in Table 17-3 reveals that a sharp distinction can be made between such countries as the United States, Sweden, the United Kingdom, West Germany, or Japan, on the one hand, and such countries as Egypt,

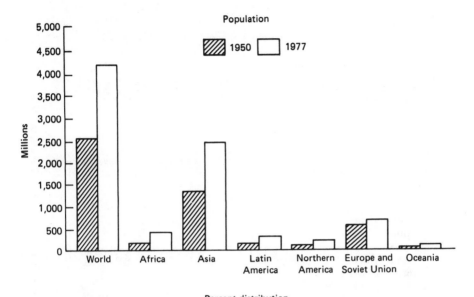

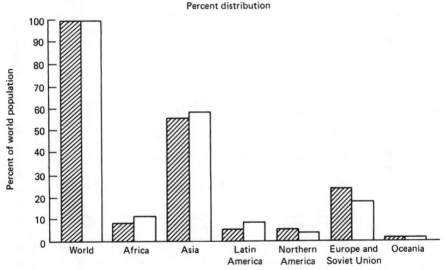

FIGURE 17-1 Population of the world and regions: 1950 and 1977 (U.S. Bureau of the Census, 1978, *World Population: 1977–Recent Demographic Estimates for the Countries and Regions of the World* (Washington, D.C.: U.S. Government Printing Office, 1978).

Ethiopia, Somalia, Nigeria, Pakistan, Vietnam, or Zaire, on the other, in such measures as rate of annual population increase or per capita gross national product. The highly industrialized, relatively wealthy countries of North America, Western Europe, Japan, and Australia are often referred to as the "developed" nations, while the other countries just listed have often euphemistically been labeled as "underdeveloped" or, more charita-

TABLE 17–3 1979 World population data for selected countries

COUNTRY	POPULATION (MILLIONS)	BIRTH RATE	DEATH RATE	% RATE ANNUAL INCREASE	YEARS TO DOUBLE POPULATION	POPULATION IN 2000 (MILLIONS)	PER CAPITA GNP (U.S. $)
World	4,321.0	28	11	1.7	41	6,168.0	1,800
United States	220.3	15	9	0.6	116	260.4	8,640
Algeria	19.1	48	14	3.3	21	38.4	1,110
Australia	14.4	16	8	0.8	87	17.9	7,340
Austria	7.5	11	12	-0.1	—	7.6	6,140
Brazil	118.7	36	8	2.8	25	205.2	1,390
China	950.0	20	8	1.2	58	1,193.0	410
Cuba	9.9	20	6	1.4	50	12.7	900
Egypt	40.6	38	12	2.6	27	63.5	310
Ethiopia	31.8	50	25	2.5	28	55.4	110
France	53.4	14	10	0.4	173	57.2	7,290
Germany (West)	61.2	10	12	-0.2	—	59.7	8,160
Germany (East)	16.7	13	13	0.0	—	16.6	4,940
India	660.9	34	15	1.9	36	1,010.5	150
Iran	36.3	44	14	3.0	23	63.8	2,180
Italy	56.9	13	10	0.4	173	61.2	3,450
Japan	115.9	15	6	0.9	77	128.9	5,640
Kenya	15.4	51	12	3.8	18	32.8	270
Libya	2.8	47	13	3.5	20	5.7	6,680
Mexico	67.7	41	7	3.4	20	132.3	1,110
Nigeria	74.6	50	18	3.2	22	148.8	420
Pakistan	79.9	44	14	3.0	23	145.1	190
Philippines	46.2	34	10	2.4	29	77.9	450
Poland	35.4	19	9	1.0	69	41.2	3,150
Russia	264.0	18	10	0.8	87	311.0	3,010
Saudi Arabia	8.1	49	18	3.0	23	15.6	4,980
Somalia	3.5	48	20	2.8	25	6.3	110
Sweden	8.3	12	11	0.1	693	8.6	9,250
United Kingdom	55.8	12	12	0.0	—	56.6	4,430
Vietnam	50.1	41	18	2.3	30	77.8	170
Zaire	28.0	46	19	2.8	25	47.2	130

SOURCE: Population Reference Bureau, *1979 World Population Data Sheet* (Washington, D.C.: Population Reference Bureau, May, 1979).

bly, as "developing" nations. While countless cultural differences exist between them, the so-called developing countries have at least the following set of characteristics in common: 1) they are still predominantly agrarian societies; 2) they are "premodern" in that they are much less industrialized than the developed countries; 3) their per capita wealth is much less than in developed nations; 4) their current rates of population growth are much greater than in developed countries; and, finally, 5) the process of urbanization has differed from that in the developed countries in speed, form, and consequences. This last distinction is, of course, most central to this chapter and will be considered in more detail later on. For now, it can be summarized that cities in developing areas are growing at faster rates than are cities anywhere else in the world and at rates that rival those in the West of the nineteenth century.

WORLD URBANIZATION

In 1950, only six cities in the world had five million or more inhabitants. In 1980, twenty-six cities were this size or larger, and it is estimated that in the year 2000 there will be sixty such cities, with forty-five of them in the developing world (New York Times, June 15, 1980). Figure 17-2 lists the 1980 population for the world's fifteen largest metropolitan areas, along with projections of the fifteen largest metropolitan areas for the year 2000. As the figure suggests, the five cities dropping from the list between 1980 and 2000 are all cities in the developed part of the world, while all of the cities added to the list by 2000 are in developing nations.

Human beings are now concentrated in cities on a scale unprecedented in human history (Frisbie, 1977). It has been estimated that the number of inhabitants in cities of 100,000 or more reached 864 million by 1970 (Davis, 1972). Eight percent of the world population and more than one-fourth of the world urban population (over 300 million people) resided in forty-three cities, each containing more than two million people. At least two metropolitan areas, New York and Tokyo, had by 1960 grown larger than the entire 1930 urban population of Africa (Frisbie, 1977). By the year 2000, it is estimated that the fifteen largest metropolitan areas will contain more than twelve million people (New York Times, June 15, 1980). The urban population of the world doubled between 1920 and 1950 and doubled again from 1950 to 1975 (Frisbie, 1977), a rate of increase that has been faster than for world population as a whole. By the year 2000, it is expected that more than half of the world population will be living in urban areas (New York Times, June 15, 1980).

Again, as in the case of world population itself, urbanization has proceeded unevenly throughout the world. Although urbanization is currently more rapid in the developing countries than in the developed countries, the developed countries still can best be described as more urban in character (see Table 17-4A). Of course, this is because the industrialized societies in recent centuries began to accelerate the process of urbanization much

1980				2000	
20.4	New York	①	Mexico City	31.0	
20.0	Tokyo	②	Sao Paulo	25.8	
15.0	Mexico City	③	Tokyo	24.2	
13.5	Sao Paulo	④	New York	22.8	
13.4	Shanghai	⑤	Shanghai	22.7	
11.7	Los Angeles	⑥	Peking	19.9	
10.7	Peking	⑦	Rio de Janeiro	19.0	
10.7	Rio de Janeiro	⑧	**Bombay	17.1	
10.3	*London	⑨	Calcutta	16.7	
10.1	*Buenos Aires	⑩	**Jakarta	16.6	
9.9	*Paris	⑪	Seoul	14.2	
9.5	*Osaka	⑫	Los Angeles	14.2	
9.3	*Dusseldorf	⑬	**Cairo	13.1	
8.8	Calcutta	⑭	**Madras	12.9	
8.5	Seoul	⑮	**Manila	12.3	

*Expected to drop from first 15 by 2000.
**Expected to join list by 2000.

FIGURE 17-2 The world's 15 largest metropolitan areas (The New York Times, June 15, 1980).
© 1980 by The New York Times Company. Reprinted by permission.

earlier than the less developed agrarian societies of the third world. Thus, as Table 17-4B indicates, each of the major areas of the developed world is more highly urbanized (the percentage of each major region that resides in places of 20,000 people or more) than any of the less developed major regions. For example, Europe, North America, the Soviet Union, and Oceania were all more than 45 percent urbanized in 1975, while the less developed areas of East Asia, South Asia, and Africa were all still less than 25 percent urbanized at that time. Only Latin America, of all the developing regions, has even begun to approach the developed world in the degree to which it has become urbanized.

Although population growth and urban growth are related phenomena, to assume that one is solely the cause of the other would be a mistake. Rather, each is more likely a consequence of still a third factor—industrialization (Hawley, 1971). Of course, relatively large cities had emerged in the ancient and medieval worlds without the benefits of industrialization. But there has been a far more direct relationship between industrialization and urbanization since the beginning of the nineteenth century. In Chapter Three, the relationship between industrialization and rapid urbanization was described as directly linked in the case of Great

Britain and the United States. Hawley (1971, p. 282) describes this relationship as functionally interdependent:

> The economics of large-scale production presuppose the various complementary services and the quick communications that only urban areas can supply. Those requisites depend in turn on the markets represented by large aggregates of consumers who earn their livings from non-agricultural activities. There is a mutually stimulating interaction between industrialization and urbanization.

Hawley further suggests an interactive relationship between population increase and industrialization. In the first stages of industrialization,

TABLE 17-4   Percentage distributions of the urban population of the world and of world regions: 1920–1975

A. PERCENTAGE DISTRIBUTION, BY REGION, OF THE WORLD URBAN POPULATION (IN PLACES OF 20,000 OR MORE)

	(PERCENTAGES)						
	1920	1930	1940	1950	1960	1970	1975
World Total	100.0	100.0	100.0	100.0	100.0	100.0	100.0
More Developed Major Areas	67.5	65.6	62.1	56.2	51.2	46.7	44.2
Europe	42.4	39.0	34.7	29.9	24.7	21.2	19.2
North America	18.0	18.4	15.4	15.8	15.2	14.1	13.6
Soviet Union	6.0	7.1	10.9	9.4	10.3	10.4	10.4
Oceania	1.2	1.1	1.0	1.1	1.1	1.1	1.0
Less Developed Major Areas	32.5	34.3	37.9	43.8	48.8	53.3	55.8
East Asia	14.9	15.9	17.1	17.6	19.4	19.6	19.8
South Asia	10.1	10.2	11.7	14.5	15.4	17.4	18.6
Latin America	4.8	5.4	5.9	7.6	9.2	10.6	11.4
Africa	2.6	2.9	3.2	4.0	4.8	5.6	6.1
More Developed Regions	74.2	73.1	70.4	64.4	59.1	54.1	51.3
Less Developed Regions	25.8	26.9	29.6	35.6	40.9	45.9	48.7

B. PERCENT OF THE POPULATION OF THE WORLD AND OF EACH WORLD REGION THAT IS URBAN (IN PLACES OF 20,000 OR MORE)

	(PERCENTAGES)						
	1920	1930	1940	1950	1960	1970	1975
World Total	14.3	16.3	18.8	21.2	25.4	28.2	29.7
More Developed Major Areas	29.8	32.8	36.7	39.9	45.6	49.9	52.1
Europe	34.7	37.2	39.5	40.7	44.2	47.1	48.2
North America	41.4	46.5	46.2	50.8	58.0	62.6	65.4
Soviet Union	10.3	13.4	24.1	27.8	36.4	42.7	46.4
Oceania	36.5	38.0	40.9	45.7	52.9	57.9	57.1
Less Developed Major Areas	6.9	8.4	10.4	13.2	17.3	20.4	22.2
East Asia	7.2	9.1	11.6	13.8	18.5	21.7	23.7
South Asia	5.7	6.5	8.3	11.1	13.7	16.0	17.4
Latin America	14.4	16.8	19.6	25.1	32.8	37.8	40.5
Africa	4.8	5.9	7.2	9.7	13.4	16.5	18.1
More Developed Regions	29.4	32.6	37.0	40.0	46.0	50.5	52.8
Less Developed Regions	5.8	7.0	8.6	11.4	15.4	18.5	20.3

SOURCE: W. Parker Frisbie, "The Scale and Growth of World Urbanization." In John Walton and Donald E. Carns, eds., *Cities in Change.* 2nd ed. (Boston: Allyn & Bacon, 1977), p. 49, and United Nations, *Growth of the World's Urban and Rural Population, 1920–2000.*

there are significant advances of scientific knowledge and its applications to industrial productivity. These help to raise the standard of living, which in turn tends to release the forces of population increase (rapidly reduced death rates, etc.). Population increase then can become a stimulant to further industrial development through the increased labor of supply of young, adaptable workers and the enlarged numbers of consumers of industrial products it creates. Of course, these are developments that tend to be concentrated in urban centers, which grow accordingly.

OVERURBANIZATION IN THE DEVELOPING WORLD

Just as the underdeveloped parts of the world can be described as over-populated with respect to the capacity of their economic and political institutions to accommodate burgeoning numbers of people, so can they be described as "overurbanized" with respect to their "premature" concentration of population in cities. While the cities of the developing nations have been growing at an unprecedented rate, so also have been their rural populations. As such countries attempt to industrialize, they are faced with the dilemma of trying to raise agricultural productivity and to reduce the number of agricultural workers needed in the countryside, while at the same time trying to stimulate industrial productivity in the large urban centers. Within this framework, large numbers of people are dislocated from rural areas and forced into the cities. But at the same time, the resources of the cities, already strained by the herculean tasks of industrialization, are not adequate to the demands of still greater numbers of settlers.

Thus, one can find huge settlements of squatters residing in newly created slums on the periphery of many cities in Asia, Africa, and Latin America, such as Mexico City, Lima, Ankara, Calcutta, Jakarta, Bangkok, and Rangoon. In these newly created squatter settlements, hunger, over-crowding, and disease are rampant, as well as extensive unemployment and underemployment. Floods of migrants displaced from rural areas gravitate to the major cities in search of employment, only to find that their numbers are too great to be absorbed by the local economy. Large surpluses of workers begin to appear in administrative and service industries, as well as in overcrowded manufacturing enterprises, and even some of the more marginal occupational groups such as peddlers, street solicitors, entertainers, beggars, and "hangers-on" of various sorts become overcrowded and unable to accommodate workers (Mangin, 1973; Bose, 1973).

This pattern of accommodating new immigrants in squatter slums on the outskirts of existing cities creates an ecological pattern just opposite that found in most United States industrial cities, where slum areas are most likely to be found in the inner city areas rather than at the outskirts (see Chapter Four). The explanation for these differences is not to be found in the logical application of "natural laws" of ecological development, but rather in the specific series of historical events associated with the popula-

Slums in Dacca, Bangladesh, sprung up as a result of the civil war between East and West Pakistan in the early 1970s. (United Nations)

tion, industrial, and urban growth of each of the world regions (Abrams, 1973). Differences in existing systems of technology, transportation, and communications, as well as culture, at the time urban growth is taking place also can be seen as contributing to distinctive differences between the ecological patterning of cities in the industrial West and the developing countries of the Third World.

PRIMATE CITIES

Overurbanization in the developing nations also tends to take on a pattern that has been described as "primacy." A primate pattern is one whereby a single, extremely large city dominates an entire nation, in terms of size, concentration of economic wealth, or political and administrative power. A primate city may be from as much as three to fifteen times larger than the second largest city in countries where primate cities dominate. For example, Lima, Peru, is approximately thirteen times larger than the second largest city of Peru, while Teheran is about six and a half times larger than the second largest city in Iran.

Berry and Kasarda (1977) hypothesize that the emergence of primate cities in developing societies is primarily a product of the imperfect mechanisms for the "filtering" or "trickling" down of urban growth from the existing urban centers outward into the smaller towns and cities. Once large cities have developed in such countries, urban growth tends to remain concentrated there rather than dispersed in a more decentralized urban pattern.

One of the principal reasons for the dominant position of primate cities in developing nations appears to have been the past colonial practices of the European powers, which had used these cities as administrative and commercial centers. As Berry and Kasarda (1977, pp. 397–398) state:

> For colonial powers to extend and consolidate their authority in alien social and geographic territories, cities had to be the base of action for those powers. British rule in India, for example, centered on capital and provincial cities both for maintaining an integrated and authoritarian administrative structure and for securing the economic base of its power—the collection of taxes and control over the export of raw materials and the import of British manufactured goods.

Partially because of this colonial legacy, the continued domination of some developing nations by their primate cities has been described as a "malignancy" by some critics and national planners. For example, primate cities have been said to have had "paralytic" effects upon the development of smaller urban places and to be "parasitic" in relationship to the remainder of the local economy. They are parasitic, according to Hoselitz (1955), because they rob the countryside of valuable labor, consume all available investment funds, and dominate the cultural pattern of a society in such a way as to lead to the breakdown of the traditional culture. They also tend to have a high rate of consumption, as opposed to production.

But not all experts agree that domination by primate cities is necessarily a bad thing for developing nations. Some argue that they may serve some very useful, or at the very least, some necessary functions. Palen (1975, p. 331) states the functional case for primate cities in this way: "Whatever its faults, the primate city is the center of economic and social change. The movements for independence received their ideas and their support from the urban population; and the present governments, even in rural countries, are overwhelmingly led and staffed by urban dwellers."

Whether primate cities should be allowed to continue their dominant roles in developing nations or should be constrained by radical national policies of population and economic decentralization are questions that are at the heart of national planning controversies among the leaders of the developing nations. One school of thought sees the dominance of primate cities as a temporary phenomenon in the urban and industrial growth of developing nations, while another suggests that primate cities could only be constrained by consciously planned radical changes in the nature of urban systems (Berry and Kasarda, 1977).

While we will cite specific urban growth patterns and urban planning policies of specific developing countries in the discussion to follow, it is still too soon to evaluate in a generalized way the full implications of and prospects for primate cities in developing countries as a whole.

With a growth rate of 2.8 percent a year in the 1975–1977 period, Africa's population is currently expanding the fastest of any of the world continents (U.S. Census, 1978). Between 1950 and 1977, its population nearly doubled from approximately 222 million people to over 430 million people. This extremely rapid growth is caused by a combination of vital rates unique in today's world—a very high fertility level with only a moderately high mortality level. In spite of these high growth rates, Africa is still the least urbanized of world continents. Not more than 10 percent of its people live in communities of 5,000 people or more (Bollens and Schmandt, 1975). Yet there is a strong trend toward urbanization, which is one of the outstanding characteristics of its present-day life. But the degree of urbanization varies drastically from country to country, varying from as low as 3 percent urban in such countries as Mozambique or Upper Volta to as high as 60 percent in Libya (U.S. Census, 1978).

It is difficult to make easy generalizations about African urbanization because of the continent's great diversity. At the far south is the wealthy and industrialized Republic of South Africa, with well-established social and political institutions. To date, these have been firmly controlled by its white minority, despite internal and international efforts to bring its large nonwhite majorities into positions of shared power and decision making. With relatively large cities, such as Johannesburg and Capetown, South Africa was 48 percent urban in 1970. North of the Sahara Desert are

Cities such as Johannesburg make South Africa more urban than most other African countries. (South African Consulate General Information Section, New York)

countries with ancient but disparate civilizations, such as Egypt and Ethiopia. While Ethiopia is only 11 percent urban, Egypt, with its large primate city of Cairo, is 44 percent urbanized (U.S. Census, 1978).

Below the Sahara region are the new nations of the continent most recently having been liberated as former colonies of the European powers. Bollens and Schmandt (1975, p. 345) describes their status:

> This vast mosaic is interlaced with a multiplicity of customs, languages, religions, ethnic backgrounds, and political institutions that defy generalization. Rapid transition and the thrust of modernization have intensified the problems of nation-building and in the process have precipitated civil wars and military takeovers. Yet, from these travails, a continent of tremendous potential is emerging.

Major cities of Africa can be subdivided into three major classes: 1) those that were founded in the pre-Christian era, such as Alexandria; 2) those founded by colonists from European countries, such as Germany, Portugal, Belgium, France, and Great Britain. Such colonization did not produce exceptionally large cities until after World War II, even though colonization was accelerated in the latter part of the nineteenth century; and 3) those that developed following successes within the African independence movement (Wilson and Shulz, 1978).

Because of rapid rates of migration into the growing cities of Africa, such cities are commonly characterized by an explosive expansion of the urban population without corresponding increases in available city housing. As a result, large squatter slums have emerged on the outskirts of most of the larger African cities. In some regions, these are called *bidonvilles,* or "tin can" cities. The inability of many African governments to expand the housing supply at the same rate at which their city populations have been growing has led observers to the conclusion that shantytowns with homes of "packing crates, scrap metal, or mud" will be part of the African urban scene for years to come (Palen, 1975). In addition to housing problems, the squatter slums experience a lack of adequate services and facilities in the areas of sanitation or sewerage, schooling, and welfare.

The Nigerian city of Ibadan is an exception to the general African city pattern of slums at the periphery. Although a large city with a population in excess of 700,000 people and a British colonial tradition similar to that of many other African cities, Ibadan's ecological structure is quite different from that just described (see Mitchel, 1961; Onibokum, 1973). In the core of the oldest part of the city, density is remarkably high, open space is negligible, roads are few, and access to many of the dwellings is by means of footpaths. Virtually all of the houses in the central area are constructed of mud and are roofed with corrugated iron. Sanitary facilities are lacking, and the water supply is obtained from communal taps.

The surrounding suburban or peripheral areas house the more affluent members of the community, including the Europeans who began to enter Ibadan after the British assumed control. Here at the periphery, the housing is better, the residential sites are more spacious, and the density is much lower. On the other hand, the poorer and less well-educated Africans, both well-established residents and newcomers, must seek homes in the crowded districts of the city core (Bollens and Schmandt, 1975). Thus, while the ecological settlement pattern is more like the pattern in the industrialized parts of the United States, Ibadan still is ill equipped to absorb an increasing number of newcomers, particularly those of lower socioeconomic status. Although it is a large city, Ibadan still retains some of the social and economic characteristics of a village. For example, Bollens and Schmandt (1975) have referred to the inability of the local political institutions to function adequately in the highly pluralistic society of the city with its many competing interest groups and diverse loyalties.

LATIN AMERICA

Latin America is characterized by a high rate of population growth as a result of moderately high fertility rates and low mortality rates. Between 1950 and 1977 the Latin American population more than doubled, from about 166 million people to over 341 million people (U.S. Census, 1978). Although fertility rates have been rapidly declining in recent years, the Latin American share of world population has continued to increase because of the momentum for growth already built into the population base. However, if recent fertility declines gain impetus and encompass a greater number of the more populated countries of the region, Latin America could exhibit a reduction of growth in the near future (U.S. Census, 1978).

Tropical South America comprises more than half of the total population of the region and is dominated by Brazil, the sixth largest country in the world and the largest country in Latin America. Middle America has the highest fertility and the lowest mortality of all the subregions in Latin America and in population is dominated by Mexico, which contains more than 75 percent of the Middle American population and is the major determinant of its total growth. Mexico is also the second largest country in Latin America. In contrast, the lowest rate of growth in Latin America is found in temperate South America, and Argentina contains two-thirds of the total population of that subregion.

Urbanization has been extremely rapid in Latin America in recent decades, and went from 30 percent urban in 1950 to 57 percent urban by 1975 (U. N. Demographic Yearbook, 1977). As late as 1930, Buenos Aires was Latin America's only city with more than one million people. But by the mid-1970s, fifteen metropolitan centers had more than one million people, and the number was expected to increase to twenty-six by 1980. Mexico City, Buenos Aires, Rio de Janeiro, and São Paulo now rank among the fifteen largest cities in the world (New York Times, June 15, 1980).

The most phenomenal urban growth in Latin America and perhaps for any of the world cities has been in Mexico City. In 1960, the population of the Mexico City metropolitan area (Greater Mexico City) was 2.8 million people. By 1980, it had grown more than fivefold to fifteen million people, ranking next only to New York and Tokyo among the world's largest urban conglomerations. United Nations projections to the year 2000 anticipate that Mexico City will again more than double to thirty-one million people and will by that time have become the world's largest urban center (See Figure 2). Interestingly, another Latin American City, São Paulo, is also expected to be larger than either New York or Tokyo by the end of this century.

Although Mexico City has many of the characteristics of a primate city, Mexico actually had thirty-six cities of over 100,000 people by the beginning of the 1970s, compared to only fifteen cities of this size in 1960 (Sanders, 1977). Such growth is due not only to natural increase but also to large streams of migration that flow toward the cities and their immediate hinterlands. Thus, Mexico City, Guadalajara, Monterrey, and the cities along the United States border, as well as the various state capitals and smaller industrial and commercial centers like Chihuahua, Cuernavaca, Puebla, Leon, and Acapulco have been among the major destination points of migrants from rural areas. Because of natural increases in the size of the rural population as well as overurbanization of the cities, there has been a sizable outflow of migrants, both legally and illegally, across the border into the United States (see Chapter Fourteen).

Fifty-nine percent of the population of Mexico is urbanized, well approaching the degree of urbanization in developed countries. The Mexican economy has also had impressive rates of industrialization in recent years, during which time Mexico has changed from a clearly underdeveloped nation to one of "middle-range" development of international significance. A large but still not fully used natural resource base, including potentially vast petroleum reserves, is expected to facilitate the momentum toward Mexico becoming a fully developed nation.

However, industrialization has not been able to keep pace with gains in population and urbanization, and Mexican economic institutions are characterized by many contradictions and shortcomings. Large inequities exist in the distribution of wealth, overcrowded housing, high rates of illiteracy, poor distribution of health care and other services, underemployment, and absolute poverty. Sanders (1977) reports that the top 10 percent of the population receives nearly 50 percent of all reported income, while the bottom 10 percent receives less than 2 percent. A third or more of the population lives in dwellings of no more than one room, dirt floors, and no piped water within the dwelling. In urban areas alone, Sanders estimates that about a quarter of a million new houses are needed annually, not taking into account rural needs as well. While Mexico City has about one doctor for each 400 inhabitants, some Mexican regions have no more than one doctor per 6,000 inhabitants, and about 1,000 inhabited locales have no doctors. Further, nearly 45 percent of the economically active population is underemployed, and the economic system produces only about 70 percent of the jobs needed to absorb the growing labor force (Sanders, 1977).

As part of a 1978 National Urban Development Plan to control population growth in Mexico's overcrowded cities, the government planned to transfer 400,000 federal government jobs out of Mexico City to smaller cities. Under the plan, the government built nineteen industrial parks to create employment outside the cities and planned to give the private sector and foreign businesses tax incentives and energy discounts of up to 20 percent to encourage them to invest in the countryside rather than in the largest cities. The plan also foresaw the construction of hundreds of regional service centers throughout the countryside, settlements of 10,000 people or more, containing all basic urban services in an attempt to lure migrants away from the large cities (UPI, November 8, 1979).

Many of the largest Latin American cities were an outgrowth of Spanish colonization, beginning in the sixteenth century and lasting well into the nineteenth century. The Spanish colonial cities were well planned according to the ideas of the Spanish Crown, and because of these common origins, they tended to develop similar physical patterns. Generally, they were laid out around a central plaza, as were the cities of Spain that served as models. The central plaza was usually surrounded by ceremonial buildings, such as cathedrals and government offices. Housing sites were of uniform shape, and the city streets were laid out in a grid pattern with rectangular blocks. This pattern offered considerable flexibility for growth, as the boundaries of the city could be readily expanded as more room was needed. This could be done by simply expanding the existing streets and adding more blocks. Also, the focus on commercial and civic activities at the center of the city allowed easier expansion at the periphery of the city because there were no physical barriers to expansion, such as walls, markets, or warehouses (Gakenheimer, 1967).

The Spanish colonial cities were rigidly stratified along social class lines, and this pattern persists somewhat to the present. Elites and higher socioeconomic groups usually occupy the most pleasant and convenient areas at the center of cities rather than in the suburbs, while the lowest-income groups occupy peripheral areas. Most Latin American cities of Spanish origin are characterized by squatter slums that ring their outer boundaries. However, with the advent of industrialization and modern transportation systems, such as Mexico City's subway system, there have been some changes in this pattern. For example, high rise office and commercial buildings have expanded at the center of Mexico City, a "zone of transition" has begun to develop around the city center, and many socially prominent and wealthy families have moved into neighborhoods at the northern and southwestern edges of the city (Haynor, 1968). Thus, industrialization and modernization may be shifting the ecological pattern of Latin American cities in the direction of that found in the industrialized urban centers of the United States. But by no means is this transformation complete.

Brazil has produced an urban pattern that does not fit the generalizations applicable to the other parts of Latin America, because of its Portuguese rather than Spanish colonial heritage. For example, Brazil is not dominated by a single primate city, but instead contains two of the world's largest fifteen cities, São Paulo and Rio de Janeiro. While Rio contains over ten million people, São Paulo is even larger with a 1980 population of 13.5

Sao Paolo, with its population of 13.5 million, is one of the largest cities in the world. (Varig Brazilian Airlines)

million (Figure 2). Brazil also contains several other cities with populations exceeding 500,000 people. The economic base of São Paulo is more typical of the large metropolises of Europe and the United States than of other metropolises of South America. It has been described as follows:

> Within its confines are over 27,000 plants and factories employing the highest paid labor force in Latin America. . . . It is served by a modern airport, 28 daily newspapers, 18 radio stations, and 5 television stations, and by such cultural facilities as 3 universities, 16 legitimate theaters, and an excellent symphony orchestra. . . . [W]ithin the metropolitan area of 2300 square miles are thirty-seven suburban municipalities, many of them industrial satellites. Squatter settlements are also found around the periphery but they are far less extensive than in other Latin American cities, including Rio. . . . Public services and facilities in Sao Paulo are among the best in Latin America. Utilities, recreation areas, transportation arteries, hospital and social welfare services, sanitation, and the primary and secondary school system are well developed despite persistent material and administrative deficiencies (Bollens and Schmandt, 1975, pp. 354–357).

But even an economically well-developed metropolis such as São Paulo has problems keeping pace with its rapid growth, and it has serious housing shortages and a great deal of traffic congestion, as well as a host of administrative and political problems growing out of its rapid growth. Between 1980 and 2000, the São Paulo population is expected to nearly double to almost twenty-six million people. By that time, according to United Nations projections, it will have become the second largest metropolis in the world (New York Times, June 15, 1980 p. 10).

ASIA

Asia contains societies as disparate as Israel, Turkey, India, Japan, and the People's Republic of China. Each major region of Asia differs in its population size and its rates of population, and urban and industrial growth. Even though Asia contains one of the largest urban populations in the world and at least six of the fifteen largest metropolitan areas in the world (see Figure 2), vast differences exist between such Asian cities as Tokyo, Calcutta, Peking, Shanghai, Osaka, or Seoul. Likewise, there are significant differences between the societies and regions of which these and other large cities of Asia are a part. Since to discuss all of Asia in this one short section is impossible, our discussion will be limited to a brief description of some of the principal cities in three of the most highly populated countries of Asia: Japan; India; and mainland China.

Japan

Japan is by far the most industrialized and urbanized country in Asia and is in the same class as the developed nations of Europe and North America in these two characteristics. With 76 percent of its population living in urban areas, Japan's degree of urbanization is virtually identical to that of the United States (U.S. Census, 1978), and it successfully competes with the United States in world markets for its manufactured goods. Japan's principal metropolitan area, Tokyo, had a 1980 population of twenty million people and was second in size only to New York, the world's largest metropolitan area, by less than one-half million people (See Figure 17-2).

The Tokyo area is one of the world's most congested and polluted. Palen (1975, p. 408) describes it in these vivid terms:

> Air pollution is so severe that it directly causes scores of deaths each year. Workers in some industries use gas masks while drug stores have machines dispensing oxygen. The level of water pollution was graphically demonstrated when a Tokyo newspaper printed on its front page a photograph that had been developed solely by dipping the negative in a chemically polluted river. Transportation is in similar condition. Subways are so overburdened that uniformed "pushers" are employed to stand on the platforms to shove and force additional people into the already overcrowded subway cars. . . . Tokyo has the worst automobile congestion in the world. Roads are in dismal shape . . . the school systems are overburdened; there are long waiting lists for apartments; and all public services are overworked and inadequate.

Pollution and overcrowding are among the most serious problems affecting Tokyo. (United Nations)

It seems paradoxical that Japan, a highly developed nation with many advanced technological and economic resources at its disposal, has not been able to control the rapid growth of Tokyo or to plan its growth in such a way as to minimize problems such as those just described. Major efforts have been undertaken, including a 1956 Capital Regional Development Law, based on Sir Patrick Abercrombie's plan for Greater London (see section in this chapter on London), which would have provided a ring of new satellite towns and a surrounding green belt at a radius of seventeen to forty-five miles from central Tokyo (Hall, 1977). But the plan failed to realize the rate at which Tokyo was growing, and it was clear in just a few years that this plan had no hope of realization. For example, areas earmarked for preservation as a green belt had already begun to be developed for residential and industrial purposes as early as 1965, mainly because the powers to prevent this from happening were simply lacking. Hall (1977) attributes the failure of planning in the Tokyo region to the strong laissez faire economic values and policies of the central and regional government, which believes city and regional land use planning must take a back seat to industrial expansion, which in the case of Japan has been of top priority during the past several decades.

Another interesting planning proposal has been the development of a completely new large city, along the lines of Brasilia, some ninety miles from Tokyo on a 116-square-mile site at the foot of Mount Fuji. A superhighway would connect the two centers, which would be within an hour's time from each other, and 200,000 government workers and their families would be tranferred from Tokyo to the new city as its core population. This plan has met considerable opposition in Tokyo, and its feasibility has not yet been demonstrated. Hall (1977, p. 239) concludes, "Tokyo's recent story, in many ways, is a chastening one for the planners of other world cities."

India

With a population of over 643 million people, India is the second largest country in the world. But it contrasts sharply with Japan in its degree of urbanization and industrialization. Only 20 percent of its population lives in urban places (U.S. Census, 1978), and it is clearly an economically underdeveloped country. With a per capita gross national product of only 150 U.S. dollars (see Table 3), it is probably the poorest of the world's largest nations. Although 71 percent of its total population is involved in agriculture, food production is not sufficient to feed the Indian population, and malnutrition and actual starvation in India are relatively widespread (Eitzen, 1980). Illiteracy rates of over 70 percent of the population fifteen years of age or older also contrast sharply with Japan's illiteracy rate of less than 2 percent (Ehrlich and Ehrlich, 1970).

The largest of the Indian Cities, Bombay and Calcutta, have a British colonial history, which may have had an important part in impeding their industrial and economic development, although these two cities taken together contain about 40 percent of all India's industrial plants (Funk and Wagnalls, 1973). Established as ports, these cities served as the conduit for trade between India and other parts of the British Empire, and little of the wealth produced was reinvested by the British in indigenous industries. New Delhi was another major city founded by the British next to the existing city of Delhi. It is now India's capital.

With a population of nearly nine million people, Calcutta has become India's largest city and is now among the world's fifteen largest (see Figure 2). Its harbor is one of the busiest in the world, and it is the terminus of several important railroad systems connecting it to the hinterlands. But of all of the world cities discussed in this chapter, Calcutta probably suffers some of the worse consequences of overurbanization (Murphey, 1977). Calcutta has long been known as an overcrowded and noxious city. Rudyard Kipling once described it as "chance-erected, chance directed," because its growth had long been uncontrolled and without plan (Van Huyk, 1967). Its recent history, including the after-effects of World War II when Calcutta was a military supply base, the Bengal famine of 1945, and the partition of the country in 1947, which produced a large influx of displaced persons from East Pakistan, has contributed to population expansion much greater than expected.

Calcutta has long had acute shortages of open space, and mass transit and roads have not even begun to keep pace with needs. The environmental problems of water, sewerage, and drainage have produced major health problems. The World Health Organization, for example, has found that the city's poor water and sanitation situation was an undoubted cause for

Lack of food and housing are among the serious problems of Bombay. (United Nations/J.P. Laffonte)

the continued prevalence of cholera and other epidemic diseases (Van Huyk, 1967).

But even more acute are the tremendous housing shortages in Calcutta. Over 75 percent of the city's population lives in overcrowded tenements and squatter slums, and more than half of all the city's families live in dwellings of no more than a single room (Bose, 1973). At least several types of slum housing areas have been identified. These include the *Bustees,* which are communities made up primarily of one-story huts containing approximately eight little cubicles, each of which in turn may be rented to an entire family. Over 3,000 such bustees contain about 30,000 huts, which house about 700,000 people (Van Huyk, 1967). Even worse are the *Pukka* slums, which consist of brick multistoried tenement buildings housing about a quarter of a million people. They lack the light and air of the bustees, and their confined nature often makes conditions malodorous and unbearable, especially when sanitary facilities break down, which is often the case (Van Huyk, 1967). But as poor as the living conditions are in these two types of slums, they are still worse for the many people living in the streets, who have no shelter at all. The city has a minimum of 300,000 homeless residents "who eat, sleep, breed, live their lives, and die on the streets without even the shelter of a squatter shack" (Palen, 1975, p. 400). The combined problems of hunger and squalid or no housing have produced riots and disorder in Calcutta, and in the mid-1970s emergency reform policies were introduced by the central government. But in many ways, the problems of Calcutta and other Indian urban areas, compounded as they are by extreme poverty, high birth rates, high illiteracy, overcrowding, and political instability, appear to be even more insurmountable than in the overurbanized areas of other developing parts of the world such as Africa or Latin America.

China

The People's Republic of China has by far the largest population on earth. Although its rate of growth in the past decade has been less than in most of the developing countries, its large population base makes yearly population increments impressive in actual numbers. Nearly sixty million people, for example, were added to its population during the three-year interval between 1974 and 1977 (U.S. Census, 1978). In the twelve years between 1965 and 1977, the number of people added to the Chinese population was greater than the entire 1977 population of the United States! The 1977 population of China was estimated at over 982 million and at its current rate of growth will be over one billion by 1981. (U.S. Census, 1978). China contains two of the fifteen largest cities of the world: Shanghai with 13.4 million people; and Peking with 10.7 million people (see Figure 2). With more than 130 million people living in cities, China probably has in absolute numbers the largest urban population in the world. But, interestingly, China is proportionately even less urbanized than India, with only 13 percent of its total population urbanized.

The Republic of China, which was established in 1949, has consistently attempted to curb the growth of its urban population by forcibly relocating skilled workers from the cities into the rural hinterlands. During what was called the "Cultural Revolution" in the 1960s, massive numbers of young people and students were mobilized as a labor militia called the "Red Guard" and transferred to the rural areas to serve as agricultural workers

Even though China contains some of the world's largest cities, such as Peking, only 13 percent of its population lives in cities. (United Nations/T. Chen)

in agricultural communes. Such measures were not always popular, but the central government seemed to have had enough power to effectively implement and maintain this policy.

China is characterized by effective political organization, not only at the highly centralized national level but at the local level as well. Agricultural communes seem to be effective in providing adequate food supplies, which are equitably distributed to all segments of the population. While information on cities is still rather meager, reports from the increasing number of journalists and other travelers permitted to visit China in the 1970s indicate that the cities seem to be well managed and to have escaped some of the worst symptoms of overpopulation that exist in many developing countries. Galston (1972) reports that the cities are clean and free of crime, unemployment is low, and street begging, which was common in China before 1949, is no longer apparent. People are well fed and clothed and the average worker lives better and is more secure than ever before. While there are still major housing shortages, one does not see the squatter slums characteristic of many of the other cities of developing countries described in this chapter. Peking, for example, has kitchens, running water, water heaters, and flush toilets in all of the newer apartments being supplied to workers (Galston, 1972). Because automobiles are extremely scarce, Chinese traffic seems less congested and the air less polluted than in cities where the privately owned automobile has become a principal means of transportation. Although the biggest cities have mass transit systems, the bicycle has become a principal vehicle for the journey to work, and Peking alone has about 1.5 million (Palen, 1975).

Shanghai, the largest Chinese city, was founded in the eleventh century, but it first became important after the 1842 Treaty of Nanking opened it to foreign trade. The city was strongly influenced by the industrial nations, such as Great Britain, France, the United States, and Japan, all of which at one time or another occupied the city or controlled its economy. This history of mixed foreign domination has produced a pattern of complex physical development, which poses difficulties for city planners in Shanghai. For example, each of the foreign settlements left behind its own pattern and width of streets, as well as its own administrative apparatus. This has made it most difficult to provide a uniform and interconnected street pattern and service structure as the city expanded. To widen or extend the streets, many buildings and houses have had to be torn down, contributing to the already existing shortage of housing. It has been estimated, for example, that the total length of city streets increased more than tenfold in the period 1949 to 1972 (Tien, 1973).

During the 1950s, major efforts were made to disperse industry from Shanghai to the Chinese interior, but the city has continued to grow as an industrial center. Textiles, publishing, oil refineries, shipbuilding, cement, chemicals, machines, paper, processed foods, steel, and machine tools are now among its major industries, and close to two million workers are employed in these industries (Funk and Wagnells, 1973). Its large port, which stretches over seven miles, handles coastal trade as well as the bulk of goods exported from China. It is also a major rail junction with connections to both the north and south of China. Shanghai has long been an educational center of China, and it has a number of universities as well as technical and scientific institutes.

When Chinese Communist forces occupied the city and made it a part of the Republic, massive housing shortages and squatter slums were as common as in many other cities in developing regions. These squatter settlements have now been eliminated and replaced with nearly a hundred new residential neighborhoods, which have been described as neat and well maintained although still somewhat overcrowded (Tien, 1973). The residents now are adequately served with clean water, sewers, and electricity. Air pollution and traffic congestion are minimal for a city of this size, mainly because of the very limited use of the private automobile.

THE SOVIET UNION

The Soviet Union has been characterized by steady urban growth ever since the inception of the communist state. Thirty-two percent of the population was classified as urban in 1939; in 1959, 48 percent was urban; in 1970, 56 percent was urban; and in 1979, urban areas were the home for 62 percent of the Soviet population (New York Times, February 10, 1980). In 1979, 27 percent more people lived in urban areas than in 1970. More than one-half of this urban growth was caused by resettlement of former farm and village dwellers, rather than by natural increase. The biggest cities, those with over 100,000 people, accounted for 75 percent of the total urban population growth in the past several decades (Hall, 1977). In the 50 years between 1920 and 1970, the urban population increased at a rate three times greater than that of the total population of the Soviet Union (Wilson and Schulz, 1978).

The Soviet Union has made persistent efforts to constrain and direct urban expansion by attempting to limit the growth of the largest cities and dispersing urban populations throughout a multiplicity of decentralized regional urban centers. These decentralization policies include the development of new towns and industrial satellites as well as the expansion of existing urban centers in outlying regions outside of Russia proper (Fisher, 1967). These policies are administered by a highly centralized State Economic Planning Commission.

A summary of Fisher's (1967) detailed review of Soviet planning policies suggests that they are based on the following basic elements, which he describes as generally characteristic of socialist urban planning:

A. Standardization. This applies principally to the standardization of housing or "living space." Housing construction is standardized through prefabrication of housing units manufactured in factories and delivered to building sites. Housing units are relatively uniform with respect to size, quality, and design. The standardization of housing is planned not only to relieve tremendous housing shortages in the Soviet Union and to maximize efficiencies of limited investment capital, but to also achieve greater socioeconomic uniformity among the residents, in keeping with even more basic socialist objectives.

B. Optimum City Size.   Soviet planners express the conviction that large cities must be contained to their present size to avoid the "inhumane" or "evil" conditions they believe to be characteristic of bigness; especially the bigness of large American or Western European cities. The critical element in determining the size of any particular urban center is to be based on the size of its labor force—the ratio of the employed population in basic industries to the total population of the community. A series of dependent satellite communities should be built around existing large cities into which surplus populations in the central cities can be dispersed, in addition to a series of totally independent new towns with their own basic industrial and service components.

C. City Centers.   Socialist planners argue that the center of a city should serve political, cultural, and administrative functions, rather than the retail or commercial functions associated with city centers in capitalistic economies. According to socialist thought, the city center is the vital core necessary to coordinate the entire urban complex, and it should receive priority in planning. The center should provide room for "parading troups and for throngs of people on holidays," as well as providing a setting for principal public buildings and monuments. A hotel for tourists, a single state-run department store, and perhaps a restaurant or coffee shop are perceived as the only kinds of commercial activities permitted at the center of the city.

D. Neighborhood Units.   Soviet planning supports the idea of an elaborate division of each city into self-contained neighborhoods, each of which maintains its own decision-making, administrative, service, and facilities structure. The goal is that the residents of each neighborhood will become a sociologically cohesive group and will become relatively self-sufficient in meeting their own economic and social needs. Thus, in Soviet city planning, elements such as the location of housing, schools, parks and recreation centers, stores, restaurants, clinics, repair shops, and meeting places will be spatially located according to the boundaries of the neighborhood unit.

Fisher (1976) has more recently reported that Soviet city planners have not fully succeeded to date in achieving these goals because of the extremely high costs of removing the devastation of the principal Soviet cities in World War II; the rigidity of the political system; a lack of knowledge of modern construction techniques and architecture; and the regime's higher priorities for industrial and agricultural development. But he further concludes that in spite of these barriers, well planned cities with attractive and comfortable residential units are being built.

Despite efforts to constrain and disperse urban growth, Moscow remains by far the largest Soviet city and is still growing. With all of the satellite cities and new towns within a forty-mile radius included, the population of the Moscow urban region includes close to thirteen million people, making it one of the largest urban complexes in continental Europe (Hall, 1977). Because so much of the administrative and political power of the Soviet Union is concentrated in Moscow, as are cultural, trade, and communications facilities, the city of Moscow has many of the characteristics and functions of the primate cities in less developed countries, although the Soviet Union differs markedly from these countries in its current rates of industrialization, urbanization, and its geopolitical history.

NORTHERN AND WESTERN EUROPE

The urban-industrial revolution first emerged in northern and western Europe (see Chapter Three). This region can best be described as mature and highly developed in the terms of this chapter. If zero population growth is a desirable goal, this region comes closest to meeting it than any other region in the world. In western Europe, estimates for the 1975–1977 period indicate that population growth has ceased entirely, while northern Europe's population growth rate is only 0.1 percent a year. A major contributing factor to the overall low levels of growth for this region is the declining population of the Federal Republic of Germany, Luxembourg, and Switzerland, plus the zero growth rate reported for the United Kingdom (U.S. Census, 1978).

Urban growth rates, which accelerated most rapidly in the nineteenth and early part of the twentieth centuries, have also slowed drastically in this region during the middle and latter parts of the twentieth century (see Table 17-4A&B). London, which was the largest city in the world at the turn of this century, is now only the ninth largest city and is expected to drop from among the fifteen largest cities by the year 2000 (see Figure 17-2). Yet the countries of northern and western Europe have been and still remain among the most urbanized in the world. France, the United Kingdom, and the Netherlands are all more than 70 percent urban; Sweden and Denmark are 80 percent or more urban; and West Germany and Belgium are both more than 90 percent urban (U.S. Census, 1978). The relative economic, political, and social stability of these countries since the end of World War II is in part a product of the well-maintained balance between population growth, urban growth, and industrial growth achieved by these societies during the postwar period.

A characteristic that the countries of northern and western Europe have in common is a high commitment to city and regional planning and to intensive land use controls. In most cases, such planning is a highly centralized function of the national government, which anticipates and attempts to guide urban growth and redistribution trends well into the foreseeable future. Nevertheless, there are countless variations in the approaches to planning from country to country and from city to city. A brief discussion of two principal European cities—London and Paris—illustrates some of the similarities and differences.

London

England has been a highly urbanized country for many decades, with three-fourths of its population living in cities and towns by the end of the nineteenth century. Yet even with its many cities, British life is still highly dominated by London, which in many ways is like the primate cities in the developing nations. It is the political and cultural capital of the nation, the center of its commerce, and the headquarters of its major financial institutions. Because it also serves these same kinds of functions in a very significant way for the world as a whole, Hall (1977) calls London one of the principal "world cities." Bollens and Schmandt (1975, pp. 341–342) describe the physical pattern of London as a series of concentric rings that produce the following pattern:

> At the hub is the ancient city . . . which contains but one square mile of territory, a night time population of less than 5,000 and one of the world's great financial centers. The traditional city and the surrounding periphery of about nine square miles lying largely within the ring of main railway stations constitute the 'central area,' the equivalent of the CBD in an American municipali-

London, with its political, cultural, and financial impact, continues to be one of the principal world cities. (The British Tourist Authority)

ty.... Beyond this core is an area of malls and closely spaced homes extending out to the ... limits of London County.... The next ring marks the limits of the area now governed by the Greater London conurbation. It encompasses 618 square miles ... and extends almost out to the Green Belt, a circle of land varying in width from five to fifteen miles and containing over 35,000 acres of open space.... Beyond the Greenbelt is the area of present expansion intended to handle the spillover from the inner rings. It is here that the New Towns, the uniquely English solution to the problems of metropolitan growth are located.

The green belt and the new towns are keys to the planned urban change in London. They can be traced back to the ideas of Ebenezer Howard and the new town or "garden city" movement of the latter part of the nineteenth century. This movement envisaged three major goals: 1) rearrangement of the large population masses of the big industrial cities in new towns of a more "human scale" of strictly limited size; 2) a better balance between the quantity of housing and the number of jobs available; and 3) public ownership of land to control land use development (Berry and Kasarda, 1977). Overall, the movement expressed the hope that green belts around existing cities and controlled decentralization of people from overcrowded cities into small satellite new towns beyond the green belts would provide a more equitable balance between town and country life, while at the same time preserving the amenities of both these alternatives. Another important goal of the new towns was that they should be relatively self-sufficient and should contain centers of employment for local residents to minimize the need for commuting. Each new town was to be made up of neighborhood units, each containing its own schools, shops, and other local facilities. Also, all social classes were to be represented in each neighborhood unit in a "well-balanced" mixture.

Several new towns actually were built outside London in the period between two World Wars, but the concepts of new towns and green belts were more comprehensively articulated, expanded, and adopted in the Greater London Plan of 1944. Sir Patrick Abercrombie, a leading sponsor of the plan, proposed that it should provide that London as well as the new towns surrounding it be developed at relatively low densities. For example, the new towns were to be built according to the English middle-class tradition of about fourteen to sixteen houses to the acre, with relatively few people housed in larger apartment complexes (Hall, 1977). This was in contrast to new-town planning in France and other European countries, which focused on the high rise apartment house and the higher density living it represented (see the following section).

Most observers (Bollens and Schmandt, 1975; Hall, 1977; Berry and Kasarda, 1977) conclude that on the whole new-town planning in the case of London has been eminently successful in achieving its goals. As examples of comprehensive and humanistic planning, the new towns have attracted admiring visitors from all over the world, and, as this chapter has already suggested, they have been widely imitated. But Hall (1977) has also suggested that unanticipated population growth in the London region has produced an "overspill" of settlements out to a distance from the city well beyond that envisaged by the planners and into privately developed housing subdivisions beyond the planned boundaries of the ring of new towns. Instead of the population being confined to a ring of new towns on an average of fifteen to twenty-five miles from London, new subdivisions now are inhabited by people who make commuting journeys as long as from forty to fifty miles to London's central area each morning. Also, many of the new towns have failed to attract substantial portions of the lower-income groups, who remain trapped in poor housing within the city. The London central area has been loosing much of its middle-income population to the new towns and newly sprawling suburbs, leaving the city mainly to its most wealthy and least wealthy residents. As a result, the Greater London Council produced in the mid-1970s a new Greater London Development Plan with broad new guidelines for the region's development. Its goals include plans to stabilize both population and employment in the central area and to supply a quality of life that persuades Londoners to stay (Hall, 1977). It is, of course, much too soon to evaluate the success of this newer plan.

Paris

Paris is known the world over for its wide boulevards, museums, parks, theaters, night spots, scenic streets, and handsome architecture. But at the same time, its 1980 population of just under ten million people (see Figure 2) is also among the most congested and poorly housed in Europe (Hall, 1977). During the decade from 1965 to 1975, officials of the French government and of the Paris region built five new towns and expanded six older suburbs within a twenty-mile radius of Paris. These efforts were designed to provide badly needed housing and to redistribute surplus population outward from the central city. By minimizing some of the overcrowding, the officials also hoped that existing Parisian neighborhoods could be renewed and modernized (Hall, 1977).

The 1965 Master Plan for the Paris region established construction areas, open space standards, and a communications network. Development was to be encouraged east of Paris, to counter the existing drift to the west. Two new types of communities were to be created: 1) those to be built on virgin land; and 2) those to be built on the base of an existing suburb (Huxtable, 1978). Each of the new units was seen as having an eventual population of 200,000 to 300,000 people, organized into neighborhood subunits of from 30,000 to 50,000 people. In turn, each of these was to be served by the appropriate political, administrative, economic, cultural, and recreational agencies, as well as by a service infrastructure of hospitals, schools and universities, art galleries, and a "lively mix of urban activities." These new towns were also to be served by a newly planned network of roads and rails to connect them to the old city, although zones of industry and commerce were also planned for the new towns to make them reasonably self-sufficient and to make their residents free from the daily need to commute to city jobs (Huxtable, 1978).

To a certain extent, the new towns of the Paris region serve the functions for which they were intended. They have been made both accessible and affordable for a worker population no longer able to afford the higher costs of the central city. The housing in the new towns has been able to absorb persons forced out of the older neighborhoods that have been going through the process of "gentrification." Gentrification has turned historic slums into costly, chic neighborhoods that the former residents can no longer afford.

The new towns offer the virtues of central heating and running water and open green spaces—amenities that were not always available to the residents in their former city dwellings. The many kinds of services and facilities just described above are also available. But most of the housing available in the new towns is contained in modernistic high rise apartment buildings that are a sharp break from the traditional Paris neighborhoods and their streetscapes. The traditional neighborhoods had always been considered attractive and exciting because they were filled with a life of constant use and activities (these qualities were discussed in more detail in Chapter Six). Thus, there is some concern that the design and architecture of the new towns may have lost some of the vitality, social interaction, and charm associated with traditional Parisian street life. Architectural and city planning critics have used terms such as "bland impersonality," "aggressive gimmickry," "empty and bleak," and "vacuous design content" to describe the new towns, and they decry the loss of the "traditional scale, character, easy functional and social mix, and elegant and sophisticated architecture of Paris, which may be the most beautiful and urban city in the world" (Huxtable, 1978, p. 167). But while the design of the new towns is highly controversial, they undoubtedly have begun to fill a widely recognized need to relieve some of the congestion and overcrowding of Paris. It remains to be seen whether their residents will be able to re-create traditional patterns of social interaction and life styles, or to invent even more satisfactory social patterns in the physical environment of the new towns, in spite of the critics' lack of enthusiasm for these developments.

SELECTED BIBLIOGRAPHY

ABRAMS, CHARLES. "The Uses of Land in Cities." In Scientific American, *Cities: Their Origin, Growth, and Human Impact.* San Francisco: W. H. Freeman and Company Publishers, 1973.

BERRY, BRIAN J. L. *The Human Consequences of Urbanization.* New York: St. Martins Press, 1973.

————, and KASARDA, JOHN D. *Contemporary Urban Ecology.* New York: Macmillan, 1977.

BOLLENS, JOHN C., and SCHMANDT, HENRY J. *The Metropolis: Its People, Politics, and Economic Life.* 3rd ed. New York: Harper & Row, Pubs., 1975.

BOSE, NIRMAL K. "Calcutta: A Premature Metropolis." In Scientific American, *Cities* (1973).

DAVIS, KINGSLY. *World Urbanization 1950–1970: Vol. II: Analysis of Trends, Relationships, and Development.* Berkeley, Calif.: Institute of International Studies, Population Monograph Series, No. 9, 1972.

EHRLICH, PAUL R., and EHRLICH, ANNE H. *Population; Resources; Environment: Issues in Human Ecology.* 2nd ed. San Francisco: W. H. Freeman and Company Publishers, 1972.

EITZEN, D. STANLEY. *Social Problems.* Boston: Allyn & Bacon, 1980.

FAVA, SYLVIA F., ed. *Urbanism in World Perspective.* New York: Thomas Y. Crowell, 1968.

FISHER, JACK C. "Urban Planning in the Soviet Union and Eastern Europe." In H. Wentworth Eldredge, ed., *Taming Megalopolis: How to Manage an Urbanized World.* Vol II. New York: Praeger, 1967.

———; PIORO, Z.; and SAVIC, M. "Socialist City Planning: A Reexamination." In Paul Meadows and Ephraim H. Mizruchi, eds., *Urbanism, Urbanization and Change: Comparative Perspectives.* 2nd ed. Reading, Mass.: Addison-Wesley, 1976.

FREEDMAN, RONALD, and BERELSON, BERNARD. "The Human Population." In Scientific American, *The Human Population.* San Francisco: W. H. Freeman and Company Publishers, 1974.

FRISBIE, W. PARKER. "The Scale and Growth of World Urbanization." In John Walton and Donald E. Carns, eds., *Cities in Change.* 2nd ed. Boston: Allyn & Bacon, 1977.

GAKENHEIMER, RALPH A. "The Peruvian City of the Sixteenth Century." In Glen H. Beyer, ed., *The Urban Exposion in Latin America.* Ithaca, N.Y.: Cornell University Press, 1967.

GALSTON, ARTHUR. "Peking Man (and Woman) Today," *Natural History* (November 1972): 28.

GORDON, THEODORE J. "Some Crises that Will Determine the World of 1994," *The Futurist* 8 (June 1974).

HALL, PETER. *The World Cities.* 2nd ed. New York: McGraw-Hill, 1977.

HAWLEY, AMOS H. *Urban Society: An Ecological Approach.* New York: Ronald Press, 1971.

HAYNOR, NORMAN S. "Mexico City: Its Growth and Configuration, 1345–1960." In Fava (1968).

HOSELITZ, BERT F. "The City, the Factory, and Economic Growth," *American Economic Review* 45 (May 1955): 166–184.

HUXTABLE, ADA LOUISE. "Cold Comfort: The New French Towns," *New York Times Magazine,* November 19, 1978.

MANGIN, WILLIAM. "Squatter Settlements." In Scientific American, *Cities* (1973).

MITCHEL, N. C. "Yoruba Towns." In K. M. Barbour and R. M. Prothero, eds., *Essays on African Population.* London: Routledge & Kegan Paul, 1961.

MURPHEY, RHOADS. "Urbanization in Asia." In Walton and Carns (1977).

ONIBOKUM, ADEPOJU. "Forces Shaping the Physical Environment of Cities in the Developing Countries: The Ibaden Case," *Land Economics* 49 (November 1973): 424–431.

PALEN, J. JOHN. *The Urban World.* New York: McGraw-Hill, 1975.

SANDERS, THOMAS G. *Mexico in the 1970's.* Hanover, N.H.: The American Universities Field Staff. Undated, about 1977.

Tien, Hung Mao. "Shanghai: China's Huge 'Model City,'" *Milwaukee Journal,* December 16, 1973.

United Nations. *Demographic Yearbook.* 1977.

———. *Annual Report: United Nations Fund for Population Activities.* 1980.

U.S. Bureau of the Census. *World Population: 1977–Recent Demographic Estimates for the Countries and Regions of the World.* Washington, D.C.: U.S. Government Printing Office, 1978.

Van Huyk, Alfred P. "An Approach to Mass Housing in India: With Special Reference to Calcutta." In Eldredge (1967).

Wilson, Robert A., and Schulz, David A. *Urban Sociology.* Englewood Cliffs, N.J.: Prentice-Hall, 1978.

SUBJECT INDEX